# Race For the World

John Todd

D1453748

## Hodder & Stoughton

LONDON SYDNEY AUCKLAND

Copyright © John Todd 1994
Photographs courtesy of A. Burton, M. Raymond and C. Ross

The right of John Todd to be identified as the author
of this work has been asserted by him in accordance with the
Copyright, Designs and Patents Act 1988.

10 9 8 7 6 5 4 3 2 1

A CIP catalogue record for this title is available
from the British Library

ISBN 0 340 60834 X

Typeset by Hewer Text Composition Services, Edinburgh
Printed and bound in Great Britain by
Cox & Wyman Ltd, Reading, Berkshire

Hodder and Stoughton Ltd,
A division of Hodder Headline PLC
338 Euston Road
London NW1 3BH

To Shelly, without whom this book, and the best years of my life, would not have happened.

# Contents

# Acknowledgments

A lifetime of travel has left me highly indebted, not just to people helpful with arrangements or met en voyage, but to dispensers of those precious commodities 'encouragement' and 'friendship' to someone shooting for the moon. Special thanks to my Guardian Angel Who kept me in one piece; to my parents, who have given unstinting support to my every endeavour; my son Nathan who has sacrificed much time rightly his both to my travels and my writing; and my parents-in-law, Frank and Sharon, who have dealt out copious amounts of backing.

This book germinated as a suggestion by David Kingdon, who, with Ivor Oakley, was a formative influence before I left Ireland. That it saw the light of day at all is due entirely to James Catford at Hodder, a very patient man. I owe David Armstrong a debt of gratitude for starting me off on the road of writing for publication.

The following have inspired, challenged, or goaded me on: John Patterson, Eric Wright, A. F. Falconer, Derek Prime, Earl Palmer, Brian Woodgate, Gus Bess, David Murphy, Henrich Brockhaus, Danny Martinson, Gordon Dunn, Colin Dye, Jack Hwyel-Davies, Lindsay Brown, Vije Khindria, Maurice Gunn-Russell, David Watters, Stuart Lynch, David Drain, Alan Scarfe, Steve Turner, Nigel Goodwin, George Verwer, K. P. Yohannan, Malcolm Muggeridge, Oswald Sanders.

It would be hard to improve on the art of hospitality as practised by the Wynnes, or my numerous hosts while on the road. When I'm travelling, an indispensable someone has to be 'back at the ranch' seeing that things run smoothly. For that I have been grateful to my brothers Tim and Philip, Marie Moss, Mary Jane Linton, Nancy Beverstock, Gerry Moscrop, and, above all, Shelly.

# Preface

## What is a Country?

Since the world consists of countries, a race for the world inevitably involves becoming a country collector. But countries, like people, come in all shapes and sizes. There are the 179 members of the United Nations, which is what most people think of when you say the word 'country'.

But although the UN includes San Marino, the Marshalls, Tuvalu, and small Caribbean islands with populations less than 100,000, it does not include Taiwan, Switzerland, Yugoslavia, Scotland, or Wales. The *Guinness Book of Answers* doesn't include Scotland or Wales either, but lists the Isle of Man and the Falklands.

Once the definition is broadened to one of sovereignty, micro states such as Andorra, Monaco, San Marino, and Liechtenstein, join the number. But when you move from small to relatively microscopic (the Vatican – a country with a great ceiling, and the Sovereign Military Order of Malta – a building set in a couple of acres, recognised by forty-three states) traditional yardsticks such as territorial integrity and policed borders are jettisoned.

Then there is politics! During the period covered by this book there have been two Germanies which became one, two Koreas implacably inimical to each other, two Vietnams united after a savage war, two Cypruses, and two Yemens which couldn't make up their minds if they were one or not. Also a Czechoslovakia which first acquired a hyphen then became two: the Czech Republic and Slovakia.

One country (the USSR) suddenly became at least fifteen, possibly upwards of fifty. But anyone who'd roamed in Latvia, Ukraine or Uzbeckistan knew that they were 'countries' all along. Ditto Bosnia, Croatia, Slovenia.

When I was eight I walked across my first border from one country (province of a constitutional monarchy, member of the Commonwealth) to another (independent republic, non Commonwealth) in the divided island of Ireland where I was born. Yet there were no guards, residents could claim either citizenship or both, and the same money and institutions were then employed by both.

The questions of recognition, ownership and access are vexed ones. As the Berlin Wall came down, a sand wall went up in the Sahara to keep Western Sahara and the Sahrawi Republic apart. Ten homelands with nominal independence within South Africa suddenly faced reabsorption, but while they existed physically they had to be counted. The four Macedonias, Armenia, and Kurdistan straddle territory laid claim to by other sovereign states. Some, like Catalonia and the Basque country certainly deserve to be counted on nationhood grounds, but lack self government.

Geography adds to the muddle. Hawaii's ancient kings certainly ceded rulership to Washington DC, but in the same way that just because you've been to Paris you can't claim to have visited Tahiti in the Pacific, or Reunion in the Indian Ocean, many country collectors and compilers of country lists include these places as separate entries, to ensure a way of chronicling progress.

Hence Pitcairn (UK), Tokelau (New Zealand), two Christmas Islands (one Australia, the other Kiribati), American Samoa (US), Macao (Portugal, pending return to China), and of course Hong Kong. In today's post-colonial world I was surprised to find how many protectorates, trust territories, dependencies, and old-fashioned colonies still exist.

Islands – singly or in groups – and 'claims' by big nations on faraway and in many cases deserted and barren pieces of rock or ice, add considerably to the number of 'countries' (or more properly territories) that any race to embrace the whole world must consider. The Chilean, Argentine and British sectors of the Antarctic overlap. The USA does not recognise other nations' claims in the Antarctic, but when you get to the South Pole the first thing you find is an American base.

No denying that these pinpoints on the map are jealousy prized by the big powers, and listed in the same way as colonies. The American ones on the list (they're nearly all American) tend to be holdovers from World War II, listed in government handbooks, and unwilling to relinquish their status as somehow different from a mere mainland base.

However, to create a new base for the US, Britain even went to the length of dispossessing an entire native population from its home in the Chagos archipelago, artificially designating the new entity 'British Indian Ocean Territory'. Although by attempting to visit (in the teeth of official displeasure) I was in effect trying to beat a ban on entering a secret US Navy defence installation, according to official gazettes when I set foot there, I was in an overseas dependent territory administered by colonial officials from London.

Perhaps the strangest category of 'country' is composed of uninhabited scraps of oceanic rock and odd reefs claimed by some government. Whilst refusing Scotland status as a country, the Guinness book lists Kingman Reef in the Pacific, a slither of rock that is not only permanently uninhabited, but submerged most of the time. A country you need a wet suit to visit!

Taken together, the criteria above extend considerably the number of entities on any list of countries. And there are almost as many lists as countries! The *Guinness Book of Records*, US State Department, *UN Demographic Yearbook*, Club International des Grands Voyageurs, and American Radio Relay League, list between 200 and 300 each. The Travelers' Century Club, long regarded as the grandaddy of country list compilers, counts 312 today, 308 when I embarked on the 'race', and 350 including deletions. (Most lists are constantly changing as the pace of both new country production and old country deletion continues unabated.)

My peregrinations in the race for the world have taken me to 379 different territories, a total which makes sense when you consider discrepancies between the various lists, and countries that no longer exist, but did when I visited (East Germany, North Vietnam, South African bantustans).

My reward, apart from grey hairs and immense satisfaction, has been a special award from the Traveler's Century Club, and a listing in the Guinness Book. But if you ask me what definitively constitutes a country, after all this, I couldn't say. I just collect them all.

# 1

# Danger Island

*Indian Ocean (1991)*

The high-level permission that we needed to reach our top secret destination, whose defences bristle with the latest military hardware, never came through. Instead, we'd set out on a clandestine voyage through these inhospitable waters. Now here we are – a full four days' sail away from the last inhabited spaces we've seen, lurching up and down in the vicious surf like Saturday night drunks. The surf has prevented a closer approach to our chosen target. We'd suspected as much, during the two days' incessant pounding our vessel took on the way here.

It's a 'go'. Donning life-jackets, we pile into two red rubber zodiacs, and plough through the swell. At a sharp command the motors are cut. We half jump, are half pushed, overboard. Crew members, fresh from paratroop and commando duty, form a human chain with rope, to bridge the distance from the first zodiac to the reef.

The elderly lawyer from Evansville, Indiana, all six foot four inches of him, is first to reach the end of the rope. 'What do I do now?' he calls.

'You'll have to swim from here,' a bronzed Israeli instructs him over the roar of the surf. 'I can't swim,' he retorts. 'Neither can I,' screams a small, balding expatriate Briton in his sixties, who's following close behind.

Both fix their gaze on me for a solution. It's every tour group leader's nightmare.

What am I doing in this crazy situation in the first place: my family 10,000 miles distant; most of the earlier contents of my stomach in the Indian Ocean; unflinching authorities who intend to keep us at arm's length; unrecoverable sums of money poured into this enterprise by passengers with big expectations which they're looking to me to satisfy. And what for? The answer partly involves: a car crash in Northern Ireland; a night in Manhattan; two eighty-year-old ladies; an odd club on Sunset Boulevard; a butcher's shop in Japan; the Cuban ambassador in Jamaica; a postcard from Peking; a nineteenth-century Greek professor at St Andrews University, Scotland; the Alexander Solzhenitsyn of Romania; General Peron; ABC News and BBC TV; some very determined Canadian mountain-climbers; the Siberian Seven; Zuulchin and the travel business generally; and above all, a benign Providence, responsive to a traveller's petitions.

# 2

# The Reds Will Get Us

*Northern Ireland (1961–7)*

I didn't discover air travel when I was eleven, but I did discover aircraft spotting.

For those not privy to this youthful hobby, it consists of recognising different civilian airliners and logging their individual registrations in a special notebook. Like many events in our lives, there was no obvious immediate explanation. Train spotting, enjoyed by many British and Irish boys, would have been more practical, since Portadown railway station was only fifteen minutes away on foot.

Our home wasn't even underneath the flight path to anywhere and family finances certainly didn't stretch to actually flying. Holidays were mostly spent at 'Miss Mercer's' in Portrush, County Antrim; days out at Warrenpoint, eighteen miles distant, from where I walked across my first border to the REPUBLIC of IRELAND. We'd been to the ISLE OF MAN for a change when I was five, by ship.

I don't remember much of this holiday, but from the pictures and family lore, it's clear I climbed a stile wearing my best Sunday suit to walk through fields near Port Erin, fed leftover breakfast herrings to grateful seagulls, endured kisses from two girls at the guest house, and was too sleepy after the sea journey to enjoy the pastries provided for our 10 p.m. arrival.

The guest house location meant that each time we took the bus into Douglas, we would certainly have passed Ronaldsway Airport and had a clear view of the two or three British European Airways (BEA) DC3s parked on the tarmac.

These wonderful thirty-two-seat machines, civilian makeovers of the World War II workhorse, and quite possibly the greatest aircraft ever manufactured, had provided the Irish Sea link and British Isles provincial services generally for a decade and a half, before retiring to secondary routes in favour of newer turbo props, especially the Viscount. But I took no notice. I was probably engrossed in my Rupert annual.

My first aircraft book, a twelfth-birthday present, was a blue-grey oblong-shaped hardback called *World Aircraft Directory*. It implanted securely in me a love of those majestic and eccentric aircraft whose time was just passing or had already ended: DC6Bs and 7Cs ('Seven Seas'), last of the big trans-oceanic pistons; Constellations ('Connies'), with their humps and distinctive triple fins; and Airspeed Ambassadors, with black patches from the puffs of smoke emitted on starting up.

I quickly became devoted to my new hobby, studying what timetables I could scrounge from Locke's – the farmers' supply outlet in town which devoted a small corner to travel agency business.

The '60s were almost history before Ulster was bothered by the jet age. Until then the four-propeller Vanguard was the largest aircraft regularly seen in what was then still a relative backwater in the aviation world.

A spotting expedition generally meant a day-return ticket in the train to Belfast, then the airport bus from Glengall Street to Nutts Corner.

You couldn't stay late at the airport in case you missed the last bus and train, so you had to study the schedules in advance to pick a good day when the more interesting planes could be expected.

Glengall Street was a true city air terminal like its West London counterpart in Cromwell Road, where people checked in their baggage, and bus departures were called by flight number. Even though I paid the correct fare, I always felt conspicuous amongst the real travellers, particularly on the early morning departures.

It was a bit of an anti-climax to watch them gather up their overcoats and pile off the bus into the departure lounge, then board the waiting Vanguard, while I headed for the spectator's gallery or the coffee shop.

I used to follow every last passenger onto the plane with my binoculars, then track the Vanguard's square profile as it lifted off into a sky that was invariably grey. After it had gone, you could see on the tarmac the black patch of spilt oil directly underneath where the wing had been. The distinctive smell of aviation fuel – like that of a garage repair-bay – always hung in the air for several minutes after take-off. Although I didn't articulate it for a year or two, I'm sure the idea was born in me on those airport spotting expeditions, that it would be much more fun to board one of those planes to faraway places, than merely to stand on the sidelines and watch.

As well as pictures of pistons, props and jets, the *World Aircraft Directory* helpfully listed headquarters addresses for all the major world airlines.

To a teenage boy hampered by finances from either flying or frequenting international airports, this offered an excellent surrogate. I began writing to as many as I could muster fourpenny stamps for, telling them of my interest in civil aviation in general and their company in particular. Not all of them replied. Those that did quickly developed into a bountiful source of brochures, route maps, badges and small souvenirs. The public relations officers who signed their names to personal letters accompanying the trinkets earned my undying support for their far-sighted and magnanimous policies.

I kept a detailed log: expenditure on stamps, envelopes, etc. This got me into trouble during a parental audit of pocket money disbursements. *Date sent, reply received:* demonstrating persuasively that most containing brochures from other continents came by surface mail. *Failure to reply:* in which the Bulgarian, Cuban, Soviet and other East bloc airlines featured prominently.

It was this notation, more than any other, which caused hyperconsternation during a routine proud-owner display of the log to a visiting relative. My uncle studied the log with incredulity. 'And did you write to Aeroflot in Moscow?' he queried, speaking slowly and distinctly, emphasising particularly the Aeroflot, and even more the Moscow.

Normal procedure on these 'show and tell' occasions followed the practice of activity directors on cruise ships filling in the hour before dinner: the question was designed to draw out an affirmative answer, a chance to elaborate, perhaps, to show off a little. It was not a high-powered interrogation by an investigative journalist.

'So that means they have your address,' he continued, and his jowls perceptibly pinkened. I knew he didn't mean they maintained a data bank in Moscow containing all the Portadown addresses.

'Yes, I wrote it on top of my letter,' I explained, 'so they could reply.' I still hadn't entirely grasped his line of reasoning, nor why he was seizing on this particular point.

All soon became clear in the explosion which followed.

'A bundle of Reds!' he exclaimed. 'The Reds have your address. They'll come and get us.' His confidence in the communist intelligence services evidently extended to their being able to infer his address from ours – maybe while they were spying on us, there'd be an incriminating piece of paper or somesuch which would lead to him.

By now he'd reached a state of apoplexy. 'You wrote to a bundle of Reds. They'll get us,' he kept repeating, swivelling his head to underline the gravity of the situation. In my mystification, I attempted to assemble the theory he was working under.

Beneficiaries of the post-1991 peace dividend era will find it hard to credit how seriously the Cold War was taken in those days by most of the population; but even by '60s' standards this was a trifle astonishing. Forget Philby, Blake, Embassy bugs, KGB operatives at large, moles in M15. Now they had a real lead: a genuine address. Just how would the approach be made? Would airline postcards be substituted for the dirty pictures which seem to have worked at Cambridge? Would there be an invitation to discuss aircraft design? Surely not. They'd already copied all current Western aircraft. Aeroflot route maps containing coded information? The mind boggled.

I was rescued by a total *non sequitur*. Someone in the family spoke up. 'Aye, and they weren't all fourpenny stamps, either. Most of them were for abroad.' I wasn't sure whether this was a backhanded reference to the earlier audit, but I took my cue and led the conversation to safer areas, such as Braniff's El Dorado route to South America and the Thai International 'Straight as a Ruler' way to the Far East.

Nevertheless, as an impressionable boy, it was some time before the gravity of a potential KGB targeting of our whole family wore off. I did have a fleeting vision of the Red Army somehow invading Britain, bypassing the major industrial cities, crossing the Irish Sea, picking out Portadown on the map, and coming straight to our house, number 91.

One letter I sent as a fourteen year old was seminal. British Eagle had entered the Belfast to London route, and when I wrote to them I told them how I'd been injured in a car accident and almost lost my life, following a spotting day out.

Back came a letter from their chairman, Harold Bamberg, prototype of the establishment-heel-nipping commercial aviation entrepreneur Freddie Laker. Both seemed to be ahead of their time. Both ultimately suffered the fate of most pioneers flying in the teeth of major entrenched interests.

Bamberg arranged a free flight to ENGLAND for me with a visit to the control tower at London Airport thrown in. I stayed with my Uncle Derrick in Wiltshire, and broke my cousins' football by kicking it into the path of an oncoming lorry on the busy London Road. My uncle's proximity to Bristol allowed me to achieve my ambition of actually flying in a DC3. The flight was only thirty miles across the Severn Estuary to Cardiff, but it did bring me to another country – WALES. The payoff for Bamberg's company was publicity, lots of it.

'CRASH LANDS JOHN AN AIR TRIP' read the banner headline in the *Portadown Times*. 'Of course we couldn't do this for every boy,' British Eagle's managing director intoned, 'but we thought in this case there were special circumstances.' The national press interviewed me at London Airport.

I almost made my first television appearance. Ulster Television assigned their camera crew – they only had one – to get pre-takeoff footage at Aldergrove. On their way to the airport, they were diverted to a breaking story: stone-throwing by a mob in Londonderry. A harbinger of things to come.

But while my television debut was still two years away, the crash and post-crash trip did open the door to local journalism. The *Portadown Times* had a vacancy for a part-time reporter for the Birches, a rural area five miles or so distant. I put myself forward. The word 'precocious' doubtless sprang to the mind of deputy editor, David Armstrong.

He eventually agreed, with three stipulations. One: my weekly reports would be 'From our Birches correspondent', and not carry my name. Two: nobody must ever know that I didn't actually live in the area. Three: it must *never* be divulged, to any reader, source, or especially to the corporate owners of the newspaper group, that I was only fifteen. My condition was bold, given that this was the sort of opportunity to offer eye-teeth for. I asked to be paid the going rate: tuppence a line.

Thus my career in journalism was born. Three days a week after school I cycled up to the paper's editorial office, where a desk, typewriter and phone were at my disposal. In the best journalistic tradition I only actually ventured out to the area I wrote about when enough reports weren't brought in to me.

The nearest we came to travel journalism was interviewing thirteen-year-old schoolgirls on their views about inconvenience caused by changing the school bus routes, or a successful campaign which I led to introduce a cheap evening return fare on the train to Belfast.

Except once, which was a bit of an embarrassment really. Domestic jet service was at last coming to Ulster and Scotland, simultaneously. British United drew up a guest list for the inaugural flights from Belfast, Glasgow and Edinburgh to London, consisting, in the main, of aviation correspondents from the national dailies, and 'leading' reporters from Scotland and Northern Ireland.

Somehow I wrangled my way onto this list. It was an experience not be missed, even if it meant skipping school for two days. I had to endure a few contemptuous looks from the Fleet Street big boys when the programme revealed me as the sole representative of a provincial weekly to have been invited. It was even more embarrassing to have to turn down subsequent invitations to press conferences and lunches from BUA in Belfast due to sixth-form Latin lessons.

In some ways travel was actually something of a hazard during my cub reporter days. Inspired in equal parts by my French teacher, Arthur Chapman, and a Parisian Jewish-Protestant acquaintance of my parents, Emile Guedj – an apple tart freak – I had opted for an exchange visit to FRANCE arranged through the school. This, and a sixth-form trip to GERMANY via BELGIUM were my only journeys abroad until three weeks short of my twentieth birthday.

Absence posed a difficulty for my regular weekly column until

I thought of an ingenious solution: I would collect enough news to last for two weeks, split the contents by the intrinsic 'ageing' of the story, and post the two columns, dated appropriately, in separate envelopes. This involved a certain brinkmanship in describing what were future events in the past tense. I had total faith in the fact-checking abilities of the sub-editors.

Unfortunately, when they recovered from the shock of receiving not one but two Birches columns from France, on the same day, thanks to the mercurial nature of the postal service, they immediately acted on the journalistic principle of 'Today's news today, tomorrow can wait', and ran one double-length column. This left an unfilled gap the following week, the only one during my whole tenure. That I never received any negative feedback from my readers about the 'reports' of events before they happened says a lot. Maybe they didn't notice!

# 3

## Scots Wha Hae

*St Andrews (1968)*

In his fiftieth year my father moved us from the town in which he and all our family had been born to a new job in Comber, County Down. For me it meant a new school, Regent House, which was kind enough to provide me with a German teacher, Owen Baxter, even though I was the only pupil in that year, so that I could continue the A-levels I'd embarked upon. One day Owen didn't come in, and it turned out he was in Germany marrying his sweetheart and bringing her back to Bangor.

It also meant, sadly, saying goodbye to my budding and lucrative career as a schoolboy journalist. The *Newtownards Chronicle* curtly informed me that they'd be glad to receive items of interest from me, but regretted they couldn't pay anything.

New vistas eventually opened up. I was asked to join the board of a nationwide UK venture, a magazine for sixth-formers, as well as write articles for it. The BBC in Northern Ireland decided its Sunday afternoon current affairs slot on television could be enlivened if the interviewers were seventeen year olds drawn from local schools. There were auditions and, despite my newness, I was selected for Regent House.

The headmaster virtually had kittens before each broadcast. I was always invited into his study for a chat, and reminded that viewers would perceive me to be representing the school. The fact that we wore school blazers underlined this, I suppose.

The other potential minefield I had to tread was my church's *Chariots of Fire* style ban on Sunday work, sports, and a list of other pursuits including television viewing. The ban was more an agreed convention than official policy, I reasoned, and it said nothing about actually *appearing* on television.

Still, such matters were taken very seriously, especially by older members. I remembered the story of my two great-aunts on holiday sitting on a wall overlooking the beach, their backs to the sea. It was Sunday, and an acquaintance, not being as scrupulous in observance, bought them ice creams. Without hesitating a moment, they threw the offending cones backwards over their shoulders to the beach below. Not being there, I often wondered if they landed on anybody's head!

In the end, nothing was said about me on television, and the number of empty seats in the congregation offered tangible proof that at least some people other than my mother watched the programme. With impeccable Irish consistency, those who held fast to their principles and didn't watch, nevertheless seemed genuinely pleased for me and congratulated me warmly.

The programme apparently enjoyed great success; or maybe novelty value is a more accurate description. Then, in the way one thing has of leading to another, media opportunities flowed in thick and fast. I was invited to be an after-dinner speaker at a prestigious gathering on the topic of 'Ulster in the year 2000'.

Even though my rosy predictions were probably way off the mark, the fact that the MC was a national newspaper executive ensured prominent coverage of my remarks next day, which in turn led to a round table discussion on ITV next night, and so on.

The mildly incestuous nature of all this media attention didn't bother me. Each occasion garnered a cheque, though I most remember a book given me after a speech. *Ballygullion* was a collection of humorous anecdotes from a fictional Irish town. The book could easily have been written as fact.

They say you always remember your first time, though, and my debut in front of the cameras was nothing to do with journalism, current affairs, or Ireland. It was a UK quiz show, *Double Your Money*, where the host, Hughie Greene, asked a series of questions, and you earned £2, then £4, £8, £16, and so on for each right answer, proceeding to compete for the jackpot after you crossed the £32 threshold.

It was really a sort of 'Double or quits', since each new try risked the stake you'd built up so far. But it wasn't money, in my case. It was a special edition where they were giving away a trip to Israel as the grand prize. I didn't win, but a viewer sent me £20, which served as a deposit towards the travelling I dreamed of doing one day.

Meantime there was the small matter of A-levels and choosing a university to apply to. I chose Cambridge, but they didn't choose me. Not surprising, perhaps, since the convention was that you waited until after A-levels to concentrate on their separate entrance exam, where you were competing with the 'cream of the cream', including the many English public schools with a track record of success.

My school hadn't had any students go on to Oxford or Cambridge; in fact very few ever left Ireland. The choice was invariably Queen's (Belfast) or Trinity (Dublin). 'Jake' Auterson, my English teacher, and Alan Knight, better known as 'Frosty' encouraged me to try again the following year. 'Just because you didn't make it first time around, doesn't mean you won't ever,' they said. This proverbial wisdom, safely tucked away, came in handy when attempting to enter off-limits countries in future years, and win the seemingly impossible 'race for the world'.

I didn't want to wait another year for college, though. The University of St Andrews, about sixty miles north of Edinburgh on Scotland's east coast, was my second choice, and fortunately they took a more favourable view of my application to study English Language and Literature.

On a clear day, you could look over from County Antrim and see the old Handley-Page Herald from BEA's Highlands and Islands Division circling to land at Macrihanish air strip, south of Campbeltown, on the Mull of Kintyre – later to be immortalised in Paul McCartney's lyrics. Scotland was barely twenty miles distant, at the nearest point. Despite that, I'd never been there, so there was an element of the thrill of a completely new country.

Perhaps my love of travel came from my family. My maternal grandfather spoke darkly of his aristocratic forebears from Spain. My paternal grandmother claimed descent from Stonewall Jackson of American Civil War fame. Whilst the idea of a soldier-mercenary ancestor certainly livened up the family tree, it left unexplained a there-and-back-again transatlantic migration.

There were aunts, cousins, and other bits and bobs in profusion in America and Canada. My own favourite theory, of whose origin I haven't the slightest idea, was that our branch of the family was linked to Abraham Lincoln's wife, Mary Todd Lincoln. She was one of the first, it seemed, to add a second 'd' to the name. Very wisely, since in German, and perhaps other tongues, 'Tod' spelt 'death'. Yet her critics insist that she claimed: 'One "d" may be good enough for God, but not for Todd.'

The lie was definitely put to this by Charlie Whitten, our baker who transmogrified himself into the losing king at the (recreated) 1690 Battle of the Boyne every 13th July at Scarva. Every Saturday we ordered two wheaten (or was it whitten?) loaves from him, and I was despatched to pick them up. Week in and week out, despite reminders, the legend engraved in ball-point on the flimsy white paper surrounding the crust was always the same: 'Tod'. One 'd'. My mother said it was because he wanted to save ink!

What was undeniable was that the Todds were a small but significant branch of the ancient Gordon clan. Did this give me the right to wear a kilt? 'You're not low-slung enough,' my rugby-playing friends advised me.

Whether or not the family's Scottish roots were plausible, I admired the Scots as a nation. They seemed to maintain a strong national identity, distinct from England, without carrying belligerence to the extreme of their Irish cousins – unless it was at Hampden Park or Murrayfield.

Strictly speaking, Scotland hadn't been a sovereign state since the 1707 Act of Union. Later in life, this kind of technical detail would become important as I ticked off countries visited.

Its absorption into the United Kingdom precluded such niceties as passports, visas, and formal diplomatic recognition, but that certainly doesn't stop many travellers signing their nationality as 'Scottish' on hotel registers abroad. Come to think of it, try asking a Glaswegian in a bar in Mallorca if he's English!

Scotland has always had its own money, church, laws, language (albeit not in majority use) and schooling system. Highers are taken instead of A-levels; and four years, not three, are required for a first degree. Scotland may not compete as a separate country in the Olympics, but its formidable rugby xv and soccer xi would take a dim view of not being regarded as national teams. The BBC gives tacit recognition to national status by describing Scotland as a 'national region' (as opposed to a 'regional region', I suppose!).

Long before I counted every country I'd been to, or checked against any list to see if the place was recognised, I knew in my blood Scotland was a country, even if not listed as such by the United Nations. Years later, such minutiae would occupy my attention closely to determine what was to be classified as a country.

But I still feel I am right to count SCOTLAND as a country, and the *Guinness Book of Records* is wrong to leave it out, but include as countries the Isle of Man, the CHANNEL ISLANDS, and a partially-submerged uninhabited reef in the Pacific Ocean which it discovered and added to its list only in 1993.

Studying for A-levels didn't leave much time to observe the disintegration in Ulster politics around me. Stridency, rabble-rousing and martyr complexes began to outshout the voices of moderation. If I'd thought about it, I may have begun to doubt that the country I'd grown up in still had a future. Maybe I was unconsciously in search of a new country that drizzly October morning as the BKS Viscount lifted off from Aldergrove and headed out over the Irish Sea to Edinburgh. Somehow I sensed in my bones that I'd never return permanently to my homeland. This premonition would give an edge to each journey I undertook thereafter. A lifetime of travelling was beginning.

St Andrews was founded by a papal bull in 1411 – something to do with a fight between rival popes. At that time there were only one or two colleges at Oxford and Cambridge; none anywhere else in Britain. So it could fairly claim to be an ancient institution.

The pulpit which John Knox was said to have 'dinged tae blads' was preserved in the university chapel, a few steps away from the magnificent ruined cathedral. A cross on the cobblestones marked the spot where over-zealous Protestant reformers had been burned, executed, hurled out of third-storey windows, or otherwise summarily dealt with by Mary Queen of Scots.

The violence seemed to have calmed down somewhat when I arrived on one of the last trains to run. Thanks to Beeching's cuts, each term thereafter you could only get as far as Leuchars

Junction by British Rail, the last five miles by intermittent bus or Shanks's pony.

Going 'overseas' to university was good preparation for what was in store for me as an international traveller. There was a welter of new people and customs to come to terms with.

We were eighteen in the Irish Students Society, outnumbered by one by Pakistani students, though I don't think they had a fellow countryman professor to invite them for tea and apple tart once a term.

Throughout my four years, I was billeted in an exceptionally comfortable hall of residence officially called St Salvator's Hall (Latin for Holy Saviour), but known to everyone as plain 'Sallies'. I even once received a letter addressed: J. Todd, Sally's, St Andrews.

Sallies was copiously supplied with reading matter in the lounge – not to mention morning coffee, afternoon tea, and maid service, all included in the fee charged to the grant awarding body at Balloo House in Bangor, County Down.

One day in my first year as I perused the *New Statesman* I came across an ad. for a summer tutorial position in New York. This was the launching pad I was looking for. It was time to start travelling, and fulfil the childhood dreams. The long summer vacation seemed an obvious opportunity. And the job would pay my expenses. It would also start me dreaming – and actively plotting – about future travels.

# 4

# Manhattan, Knights and the Colonel

*USA, Canada, Malta, Libya, SMOM (1969)*

It was a blisteringly hot August night in Manhattan. The apartment on East 73rd Street broiled like an oven; all our windows were open, to catch even a breath of cooler air. The noise, smells and commotion of the city wafted in. From a distance came the strains of the hit song:

> In the year 2525
> If man is still alive
> If woman can survive . . .

I turned into the living room from the tiny kitchen, glass of ice-water in hand. Rounding the door took some finesse since space was at a premium. Indeed what passed for the living room was little more than a passage connecting the entry lobby to the bedrooms. The kitchen seemed like an afterthought.

Yes, it was cramped, but this was New York's Upper East Side. Not bad digs for a foreign student summer visitor. It came with the job: shared with Jim, one of the two patients I 'minded'. Actually with Jim, I didn't have any real duties. The apartment was paid for by his family, and since he was 'cured' enough to hold down a daily job, I could live there in the evenings during my three-month stay.

Fred was somewhat different. The clinical intern, a pleasant Puerto Rican called Juan, was billeted in his quarters. During the day, while Jim was at work, Fred was in my charge: this applied to daylight hours only. By 5 p.m. I delivered him to his apartment a few blocks away, and returned to Jim and the tiny kitchen.

With Fred, the duties couldn't have been more pleasant. Sight-seeing trips to the countryside and playing golf and tennis, accounted for most of our time together.

Afterwards, it was explained to me in what seemed very Freudian terms. Fred's ego had been damaged by LSD. He'd been treated in hospital and discharged; now he needed a normal person to borrow from, until his own personality could be rebuilt.

Simultaneously I eased myself down on the black moquette sofa, and flicked on the 14″ Panasonic television: a relatively easy manoeuvre, since they were virtually cheek-by-jowl. In front of the television set was the window to the courtyard; behind the sofa was passage for one: two by arrangement. The programme was boring. My concentration wandered. How had I been selected for this job? My thoughts went back to the time, three weeks after I'd first perused the ad., when I found myself being interviewed for the position in London by a James Bagby, Ph.D.

Doctor Bagby, a quiet, refined middle-aged bachelor, stressed that he was a *psychologist*, not a *psychiatrist*. Not clinical, he sniffed, no white coats and all that: 'I wear a suit.' His practice apparently consisted entirely of a few wealthy clients; more precisely, of their offspring. Names were dropped, which I was meant to recognise as belonging to scions of the noblest and best on the East Coast.

They certainly had to be wealthy to pay his hourly consulting fees, which seemed astronomical to me then. His client base and fee structure allowed him to keep comfortable office hours (Monday afternoon to Thursday morning only), and to spend his leisure time unwinding in his plush estate backing on to that of the former UN Secretary-General, Dag Hammarskjöld, in Brewster, upstate New York.

I never quite understood the relationship between the 'tutoring' as described in the ad. and what I actually did, except that there was some very important tax connection.

Nearly every student from the British Isles who aspired to visit America flew by one of the many student charters. I had even dropped into this sideline business myself, representing an enterprising firm who, now that the jet age was firmly here, figured older and slower turbo props would mean cheaper fares, and students wouldn't mind.

The posters I affixed to college walls were blunt: 'New York £45. Why pay more?' They contrived to make the official student travel office irate, since they drove business away from their jets. But Dr Bagby wouldn't hear of charters. I noted, too, that he didn't use aerogrammes for his international mail, just a regular letterhead in an ordinary envelope which, of course, cost twice as much.

He offered me choice of airline. My sole reason for picking Pan Am was because they made a stop in Reykjavik, ICELAND. Who knew? Maybe they'd have a mechanical failure and the enforced layover would give time for sightseeing. In the event, all I saw of Reykjavik was some garish lights at about 3 a.m. Even when operating on time the Pan Am schedule was not the most convenient. The 2 p.m. departure from Prestwick effectively ruled out the 1 p.m. connecting flight from Belfast, leaving the 6.45 a.m. as the only alternative (4 a.m. departure from home).

Even then there was the nonsense of flying into Renfrew, taking a bus to central Glasgow, and embarking on another bus for Prestwick, thirty miles away in Ayrshire. When I arrived, I was in loads of time. The kindly Pan Am check-in agent, referring to the anticipated delay, said: 'The best thing you can do is go away, and come back about 7 p.m. or so when I'll have more news.' I had nowhere to go, so I watched the BOAC and Air Canada flights depart and the airport gradually empty. At 5 p.m. the Pan Am 707 hove into view, but only on its outward run to Copenhagen. At 11 p.m. it returned, and just before midnight we finally got airborne, about ten hours late.

What I most remember about this first introduction to American commercial aviation were two things. First, there was no attempt at an apology for lateness; if there was, I missed it hidden amongst the hyperbole and hubris. The captain: 'Good evening, ladies and gentlemen. Welcome aboard this fabulous Pan Am Clipper Jet bound for New York City, the greatest city in the world.' Then, when I asked the stewardess (they were still called that) for an orange squash, she said: 'Well, I've no idea what that is, but I'll try to make it for you.'

Now here I was in Manhattan, and all in all, the Jim and Fred job had proved rewarding. There was time off, too, during which I represented Britain at a student United Nations conference in the UN Building. I must not have been wholly orthodox in my dealings with Fred, because one day shortly before I left he said: 'I am a bit crazy, I suppose, but you're *definitely* crazy!'

My attention jerked back to the long-forgotten television show in East 73rd. Something caught my eye: it was a preview of EXPO 70, to be held in Osaka, Japan, the following year. Right then and there I knew that would be my next major destination. I had no capital or income, except what would be left at the end of this summer job . . . but I would go. And I'd also tour many of the neighbouring Asian countries, for good measure.

I was unaware then that this insatiable curiosity to see the world would place me, twelve years later, in the 'top ten' of world travellers of all time, and position me for a keenly contested race to the very last place on earth. Similarly, I only dimly realised how great an asset lack of capital would be. It would force me to be creative and well planned, if I was to achieve with a penny what others did with a pound.

I began tentatively to strategise. Since my needs were adequately provided for in term time, I would concentrate on the long summer vacations initially to work my way around the world. I would use this summer's cash as seed capital, but seek to find a job each summer to replenish the pot for future summers.

*Every year I would attempt to do something useful, so that travel didn't become an indulgence or an end in itself.*

Each chance I got, I would take in neighbouring countries to the one I was in, both in case I didn't get a chance to return to that area, and because I figured out that this gave 'the most bang for the buck'. A side trip might only cost £40 for example, from wherever I'd travelled to, but £400 or more to return to directly from Britain.

Thus, in Manhattan, a dream was born.

On my way back from New York I was determined not to fly Pan Am. I was equally determined to see exactly how much more in terms of additional countries (one) and destinations (several) I could extract from the ticket value.

I came away from the travel agency feeling I'd done well. A single New York-Glasgow coupon was traded for

New York-Rochester-Buffalo-Niagara-Toronto-Ottawa-Montreal-Halifax-St John's-Glasgow. More importantly, I'd learnt a lot about fare construction and things called MPMs (maximum permitted miles) which would stand me in good stead for future long-distance journeys.

It was a lightning trip, mostly on Air Canada, with hours rather than days in each place, since I wasn't flush with funds for hotel overnights. But I did see all the basic sights, and I had two full days in Toronto with an Irish uncle who took a day off his construction job to show me round.

As we neared City Hall he suddenly slid back in the driver's seat so that his knees were almost level with his head. The effect was rather like one of those party games where you're blindfolded and have to use your outstretched arms to stick a tail on a donkey's backside. He also pulled his baseball cap on very tightly. 'My crew was supposed to be working around here today,' he muttered.

The single disappointment was Niagara Falls, which had been turned off while some repairs were done. In the same spirit of hubris demonstrated by the Pan Am pilot, a large notice informed me that this was the opportunity of a lifetime, to stand where normally thousands of tonnes of water cascaded down.

But what if you'd actually come all that way just to see the water?

Back from Manhattan via CANADA there were three weeks left before the academic term started. My father had just won one of those 'Salesman of the Year' incentives. The prize: two weeks for two by scheduled airline in MALTA and GOZO. My mother had to drop out, so I was the fortunate companion.

I got to work immediately to maximise the opportunity . . . SICILY on the way down, ITALY at no extra cost; flying back on Nigeria Airways VC10 from Lagos which picked up passengers in Rome.

And LIBYA, of course, since it was only forty minutes' flying time from Valetta, the Maltese capital, in one of Colonel Gadaffi's brown F27s. The Colonel wouldn't mind if we dropped in, as long as we didn't stay long.

Surprisingly, it all worked out fine. Even the two countries wholly contained within the boundaries of Rome itself. *Two* countries? Which you could walk round in an hour? VATICAN CITY of course. What other country could boast such a marvellous ceiling? But there was also one other little-known 'sovereign state': the SOVEREIGN MILITARY ORDER OF MALTA, SMOM for short.

Believe it or not, SMOM has diplomatic recognition from over forty states. Its buildings don't cover more than an acre or two, but it exchanges ambassadors, issues coinage and patronage, and jealously guards its long and fascinating history of combat.

Its *raison d'être* was the Crusades. Afterwards it held power in a number of Mediterranean centres, not least Malta itself, before settling its rather secretive secretariat in a quiet Rome side street. Today the work of the knights is mostly charitable. Recently SMOM elected a Scot to head their order – the first non-Italian in centuries. So they can't be all that bad!

# 5

# World's Safest Airline

*Egypt/Gulf (1970)*

I don't know who Mr Walker is or was, but he created a handsome trust, the sole purpose of which was to distribute travel bursaries to worthy students at St Andrews. Happily, I qualified as one, after submitting my travel project to the selection committee.

I didn't feel it would carry much weight if I said to them my purpose was to visit EXPO 70 in Japan, so in the application I fell back on the old chestnut of 'seeing and experiencing at first hand another culture'. I think I can say without hesitation that I fulfilled that goal.

With £100 in hand from the good Walker Trust people, I set to planning my route. The scheduled return air fare to Tokyo from London was £656 in economy class. Then I spied a tiny notice about a student charter via Cairo, departing in early July.

Family and friends were sceptical. 'Don't the flights to Japan go on that "Great Circle" route through Asia? Or the new way via Alaska and over the North Pole? Or maybe Russia. Surely not via Cairo?'

But Cairo it was, for the ticket was on United Arab Airlines (wags said the initials actually stood for Use Another Airline), who had recently acquired the route from their home country of Egypt to Tokyo, and proposed to feed into it passengers from the cities they served in West Europe.

At first, I didn't twig to this. After I'd paid, and with no sign of any ticket being delivered, I became increasingly worried. The student office could only tell me the ticket would come a few days before departure. It actually came the evening before.

To be a charter, I assumed the whole plane was on a dedicated point-to-point journey, every last seat filled by student organisers, and therefore at a one-off price. But we were leaving from Heathrow on a regular flight, with choice of dates and stopovers. Some of the students looked suspiciously old, to say nothing of the German train driver.

When the penny dropped about the underlying economies, a whole new vista opened up for me, both as a travel consumer and in my rapidly developing sideline as a part-time travel agent, brokering discount price tickets.

The commercial proposition was pure marketplace. All the large airlines, mostly state-owned, from the main countries of the world, regularly met together to fix cartel-style tariffs for travel on international routes. They then met bilaterally, not only to reaffirm prices between their two capitals, but to divide up or pool together capacity; and as much as they could, prevent airlines from other countries officially picking up or setting down passengers for gain between their two countries.

There were some exceptions, but by and large the home airlines, for example, of India, Japan and Kenya, could expect fifty percent of revenue, (accruing, mind you, at prices they themselves had set) on the routes from, say, Britain to their respective countries. The theory no doubt held that those who wished to fly paid the full price, and frequencies were set accordingly.

To this day, under these restrictive bilateral government agreements, it's often very difficult for an airline which gets a bigger share of the traffic than its partner from the other country, to persuade the other to allow it more flights, if the other would lose further market share by agreeing.

Wasn't there, then, scope for a canny operator to tap a market of those who would fly if it was cheaper? And that's just what the third-world airlines, especially those from Arab countries and Africa, were quietly doing. They were quickly followed by East European carriers, and unpopular airlines generally, until a whole industry developed of 'unofficial' or 'bucket shop' prices for flights, invariably on less-direct routeings.

EGYPT was strategically placed for this operation, since its national carrier had a licence to fly to countries such as India, Japan and Kenya, as well as to carry passengers from London and elsewhere in Europe to Cairo. Adding together two legs then, you got a through – but not direct – journey. With keen pricing an airline could then sell tickets to Japan-bound passengers in London, even though they technically were not flying on that route.

Many years later the US domestic airlines would do the same thing – send you from Los Angeles to New York via St Louis, Denver, or Memphis. Only they dubbed it a 'hub and spoke' system. And they claimed it to be a new invention.

Of course the indirect airlines had to charge the same as for the direct routes, said the rules. This was easily achieved by printing the full price as face value on the ticket, marking it 'Non endorsable without reference to original issuing office', and then doing some fancy internal accounting.

The practical effect was that airlines seeking this cut-price business selected one main agent or consolidator on which to dump their tickets at an agreed wholesale or bulk price, leaving this agent to do the reselling through other outlets at its own marked-up price, which was still considerably less then the price charged by the very same airline for the very same ticket if you bought it from the airline itself!

The 'United Arab Airlines' designation came about through one of Egypt's periodic mergers with a neighbour, usually Syria or Libya, accompanied by declarations of undying unity, inseparability, brotherhood, etc. The name quietly reverted to Egypt Air shortly after the breakup of yet another of these 'unbreakable' unions.

UAA, and Arab airlines in general, were among the few buyers of the British Comet, a jet-age pioneer that was now beginning to look dated. I was looking forward to flying in this venerable machine again (it had replaced the Vanguard on some Belfast-London runs) but UAA were now utilising their spanking new Boeing 707s.

Sixteen stops, flexible return dates, £212. Almost too good to be true! It was on our late evening arrival in Cairo, that the overbooking became apparent. Departure for Doha, Bombay, Bangkok, Hong Kong and Tokyo was set for eight o'clock next morning. The ground staff looked at our connecting tickets, muttered about a hotel, and told us to go through customs and immigration.

I'd spent the pricely sum of £8 for a full tourist visa for Egypt for my stopover on the return journey, complete with stamps supporting the Aswan Dam project, and other forced contributions to the cultural heritage of the country. This outbound ten-hour transit was free, I knew, and I was glad to see the passengers in front of me simply having their passports rubber stamped, with no questions asked.

As luck would have it the officer opened my passport right at the page decorated with the Temple of Thebes, and the inscription of the Egyptian Consul in London, and proceeded to obliterate it, over my strenuous objections. 'You may enter,' he said. So much for advance planning!

Collecting the luggage and other matters took a while, and it was after midnight when I found a manned UAA desk. Already about forty 'students' bound for Tokyo were surrounding it. From a distance the omens were not good: I could hear raised voices and murmurings of discontent.

The unease expressed had been on account of only one hotel voucher being dispensed – in theory it was for a group, but no one could read Arabic to decipher it. The UAA man packed up and went home. 'Be back at six in the morning,' he said. It was already almost 1 a.m.

One of our number attempted to interest a somnolent taxi driver in taking us to the hotel. 'Bus, bus,' he repeated. A bus did eventually show up, at about 2.30 a.m. By now our numbers had dwindled as several of us had given up and gone back into the airport to grab some shuteye on the benches. The rest of us quickly boarded, only to find the driver disembarking.

'Break,' he said. At 3.15 he returned. He hesitated before putting the key in the ignition, and turned to address us. The import of his words was that it was now so late that there was no point going to the hotel – why didn't we enjoy a night tour around Cairo? He'd give us a very good price.

Sensing that his words were falling on a less than receptive audience, he quickly turned back to the wheel and set off. Our relief in arriving at the hotel reception was short-lived. The presence or absence of a voucher seemed to make not the slightest difference: the number of bodies sprawled around the lobby indicated that room space was at a premium.

I approached the man behind the desk. He raised his hands with a doleful expression and said: 'Sir, it's like this every night. No rooms.' I put my head together with an Indian doctor, a Swede, and a Belgian teacher. Together we scraped up some baksheesh, and were given the key to a tiny room on the fifteenth floor.

It was a Pyrrhic victory. 'Look,' said the Swede, 'we have to leave in forty minutes anyway. Let's freshen up, and share a taxi back to the airport via the pyramids.' The driver had scarcely begun to offer us this alternative when he realised that that was exactly what we were indeed asking for.

Anyone who has ever physically been to the pyramids knows the answer to at least one of the great questions of the ages: Why were they built? What was their purpose? To extract tribute, of course, from an advanced yet gullible species called 'tourist'. This particular creature, unlike the legions of slaves in centuries past, whose dedication to every command of their master was taken as read, needed a degree of cajoling to be parted from their earthly treasures.

The cajoling began immediately the taxi drew alongside a rag, tag, and bobtail outfit squatting by the Giza road. The sun was just making its appearance, a pale shadow of the desert intensity it would display in a handful of hours. Yet despite the earliness of the hour, the mere approach of the taxi galvanised the twelve scurrilously-dressed local inhabitants into such rapid-fire action that, in my view, they should have been given a chance at running the administration of Cairo Airport, the local hotel trade, or perhaps both.

With no predetermined expectation on our part, we were clearly outmanoeuvred in the subsequent negotiations, in addition to being both outnumbered and at a disadvantage in terms of not being on home ground.

Everything: the camel to ride upon, the appropriate headgear, the garments draped around our shoulders, the small gifts pressed upon us – 'It's nothing, sir, just a very small reminder of your visit here' – was at first presented, and received, in the spirit of Arab hospitality. But anyone with even a rudimentary training in transaction analysis would have discerned on the one side the consumer pleasure mingled with fears of unsanitariness and 'How much is it going to cost?'; and, on the other, the 'How much can we clip them for?' of the ingrained monopoly supplier, to whom each new customer was fresh bait for the same old line, together with hook and sinker. Only the precise tariff was withheld until the final *dénouement*.

In world-record beating time my colleagues and I were separated, accompanying hand baggage left with a one-eyed man on the ground for 'safe keeping' (also doubtless for their value as inanimate hostages), and each of us suddenly hoisted what seemed like thirteen feet into the air, while maintaining a death grip on the camel rein, then pointed south towards Johannesburg with an enormous stretch of the Sahara Desert intervening, and no bottled water supplied.

At this stage the escort, who was holding the other end of the camel rein, became a very important person in the lives of each of us. His role encompassed many skills, of which the most important was reassurance that he wasn't going to let go.

He was all smiles, full of friendship. If we would pass down to him our cameras he would duly take pictures of us. As well, of course, as adding to his bargaining power in the coming financial negotiations. Actually those negotiations began precisely at the nerve-racking point of the camel's first clumpy steps. The pyramids seemed still a long way away; the stability, comfort and normalcy factors were not high, the super eight movie camera had been handed down. We were definitely committed.

Negotiations, in a sense, is the wrong word. They took the form more of a monologue on the part of the escort as to how poorly he was paid, how ill his sister was, how much he admired Britain, Ireland, Sweden, etc. as appropriate, how generous previous riders had seen fit to be, and other miscellaneous remarks calculated to induce in his charge one clear and unequivocal message: 'Give me.'

What do you, as a privileged tourist from a perceived wealthy country, say to a grubby third-world camel boy who at this precise moment is your one surety that the camel underneath you won't bolt off in the direction of southern Africa, who's holding your camera, and whose arguments, after frequent repetition, even begin to sound plausible? Try as you might to steer the subject of conversation away from money, you do not succeed, and you end up acquiescing to the polite, but incredibly persistent, demands. The pyramids seen, the camel-ride over, the payment made, and finally reunited with your friends, you attempt to retrieve your belongings and leave.

That's when the financial boom is lowered. These friendly discussions to and fro while on the back of the camel turn out to have been side issues, such as the tab for having your picture taken, and the tip to your escort. Now there's the serious business of paying the camel owner for hire of his beast, plus the official visitor's tariff for the pyramids.

A Custer's last stand is called for. We form a phalanx and deliberate as a joint team. No headway; then a brainwave: 'We've no dollars or pounds, or Egyptian currency. Just kroner and these Belgian francs, anyway,' producing two largish notes. Any hope that this could bring a favourable conclusion to the proceedings is quickly squashed. The littlest boy sends for a medium-sized boy who in turn fetches a bigger boy. He goes to a tent behind the camels and is admitted. In moments a rotund man, clad with an equal degree of decrepitude to all the others we've so far seen, emerges and fishes from underneath his off-white robe a gigantic wallet, its many compartments bulging with thirty to forty hard currencies.

He taps the imbedded calculator for the Belgian franc exchange rate, quickly snatches the new addition to the right side of his wallet, makes change and cheerily waves us on our way. We are well and truly beaten, and we know it.

Compared with the scene greeting us on arrival at Cairo Airport this Sunday morning, the previous evening's chaos was as nothing. Boxes are piled to the ceiling in front of all check-in positions. Even finding the correct check-in position is daunting. Live people (whether passengers, wellwishers, or mere hangers-on, isn't clear) scurry between what look at first glance like dead bodies. On closer examination these recumbent forms are hapless delayed travellers who've slept on the floor, and are not yet fully awake.

There's a constant din in which it's difficult to distinguish official announcements from mere chatter. We inch our way towards a desk, wondering why in retrospect we hadn't traded our pyramid and hotel adventures for making a start on the check-in procedure last night. Our spirits aren't lifted when we're given what look like very flimsy slips of paper in lieu of boarding passes to present at the boarding gate once through immigration. The suspicion of gross overbooking begins to harden. After all, how many tickets do you need to sell at a seventy percent reduction to break even? Any answer above one hundred percent is very disconcerting! It's now five minutes to departure.

Pushing and shoving through the outbound customs and immigration formalities leaves us with the feeling that the airline staff are confident sufficient would-be passengers will be weeded out at this stage to more than solve the overbooking problem.

A stern man in uniform appears in the departure area – having obviously been airside, and now returned. It's the captain of our aircraft, not at all happy that departure time has come and gone, and his plane is still largely empty of passengers, while more than it can hold are attempting to break through the departure log-jam.

The initial euphoria of incipient rescue quickly gives way to perplexity as he strides past the official at the head of our queue, still a long way off for us, and begins jointly upbraiding all of us in line: 'What are you doing here? You should be on my plane.' Without waiting for a response, or, as seems to us even more logical, interceding with the official, he bounds back to the exit and disappears onto the tarmac.

Somehow his amateur theatrics work, the line speeds up, and I reach the last obstacle – the podium right at the gate. 'We're already full in economy class,' the ticket taker says, looking at my *ersatz* boarding pass, and simultaneously scanning his seat plan – a sea of white now that all the coloured sticky tabs have been removed and placed on the boarding passes which got there first!

'So I'm afraid you'll have to go in first class,' he continues laconically. Before the shock registers, I'm on board, chocks away, and the white tablecloth is being spread for the first of many feasts on the two-day journey. Who said student charters were spartan affairs?

Before Asia proper is reached, the stops all seem to be at sweltering dots in the desert: QATAR; KUWAIT. If their main product was carrots, would they now be so well known? Would they be recognised as individual countries?

In between feasts the male steward brings reading matter to my seat – mostly old copies of *Al Fatah*. He takes great pains to make sure I understand Arab politics. 'Relax,' he says 'It's only Western and Israeli aircraft that are being hijacked. You're on the safest airline in the world.'

# 6

# The Butcher's Shop

*Japan (1970)*

JAPAN was a crash course in cross-cultural understanding. They say that even when foreigners manage to master: kimonos; the four alphabets; 2,000 written characters; ceremonial bows; types of tea; slipper etiquette; business protocol; strange toilets; communal bathing; miniaturisation of everything including living space; packed commuter trains . . . and SUSHI, they're still never fully accepted or integrated into Japanese society.

I was spared the initial harsh impact of unintelligible street and station signs, and a numbering system of buildings that relates to age not sequence in any given road, by the lady designated to meet me at Haneda Airport.

She was a diminutive, recently widowed American who'd volunteered to do a stint as guest house hostess in Tokyo, meeting and seeing off Westerners in transit.

'Well, I never,' she exclaimed in her southern drawl. 'How many people were on that plane? Didn't look like Egyptians to me, most of them. Now we're gonna have to hurry on back home.'

She nodded to me to wait while she stood in line at the ticket counter to buy our train tickets. Arriving at the booth, she suddenly raised her voice to boom in the verbal equivalent of capital letters – English, of course – while holding up her fingers to demonstrate the number of tickets she wanted. A veritable posse of polite Japanese surrounded her and translated for the clerk. She returned to me smiling. 'It's easy, once you get the hang of it,' she said proudly. 'Now the only thing to watch is that we catch the semi-express, not the one that stops at every station.'

She bobbed up and down in the crowd, trying to see over the heads of the Japanese travellers, themselves not tall. I felt conspicuous at six foot two inches. She dragged me to one platform after another. Finally, after many discussions with bystanders (again in English) we chose one particular train. She was delighted to see the countryside start to flash past, proof this wasn't the dreaded local. Her joy was shortlived as she recognised after much bobbing up and down (we stood most of the way) our stop approaching, then receding at an alarming pace. Clearly this was the express, not the 'semi'.

Three hours and a detailed knowledge of the Tokyo railway system later, we made it to the guest house. An acquaintance with low ceilings and bangs on the head – which was to last throughout my stay – began in earnest, as I navigated my way to a second-floor bedroom. I couldn't get acquainted with any Japanese, since all guests were foreigners.

Amongst other forms of acculturation, this delightful lady took me to a concert given by a touring troupe of young scrubbed Americans who went by the name of 'People to People' or some such. They sang: 'Raindrops keep falling on my head', and other edifying nonsense. Presumably the Japanese in the audience received it generously. I was unable to tell, since I was surrounded by other admiring American matrons, who kept muttering how nice it was to see clean young people who weren't on drugs, and how important all this understanding of each other's culture was.

Even EXPO 70 – the fulfilment of the first part of the Manhattan dream – was disappointingly like any big-scale international exposition. English was much spoken, and there were so many exhibits and events relating to the Western world I was familiar with, that you could be forgiven in the middle of it for not knowing which country you were actually in.

I didn't even get to sample the famous Bullet Train, or to give it its proper designation, the New Tokaido Express: 347 miles to Osaka in 2 hours 58 minutes. I had a Japanese Youth Air discount card which gave me fifty percent off domestic flights, and I wanted to sample both Japan Airlines and All Nippon. Although they hadn't yet graduated to 500-seat jumbos and seventy, yes *seventy*, flights per day in each direction between two internal cities, I had a feeling, even then, that the future of commercial air transport would be written there, when the Japanese took a breather from eighty-hour weeks and country rebuilding and launched out on leisure trips.

The culture shock which until now had been like a pulled punch, was about to sock me with full force. I flew to Hokkaido.

Hokkaido, the north island, to Honshu, the main island containing Tokyo and Osaka, is as Scotland to England, or the wild west to the eastern seaboard of the United States.

Even today, with an undersea rail link and booming domestic travel (some four million annually at last count) between the two islands, few Europeans and Americans are aware that in tightly packed, congested Japan, there exists an underpopulated area of over 30,000 square miles of cattle ranches, pine forests and fertile valleys: twenty percent of Japan's land area, including some of the most ruggedly beautiful, shared by only five percent of the population.

The only three facts in my possession about Hokkaido before I got there, were that every February they hosted a huge Snow Festival (I'd seen pictures of the breathtaking ice sculptures); that they'd been selected as the site of the 1972 Winter Olympics, and that a UK friend of a godson of a friend was on a two-year contract at Sapporo University and had a large home to himself in which I could stay.

Summer 1970 was too early to be concerned with 1972 games, I mused. I was wrong. Following an initial fill-in job teaching English at Sapporo's International Academy of Youth, I was invited to teach at an Institute for Japanese teachers of English, and this led to a job teaching English to the television technicians, air traffic controllers, mayor's office, and others anticipating the Olympics.

And all because of the butcher's shop. You see, my English friend, John Landon, was still on holiday when I arrived. He arranged for me to stay with a Japanese family meantime. When it became noised abroad that there was a 'gaigin' in the neighbour-hood, a few enterprising parents decided their children should take advantage of English lessons from a native. They didn't want to pay a private lesson rate, and there weren't quite enough to form a quorum for a class so naturally it was suggested that a suitably worded ad. be placed in the butcher's at the corner. Apparently that was the drill. It worked: for three afternoons a week I taught a form of English to neighbourhood children in Mrs Ishihara's living room.

Mr and Mrs Ishihara were both schoolteachers, who seemed to work all the hours God sent them. Living with them was an education in itself. The genuflecting came naturally due to the height of the doorways. You couldn't be so crass as to wear outdoor shoes inside when an army of slippers greeted you at the door. Elaborate tea ceremonies were not *de rigueur* for everyday usage – you just had to memorise which kettle and which size of cup went with which colour of tea. Fortunately, I was more consumer than preparer.

But it was the more intimate aspects of life that were hardest to grasp. Bathing was full soap and complete rinse before gingerly easing into a scalding barrel of water shared by the whole family, one after another. Sometimes you had the privilege of going first. The only advice I'd had before coming, 'Be deft with the use of the towel', I discovered was more apt for the mixed communal baths and public hot springs.

And I could never quite remember whether Beethoven's Ninth Symphony was the one played by the van which came on Mondays to collect rubbish, or on Wednesdays to do the weekly pickup from all the neighbourhood dry toilets, using a giant suction device. I knew once he arrived, but by then it was too late.

As a special treat, on the Ishiharas' sole Saturday off that month, we took a train to the seaside and ate something mixed with seaweed in a ball of rice. It felt odd to be both sitting surrounded by seaweed, and eating it at the same time. Or maybe it was just meant to be wrapping.

On the first day at my Institute, I popped into the washroom to 'spend a penny'. As I emerged, I was intrigued, on crossing from stall to washbasin, to see the receptionist putting on lipstick in front of the mirror. The washbasin was directly in front of the urinals. She said: 'You must find our customs strange.'

After some weeks of teaching students the same age as me, I tired of Mr this and Miss that and I asked if I could call them by their first names. 'It's not our custom,' they replied. A week later three of them brought me a gift and said they'd thought about it and now that we were friends we could use first names.

The gifts were the best part. Every class I taught gave me gifts at the end of their course, or when I left. On my twenty-first birthday I even had bouquets of flowers brought by my female students. Sapporo TV gave me a lantern too heavy to carry back, and the mayor held a ceremony for me involving much bowing, and putting an official emblem on my lapel. I had to be careful to bow low enough during the ceremony to be pinned but not so low that I was jabbed by the pin. Who knows? Maybe that made me a freeman of the city of Sapparo, or entitled me to lesser privileges I haven't yet taken up.

My talents weren't universally appreciated. I found the materials used in the Teachers' Institute a bit stuffy, and decided I could liven up their lessons with some ad-libbing. After one of these impromptu lessons I was taken aside by the management. They demonstrated how the lesson should be taught by opening the manual and reading verbatim in robot-like voices. Perhaps an inanimate version of me would have done. Other times I tried to inject some hilarity, using well-worn jokes. None of them worked. If there's anything more mortifying than a totally uncomprehending silence after you've delivered the punchline, with the prospect of then *explaining* the humour in translation, I'm not sure I know what it is.

Then, incongruously, I would explain that my friend John Landon lived in London. Immediately mirth would erupt classroom-wide, and there would be much slapping of knees and repeating, beween gales of laughter: 'His name is *Randon* and he lives in *Rondon*.'

I gathered it was some sort of play on similar words, but couldn't come up with any other jokes along the same lines.

Actually the whole John-combined-with-teaching-English situation was mildly amusing in itself. At that time in Sapporo there were four British expatriates living in the city. Doubtless there were more – I only knew four. All four taught English; three were called John; three at one time lived in the same house.

This accomplished two things: first, it made for great difficulty answering the telephone: 'John, it's for you. I think it's John.' Then, it convinced legions of Hokkaido students that all 'Englishmen' (they refused to distinguish Scots, Irish etc.) who taught English were called John.

Undoubtedly my favourite class was kindergarten – five to eight year olds – even though it gave me the most headaches, since I didn't have enough Japanese to tell them what they were supposed to do. Usually if I ran up against a wall, I'd tear out to the corridor and the receptionist (the one I met in the Gents) would come in and translate.

One day I'd been getting on particularly well with page four where I'd said, 'What is this?' and they'd repeated:

'What ees thees?'

Now page five invited me to ask them, 'What is this?' – holding up a pencil – and they were to reply:

'Thees ees a pencil'; only to a man (or rather boy and girl) they repeated:

'What ees thees?' as I'd been encouraging them to do formerly.

Note for teachers of English in foreign parts: before embarking, learn in the native tongue a means of describing clearly that you're switching from the demonstrative to the interrogative. You can't be certain of bumping into a willing helper in the gentlemen's loo.

If you've dreamed as a boy of travelling far and wide, you don't go straight home from Japan. My UAA ticket was going to be used to 'race' through Asia, I determined. I may not have been fully conscious at that moment of why I wanted to stop at each point I could along the line. I just saw them on the map, and figured: 'Why not see them in real life?' I couldn't think of a suitable objection to that.

# 7

# War in Progress

*East Asia (1970)*

HONG KONG was the first of the dozen Asian countries I sand-wiched between the Japan stay and home. I stayed in an empty flat whose inhabitants were on holiday, near a couple from Perth who gave me breakfast in their flat; they played Rolf Harris records continually. It was quicker to sprint over the adjoining roof to get there, than to go down sixteen flights to the street, and back up fifteen in the neighbouring building.

Coming in to land at Kai Tak presents you with an instant thumb-nail sketch of the place. As the 707 dips below cloud cover you see Hong Kong rushing up towards you – commercial towers, row on row of tenement blocks, the ancient walled-city-slum claimed by Peking in 1963, even the sampans jostling for space in the South China Sea.

From a window seat the buildings positively scream past as you screech into a landing on the runway that juts way out into the sea. The whole effect is perilous, like the very idea of six million souls dwelling in so few square feet, or the brevity of the ninety-nine year lease, and the looming shadow of the big Red Dragon on the horizon.

I took the tram to the Peak, had tea on the rooftop of the YMCA, counted the Rolls Royces in circulation to see if there really were more per head here than anywhere else on earth, crossed to and fro on the Star Ferry at tuppence a time, and enjoyed easily the best Chinese food outside the mainland.

But I'd come specifically to see one icon. Not so much sight as symbol. I took a bus out to the New Territories, passing fields and landscapes which gave me much more idea of what China itself must be like, thoroughly rural.

Eventually we pitched up at the border river, Lok Ma Chau. I climbed a small hill and trained powerful binoculars towards the watch towers on the Chinese side. In between the guards, peasants in conical hats worked the fields as they likely had done for centuries.

'Some day I'll cross that border,' I thought to myself.

Next day I flanked the skirts of the People's Republic from another side. The hydrofoil had been introduced on the run to MACAU, but I chose the slower ferry, for a more stately procession through the lighters, junks, sampans, and merchant ships, forty miles to the west across the mouth of the Pearl River.

The city of Macau, an ancient Portuguese possession, occupies a tiny two square mile peninsula jutting right up to China. Its old colonial facades, though now decaying, were colourful. The cathedral must have been a splendid landmark in past centuries.

I hired one of those pedal cycles to go as close as allowable to Red China. There was a gate with a large red star on top. A sentry was on duty; he barked out something to the cycle operator when we approached within a hundred yards. Whatever it was, the cycle operator turned around sharply, and pedalled away; I snapped a hasty picture on the turn.

'You see that river,' my escort said as he pedalled. 'Many people they try swim over. Guard shoot. Bang bang. Dead.' It seemed vivid enough. Here was a man-made cordon thrown over a huge land mass, with a quarter of the world's population behind it. My determination grew: on a future trip I would cross that border and visit the people on the other side.

Strictly speaking there was only one other UAA stop before India and home: Bangkok. But THAILAND, the exotic uncolonised kingdom, was so conveniently placed that routes radiated from its capital, north, south, east, west, inviting visits to countries tantalisingly within reach.

After an all-night train journey up country to Chiang Mai, past droves of sleeping water buffalo, then a bus further north and east to Chiang Rai, I fell in with a British missionary who directed me to two of his American colleagues living right on the border with Laos. It took quite a few jaunts by rickety minivan to reach their riverside hut.

Verna had just finished baking a tray of cinnamon buns – quite a feat in their one-room quarters. I was so hungry after an enforced diet of intermittent roadside rice and vegetables, that I'm ashamed to say I gobbled up half the contents at one sitting. The cinnamon aroma seemed more appropriate for a real-estate agent's set piece – a beautiful show house on a weekend afternoon – than a hut overlooking the brownish river where the entire local populace seemed to be engaged in washing themselves, their animals, or their clothes at the same time.

In the morning Verna's husband accompanied me on a dugout canoe across the river, with a handful of locals. I was in LAOS, on one of the easiest border crossings imaginable. Despite weeks of pleading and cajoling officials of Royal Lao Embassies in three countries, and the impressive full page visa that resulted, nobody seemed bothered enough to check.

I'd been warned that internal transport schedules were erratic in parts of South East Asia. In Laos they seemed non-existent. At the edge of the airstrip at Ban Houei Sai I waited for the promised Royal Lao Airways DC3 to show up. And waited and waited and waited. The town office (a boy with holes in his tee shirt, sitting at an empty desk) had no further information, so I reluctantly retraced my steps to Thailand, leaving the capital, Vientianne, for a future visit.

The plan had been to obtain visas for Vietnam and Cambodia in Vientianne, on the assumption it might be easier there. I'd already drawn a blank in Bangkok and Hong Kong.

Fortunately a rare chance to visit BURMA (now Myanmar) opened up, as the government reversed its closed door policy of recent years and permitted limited entry by air, if you flew in on their national airline from Thailand, and back the same way, or on to Calcutta. The courteous offical at the Burmese Embassy firmly explained that with the visa affixed in my passport I could now go to the Union of Burma Airways office to book a flight, but that if I tried to enter by road I would be shot. I opted for the air method.

The expectation of colourful exotic mysteries emanating from a previously hidden country was rudely shattered when I boarded the Boeing 727 at Don Muang Airport. I'd been expecting the venerable forty-seat turbo prop Fokker F27, well used to nipping in and out of jungle clearings; not this production-line American jet, which looked as if it was fresh from California.

It was fresh from California. So was the pilot, on a 'wet' lease from Western Airlines. 'Welcome aboard Union of Burma Airways,' he said, in a voice you expected for a Denver-Seattle or Boise-Los Angeles flight. It was a pity the flight schedule only allowed two days in Rangoon, because almost all of one of them was taken up filling in forms declaring suitability to be admitted, having watch and camera particulars entered physically on the passport page, and counting out all foreign currencies to onlooking customs men.

In the limited remaining time after passing through formalities and finding a room, I saw around the Shwe Dagon pagoda (more guides than tourists) and was besieged by residents eager to find a foreigner to talk to who might act as postman, bringing in news from the outside world, and possibly carrying out their news and views.

Yet another transit stamp at Don Muang set me on course for MALAYSIA and SINGAPORE. Even though many of the generation just before mine had been given posts on graduation tantamount to administering huge chunks of territory overseas in the still-extant Empire, it was here that I found visible evidence of the rapid pace of de-colonisation.

The whiff of colonial estates and absentee-owner rubber plantations was nowhere in the air. All around you saw bright, eager students going for Ph.D.s and professional careers, full of verve, drive, and growing self-confidence. Modern buildings, clean streets (£500 fines for littering), a dynamic future. MSA hadn't yet split into Malaysia Airlines in red, and Singapore Airlines in gold, but it was trading in its old Comets for new Boeings.

British and New Zealand university lecturers, who'd been thrown out of China when Mao came to power, were now teaching here. They spoke with awe of the prowess of their determined students.

I stayed at 2 Cluny Road. At tea one afternoon I reported to the other residents my singular lack of success in getting a visa for

Vietnam. I'd just returned from a markedly unproductive visit to the Vietnamese Embassy where a senior official had rounded on me for the impertinence of even asking for a visa.

'Don't you know there's a war in progress?' he'd sniffed. 'We don't want tourists or visitors.'

'Have you tried getting a transit visa?' asked Michael Griffiths, innocently. Michael was a Cambridge graduate and a logistics supremo, responsible for operations in a dozen Asian countries. We'd been sharing Japan stories: his was of escorting twelve new teetotal missionaries on a freighter, where he'd been stressing the importance of cultural adaptation and of not giving offence. The crew, as a farewell, offered them all champagne or whisky, nothing else.

'I won't be in transit,' I said lamely. And then the lightbulb came on in my head. I wanted to go to Vietnam, so my application to Cambodia was just to transit there on the way to Vietnam. Vietnam was going to be a bit more difficult, but the principle was the same. Transit from Cambodia, on the way to Thailand, maybe?

After some tweaking of existing airline schedules, I presented my case to both embassies, and both gave me seventy-two hours in their respective countries. It was a marvellous suggestion from Michael, now migrated to Vancouver, and I've honed its use for over twenty years in various parts of the world.

I celebrated with a side trip to SUMATRA. The non-appearance of my contacts at Medan Airport was puzzling, since I'd sent a telegram three days before. A helpful airport worker guessed whom I was there to visit. 'I'll take you to the foreigners,' he said. 'Hop on.' So he, I, and my suitcase, balanced on his bicycle for two miles. The mystery of the telegram's non-arrival was solved when I left two days later. As my host deposited me at the airport, he checked his post box there. Inside was my telegram. I'd sent it to what I thought was his address. Now I know that 'd/a Kantor Pos' means 'Care of the Post Office'.

Poor old CAMBODIA! It found itself stuck fairly and squarely in the middle of a war it didn't want, but was powerless to prevent. There was something noble, as well as pathetic, in the banner displayed in the arrival hall at the airport which proclaimed to all the world: 'Hands off Cambodia. We want to live in peace.' All the world that is, which made the effort to get there. They were the only ones who had the opportunity to read the sign, and more importantly, observe at first hand what was going on. What did others know, or even worse, care?

Only eleven of us piled off the Cambodian Caravelle jet, long since surplus to Air France's requirements. After Prince Sihanouk was deposed, they kept the Caravelle and painted over the 'Royal'. But they didn't do a very good job, and you could still see the faint outlines of the letters from close up.

It's difficult to adequately describe how I felt: a curious twenty-one year old dropping into the war in Indochina, with no preconceptions and a great deal of naivety. Americans of my age were fighting and dying in the next country. Yet very few people could accurately analyse the situation in Cambodia. Were they baddies, goodies, or neutral? Was there such a thing as neutral?

Not for the last time, I reflected what a unique privilege it was to be on the spot, see for myself, and carry back impressions to report. Intangibles, yes, but stowed away in my mind as securely as the shopaholic cossets her latest purchases. With the urge to see, came the impetus to understand; the desire to communicate what was seen.

Siem Reap and the magnificent Angkor Wat temple complex were out of the question. Getting in and out of Phnom Penh alone took some finessing. So the three days were spent largely in and around the capital.

I walked around in something of a daze. There were nightclubs and bars without customers; moneychangers who became violently angry with me for just wanting to exchange $10 when I was their only client of the day; shops that nobody seemed to be patronising. Everything looked normal on the surface, but if you scratched underneath a little it had more the appearance of a Potemkin village, or a Hollywood studio lot: facade and not much more.

I stopped at one of the guardposts dotted throughout the city. This one, like all the others, was manned by a boy who could have been eighteen, but looked fifteen. I asked if he minded if I took his picture. Misunderstanding, he took off his rifle – still fully loaded – and draped it around my neck, to take a picture of me up against his sandbags. We chatted for a bit, of this and that, families, hobbies. His neighbour, in the next bunker, called out to me cheerily: 'Tell the world we want peace.'

Around the next corner, I was more sternly received by an

officer who was a few years older: perhaps nineteen passing for twenty-two. He objected to my super eight camera. He could see I'd been filming. Meekly I put it away, and that ended the altercation.

My contacts had gone 'somewhere else' when I got to the house at which I was staying. Only their grandparents still lived in the basement. It was a city of the elderly and the tragically young, a city in the eye of a firestorm spreading through Indochina. This gentle nation didn't deserve Pol Pot and the 'killing fields'. In life you don't always get what you deserve.

The combined might of the US and South Vietnamese airforces may have been hurling the latest in aircraft design into the air for the battle against the Viet Cong, but for civilians it was somewhat different . . . an ancient four-propeller DC4, 1940s vintage, with crudely painted lettering spelling Air Vietnam. After an uneventful landing it seemed to take hours to taxi to the terminal, dodging and giving way to military aircraft of every kind. This was Tan Son Nhut, nerve centre of the war.

Two things happened in short order. First I was arrested, then I was roundly cheated by the first GI I met, after securing my release. The arrest was bizarre. It just seemed to the immigration officials that it was too unlikely I would turn up without a nefarious purpose. The last student who'd arrived had apparently held a demonstration in Saigon in favour of the North. They detained me for a while, but eventually they satisfied themselves of my bona fides, grew tired of holding me, or both.

Neither my British nor my American hosts could pick me up, so I had to change some money. A US sergeant obliged . . . at the officially posted rate, making himself a tidy 400 percent profit. My American host's wife Maida Contento was full of sympathy when she heard this, and offered to make good the difference to me. Her husband Paul exploded: 'Let him learn the hard way.' His furious driving and swearing at the traffic were legendary.

Two decades later I tremble as I remember his stern injunction to me the first night: 'I hope you're not going to write about any of this after three days here. Don't even think about it till you've been here a year.' For all his harshness and swagger, he was much beloved of his Vietnamese students. I remember one who would have done anything for him. He already held down a full-time job to support his family, studied full time, and in his spare time ran a national youth organisation, apart from coping with the war.

Michael Meadows from Dorset was an altogether gentler sort. On my last day he invited me to go swimming with him in the British Embassy pool; but when we got there, all the water had been drained out. A bit like the country, in its headlong race to destruction.

But don't ask me: I was only there for three days. And the nearest I got to combat was when I thumbed a lift from a GI up country, and the traffic was going too slowly for him. Exasperated, he thumped on his siren, and we proceeded in the fast lane unhindered. Yes, there was a war in progress, but I was just in transit.

# 8

# No Snakes Please

*India/Nepal (1970)*

'You can't possibly do justice to INDIA in two and a half weeks,' Phillip Morris upbraided me, as we made our way through a none too salubrious suburb of Bombay; a sort of teeming sub-section of a teeming city in a teeming country.

Phillip ran the warehouse for 'Educational Book Exhibits', which sold cheap versions of English texts throughout the Indian subcontinent. This was one of a myriad of worldwide branches of Operation Mobilisation, whose slogan was: 'Bringing hope to the peoples of the world'.

Operation Mobilisation (OM) was founded by George Verwer, a charismatic New Jerseyite perpetually bubbling with energy, who wanted young Christians from the West to spend their summers abroad, and have their eyes opened to the needs of the world.

He bought a clapped-out but still seaworthy freighter, and had it transformed into an ocean-going combination of school, dispensary, and bookshop. Literature was his passion. He wanted everybody in the world to have a chance to own a Bible and a good library.

George was also the first person I met who liked to *give* books away, as well as sell them. I met him when he came to recruit in Ireland. I didn't sign up (before he bought the ship, the overland trip to India in the back of a lorry sounded quite arduous), but he did say to look in on his Indian operation if I got there under my own steam. So I did, on the way back from my summer in the Far East.

That was the start of a lifelong friendship with George and his colleagues around the world. Over the years OM and a plethora of church contacts like them would be extremely helpful in my trips, supplying local contacts, fellowship, and a perspective on countries visited.

Phillip was right about India needing more than two and a half weeks. I had to go back again and again, not just to cover the vast country itself, but because so many other territories and quasi-countries could only be accessed from there.

ASSAM, BHUTAN, ANDAMAN, NICOBAR, LAKSHADWEEP, SIKKIM, KASHMIR; the names rolled off the tongue like inventions of a Kiplingesque cartographer; exaggerations from bygone days of the Raj. But they were real places, not inventions. Each had their own easy or uneasy relationship with the Indian authorities, and their own peculiarities of approach.

When I would later start the 'race for the world' in earnest, I would find that all these territories, because of special status, would count separately. Now I just wanted to visit them because they sounded so fascinating. I didn't want to miss any travel experience that was within my reach.

There was the obligatory master visa first for India itself, of course, which always bore the legend: 'Not valid for any restricted region or territory requiring separate permit.' Since all the fascinating areas with any degree of autonomy fell into this category, the trick was to find a way, some way, any way, through the tedious bureaucracy of this additional step, which required an elasticity both of approach and time.

The temptation was simply to allow a pen mark, or even a decent-sized smudge to cover the word 'not', thereby logically rendering the visa 'valid for any restricted region', without the bother of the application for a separate permit. This didn't work, since apart from not having the extra paperwork all present and correct when challenged en route at a border or police post, other matters were involved in the permitting process.

I knew this from some of my first attempts to get into places on the semi-forbidden lists, when I had invitations from them, but not the necessary interior permits. Result: turned back before being able to cross the last stretch of Indian territory. Reading the lurid accounts in the Indian press of decapitations and other grisly murders which seemed to be a staple of some of the northern and eastern border regions, and paying attention to the days of the week when rare permits were most often granted, I formed my own theory.

The thesis was very simple: the rule of law didn't fully stretch to the borders. There were unpredictable people with a mind of their own operating in these regions; and they were armed. The Indian authorities acted on the reasonable assumption that the tourist-visitor's direct contacts and bargaining power with these people were limited. The government therefore pooled the money obtained from permit applications and used it to negotiate a series of ceasefires on certain dates, with guaranteed safe passage for a small group in a marked and identified vehicle.

Security for foreigners on these remoter roads was an important concern because as yet there weren't enough visitors to build up an infrastructure to cope with tourists as regular occurrences, and the last stages were invariably performed by road.

But what roads and what staging posts: Darjeeling, Siliguri, Bagdogra. Even the spectacular forty-minute flight over the lower Himalayas and into the Indus Valley from Leh to Srinagar was hard put to beat the slow ascent up to 7,000 feet, dominated by majestic Mount Kanchenjunga, then the winding drive to the Ghoom Monastery at Tiger Hill, and a stop at the institute where mountaineers trained in a setting that put their goal on their doorstep.

Sometimes you felt you didn't actually need to go there; reading the itinerary was such a thrill in itself: 'Rumtek is the seat of His Holiness The Gyalwa Karmapa, the head of the Kargupa sect of Tibetan Buddhism. Afternoon visit to Gangtok Town, Enchey Monastery and Institute of Tibetology. Drive to Kalimpong to see the monastery called Dzong-dhog-palri-phondog.'

Nowadays you can fly by Vyadoot out to Kavaratti, and reach the LACCADIVES by launch from there, avoiding the slow and woefully unpredictable boat from Cochin. You can board a Druk Air plane in Delhi for a direct flight into Bhutan. It's much more convenient, but you miss the thrill of the ground-level arrival in the Paro Valley, and the slow stately progress to Thimphu, the capital.

I wanted to see the hill stations of the Raj so badly that I could almost taste the cool environment that lured the former ruling classes away from the sweltering lowlands for their annual rest and recreation, and where generations of expatriate schoolchildren boarded. The names tripped off the tongue like a roll call of past and distant glories: Ootacamund (Ooty), Manali, Kulu, Simla the summer capital, and Kitchener's Kufri. But the two and a half week time limit forced me to shelve that option, and be more realistic about what could be done.

To start with, there was the question of getting to Delhi from Bombay at all, on which all subsequent plans seemed to depend. Internal flight bookings were not computerised, and seemed to be full for weeks ahead. I'd almost given up in despair, when a friend of Phillip's burst into the Bombay warehouse where he was chatting to me while taking inventory of his educational books.

The friend's parents were on their way out to visit him, on a flight which rivalled mine in cheapness, but didn't offer as many stops: just one in fact, Aden. The Brothers Air Service Company (BASCO, as it was affectionately known) had one antiquated DC6, and when it burst a tyre on landing at Aden, it seemed the passengers were going to be holed up there for some time, while a replacement was sought.

That meant – unfortunately for them, fortunately for me – that they couldn't take up their prebooked seats to Delhi, so I bought one of the two tickets, and was airborne in a matter of hours.

No journey to India is complete without a long train journey, in which to watch the bullocks, the ancient ploughs, the subsistence farmers, the whole rural panorama slowly pass by. Indian Railways is an amazing institution. Day after day it squeezes yet more service out of well-used trains ('600 sitting, 700 standing,' officially; unofficially I never saw fewer than 3,000 on any given train), as they descend on Lucknow, Howrah, Hyderabad, or Udaipur. 'Passengers must not carry their snakes into the sitting compartments with them', proclaims a station notice.

Securing both a seat and a student discount on my eastbound train gave me plenty of opportunity for a quintessential Indian experience. I visited seven different offices, including one which could furnish the student discount application, and one which could verify that status . . . but neither of which could sell me a ticket on the train. The cumulative result of all seven, however, was that I had all the bits of paper I needed. Speaking of bits of paper, the dividing wall in the fourth office I visited was composed entirely, floor to ceiling, of papers that clearly had once been working files which were allowed to pile up vertically from the floor until in height they rose above the clerks, and assumed their new role as partitions.

Each arrival at a station followed a familiar pattern. First of all those who had been happily sitting on the carriage roofs, paying no fare and suffering only occasional disturbances at unexpected halts and random inspections, jumped off, sidled down, or otherwise made themselves temporarily invisible. It was obligatory for all passengers to stick their heads out of windows and enquire about length of stop, or offer opinions on a variety of subjects.

That's when the women would scurry along the platform, hold up babies to the passengers, and look with imploring faces. It always looked as if they were stretching all the way up to offer to sell their baby to you, rather than simply begging, which is what they were doing, with the child as a necessary prop. At one station I called one woman's bluff, said 'Thank you,' reached down and lifted the baby towards the carriage. All at once an ear-piercing scream was heard from the other end of the platform. The real mother rushed up at full steam to retrieve her child. Clearly the prop had just been on loan.

The Ganges had no particular effect on me. It was brown and muddy, and people were bathing, drinking, defecating, and being cremated in the same general area. Varanasi was my jumping off point for a side trip to NEPAL, a Hindu kingdom that still really had no truck with the modern world.

On the return, I was waylaid by an enterprising businessman who asked if I wanted to stay in his hotel. On the way to it he told me he hadn't finished building it yet. The shell was complete, but no furnishings. In fact, workmen continued plastering the walls surrounding me during the night.

In the morning I asked what the price was. Quick as a flash came the retort 'Whatever you like, sir', his face bearing that look of profound awe that any gratuity should be dispensed. After I offered him an appropriate number of rupees, taking into account the 'unfinished' discount, another look of profound gratitude, perhaps shading slightly into the 'How could you insult the friendship, and my excessive expectations by proferring such a paltry amount?' look.

Fortunately Indian Airlines was not as heavily booked on the Patna-Varanasi-Kajuraho-Agra-Delhi run as the Bombay-Delhi sector. In fact, since I was the only passenger, the captain invited me up to the cockpit of the Viscount for the landings. Overbooking or else the opposite extreme appeared to bedevil the airline's pre-automation operations. But they did a good job, given the demands placed on them. The in-flight literature gave no indication whether snakes, banned as carry-on baggage on the trains, were allowed in the aircraft cabin.

A switched-off Niagara Falls and empty British swimming pool in Saigon should have alerted me, but the glimpse of the Taj Mahal from the cockpit sent me heading there as soon as the Viscount taxied to a stop. It was everything the posters had promised . . . shimmering in the moonlight. Wait a moment. Something was missing. What was it? Some feature remembered from postcard views. The *reflection*, that was it! The Taj was artistically designed so that its reflection was cast the whole length of the lake between you and it. No lake. No reflection. Again the water had been drained out before I got there. This was getting to be a habit.

As with the pyramids, souvenir buying somehow happened, even if not pre-planned. The reflectionless Taj was my last stop before Delhi and home, so I asked the taxi driver to be as quick as he could. After about 300 yards he stopped at a shop. 'My uncle,' he said. 'Have a look inside.' I didn't want to have a look, and I became annoyed when this behaviour was repeated 200 yards further on.

'How much do they pay you?' I asked. He affected surprise at first, then indicated the amount of commission earned for producing a foreign customer at each shop. 'Right,' I said. 'We'll stop at as many as you like. You'll earn the commission. I'll have the same amount reduced from my taxi fare.' It was a winning strategy. Almost! At the fourth shop the fare was about to be reduced to zero. At the fifth shop I made some purchases: little wooden Taj Mahals (no reflection) to join my Egyptian camels. Both broke into tiny fragments before reaching London.

I almost didn't meet K.P. Yohannan. Delhi belly finally caught up with me on my last day in the Indian capital. I was weak after a night of diarrhoea and vomiting. He took it upon himself to clean up the mess, attend to my needs, see that I made the plane in time, and was able to make the journey. He brought a farewell gift. There was no justification for such astonishing kindness to someone he'd never met before. It seemed to be his nature. He told me how he lived a simple life, travelling from village to village as an itinerant evangelist, often barefoot. He loved his calling, but one day maybe he'd have a chance to study more. We became friends. I promised to write.

Three years later in Scotland I got a letter from K.P. He felt he needed further education: did I know anyone in the West who could help? I showed the letter to a big-hearted Texan, E.A. Gresham ('my friends call me Easy'). K.P. got a place at a seminary in Dallas. When I next caught up with him he was pastoring a small inner-city native American church, but feeling restless to be involved with India again. I hoped he wasn't another brain-drain casualty.

A few months ago a friend sent me a copy of K.P.'s first book. He's used the intervening years to set up an organisation in America persuading people to send him the equivalent of one cup of coffee a day money, about $30 a month, and he uses this to support one Indian living a servant lifestyle, bringing the good news to his own people, and helping meet a variety of needs in the same way he himself used to do. Only now the effect is multiplied. At last count he was supporting 8,000 fellow countrymen.

# 9

# Price On His Head

*West/South Africa (1972)*

People frequently ask: 'How on earth did you start travelling so extensively? What motivated you?'

Looking back, I can't honestly say there was one moment that transformed me from normal person into travel nut. Certainly, it was only *after* I'd been virtually everywhere that I discovered the Travelers' Century Club which named me one of the top ten travellers of all time, and motivated me to become the top one. It did provide a quasi-definitive list of territories to check off one by one: a measurement of progress in the race, as it were.

But at the start, it was much simpler. An insatiable curiosity about the world beyond my doorstep. Friendship with overseas students, and invitations to visit their home countries. A concern for persecuted individuals in 'closed' countries, and a desire to help them by going to visit them, when they were unable to leave.

Also, the enrichment I received from the first two summer vacation trips in which I'd already been to North America, Europe, North Africa, the Middle and Far East, convinced me that it was possible to travel far and wide on a shoestring budget, and benefit immensely, without freeloading or exploitation.

I clearly did have a dream in those student days; long before being entered in any race to cover a particular list of countries. Perhaps its intensity was stronger than I realised, for I began to anticipate the thrill of the following summer's journey all through the college winter and spring terms.

Africa – especially sub-Sahara Africa – was the next major continent I'd set my sights on. I did a lot of itinerary planning and searching for summer employment in the first six months of 1971, but at the last moment everything fell through.

I'd been so single minded about Africa that I'd ignored every opportunity to travel elsewhere, until the day I was packing my bags to leave St Andrews for home and Bill Shannon phoned from Perthshire. He asked if I wanted to go to California to work with a student group called Seekers (not the Seekers).

There were only two qualifications: you had to be Scottish and Presbyterian. Strictly speaking, I was neither. He assured me the conditions could probably be loosely interpreted, and I soon found myself in Fresno, the 'biggest little city in America'.

After a summer of puppeteering, drama in the park, presenting seventy-five radio shows, and being a high-school camp counsellor, I took off on a regional airlines airpass to forty-seven of the fifty states. Ninety-one flights, a month of aeroplanes, and all for $149. It took five connections to get to Florida, about eight coast-to-coast, but I wasn't complaining. Hughes Air West of Howard Hughes fame (also known as the yellow banana) actually served wine and cheese even on short twenty-minute hops. I think I ate more in food than the price of the ticket. Tip: always pay the foreigner's price to fly in your own country: it's usually cheaper!

This incredible value ticket even allowed me to travel to ALASKA. Between Nome and Kotzebue the pilot diverted to fly out over the Bering Strait so that we could see Greater and Lesser Diomede below: on one side the USA, on the other Siberia. This was as far as you could go without slipping across the International Dateline to tomorrow.

Twelve months later, in the early summer of 1972, it was time to graduate. Her Majesty's Government was always in search of fresh faces, so two days were arranged when prospective graduates could shadow a senior civil servant at Whitehall to see whether the job appealed. I got in on the Foreign Office briefings, but was actually assigned to an official at the Ministry of Defence.

'First question,' he said as soon as we met. 'Do you take sugar?' Preferences were jotted down and orders telephoned for morning coffee and afternoon tea. Lunches were grand affairs at a pleasant eaterie adjoining Trafalgar Square, with several of his colleagues from neighbouring offices. In fact, we did seem to spend a lot of time eating and drinking. 'Some days are very busy,' he reflected, 'and others are, well . . .'

As with anything even this harmless in Britain, of course, we had to sign the Official Secrets Act. I couldn't quite see the point. One presentation we were supposed to sit in on, and be subject ever after to strict secrecy on, we all got lost on the way to. Another meeting my officer took me and two others to was part of his routine, but at the end the man in charge came up to him and whispered in his ear: 'I don't think they are supposed to be in meetings like this.' Too late!

The reason we failed to get to the meeting we were supposed to be at was the absurd door numbering system. We weren't sure if it was deliberate obfuscation, or just a shambles that had gradually come about. You'd be told to go to Room 2322, and it would be locked tight, whereas the door to Room 2323, which bore the legend in bold: TOP SECRET. DO NOT ENTER. ALL ENQUIRIES TO RM. 2322 would be wide open, with officers, clerks, secretaries and messengers traipsing in and out.

Even this didn't take as much getting used to as the confusing administrative hierarchy. We knew it was the War Ministry under Churchill, and now in peace time there was no such thing; but instead of Admiralty, Air Ministry, and Army becoming conjoint in Defence, we rather formed the opinion that a fourth level had been added, and the existing structure stayed intact.

I came away from Whitehall with three convictions. First, whatever might be averred to the contrary, top Foreign Office recruitment was confined to public school, Oxbridge, 'one of us'.

Second, analysis of geopolitics, territorial disputes etc. seemed to hinge on their evaluation of whether the protagonist was 'a good chap'. The Shah was always mentioned as basically 'a good chap'.

Third, if you get into difficulties overseas, don't depend on your government to bail you out.

In June I refused a job with the Civil Service; this meant a certain amount of brinkmanship. I'd been offered a place at Oxford from October for a postgraduate degree, if I got a first-class degree. But the results wouldn't be known for a while. I decided to spend my first summer after graduating in the same way I spent the other three while a student – travelling.

The deferred three-month Africa trip was now ready for realisation, except for one thing: money! After weeks of perusing schedules for connections, I went ahead anyway and booked the ticket with thirty-two stops. Out in early July, after the results and graduation ceremony. Back in October to start two more years of study. No single airline wanted to have the bother of writing out tickets for all the other airline flights, but finally the manager at the new British Caledonian office in Belfast took the itinerary home with him and wrote the ticket out by hand. I was very grateful to him.

On the eve of departure I stayed with a chaplain at Heathrow, whose house was conveniently at the end of the runway. I arrived in time to take a phone call from my bank manager asking if I knew that there wasn't enough in my account to pay for the ticket. I told him funds were coming. The next phone call was from my parents – a cheque had arrived from the University. I'd been awarded the Samuel Rutherford Memorial Prize for outstanding work in the Faculty of Arts. Rutherford had been Professor of Greek and Mathematics at St Andrews over a hundred years ago, and was buried in the vicinity of the ruined cathedral.

My first 747 flight was on VIASA, the Venezuelan airline, to Madrid. Whether this was immediately apparent depended on which side was visible on landing, because only one side was painted in VIASA's colours. The other side was painted KLM, and registered to the Dutch airline. I suppose that was fair enough if they only paid to lease half.

SOUTH AFRICA was the ultimate destination, but I took the opportunity to hop down the west coast via GIBRALTAR, MOROCCO, MALI, IVORY COAST, NIGERIA, TOGO, BENIN, CAMEROON, ZAIRE, ZAMBIA and BOTSWANA. I also spent time in GHANA and LIBERIA.

These countries were the source of the only two invitations I ever received to dine with a head of state. Sadly both were deposed before I could take up the invitations. When Sergeant Doe took over, he unceremoniously dumped President Tolbert's body on the beach at Monrovia. In the case of Kofe Busieh, it was rumoured in Accra that there was now a price on his head, and he'd been seen around Oxford.

Two of the flights were memorable. On Air Mali the galley

wasn't secure, and food trays (full) went scuttling down the aisle as the pilot climbed out of Bamako. The crew were otherwise occupied, crouching behind their curtain dividing out the duty-free goods they'd purchased in Paris.

After four hours on an Air Zaire DC8 I was surprised to find us landing right back where we started from, at Kinshasa. A forced nightstop and three attempts to fix the problem later, they gave up and put us all aboard a domestic Caravelle flight down to Lubumbashi. As air services across the border to Zambia had been withdrawn due to some political argument, I had to fend for myself the next hundred or so miles through the bush to the Copperbelt.

By rights the airline should have picked up the tab for the overnight expenses in Kinshasa. But all Air Zaire personnel from whom I enquired directed me to the Pan Am office upstairs. Pan Am? What were they to do with it? Intrigued, I wandered through an empty outer office, which hadn't been locked. It was late at night but four or five people were visible in the back office, heads down, studying something very intently.

At my approach there was the kind of mild panic where the whole production line is caught slacking by the boss, followed by a quick regrouping as one of their number led me away into a third office. The legend on his jacket said Station Superintendent. When he discovered I needed a voucher to cover my hotel costs due to airline equipment failure, he was visibly relieved.

He called in an assistant and watched, intrigued, while she found the correct stock from which to issue the voucher, and speedily completed it. He handed it to me, turned on his heel, and rejoined his colleagues. It was clear he didn't know very much about the airline business. What exactly was he doing there? I'd heard of shadowy Central Intelligence Agency operatives in odd places, using civil aviation as cover. Maybe the letters CIA were a better description than PAA (Pan Am) . . . or maybe he'd just borrowed somebody else's jacket that evening!

Come to think of it, he wasn't the only strange American I encountered on this trip. My plane was late into Douala, the Cameroon capital, after nightfall, so there was no possibility of continuing my journey up country to Buea where Tim Steer, my friend from the ORKNEY ISLANDS, was a lecturer at the Education Institute.

I remembered how much fun it had been acting as groomsman at Tim's brother's wedding in Stromness; I looked forward to seeing him again.

There appeared to be an acute shortage of rooms in Douala; at least, so I gathered from a Jewish young woman from New York, who was stranded at the airport. Her father was a bigwig in the Nixon administration. When I asked her what she was doing in Africa, she opened her handbag, and pulled out screeds of multiple tickets on every airline which flew to the continent, which one person could never have used up. 'Just travelling,' she said.

She tagged along while I went in search of accommodation. Finally I succeeded, with impeccable schoolboy French, in persuading the headquarters of the Catholic Mission to Cameroon to reopen their doors, which had been shuttered for the night. They were kind enough to come up with first one bedroom, then in response to my 'Nous ne sommes pas mariés', a second. It would never have done for the Catholic authorities, albeit unwittingly, to have sanctioned a night of apparent sin under their own noses between a Jewish American and an Ulster Protestant!

# 10

# Dodging Idi Amin

*East Africa (1972)*

For two months I led a double life in apartheid-ridden South Africa; a respectable suburb in Pretoria at weekends, Soweto during the week, occasionally helping Billy Farr, a jolly Irishman whom the Africans loved. I stayed with dyed-in-the-wool Orange Free State farmers, leaders in Helen Suzman's party, angry young Indians, English migrants. There was usually only one subject on everyone's lips, even when they tried to avoid it. How could it be otherwise when the first and third worlds collided head on, and people were stripped of their dignity day in and day out?

Unilateral Declaration of Independence RHODESIA was a joke. Sanctions didn't allow you to go there at all in theory, but all that was required to defeat that was to fly via South Africa, which most people did anyway. When you asked the locals how they fared under the oil embargo, they guffawed, 'Didn't you know we grew our own petrol here?' They clearly had no difficulty thumbing their collective noses at Harold Wilson, the British prime minister.

The early stages of my Cape to Cairo odyssey were uneventful:

- side trips to SWAZILAND, CISKEI, TRANSKEI;
- a visit to XHOSA territory to see their vivid red blankets and perfectly rounded huts, and to hear those incredible clicking sounds produced by sharply pulling the tongue from the roof of the mouth to the teeth;

- a horseback ride into Maseru, LESOTHO, the 'Switzerland of Africa', with its fast-flowing rivers and spectacular mountains;
- MOZAMBIQUE, before Lourenco Marques became Maputo;
- gentle MALAWI, under President-for-life Hastings Banda, full of expatriate Scots, and with a perfectly adequate low-key capital at Blantyre, before the seat of government moved to the tongue-twisting Lilongwe;
- Julius Nyerere's self-reliant TANZANIA, where I'd never have found a place to stay if I hadn't been taken under the wing of a visiting trade union delegation;
- and ZANZIBAR, an exotic chunk of old Araby, deposited off the East African coast.

In KENYA I produced programmes for Schools Radio. I used to take the bus in and out of Nairobi. Basically this involved a life-or-death struggle to join the suffocating crush on the running board or entrance step, if you didn't particularly care to climb on the roof. I never quite figured out how those passengers already inside had boarded, as buses only seemed to arrive anywhere fully laden.

One night I was running particularly late, and the buses were particularly full. When I asked around the bus station for the nearest phone, to let my hosts know I'd be a while, I was directed to the nearby hospital. After negotiating seemingly endless corridors, I ended up in the only place with a phone – the labour ward in the maternity unit.

Around the time the first pictures began appearing on British television of the psychotic mixture of buffoon and bloodthirsty despot that was 'General' Idi Amin, I was squatting in a hut near Mount Kenya, trying not to finish my goat's milk without offending the Kikuyu village elders. Their attention momentarily diverted, I tossed the remains out through the hut window.

I'd just finished a circuit of highland villages in the company of a friend from Dundee, Jock Stein. Since he was ordained, and his wife Margaret was one of the first female Church of Scotland ministers, letters addressed simply to Rev. Stein were often fought over in their household. On the other hand, envelopes dropping on their doormat sometimes bore the legend: Rev. and Rev. Stein.

Jock was in charge of the annual field conferences, when his arrival would be announced months in advance, and all villages within ten hours' walking distance would be alerted to send delegates to a central location for a full day of teaching: three sessions, minimum three hours each. Then the conference format and contents would be repeated next day in another region.

I didn't realise that accompanying Jock meant I was responsible for the evening session, after he'd finished his six or more straight hours. Judging at least from the hospitality afterwards, my impromptu three hours went over all right. In fact it was more like twenty minutes, followed by answering questions that flew thick and fast from an audience hungry for knowledge.

Traces of the goat's milk were still visible as we moved outside the hut to collect our live chicken, presented to us three villages back. Transporting him in the back of the car between stops was easy enough, as was releasing him at each village. Rounding him up again prior to departure was the amusing part. Back at base Margaret cooked him. I don't remember what we drank, but it wasn't goat's milk.

It was to be my last night in Kenya – my tickets for UGANDA had arrived. Departure was set for next day. During the night I woke with a start. I felt a sudden, searing stomach pain and the cramping became more severe as morning approached. I had no choice but to postpone the trip to Kampala, mentally trying to pinpoint the culprit.

I sat in the Steins' living room that evening watching the television news, eternally grateful for either the chicken or the goat's milk. The scene was Entebbe Airport: there, large as life, was Amin, striding out to scrutinise arriving passengers off the very flight I was due to take. As the cameras rolled, he selected British passport holders to be led away, to what fate was not specified.

It may have all been for show, a public retaliation for some imagined slight by the British press perhaps, or a Foreign Office note he didn't take to. But that was one occasion I was glad I wasn't there in person to find out. In a peculiar way, I felt protected: a feeling I'd know again and again in my travels.

Three days later, feeling up to snuff again, I did land at Entebbe, this time en route to RWANDA. All I saw of Uganda though, was a brief glimpse up through the big oval window of the Fokker

Friendship, from the floor. I was hiding behind the back seat, because I didn't want to tempt fate (or Idi) on the ground. The cleaner was quite startled.

From Rwanda I tried to cross the border into Burundi, but was turned back. The large man in charge refused to see me, dealing with me only through his teenage assistant. As if letting me in on a great secret, the boy flipped through my passport till he reached the offending page, where he pointed out the South African entry stamp. This was the absurd 'guilt by association' notion that wreaked havoc to a neutral traveller's schedule. It was bad enough when country X declared 'we hate country Y and all its policies so much that we won't allow any of its nationals into our country.' After all, many nationals of Y might hate their government's policies also, but be powerless to overturn them. But to go further and ban a national of country A from entering X as a retaliation for visiting Y, is a mite unfair, especially for anyone with a desire to visit both countries and not be forced to choose between them.

As with many things in life, there was a solution when you stood far enough back from the problem to view it impassively: an approach from a completely different perspective was called for. But not here, not on this dirt road, not now. Thirteen years later I would cross easily into Burundi. For now, a dignified retreat was the best I could manage.

Much later in London I would solve this and allied problems: Israel/Arab states; China/Taiwan; India/Pakistan; Argentina/Falklands; using the old maxim: 'Avoid giving offence'.

Strictly speaking, the Burundians did not want to totally and irrevocably deny me admission just because I'd had the bad sense ever to have been to South Africa. They simply wanted me to present to them a travel document which showed absolutely no evidence of having been there. This was a different matter. Achievable. It involved a new passport: no visa in it issued by a South African consulate and no entry or exit stamp from any South African border post.

The first was solved by a special petition through my future employer, the BBC, to the Passport Office in Clive House, Petty France, SW1. The second by holding one of the only four passports in the world which did not require a visa to enter South Africa. The third, by offering, on my next trip there, a small piece of blank paper to the immigration officer, and asking if he'd kindly stamp it instead of my passport.

As an extreme precaution I would also take care, on all future trips to independent African countries, to remove all traces of evidence of having been in the RSA before leaving: boarding passes, airline coupons, baggage tags, hotel receipts, credit card slips, souvenirs, letters addressed to me there, and so on.

This also meant having any airline tickets which had been issued in Johannesburg rewritten in a friendly neighbouring state. Quite a dilemma, because the combination in Johannesburg of major airline offices with tariff experts who could issue long, complicated tickets, and an enviable rand exchange rate due to the country's pariah status, was irresistible.

Of course you couldn't simply march into the Air Malawi office in Blantyre with: 'Here is an international Cape Town to Inverness ticket issued on South African Airways paper, with forty individual sectors. It might cause me embarrassment elsewhere in Africa. Please reissue it.'

A little diplomacy was needed. You had to have a change of heart about your original destination, opting for say, Iran instead of Scotland. Even if you were only flying to London you always specified Aberdeen or Inverness to gain extra allowable miles in the calculation, and sometimes a free or at least greatly reduced price domestic connection.

The change of heart to Iran would achieve twin objectives – maintain a similar through fare based on distance, and keep in place most of the stops you wanted, whilst causing the whole ticket to be reissued from scratch. If you merely altered a sector or two, this was sometimes done the lazy way by inserting a new coupon for these sectors in the original ticket, leaving the offending orange and blue covers of the Springbok airline clearly visible.

A frequent bonus occurred if the reissuing airline took a more favourable view of, say, a side trip to Bujumbura, counting it as part of the through journey, rather than levying a full local fare at a much higher rate. When it worked the other way – to your disadvantage – and you were now required to pay extra for sectors which had previously been included in the international ticket, you were simply stuck on the wrong side of the two-edged sword you had chosen to employ.

Naturally you took into account where you actually wanted to end up. In my case, furnished with a student special second-class railway ticket from Teheran to London via Turkey, Bulgaria, and most of East, Central and West Europe (seven days £35, bus connection from Kabul £8 extra), either Iran or Afghanistan were suitable terminus points. The last leg would preferably be a flight between them, to keep my options open.

If you were flying all the way to the UK it was still often prudent to book first to Iran, then extend to Britain on the reissue. This was because if you asked for too much at first, no airline reservationist ever believed you or wanted to help, even if it was perfectly legal and permissible within the tariff structure. Further, the extra cost of the Middle East to Britain portion on a long-distance ticket was a fraction of the cost of a separate ticket for that journey. And you enjoyed the benefit of all the stops you'd already booked up to Iran, plus any new ones you were able to now fit in.

I should add that such machinations were only possible with an extremely detailed knowledge of available airline publications such as *ABC World Airways Guide, Official Airline Guide* (green version for international flights, not blue), and *Airline Passenger Tariff*, usually abbreviated by those in the know to *ABC*, *OAG*, and *APT* respectively. These gave you a great starting point; but, since they weren't infallible, it paid occasionally to try to sneak behind the counter at major international airports to double-check details in the individual airlines' own tariff and rule manuals.

To have any chance of convincing an airline that your plethora of stops could all be included in one through fare, you needed to come equipped with a knowledge of all carriers serving your en route points, and the interline agreements between them. Each airline had a list of designated carriers whose flights were allowed to be written up on their ticket stock; and if even one airline on the route hadn't entered into such an agreement, the whole itinerary was rendered impossible, at least without paying twice over.

Then there were official published mileages, often differing from actual geographical miles, and the complicated grid by which you paid increments of five percent to twenty percent over the published fare, but additional allowable flown mileage was scaled on a different basis.

The big spoiler was when an en route city had a higher fare than your destination, since this upset the calculation. There was a way of dealing with this, but for both administrative ease, and to maximise revenue, an airline invariably broke your journey calculation at this point, resulting in two higher priced tickets.

As if all this wasn't enough, it soon became necessary to find a way to standardise tariffs in all the different world currencies, and somebody dreamed up FCUs (fictitious currency units) to count in. These later evolved into NUCs (neutral units of currency). As my travels became more extensive, so did my knowledge of fare construction. Flying from Europe to the bottom of the African continent was always a challenge to see how many of the intervening fifty-two countries you could fit in.

Managing thirty on this first African jaunt was not too bad, I reflected. A pity about that incriminating passport stamp. Yet it was incredible, with feelings running so high at the time, that I visited every frontline state, and just about every major independent country in West, Central and East Africa that led the fight against South Africa, without problems – apart from tiny Burundi.

There may have been other considerations. It wasn't long since widespread massacres had taken place in Burundi, as part of the Hutu/Tutsi internecine violence which had erupted sporadically since independence. What little news of the brutal slayings had reached the West was disturbing in the extreme, and highly unfavourable to the regime in power. They were perhaps cautious about visitors who could tell tales.

Ironically it was an English friend, George Hoffman, who had not long since risked his life smuggling out details and pictures of the massacres. Later he was awarded an OBE for his fearless charitable, relief, and development work for TEAR Fund in numerous third-world countries in crises of one kind or another. Despite scores of journeys in and out of war zones over the next twenty years, notably Croatia and Bosnia, he died struck by a car as he crossed the road in England.

Snags now began to multiply as I tried to get out of Rwanda. East Africa Airways informed me there were no seats available for two weeks out of Kigali, the smallish capital. As things stood, they only operated one flight per week with forty-four seats, backed up some weeks with a second. With Uganda to the north, and Burundi to the south, things didn't look too hopeful.

When I turned up at Kigali Airport in the hope of a cancellation, the news was bad. One of the two engines on the F27 turbo prop had died, and the airline's solution was to fly the plane back to Nairobi on one engine with just the pilot and stewardess on board, leaving all forty-four passengers (forty-five if you counted me) well and truly stranded.

'There'll be another plane next week,' said the pilot, as he started up his one good engine. To my immense surprise, nobody demurred. Forty African would-be passengers melted away, seemingly into the nearby bush. Four remained: a Swiss white hunter, a Swedish flight attendant, an Indian lady and her teenage daughter.

The five of us put our heads together to figure out our next move, as the two-engined aircraft, operating as a one-engined aircraft, disappeared from sight. There wasn't another scheduled plane of any kind due for three days. Kigali, with a population of 16,000, had more the look of a sleepy village than a capital city. No buses or taxis seemed to exist, and cars were few and far between. When the airport closed at dusk, we managed to hitch a lift into town with the Belgian who manned the airport control tower, and found hotel rooms.

At first light we walked back out to the airport. It gave us something to do, and held out some hope, whereas in town there was no hope. All day we sat by the edge of the runway, to no avail, returning to town at nightfall.

The following morning the control tower was abuzz with excitment – an airliner was due to land to refuel. It hadn't been listed as expected, so no other details were forthcoming. Five pairs of anxious eyes followed the speck on the horizon as it grew larger, turned to execute a flawless approach through the admittedly uncongested skies, landed, and taxied up to where we sat on the grass.

It was a singularly unprepossessing silver DC3, empty except for two pilots. The Ugandan, offically the captain, climbed out of the co-pilot's seat. From the pilot's side a genial Irishman disembarked and strode over to us: 'Hello. I'm Idi's pilot. What are you doing here?'

After I recovered from the shock, I talked him into giving us a lift. He was returning to Uganda.

The Indian family became visibly frightened as we circled to land at Entebbe. Even more so, when they discovered that the main business of the day was a series of special flights expelling Indians from the country.

Mother and daughter quaked with apprehension as we were led into a special waiting area on arrival. From the enclosure we could all see the customs men helping themselves to whatever they liked from the possessions of the exiles, who could offer no resistance.

I only became alarmed when dusk fell, and – after a whole day at Entebbe – we were summoned to join the tail end of yet another group of departing Indians as they boarded the EAA VC10 in front of us. The flight was announced for Bombay.

On board I tabulated the passenger list: 128 Indians being expelled; two Indians not being expelled; one Swiss, one Swede, me.

We'd only been airborne for twenty minutes when the pilot throttled back on the engines, descended . . . and dropped the five of us off in Nairobi, before resuming course for India.

I determined to give Idi a wide berth after this.

# 11

# The Lion Emperor

*Ethiopia/Sudan (1972)*

One of the first targets for takeover by Colonel Mengitsu's gang, when they seized power in Ethiopia's Marxist coup, was the RVOG site at Addis Ababa, one of the oldest broadcasting sites on the African continent. RVOG had been established by Lutherans from Scandinavia, initially for round-the-clock short wave broadcasting worldwide. Over the years the station had built up a loyal local following, too. They had asked me to contribute to their output while I was there.

I stayed in guest quarters in a hospital compound, peopled by all sorts of old-time British expatriates. One was the widow of an author I half remembered from dusty volumes on my father's bookshelves. All had double-barrelled surnames.

This was odd, because ETHIOPIA struck me as perhaps the most uncolonised country I'd been to in Africa so far: there was a completely different feel to it. Whereas other nations, especially in their capitals, bore a clear colonial imprint – through names, building styles, government administration, atmosphere – Ethiopia seemed to exude an ancient, proud, unconquered Africa.

Mrs Rendle-Short drove me to the market place, where Amharas, Wolayta, Sidamo, Hararis, Gurage, Nilotes, Oromo, Afars, Issas, Somalis – tall, slender descendants of noble warriors of the past – mingled and haggled. The colours of their clothing were sometimes so vivid they knocked you back as you stared at them.

But I had little time to savour the delights of this ancient country, proud of its ancestry stretching back to the alleged union of the Queen of Sheba with King Solomon of Jerusalem. As soon as my RVOG broadcasts were complete, Jock Stein had arranged for the Third Secretary at the British Embassy in Khartoum to meet me off my next-country flight, and to spirit me through customs with no visa formalities.

Wrong! First, the ageing Sudanese 'White Nile' Comet had a series of mechanical malfunctions and couldn't take off. Second, the proffered replacement, an East German Ilyushin, despite being empty, wouldn't board me if I wasn't going through to East Berlin, forty minutes after arriving in Khartoum. Third, Ethiopian Airlines, they of the beautiful splashes of green, red and yellow on the tail, after at length agreeing to accept my now much-thumbed ticket, refused to recognise my visa waiver for Sudan. So it was back to the drawing board.

As I returned for a second, unscheduled week in Addis, staying this time with the Reuters correspondent, I walked into a crisis. Both the way it came about, and its resolution, spoke volumes about the system of governance in Ethiopia, unlike anything I'd ever seen before.

Supreme power and authority rested with one man: Haile Selassie, Power of the Trinity, King of Kings, Emperor of Abyssinia, Conquering Lion of the Tribe of Judah; now in his eighty-first year, for the last forty-two of them he had been absolute monarch in the land.

From him power flowed downwards – through the imperial family, palace officials, those well-connected in the capital; and, in the regions, provincial governors he appointed, and their entourage.

The poor, the dispossessed, the swarms of beggars cleared from the centre of Addis every time an international conference was held there, the walking wounded, the hideously-deformed lepers, the ordinary masses, did not enjoy any of the fruits of the imperial reign, scarcely even access to basic justice – except for one archaic procedure.

My hosts related to me how the Emperor's entourage was a frequent sight around the city. Flanked by an Imperial Guard escort front and rear, the Emperor's gleaming Rolls Royce would often be halted as a citizen would fling himself in front of the leading car.

The scenario was always played out the same way, they told me. The armed guards from the front car would jump out, and form a protective circle. The man performing the death-defying leap from the shrubbery at the side of the road was neither attacker nor would-be suicide. He was a petitioner, to the court of last resort, the Emperor. His rolled-up piece of paper would be passed through the window to Selassie's aide, the convoy would resume, and the same drama would play out a few yards further on. His Imperial Majesty was thus at one and the same time totally remote and totally accessible.

As Selassie aged and became less progressive and more reactionary, the man lauded internationally as the champion of Pan-Africanism and founder of the Organisation of African Unity, had appeared to lose his once-secure touch within his own country. More and more of his middle-tiered officials acted corruptly, in his name.

The Church reflected this strict hierarchy. Much of the cosseted Orthodox establishment resented the incursion into what they considered their exclusive preserve, of Lutherans and other Protestants, popular radio station or not; and especially the growing numbers of Pentecostal Christians, who to them were a sect – at best unfathomable and iconoclastic – at worst dangerous to accepted traditions and doctrines.

Wave after wave of mindless persecution launched against the Pentecostals had been tolerated, suffered, endured; sometimes beaten back by appeals to the Emperor. Now that Selassie was abroad, attending a conference in Europe, some Orthodox functionaries opted for quick action, ordering raids on churches they didn't take too kindly to, and imprisonment of their members.

Their only crime, it appeared, was holding unauthorised prayer meetings. My hosts were concerned to help, yet mindful of their need to continue to function in this society. I was recruited as the visiting fireman journalist, who would ask the awkward questions.

So I began a trail through a different Ethiopia, one well off the tourist route. All I got for my trouble was the cold shoulder; my enquiries through normal channels were rebuffed time after time. There was nothing for it but a visit to the jail itself.

I roped in a sceptical colleague, and together we presented ourselves at the entrance to the city prison, for searching. In front of us was a pile of Bibles and hymn books, waist-high, which had been confiscated from the new prisoners on entry.

We met the prison authorities, who were cordial even when we implored them to release the believers. That was up to the police, they said. We spent time with the prisoners, alerting them that many people in the outside world would be aware of their fate. This was amazing news to them, and seemed to buoy their spirits.

The prison visit was my last act in Ethiopia before a renewed try at Sudan. The day after I left, a clipping from a European daily, datelined Addis Ababa, was shown to Haile Selassie, featuring the arrests. A telex was sent from His Imperial Majesty. The Pentecostals walked free. I suppose it was the journalistic equivalent of jumping out in front of the imperial Rolls, and pushing a scrap of paper in through the window.

I didn't of course know it then, but Ethiopia was on the brink of a vicious downward spiral. In less than a year, the full force of the famine at Wollo would emerge – the distended stomachs of the children and pathetic skeletal forms desperate for food would burst on television news bulletins with sickening force.

Another year, and the Conquering Lion of the Tribe of Judah would be whisked from his regal surroundings at the Jubilee Palace in a small blue Volkswagen, to face imprisonment. Eleven months later his death would be announced by the ruling Marxist committee. No one ever found out how he died, or where he was buried.

The next decade would see Ethiopia face appalling suffering as Mengistu Haile-Maryam's revolution took hold. Red Terror, White Terror, counter-insurgency, torture, murder by death squad, fighting in *Eritrea*, *Tigre*, *Ogaden*, *Somalia*. These had been peaceful side trips for me from Addis or Nairobi. And all the while, famine stalking the land.

After the Emperor was deposed, the new regime showed its vindictiveness by rounding up all the members of his extended family. Those who were not shot were incarcerated behind the very same walls where I went to visit the Pentecostal prisoners. No distinction was made between immediate family who exercised power and enjoyed their perquisites, and more remote relations who simply bore the wrong blood line, and found themselves on the wrong side of the revolution.

It was these unfortunates who exercised my mind, long after I left the country. I never believed in just flying in to a country, then leaving and forgetting about the people I met and the situations I encountered there. But what could I do from a distance?

By way of answer, a fellow-traveller turned up to have lunch with me one afternoon in Edinburgh, a few years after this trip. He'd heard about the release of the Pentecostals, and wanted to share details of his undercover work in Ethiopia since that time. Whereas many tourists swap yarns and slides, we got down to serious details of who was being persecuted, and how we could help.

For many years afterwards my friend kept in touch with me, informing me of progress on aiding Selassie's suffering family members: his attempts to visit blocked by the regime; occasional successes getting a blanket or favourite book into the prison, and messages out; and publicity in Britain and America about the royal family's plight. It took the better part of a decade, but all eventually escaped, or were set free.

Meantime he was engaged in assisting an entirely different group in Ethiopia, one that history seemed to have played a trick on – the black African Jews, known as Falashas, whose temporary homeland I'd seen in my visit. Their name was a good indication of their status, meaning a stranger, emigrant, or someone without rights. Their origins are mysterious, but they'd been in mountainous northwest Ethiopia for close to two millennia.

Though they rejected the term 'Falasha', and referred to themselves as 'house of Israel', the dilution of their distinctive culture, loss of Hebrew, lack of knowledge of their existence by the outside world, and the post-war state of Israel's preoccupation with its own survival and repatriating holocaust survivors, all combined to frustrate their deep-rooted desire to migrate to Israel, their personal promised land.

True, forty leading rabbis in 1906 sent a message to 'the sons of Abraham, Isaac and Jacob who dwell in Abyssinia', showing that some sections of world Judaism were aware of their existence.

Then, just after my visit, the Chief Rabbi of the Sephardic Jews of Israel announced that the Falashas were accepted as part of the lost tribe of Dan. In 1975 Israel went further, and declared that they would come under the Law of Return, which allows all Jews, of whatever race and colour, the right to enter and settle in Israel. This was of limited practical use to a poor minority people struggling under a communist regime which discouraged emigration, and surrounded by Muslim neighbours. Diplomatic relations between Ethiopia and Israel had been cut.

For my friend, these were mere obstacles to be overcome. He wasn't Jewish, he was Christian. But he'd taken on the Falashas' longing for freedom to repatriate as his own cause. And he prosecuted it with vigour. He talked excitedly of these resilient people, in threes and fours, slipping away from their individual villages by night, rendezvousing at or near Gondar, then descending 165 miles of mountain trails to the blistering heat of the Sudanese Desert, and transit refugee camps around the town of Gedaref.

From this point they'd be ferried to Khartoum just in time to catch special flights to Europe, timed to connect with an onward flight to Israel. All this was done under a veil of secrecy.

Thirteen thousand Falashas reached their new homeland in this way before the exodus was publicised, and Sudan's Vice President, General Omer Muhammad al-Tayeb was put on trial for treason for his part in the affair. The migration halted abruptly, stranding many thousands of would-be travellers.

The final dramatic chapter came with the airlift of those stranded, breaking all previous records for passenger occupancy of a Boeing 747. Sadly, the assimilation of the Falashas was not without hiccups. Because of their intermarriage and long isolation, there were demands for them to go through a 'reconversion'. And, despite the selfless involvement of my friend and other Christian volunteers, Christian Falashas were deemed unwelcome, even when this decision split up families.

I did finally land in SUDAN, on my way out of Ethiopia, but I wasn't allowed through immigration. They despatched me on the next plane to Egypt. For all I know, the Third Secretary's still waiting! I wondered what Egypt held in store for me this time, and if I'd make it to Lebanon and beyond.

I viewed another landing at Cairo with some suspicion. After all, I was primarily interested in new places which I hadn't been to. And the previous two visits to Cairo had been so traumatic – the first a tour of the pyramids by night, the second a sea of wailing and gnashing of teeth on the occasion of Nasser's death; grown UAA male stewards, dressed in black from head to toe, sobbing; everything shut down. What surprises did Egypt and the rest of the Middle East hold in store on this occasion?

# 12

# Beirut and 'Straight' Street

*Middle East (1972)*

For some people the extensive African trip I'd just finished would have been enough travelling for the time being, before heading back to the creature comforts of home. But I had the bit between my teeth. There was no stopping me: I wanted to see and experience as many countries as I could. It wasn't a conscious attempt at all to get into the record books. More the fascination. I was hooked! I couldn't get enough travel. So, despite any misgivings about Cairo, there was a certain 'frisson' of excitement as I contemplated a Middle Eastern adventure on my way back to Britain.

Like my last visit to Egypt, it was beginning to look as if everything had shut down this time also. The Six Day War was not long finished and there'd been a raid or two in the Israeli-Lebanon corridor, making air travel (civilian or not) potentially risky. All European airlines, and even UAA, suspended their flights for an unspecified period.

I'd hoped to travel on an Alyemda DC6, on the last leg of its Aden-Cairo-Beirut service. It never made it in from Aden. So I was stuck, in the transit lounge, with upwards of a thousand passengers from the cancelled flights, trying to fight my way onto the only plane with any hope of going to Beirut: a Middle East Airlines 707.

Conditions in the packed lounge bordered on outright chaos,

returning most of the time to merely normal chaos. The wait was alleviated by syrupy orange drinks which were for sale. Fearful of losing one of the few chairs I sent payment up to the counter with another foreigner, plumping for two glasses. His pointing must not have been very good, because moments later a waiter appeared at the seat beside me with two glasses of orange for the adjacent passengers. They accepted gladly. It was afterwards I found out they were my drinks.

A carefully folded note, with the appropriate 'note' inserted, carried to the ticket desk outside brought a uniformed MEA gent through the doors to inform me that I was one of the lucky ones with a seat on his Boeing. Lucky? Flying along an air corridor boycotted by every other airline, where a non-friendly Israeli jet might at any stage take a potshot at us? But then, the alternative was an indefinite sojourn on the floor of the transit lounge at Cairo Airport, maybe without even the pyramid tour option to liven things up.

I took the boarding pass gratefully. The nice MEA gent even showed me my name on the manifest, so I'd be confident I wouldn't be left behind. A pity he wasn't the one collecting boarding passes at the departure gate. Just as I was about to board, a burly hand pushed me back, declaring: 'You have already boarded'.

At first nonplussed, I eventually drew out of him the implausible explanation that indeed I, J. Todd, had boarded and been checked off.

'Look, there's your name, with the tick.'

My brain roared into overdrive, not so much to work out which of the permutations of the who-stole-my-seat-mystery were accurate, as to figure out another means of approach. I opted for shouting and hand waving.

Eleven minutes of lung-piercing yells (the hand waving didn't seem to do any good) persuaded the man with the burly hand to refer me to an airside official. That was all I needed. Especially when I saw his driver's pass.

'Take me to the plane,' I ordered.

'No seats.'

'To see if there is one.'

'OK. We walk through plane. I show you full.'

The official and I paraded from front to back of the 707. Finally, in row twenty-one, an empty seat. Diligent enquiries confirmed that no one else was entitled to it, so I plopped down. 'You'll never believe the excuse they gave me,' I said to the lady beside me, who was busy filling in her disembarkation card for LEBANON. 'They told me they'd already boarded J. Todd.' I glanced over as she completed her details on the card: 'NAME: Mrs J. Todd, OCCUPATION: spouse of diplomat'.

Beirut itself was almost an anti-climax after the ordeal of getting there. Those were still the days when it was a major banking centre and cosmopolitan oasis in the Arab world, before all the buildings, including the one I stayed in, were blasted out of existence by misguided zealots.

Most nights it was so humid I didn't sleep in the seafront building, but on the rooftop. It was worth it alone for the Mediterranean sunrise. Lebanese friends drove me to Tyre and Sidon. I remembered that Solomon's temple in Jerusalem was indebted to Hiram, king of ancient Tyre, 'which brought from Ophir a very great amount of almug wood and precious stones. No such almug wood has come or been seen to this day' (I Kings 10).

On the way back from Tyre we were stopped several times by security patrols. Even then they were omnipresent. But at least I didn't have to ride around Beirut blindfolded in a refrigerator like Terry Waite. It seems awfully cliched to say it, but Beirut was beautiful then.

Some heated arguments were going on between Jordan, Lebanon and Syria about air agreements, so flights between their respective capitals were continually interrupted. Only one Aeroflot Tupolev 134, once a week, was allowed to pick up passengers between Beirut and Amman, for example, after offloading through passengers from Moscow. The waiting list was a month long. Taxis were fortunately plentiful, so the rest of my brief Middle Eastern odyssey was performed by car.

To be precise, they were shared taxis. The kind that lure you into the back seat with a promise of an imminent departure, then wait until the vehicle is stuffed to capacity before taking off on a slow hot drive, accompanied by the driver's choice of 'wailing' music. Food is usually lots of pitta bread and hard-boiled eggs (bring your own).

In this way I traversed JORDAN, got to the border of Iraq, and spent time in SYRIA. My miraculous railway ticket offer from Teheran had evaporated, so I had to retrace my steps to Beirut for onward flights.

Syria was like walking into a tale from *1001 Arabian Nights*, and not being sure which one. It's a country that's always fascinated me: Palmyra, the oasis of beautiful Queen Zenobia, who took on the Romans 250 years after the birth of Christ; Aleppo with its magnificent citadel; the definitive Crusader fort at Krak des Chevaliers; and Damascus, perhaps the oldest continually inhabited city in the world. People were friendly, yet cautious. The country was open, if you had the right key, closed fast if you didn't.

I'd been warned in Jordan, for so long a reliable pointer to conditions to the immediate east, that it might not be wise to associate openly with my contacts in Syria. 'Use discretion,' my Arab hosts warned.

I did. When my shoulder bag burst open in a main thoroughfare in Damascus shortly after I arrived, and a cheery fellow came up and offered to help me pick up my belongings which spilled out helter-skelter, I declined his aid. He walked away slightly baffled. I was even more embarrassed when I reached the house I was looking for, to find my would-be helper there. He was the son of the man I'd come to visit!

In some ways Damascus has a more biblical feel than even Palestine. I rode a bus part of the way, and walked the rest, down 'the street called Straight', where Ananaias was deputed to visit Saul. Saul, you will remember, had come 'breathing fire and slaughter' against followers of the Jesus sect, but he'd been blinded on the Damascus Road. Now he would watch the scales fall off his eyes, for his sight to be restored. Straight Street was a mile and 2,000 years of merchandising. The bag I bought there to replace my burst shoulder bag itself broke before I reached London.

Saul the threatener, with letters of permission from the High Priest to kill the detested Christians at Damascus, was now transformed into Paul the intellectual advocate for Christ; apostle to the Gentiles. Changing allegiance so suddenly, as cross-bench politicians know all too well, is a recipe for making even more enemies. I was taken to see the spot where Paul made a hasty escape over the wall in a basket.

I too retreated from the Middle East, not in a basket but in a battered Syrian Arab Airlines Caravelle to CYPRUS, then on to RHODES. The Caravelle deposited me into the arms of a waiting Armenian family – citizens without a country. There, on sunny beaches, they whetted my appetite for a view of snow-covered Mount Ararat in their former homeland. To go there, I'd have to get to Moscow first.

The USSR wasn't on the home stretch of this Africa-Middle East-Europe itinerary. I was due back in Britain in less than a week, to start postgraduate studies at Oxford. But I did manage to fit in flying visits to BULGARIA, HUNGARY, CZECHOSLOVAKIA, AUSTRIA, LUXEMBOURG and HOLLAND. My first tantalising glimpse of Eastern Europe made me determined to return and get to know people there, people who were trapped in a monstrous system they no more deserved than you or I did. I sampled the first-ever commercial Russian jet, the Tupolev 104, on the Prague-Frankfurt sector, and, by way of contrast, the pristine DC9s of Austrian Airlines. I'm convinced they employ an extra crew member just to make sure no one tarnishes their image by inadvertently dropping a sweet wrapper, or leaving a pencil mark on the lavatory wall.

Czechoslovak Airlines (CSA) so enjoyed its assigned code letters of 'OK' that it painted them on the tail. Each of its planes was then an 'OK Jet'. The Bulgarian airline which flew me to the Black Sea has since been renamed 'Balkan', but at that time rejoiced in the name 'Tabso' – an acronym of course for some state aviation organ, but sounding like the sort of potion you had to take twice a day to ward off various unwanted infections!

Tabso, metamorphosed into Balkan, had two claims to fame. Its executives were second only to the Soviets as targets for Foreign Office expulsions from the UK for spying, and amazingly, it became the first communist airline to regularly fly to Belfast, transporting Ulster holidaymakers direct to the delights of Sunny Beach and Golden Sands, on the Black Sea.

Bill and Eileen Laird will never forget their first Balkan flight. When they boarded the Tupolev at Aldergrove, they found that their seats had been double-booked. The stewardess indicated a crate in the cockpit, barely big enough for one. They shared this for the four and three quarter hour flight, each taking turns, while the other stood. 'They brought our meals as though we were normal passengers,' said Bill. On the return trip, there wasn't even space on the crate. Only Eileen was boarded; Bill had to wait for two more days, and then take an indirect flight back with two changes of plane en route.

Personally, I found the Bulgarians most accommodating. I stayed in someone's house who didn't speak a word of English. At one of the state bakery stores I watched the routine as people obtained a ticket for the precise amount of their purchase, then handed this over as payment, describing the desired object.

I decided to give it a go. Indicating the particular cake of which I fancied a slice required a great deal of pointing from the far end of the shop to the cashier, but everybody obliged. It was astonishingly cheap, considering that when my purchase was handed over it was not a slice, but the entire cake!

Back in Oxford I took stock: it had been an incredible summer of travelling and adventures, in more than forty countries. But was my globetrotting about to be curtailed? Postgraduate studies would mean shorter holidays, tighter budgets.

That's when I saw the ad. for a long weekend in TUNISIA for £29, including flights. Incredibly, the Tunisians in developing their tourism industry built five-star hotels first, so that was the only available accommodation, even at budget prices! Combined with the almost-bankrupt Court Line Aviation, who flew purple BAC111s from Luton, it was irresistible. And ALGERIA, a neighbourly hop, filled another gap in my North Africa personal travel map.

But there were still whole continents on which I hadn't set foot.

# 13

## General Peron's Guest

*South America (1973)*

If I were, say, a prime salmon or a large juicy trout, and you were a fisherman, all you'd have had to do at this stage was put out the bait . . . a new continent to visit, a worthy purpose for the journey, a base from which to operate for a few months, and plenty of side trip possibilities.

I'd have been yours, hook, line and sinker. Call it fascination, call it obsession, call it what you will. I began to have itchy feet every time the though of the three-month summer break entered my mind.

Realistically, at this stage in my career as a penniless student traveller I could have taken one of two views. A: I've been fortunate enough to cover a decent chunk of the world. Time to get back to serious studies. B: Granted, I've been to parts of Europe, North America, Asia, the Middle East and Africa, but apart from the gaps in those regions, that leaves South America and Australasia to go. Which shall I do next? It's an awfully big world out there, and I mustn't lose momentum.

What drove me to seek out these travel adventures? I don't fully know. I just know it was something I had to do, just like some people live for golf or mountain climbing.

I chose B and listed South America as the next target area, followed by Australia/New Zealand as the 'big one' – the far end of the earth. Communist strongholds beyond Europe seemed unreachable, unbreachable, and I didn't pay much attention at that time to the islands, with various claims to sovereignty, dotted profligately across all the oceans. Arctic and Antarctic regions appeared to be for explorers only. And going to the Pole . . . give me a break!

For a time I felt defeated. There didn't appear to be summer jobs opening up in South America, especially for non-Spanish speakers. The Oxford University Tango Club and various cultural groups proved equally non-productive. By being frugal, I could suppport myself once there, perhaps even without working. But what about the cost of getting there?

The eventual solution was so bizarre that if I'd invented it, I'd have been told it was too unusual to be credible. As with many things in life, you try in vain to bamboozle your way into something, then the prize drops into your lap, because of something else you've done, totally unconnected.

It all started with a telephone call from the Third Secretary at the Argentine Embassy in London. (I never seem to graduate to First, or even Second, Secretaries.)

Actually the phone call was to the porter's booth at Lincoln College, the cosseted luxury of student life not stretching quite to all modern conveniences such as a private phone. A message would be left in your pigeon hole to return a call, unless you happened to be passing at the exact moment the phone rang.

In this respect I was fortunate the following year to acquire 'rooms' (they were always called 'rooms', but there was only one) above the Mitre in Turl Street, close to the corridor payphone. When I was attending lectures in the mornings, the lady who cleaned the room would often answer for me, and got to know my regular callers. This helped as my sideline travel business developed. But I was only awarded the room in the Mitre the following year because of the typhoid cataclysm that befell me later in this story. This year I was dependent totally on the porter.

He coped with the routine messages with panache. The ones with business overtones gave him more problems, especially when I forgot to apprise him of the earlier parts of transactions.

One message from my fledgling travel business sticks in my mind. I'd neglected to inform him that I was tendering for quotes from whole aircraft charterers, to bring deprived children from Belfast over to England for a holiday. He greeted me with a quizzical eye, as

I entered the quad, gesturing to a piece of paper. On it was scribbled: '£2,481 *including coffee and biscuits*!'

When I returned the Third Secretary's phone call, he asked if I could come down to London to meet him. A date was set, and I duly presented myself at 53 Hans Place. Over a cup of tea he asked if I'd like to be considered for a scholarship to ARGENTINA of three months' duration, dates flexible. My fear that I said 'Yes' too hastily was dissolved, as he relaxed. He pushed a single sheet application form over to me, signalling the end of the interview.

Several questions presented themselves to me on the train back from Paddington. How many people were applying? What was the closing date? He'd said 'As soon as possible'. Who had given them my name? And did every applicant secure a personal chat with the Third Secretary just to receive the application form?

The mystery was partially solved that night at a party in Commonwealth House, Pembroke Street. As part of my volunteer activities I helped co-ordinate social events, homestays and orientations for new foreign students at Oxford. June from the British Council acted as liaison, providing lists of arriving scholars and seeing that they were met off the train and helped to find their way around. She called me over.

'Did that Argie bloke ever get hold of you? He rang us up asking if we knew anybody interested in studying there, and I gave him your name. I knew you'd been talking about going there.'

Thanks, June. You're a brick! That calls for a poncho to be brought back – if I get the scholarship. Better get the form filled in tonight. Which reminds me: it's in Spanish. Maybe the Basque girl from the Overseas Club will help me translate. Better bring two ponchos back.

The other part of the mystery cleared itself up one day after I sent in the form. The Third Secretary rang again: 'Can you go round to the Aerolineas Argentinas offices in Bond Street and pick up your tickets?'

I was incredulous. Was there no selection process? No telex-conferencing with Buenos Aires about suitable candidates? No screening of subject matter proposed for study? It was perhaps unfair to congratulate myself for winning. I was obviously *the only candidate*.

A letter a few days later spelt out the details: airfares, international and within the country, would be paid (that bit was obvious: I already had the tickets!); a grant for accommodation; a stipend while in Argentina; and necessary project expenses. Was I dreaming, or what?

How did the whole scholarship business come about, anyway? Every other year the British government, through the British Council, awarded a highly competitive scholarship to an Argentinian scholar for work in the UK. It was said that, on impulse, General Peron had asked how many British scholarships had been provided by his government. A check revealing none led to a hasty search for a suitable person to remedy the balance. I was in the right place at the right time.

I almost didn't make it. After the tickets were issued, and my acceptance confirmed, I got another diplomatic call – this time from the UK Foreign Office. They pointed out that they'd just cancelled a British sports tour to Argentina, and were putting any official goodwill visits on hold, due to the political situation there. They suggested I should cancel my study trip, because it had 'official overtones'. I agreed to delay it for a few weeks, but had no intention of giving it up altogether.

So in mid July, I found myself, with General Peron's obvious blessing and to British government disapproval, ensconced in a penthouse apartment atop a deserted six-storey building, during the 'dirty war', when anyone without impeccable fascist credentials was liable to find himself doing a disappearing act. And I didn't even speak Spanish!

I had an excellent minder in the Foreign Ministry – Manuella. She phoned at least twice a week, but always on the eve of any planned riot, demonstration or disruption. She had an uncanny knack for pinpointing any potential flashpoint, and timing it with great accuracy.

Our conversations would go something like:

'Mr Todd, do you have a good book?'

'Yes. Why?'

'You might want to read it tomorrow, instead of going out. There'll be a "spontaneous manifestation" tomorrow at 2 p.m. in the Plaza de Mayo. Without fluent Spanish, you'll be at a disadvantage.'

Thanks to Manuella's early-warning system, the closest I came to trouble was trying to pretend I wasn't in the back row of the cinema during a showing of *Estado de Sitio* ('State of Siege'). At the point where the American Ambassador to Uruguay was kidnapped, the whole audience rose as one man to cheer and exult.

The newsreels before the main feature helped set the scene. They consisted of Argentinian generals flying down to the Antarctic to inspect newborn babies, reinforcing sovereignty claims over a large barren waste; inflammatory comments on a border dispute with Chile; and posters and display material clearly announcing 'Las Malvinas son Argentinas' (the Falklands are Argentinian).

Other highlights were travels in PATAGONIA down to TIERRA DEL FUEGO; a meeting with Jorge Luis Borges, the blind poet who repeated to me his marvellous joke about the Falklands, that it was like two bald men arguing over a comb; and 'dulce de leche', a sort of untranslatable caramel dessert every afternoon at four.

You may wonder how I had so much spare time from my studies during this study trip. There were two main reasons. The first was that only seven days of my almost three-month sojourn were actually totally free of any form of 'huelga' (strike), 'manifestacion' (demonstration), or other disruption on campus.

The second reason was that my scholarship clearly stated it could only be pursued at a government university. I'd given as my subject the teaching of English, which was only done at the 'profesorados' (teacher-training colleges). These were not approved in the scholarship's wording, but nobody seemed to mind.

A small bonus was the fact that the air ticket was not restricted to the state airline, but open for any international carrier along the length of the route. I was thus able to parlay the largesse of the Argentinian government into additional country stops – BRAZIL and PARAGUAY on the way down; side trips to URUGUAY and CHILE, BOLIVIA, PERU, ECUADOR, PANAMA, VENEZUELA, COLOMBIA, and over a dozen Caribbean islands on the way back: BRITISH and US VIRGINS, ST KITTS, MARTINIQUE, ST LUCIA, ST MAARTEN and ST MARTIN, PUERTO RICO, DOMINICA, ANTIGUA, BEQUIA, TRINIDAD, BARBADOS.

Using my Aerolineas airpass I touched down at every city they flew to: Comodoro Rivadavia to Mendoza, Neuquel to Rio Gallegos, Bahia Blanca to Cordoba, San Carlos de Bariloche to Rosario. The side trip to the FALKLANDS twice a month was operated by an Argentinian Air Force F27. On an Austral shuttle flight over to Montevideo my boarding pass had the winning number encoded, and I won a purple flight bag.

There were so many wonderful qualities to Argentina that even with the strikes, riots, kidnaps, protests, murders and general mayhem, it was hard to leave the many friends I made there. If I'd hoped things would be easier on the rest of my passage through South America, however, I was mistaken.

Tourists undoubtedly recall Iguacu Falls, the mighty Amazon, Copacabama Beach or Manchu Picchu among their highlights from this continent. Me?

A school bus which caught fire near Lake Titicaca, and the resultant exit stampede of forty boys who charged straight over the two seats I was wedged tight between while I ducked under the blows of their passing shoes. They'd earlier given me a lift from La Paz, Bolivia.

Being misdiagnosed as suffering from typhoid in an Indian hospital 11,000 feet up in the Peruvian Andes. The doctor's aides had misread the blood results by a factor of ten. I headed for sea level where I felt better. The diagnosis, however, ensured both a late arrival back to Oxford for my second year, and the keeping for me of a central room in Turl Street, when I cabled to say I was sick.

Being shown to the door of my room at the radio station compound in Quito, where I was broadcasting – opening it, and immediately blanking out from the altitude sickness peculiar to those parts. I didn't remember anything for the next forty-eight hours.

Narrowly escaping torture, death or worse in the soccer stadium in Santiago, twenty-four hours before Salvador Allende was shot. When every business and mode of transport is shut down, people are chaining themselves to the palace railings, and the currency is becoming worthless, you know something is afoot. I didn't stay to find out and become one more deadly statistic. Together with a Brazilian, Italian, and two Germans, I hired a minivan and we escaped over the nearest mountain pass, dumping our now worthless shopping bags full of pesos at the border.

Perhaps my introduction to South America was atypical. Certainly there was never a dull moment. I don't think my two-page report to the Third Secretary did full justice to it.

Career choice time was upon me, as Oxford days drew to a close. I beat out a few thousand hopefuls for a plum job at BBC News to start in October 1974.

But I needed to travel some more, add to the countries I'd been to, visit those that were more difficult to reach. Cheekily, I asked for a year off; they gave me nine months. Now at last I could tackle the forbidding and forbidden countries. But why did I start by being accused of conspiracy against the state?

# 14

# The Dissident and the Stolen Passport

*Aaland/Romania (1974)*

AALAND is a medium-sized island midway between SWEDEN and Finland, capital Mariehamm, population 50,000. I know this because it's approximately where I was relieved of all my then worldly goods. If you ever have the misfortune to have your passport, tickets and traveller's cheques stolen, try at least to arrange such a mishap towards the end of your trip and not, as happened to me, at the beginning.

At the end of the summer I'd planned to start my big almost-one-year around the world effort, visiting off-limits communist countries I hadn't been to, such as Cuba, China and North Vietnam. Meantime I was on my way to 'limber up' with short trips to East Europe.

I was more heavily bitten by the travel bug than ever. But it wasn't just travel for the sake of travel, whatever that is. I felt that behind the headlines of the Cold War, there were real live flesh and blood people, enduring lives of quiet desperation under tyranny of one kind or another. In a naïve sort of way, I felt that if only I could make contact, I could help in some way. At least it was worth a try!

I fell asleep in the Gulf of Bothnia, on board Silja Line's nightly Stockholm-Helsinki ferry, with onward tickets to Denmark and Germany, £95, and the stiff-backed, distinctive navy document with the polite request from Her Britannic Majesty, that border officials should grant passage to me across their respective frontiers without let or hindrance, all safe in the inside pocket of my light cream-coloured jacket. And woke, about to dock at Helsinki, minus all of the above.

The immediate cause for concern was the lack of a disembarkation card to prove I'd paid for my passage. I solved this by muttering 'Police' to the collector, who referred me to the dockside security office. So, unlike past Russian Tsars from the east, and Kings of Sweden from the west, I was unable to make a grand entrance in my march into Finland. Instead I caught my first glimpses of Helsinki from inside a Black Maria police van, accompanied by a couple of overnight drunks they'd picked up.

Filling out the police report to document the theft (in Finnish) was difficult enough. But it was nothing to my reception in the British Embassy. To them I was simply nuisance number one of the day – a problem to be ignored in the hope that it might go away; and, if it didn't, to be rudely and summarily dealt with by the book.

How narrowly I averted forced repatriation I don't know, but it was mentioned again and again, as their preferred solution. It was only by the generosity of the Finnish welfare state that I ate breakfast and had the bus fare to even get to the British Embassy. It was clear I couldn't look to my own consular representative for another sixpence, even as a loan, without agreeing to be sent back to Britain as a *quid pro quo*.

In those awful three days – especially the first – I knew what it must feel like to be a Manchester United football supporter after a match on the continent, running into difficulty with the law. As soon as you misbehave, the host country can make your life miserable – the British Embassy can make it unbearable. Problem is, a misfortune that arises outside your control can be treated in exactly the same way as if you'd misbehaved.

Getting into such scrapes lets you, even for a brief moment, share a tiny glimpse into the daily life of a majority in two-thirds of the world, who have no representation, no clout, and no hope outside of God. I was able to have emergency cash forwarded inside seventy-two hours, and escape from the clutches of embassy bureaucrats. That solved the pressing problem of being indigent far from home, but what of the journey I needed to embark on?

The best I was able to secure from the consular folk was a new, highly limited passport, on the third day after my misfortune. I left town quickly before they changed their minds.

I'd been due to rendezvous with a friend from Oxford, Lindsay

Brown, in SWITZERLAND. Amazingly, despite the delay, I bumped into him in the street in Zurich. While he was waiting for me, he in turn ran into a former Hindu guru from Trinidad, Rabindranath Maharaj, who had teamed up with a Swiss colleague, Heinz Strupler, to found a coffee bar where street people could come to talk, and be weaned away from drugs and other dependencies. They invited us to stay at their place, and Rabi got so excited by my proposed Cuba visit that he offered to accompany me on the first leg through the Caribbean.

On our way to what was still a federalised YUGOSLAVIA, even though you could clearly see the differences between the constituent republics, I left Lindsay for a few hours on the beach at Rimini, while I made a thirty-minute visit to one of Europe's delightful tiny countries, SAN MARINO. I did this just because it was there. The idea of a postage-stamp sized place calling itself a country, and earning its revenue from selling postage stamps, fascinated me. So did the historical background, and the survival of such mini potentates in a sea of consolidated modern nation states. LIECHTENSTEIN had been easy to visit since it was virtually at the Struplers' back door.

We'd planned only a two-day side trip into ROMANIA. It was already late in the summer. Lindsay was due back in England. I had negotiated a block of seventy-five seats on a flight from Luxemburg to the Bahamas the following month for a Swedish choir giving concerts in the Caribbean, and Rabi and I planned to use the free escort tickets for the first stage of our journey. I knew visas would be more difficult this time, and these communist outposts would take more than a summer vacation to get to.

But even my strong curiosity to see and explore new places was always subject to greater priorities. And one of these stared me in the face the moment Lindsay and I set foot in Cluj, the beautiful university town in western TRANSYLVANIA, not far from the castle of Vlad Tepes which gave rise to Bram Stoker's Dracula legend. Some Romanians still get visibly upset over the transformation of their good Count into a late-night horror movie prototype.

We were visiting a family we'd sent some books to from Oxford. While Ceaucescu cultivated a liberal image abroad – slight diversions from Moscow-approved foreign policy, non-participation in Warsaw Pact manoeuvres, and other gestures – he was ruthlessly tightening the screws on his own populace, censoring and forbidding anything which didn't toe the party line.

But whereas certain 'decadent' Western books, especially religious ones, were banned, couldn't be bought inside Romania, and would be confiscated if carried across the frontier in luggage, we'd found that a sure way to supply the intellectuals and believers who suffered this shameless discrimination, was simply to send one book at a time by registered post from England. You could also verify that the books arrived by the delivery receipt signature.

We'd been taught this trick by Josif Tson, the Alexander Solzhenitsyn of his country. As a Baptist pastor he knew he had no hope of a university-level theological education under the communists; so he took a daring gamble. He got a weekend visa to Austria, leaving his wife behind (the authorities believed very strongly in the hostage principle).

From Austria he made his way to Oxford, where he was quickly enrolled in Regent's Park College thanks to the generosity of British Christians. I met him at a conference of all universities at Swanwick, in the Derbyshire Dales, and sat enthralled as he related stories of life back in Romania: the hardships, the oppressions, but above all the underlying joy and confidence his people had that Ceaucescu would not write the final script, that those who had hope and faith would transcend their temporal reverses, and triumph in the end.

Josif gave a completely trustworthy account of the situation on the ground in Romania. He furnished names and addresses for the book parcel scheme. It seemed a simple way of helping, and becoming personally involved.

I was struck by the fact that Josif rarely mentioned his own situation – three years' separation from his home, no visible means of support, the impossibility of his wife Elisabeth joining him on or after graduation. And then the magnitude of what he was doing dawned on me. He was going back. He'd planned it all along, and his wife trusted him implicitly. A subterfuge in the visa was necessary – it was the only way out. But his people had actually worked around the fiendish restrictions. They'd commissioned him to be the first graduate from the West, who'd return to train them and lead their cause with enhanced skills.

Nevertheless, it took guts to follow through. To sample the easy life in the West, and then forsake it. To follow his destiny, leaving his homeland, then returning to it under a cloud, not knowing what lay ahead.

*     *     *

The Cluj family set about alerting their network that visitors had arrived. We were invited to a friend's house for a slide show of the frescoes, icon paintings, and other regional works of art of which the Romanians were so proud.

The slides popped up on the blank wall (no screen) one at a time. Each one seemed to take an age. I was faint from hunger, tired from two nights' bus travel. I fought off sleep, but not too well.

The narrator would display the next slide, pause, and say something like: 'The face of Jesus', or 'Christ on the Cross', and the whole room would fall silent and gaze reverentially for an extended period.

Even the belated realisation that this was their only means of unsupervised worship (the churches were full of secret police informers) couldn't overcome the pangs of drowsiness to which I eventually succumbed. What made it worse was being given the place of honour in the front row where everybody could see me.

Our friends were gracious. No reprimands. They spoke of how much they valued the books. Then Josif was discussed in hushed tones. No one knew exactly what he'd had to go through on his return. The government no doubt took it as weakness, a caving in, he couldn't take living in the West any longer, or they'd discarded him – not for the strength of character and purpose which it was. But he'd managed the return, and was quietly teaching and preaching, sharing what he'd learned.

Word leaked out from time to time of difficulties resurfacing between Josif and the authorities; such were doubtless inevitable, given his determination. And perhaps the calculating approach of the police on his return had been no immediate action, just the threat hanging over him that if he didn't behave, now that he was back in their power, they could always resurrect charges based on his illegal stay abroad. According to their strain of thinking, this could act as a permanent muzzle.

Monica, the daughter, took me by the arm and whispered: 'Go and see Josif. Something is afoot. Your visit is very timely.' We left on the night train to Bucharest, unsure whether even contacting Josif would put him in danger, but feeling that we had to follow through on our instinctive urges, and the guidance of his friends. Lindsay would only be able to turn around, as he had to leave that same day to be back in Oxford. I had planned to return with him, but was beginning to be less sure now that I would actually accompany him.

Josif's voice was strained on the telephone: rigid, correct, pleasant, but without the warmth I'd known in Oxford. Straight away I knew he was afraid of the omnipresent bug, not so much for himself (he'd come to terms with it), but for the way in which it might implicate me in what he was planning. Just exactly how I was to be implicated was still hidden from me, but not for long.

He suggested a meeting. We spoke of the railway station, and our imminent departure. Normally he would have said he'd wave us off, and express his regrets, for the unseen listeners, that we couldn't stay longer. But he seemed eager that we come to his house.

When he met us on the doorstep there was no small talk. His eyes danced as he came straight to the point. 'I've written a paper against the government, John,' he said. 'You'd better stay around for a while. As long as you're here they won't put me in jail. But if you go . . .'

I thought of the free tickets with the Swedish choir, the lengthy preparations needed for Cuba, never mind China, the time that would be eating away into my part-year off before starting a career that I imagined would curtail my long-distance travelling somewhat. But only for the split second necessary to know where my duty lay. I had freedom of movement, access, some clout in the West. He had none of these. His stand might produce greater freedom for the long-suffering faithful Romanians. I had to stay.

This wasn't the first time my well-laid and intricate plans in my quest to cover the whole globe had to be turned aside. As individual destinations became ever more difficult to reach, requiring advance commitment and a tiny window of accessibility (maybe only a single opportunity in one, three, or even five years), any such clash with another imperative put me even more agonisingly on a rack of turmoiled indecision.

But I always followed what I knew deep inside to be the right course, even if another chance didn't come along. Often one did. You never know when your travels might be transformed from personal meanderings to predestined appointments. This looked like one of these times.

My special privilege, in three decades of travelling, has been to be now a messenger, now a witness to history, now a visitor, in the right place at the right time, now a catalyst maybe for another's action, now a 'teller of tales' both about key figures in other cultures, and especially, on behalf of those who for whatever reason can't speak for themselves.

Josif's 'Manifesto' was as simple as it was radical. He argued that communism had tried, and failed, to produce a 'new man'. Instead of ridiculing, persecuting and demeaning their enemies of other persuasions, they should allow people of faith, opposed to communism, but accepting their rule, to make their contribution to society through civic virtue. Give Caesar his rights, in other words. But give God His, too. So hands off manipulating church congresses, infiltrating their leadership, and dictating limits on Sunday schools and services.

It was nothing if not bold for its time, In all the East European countries there was no open debate of this sort, no questioning the government line, which was party policy. Dissent was squelched, by intimidation, bribery, force, or manipulation. Josif waited to see what action would be taken against him.

'I'm going to send you to the number two dissident in our nation,' Josif announced at noon, after Lindsay's train had left. So began a two-month stay in Romania, the first of many, shuttling between attics and basements, sometimes out in the open, sometimes in concealment, always keeping an eye over my shoulder to see who was watching.

I was introduced to the double lives people were forced to lead. Pavel Niculescu showed me his bookcase, full of the works of Lenin. A secret panel swivelled these round and replaced them with Solzhenitsyn. His Ceaucescu wall calendar similarly reversed, to reveal pictures of prisoners in the Soviet gulag.

I met university professors working as garbage collectors because of their failure to spout Marxist dogma at every turn; children denied education because their parents' political credentials were suspect, widows whose husbands had been involved in a fatal car crash after falling out with the securitate (secret police), and droves of ordinary folk whose lives were circumscribed beyond measure by the iron grip of the Ceaucescu machine.

But I also fell in love with Romania and its people, and did all I could in the succeeding years to alleviate their plight. Years later I was delighted when my radio reports from Bucharest were selected first for BBC's *Pick of the Week*, then *Pick of the Year*.

Josif was indicted for conspiracy against the state. But he kept one step ahead of the authorities for a long period, before eventually being forced into exile. From outside the country he became one of the most popular broadcasters into Romania on short wave. It was said whole streets in towns and villages emptied to listen to his talks. He got books translated and smuggled in, and set up training programmes for his countrymen. To his everlasting credit, as soon as the Ceaucescus fell, he gave up a privileged existence in the West for the second time and returned to his people. He now heads a new private university in Oradea, and has helped start new schools, a printing press, and numerous other facilities.

I was reputedly named as co-conspirator in the indictment, and told by Her Majesty's Government that 'it would not be advisable to return to Romania, in our view.' But since I was never officially declared *persona non grata* by the regime I took the optimistic view, and returned a dozen more times.

Mind you, I usually took care to arrive in the country on a Friday afternoon by train, knowing that the record of my visit would probably not reach Securitate HQ until Monday late morning, by which time I'd usually be safely on a Tarom flight out of Bucharest, bearing a transcript of a prisoner interview, a new 'appeal to the West', a tape for immediate broadcast, or other sensitive documents.

On this occasion, however, it was the first time for six years I didn't have the pressure of being back in Scotland or England by early October for the start of the university year. I'd lost my Swedish choir free seats, and hadn't begun the process of applying for a Cuban visa. To the best of my knowledge, you couldn't actually even apply for a visa for China or North Vietnam.

So I opted to take the long way round by train, through the USSR, giving me my first view of Lenin's workers' paradise close up. I applied for a visa at the imposing Soviet Embassy in Bucharest. They curtly informed me I had to have a telexed confirmation from Intourist in Moscow of prepaid accommodation, normally a three-weeks-in-advance procedure.

Carpati, the Romanian tourist organisation, was the local agent for Intourist, so I tried my luck with them. The girl behind the counter was sympathetic. 'You just need a confirmation *number*,' she said. She accepted payment, ran to the back room, and returned with a number she'd plucked from somewhere. 'That will get you the visa,' she said. It did.

The number two dissident and the number seven dissident came to see me off at the railway station. As he left, number two slipped an envelope into my hand. I assumed it was an article for publication in the West, or a message to be smuggled out. When I opened it on the train I was touched to find money 'to buy food on the train'. He was Ph.D. level, living off a manual worker's low wage, devoting all his free time to campaigning for human rights.

In my compartment a middle-aged lady, a soldier and his young wife were sharing a farewell drink. Hearing the whistle, the soldier bolted off, leaving the two women. I forgot that the Russians didn't segregate their train sleeping accommodation. They got off in Kishinev, capital of the then Soviet Republic of Moldavia, now independent MOLDOVA. Through the UKRAINE I was alone. BYELORUSSIA and LITHUANIA seemed slightly more Westernised, POLAND more open still.

My ticket, being a cheap rouble one, ended in EAST GERMANY, but five marks took me from one Berlin to the other. I was back next day though, at Schonefeld to fly on the Interflug Ilyushin which had denied me boarding in Ethiopia. In those days you bought tickets in the West from an East bloc airline at advantageous rates.

As we taxied off, a Cubana IL62 nosed alongside, arriving from Havana via Gander. What did it take to get aboard one of those? Whatever it took, I'd do it. I'd met two Cubans at a conference in Sweden before losing my passport. I knew their trip was a once in a lifetime experience for them. They'd invited me to visit them: I would, before the year was over.

# 15

# The Cuban Ambassador

*Cuba/Caribbean (1974)*

The consular section of the Cuban Embassy in Kensington Gardens was not a hive of activity at the best of times. You tended to become well known after turning up there three or four times. You also knew the inevitable disappointment in store if you hoped that this time they'd say yes.

The silver lining in the Cuban Embassy cloud was that Nigel Goodwin's flat in Hornton Place was just around the corner, and you could always be sure of a cup of coffee from him or his wife Gillie.

Nigel had gone from Shakespearean actor to television hospital soap (*Emergency Ward Ten*) to co-founding with Cliff Richard the Arts Centre Group – a meeting place for arts and media professionals. I qualified for membership, even with my nine-month BBC deferment. When he discovered that I took the train down from Scotland to attend functions, Nigel took to making up a bed in his spare room for me. He was like that. An encourager in word and deed.

One October Monday I attended a regular ACG meeting at Nigel's after another Cuban rebuff. Summer festive occasions were held on the lawn at Cliff's country house in Essex, Battailles. Now we were back in town for winter gatherings.

It was an eclectic bunch. Sometimes 'name' stars such as Derek Nimmo or Thora Hird would turn up. Young Turks of burgeoning potential; film director Norman Stone; poet and *Rolling Stone* columnist Steve Turner; Dan Wooding from the *Sunday People*, full of exposés of naughty vicars and sacked football managers; dancers, musicians, designers, television presenters. On a good evening Cliff might be importuned to do a 'living room' performance of 'The Young Ones' or 'Travelling Light', without a backing group.

I don't remember what was discussed that evening, but I do recall looking around the tightly-packed throng and thinking how the success of nearly everyone in the room superficially was attributed to talent, but in actuality consisted of large doses of perseverance in the face of rejections and upsets, the ability to get up and go on.

That's when the verse popped into my mind:

> Ask and you shall receive.
> Seek and you shall find,
> Knock, and it *shall* be opened unto you.

I would keep on knocking at the door of Cuba. The best evidence of my determination to do so would be if I headed in the direction of Havana, without waiting for ever at the starting blocks.

So a grey, drizzly November evening saw me board a Varig DC10 at Heathrow for PORTUGAL where I caught a Surinam Airways DC8 to CURACAO, and on to ARUBA with a few additional layovers. The stop in Lisbon gave me enough time to look up an old friend from Feijo. He gathered a cluster of neighbours to wish me bon voyage. 'You'll get to Cuba, no problem,' he averred. My spirits were buoyed up no end.

For weeks I criss-crossed the Caribbean, taking in islands that were new to me: ST VINCENT, GRENADA, GUADELOUPE, MONTSERRAT, VIEQUES, and revisiting many old ones. I noted that Leeward Islands Air Transport painted their planes the same wild colours as the collapsed Court Line which took me to Tunisia for £29 in 1972. It wasn't an island-hopping pleasurama – it was a pursuit of anyone with Cuban connections.

At each island embassy there was the same impasse. They must telex Havana, and await a reponse. Either the response never came or, more likely, the telex triggered the file labelled 'Visa Already Refused'.

In GUYANA the family I stayed with loaded me down with leather goods as barter for the foreign exchange they desperately needed. They directed me to a Dutchman who lived in a hut in the jungles of FRENCH GUIANA, who'd allegedly made a trip to Cuba. I found his hut, but he wasn't in.

It was a great surprise when Rabi Maharaj came walking down the aisle of the Pan Am 707 during a transit stop in the DOMINICAN REPUBLIC. He'd boarded in Santo Domingo, not knowing I was en route from Puerto Rico to HAITI.

In Port-au-Prince we both stayed in a desperately poor neighbourhood at Ernst Cassy's Good Shepherd Orphanage, where Ernst, a local bachelor, cared for eighty deprived children. We went to church together on the Sunday morning, and were invited for refreshments at the church hall after the service. Scarcely were the plates of food put on the tables, when a throng descended on them as one. Everything edible was gone in seconds. My heart went out to these poorest of the poor. Worse by far were those in the grip of voodoo practices. Lying in bed at night you frequently heard the wailing and frenzied screaming.

In JAMAICA at last I got the break I needed. Michael Manly's socialist revolution had brought to power a government favourable to Castro. The first ever Kingston-Havana commercial flight was scheduled for the week before Christmas. I booked a ticket on this inaugural service.

The Cuban Ambassador in Kingston was all smiles when I dropped round for the small matter of the visa. Maybe things were more relaxed with the new flight. I held my breath. On the second visit the smiles had gone; he was now aware of the prior refusal. No visa, but I looked on the bright side: my ticket wasn't revoked. So I proceeded to the airport for the 6 p.m. departure. Check-in was effortless; then, boarding pass in hand I cleared customs, and waited at the gate. The only other passengers seemed to be six Cuban diplomats. A seven-hour delay was announced. Finally, well after midnight, when the entire airport had shut down otherwise, the ancient Belfast-built Bristol Britannia 312 turbo prop, staple of 1950s Atlantic crossings, lumbered in.

I tried to suppress my excitement and relief as I handed over my boarding pass and stepped anxiously towards the plane. Had I really slipped through the net? Out of the corner of my eye I spied a black Mercedes speeding towards the plane across the tarmac.

It stopped when it reached me. The Cuban Ambassador jumped out, collected my boarding pass, handed it back to me, ordered my two suitcases already on the aircraft offloaded and the plane door shut.

The Britannia and the diplomats took off for Havana. The Ambassador drove back to Kingston. I slept on a bench at the airport for the rest of the night, as technically I'd left the country. The Jamaican immigration officers had all gone home, and there was no one to stamp me back in.

Early next morning, I heard my name being called over the airport loudspeaker system, I was peremptorily summoned to a meeting in the airport administration office, a shabby place with paint peeling from the walls. I shivered slightly as I entered, from the temperature change as the sun came up.

The ambassador was there, the Cubana airline manager, and three or four Jamaican officials, whose role I couldn't quite figure out. They were drinking tea, but didn't offer me any. They were all ranged on one side of a table across from my lone seat, facing me like an inquisition.

The Cubana representative spoke first, offering to endorse my ticket over to another airline of my choice, since I wasn't able to fly on his. The ambassador backed him up, expressing regret that I couldn't visit Cuba. The Jamaicans remained silent.

I felt like asking why have an airline if nobody could use it except its own diplomats; why have embassies whose only function was to turn down requests for visas? But I knew it would be futile to do so. For I was dealing with organs of a government run by a party specialising in political double-speak.

'Democracy' to them meant rule by one man, 'freedom' meant Cubans could have an assigned job, but not visit their relatives overseas, and 'normalised relations' with other countries meant visas were compulsory, only issued to carefully screened individuals who were known in advance to be in agreement with the party line, and definitely not for the likes of me.

Instead of a point-scoring declaration, what came out of my mouth was a mildly exasperated plaintive appeal. 'But I'm not going to Cuba. I'm simply flying through Cuba on my way to Mexico.'

Perhaps I was relying too much on the success of this ruse I'd employed in Vietnam and Cambodia. This time it didn't look as if it would work. My adversaries pointed out three potent facts: first, there were other flights to Mexico that avoided Cuba, so I couldn't claim it was a necessary transit; second, the timing of the Cubana flight required a night stop for which there were no facilities at Havana Airport. Third, and potentially most damning, to allow transit without a visa, my onward Cubana flight must be confirmed before I embarked for Cuba. He motioned to my ticket lying on the desk in front of him: 'It says "Open" for the Havana-Mexico City sector'.

It was useless to retort that if bookings on the Kingston flight were any indication, I didn't think I'd have trouble getting a seat, or that instead of putting obstacles in my way, he could have easily obtained for me such a confirmation from his head office.

Instead, I reaffirmed my choice of carrier and route, and asked how the Mexico City flight could be confirmed. 'Not from this office here, only direct from Havana,' came the catch-22 answer, and the meeting abruptly broke up; they perceiving they were dealing with a lunatic, I pondering what to do during the week I'd have to wait in Jamaica for the next Cubana flight, and wondering whether an identical scenario would present itself then, too. It was 20th December; their second-ever flight would be on the 26th – Boxing Day!

My schedule for the intervening week soon became clear. Rabi Maharaj had been among a small crowd of well-wishers seeing me off the night before. I phoned him from the airport and told him I hadn't made it to Cuba. My news fell on deaf ears – he was clearly preoccupied by something else which excited him greatly. 'Wait at the airport,' he commanded, 'we'll pick you up shortly.'

The 'we' turned out to include Menzie Oban, a Jamaican returnee from London, a quiet giant of a man. Not that he was of above-average stature; just that somehow underneath his calm and very ordinary external demeanour surged the charismatic heart of a visionary. In the UK he'd been to all intents and purposes just another black West Indian, leading a nondescript life. Back to no particular welcome in his homeland, he'd taken on the cause of the underdog with a vengeance. No prisoner serving a sentence, no drug addict, no lady of the night was safe from his reforming zeal. He'd help them, give them money, food packages, medical assistance. If they'd no place to call their own, he'd give them shelter in his own house. All he lacked to carry out his grandiose vision was larger quarters.

Until yesterday! While the Cuban ambassador was speeding

towards me in his Mercedes, Menzie received a phone call from the English owners of a resort near Montego Bay. They were selling up, leaving to return to England, had heard of Menzie's plan to acquire land to rehabilitate drug addicts and ex-cons, and had decided to *give* him their land, complete with buildings, completely free. Actually the nominal rent was set at $1 per year!

Menzie, bursting with excitement, was on his way to inspect his new property. Rabi and I went along for the ride. I'd nowhere to go for the next week, anyway! In lulls between conversation Menzie would break into spontaneous negro spirituals, often improvising lines as he went along.

Rabi and I were dozing off to the accompaniment of a spirited rendition of how 'It will be worth it all, When we see Jesus, Life's trials will seem so small, When we see Him,' one of the songs that kept cotton-picking slaves' hopes firmly fixed on the much brighter future that awaited them in the hereafter.

Suddenly we both snapped back to consciousness. Menzie was banging the steering wheel with both fists, while continuing to drive. 'Nonsense, rubbish, tripe,' he yelled. He clearly was excited about something. Did he feel uniquely the injustice of the past, the system of slavery, colonialism, the sentiments of the song? Then why had he been singing with such abandon? Had he had a reverse conversion experience in a few seconds?

'Nonsense,' he repeated now that we were fully awake, and he had our undivided attention. 'It's worth it all *now*! *Now*! We don't have to wait for the future.' And in that moment of epiphany, in a bumpy jeep on the road to Montego Bay, I encountered a true believer, whose hope was no pie-in-the sky, but a daily experience that was the source of both his power, and his settled joy.

After we returned to Kingston, Menzie introduced me around his church friends. They could all sing like him. To them my Cuba trip became a David and Goliath struggle. Goliath had everything going for him, but we all knew who won in the end. The only slingshot I had to hurl pebbles at the giant, was a telex direct to Havana requesting a confirmed seat to Mexico City on 27th December. I sent it, and waited.

Two days before Christmas Menzie insisted I accompany him to a Full Gospel Businessmen's Fellowship breakfast at the Hilton Hotel. I'd not come across this group before, I listened spellbound as managing directors told of 'laying hands' on broken factory machinery, praying for it to restart; salesmen spoke of receiving promises from Bible verses, and watching their performance rise; union leaders shared stories of industrial disputes being settled by prayer and conciliation instead of conflict.

My bacon was already cold. I hadn't touched it. 'Someone else here today needs a miracle,' the MC called out. 'Amen,' said Menzie, nudging me forward to the rostrum to make an impromptu speech. I explained my desire to visit Cuba, for no other reason than that I knew people there had needs, and couldn't come to visit us. I reminded the audience that Cuban believers were just as much part of the community of faith as us. Couldn't we use our freedom just to visit them, and say we thought of them?

US-led sanctions must be hurting them. I had no sinister motives, no political agenda. By now, after months of trying, multiple visa rejections, and last week's rebuff at the steps of the plane, I was more than ever determined just to go there, and see for myself.

The audience was highly receptive. Several people offered various of their possessions to add to mine as donations. The organisers of the breakfast formed a circle around me. After a hush one of them announced: 'This young man will go to Cuba, and an angel will accompany him.'

The breakfast broke up and I walked through the lobby with Menzie. On an impulse I went to the reception desk to check for the umpteenth time if my telex had been answered. It had! With trembling fingers I unfolded the paper and read the magic 'OK' letters beside the CU flight number and 'HAV/MEX 27 DEC'. Clearly the angel had been on the job!

The second ever Cubana flight to take off from Jamaica since Castro's 1959 revolution differed from the inaugural in that there were eight passengers on board, and this time I was allowed on. No scenes, no screaming Mercedes, no obstacles in the way. The in-flight catering even stretched to turkey and trimmings, making Fidel's Britannia one of my more exotic Christmas-dinner locations. As I ate, I mused about what might happen on landing. After all, I had a confirmed seat on the next evening's flight to Mexico City, but still didn't have the elusive visa.

One of the uncertainties about overnighting at a transit stop without a prearranged visa was whether you'd be allowed outside the arrival lounge at all. Each country and each airport had differing policies. And each immigration officer appeared to interpret these policies differently.

The Cuban official who processed the seven passengers ahead of me took one look at my passport and indicated, with a jerk of his hand, that I was to return to the combined arrival/departure lounge through which I'd just passed. Had I come this far only to fail? If I'd just been interested in ticking off new countries, this wouldn't have bothered me. I was in CUBA: I'd reached it, I was there. But I had a mission to accomplish, people to see, gifts to deliver on behalf of the generous Jamaicans.

Reluctantly I returned to the lounge. Oddly, the windows which ran the entire length of one side formed the exterior of the airport building, so that families awaiting arriving passengers could line up and press their noses against the glass to catch sight of loved ones. Amongst the now-dwindling crowd I saw two figures, a middle-aged man and his daughter, pointing in my direction. I looked around to see if they were gesturing at someone behind me. No. I was the object of their attention.

I looked more closely, and gasped. It was Herberto, the man I'd encountered in Sweden, who'd invited me to visit. How on earth could he have known I would be arriving tonight, especially since I'd planned on coming six weeks ago, then counted on it last week? But there they were. We couldn't hear what each other said through the glass, so there was a continual pantomiming on both sides, interrupted by repeated trips on my part back to the immigration officer to see if he'd changed his mind, perhaps.

After some hours of this, it grew pitch black outside, my would-be greeters and welcomers gave up and went home, and I settled down to spend the night, somewhat disconsolate. Where were the angels when you needed them? I thought. Then a voice inside me said: 'Ask! Seek! Knock!'

'But I did,' I retorted lamely. 'Keep on knocking till the door is open,' the voice replied. It was now well after midnight. I took my courage and my suitcases in both hands and headed for the immigration control one more time.

The previous officer had been replaced by another. I reached the counter with my heart in my mouth, pushed my passport over to him with the ticket and telex showing my onward flight, and said the one word that (give or take a vowel or two) was recognised in most travel languages: 'Transito'.

He scowled slightly, wrinkled his brow, leant back and stifled a yawn. Then he reached for his inkpad and plopped the rubber stamp squarely in the middle of page fourteen. This time the direction of the hand jerk was outbound from the lounge. A surge of relief and exhilaration washed over me. I felt like the little engine which turned 'I think I can, I think I can,' into 'I know I can,' as it crested the hill of difficulty. From that moment I've had less difficulty believing in good angels.

The problems to be solved now were minor: small details such as transport, a hotel, money changing, and finding my way around during the hours of darkness. I only had the office address, not the home address, of my friend. Getting into a restricted country took so much effort, I almost never gave thought to the difficulties of getting around, taking them as they came.

A taxi driver helped me find a room in a crumbling colonial edifice, benefiting from the enhanced exchange rate that can be levied when banks and all other forms of competition are closed. 'No pounds. Dollars,' he said. But he only accepted Canadian dollars. This was the only place so far in all my travels that the US greenback was unwelcome.

It would be nice to record that next day I saw something of the alligator-shaped island declared by Christopher Columbus to be 'the most beautiful land I have ever seen'. Especially after all the trouble of getting there.

But not for me the haunts of Hemingway, tours to the opulence of the former DuPont mansion, the Spanish basilicas, colonnades, plazas, or palaces, or indulgence at the Tropicana nightclub; no visits to cigar-rolling workshops or rum factories, no side trips to the cobbled streets of Trinidad, not even a chance to relax on the twelve miles of white sand beaches at Varadero.

Instead I struggled with local buses in Havana to find my friend's office. It was clear to me from even minimal observation that sanctions were indeed biting deeply. On each side of the street open spaces between houses seemed to be improvised builders' yards or scrap metal dealerships, as individuals cobbled together every part that might be forced into service for future needed repairs.

The lorries looked as if they had gone missing from their army convoys. Each bus I took was of the squat appearance that betrayed its age. The cars on the roads were mainly ancient Chevys. The whole appearance could have been Harry Lime's post-World War II Vienna, if it hadn't been for the gentle tropical breezes from the waterfront.

I got a double shock when I caught up with my friend, Herberto, for in his office was the other man I'd come to see, and given up on, because he lived so far out of town. Perhaps that's why I'd been delayed till now, so that I could catch up with both of them.

They greeted me effusively but with an element still of disbelief, like one who finally encounters an oasis after so many mirages. They wanted to take me out to lunch immediately, but practicalities stood in the way.

First a visit to the Cubana office to have a confirmed sticker put on my ticket, and check the flight time. With only one or two flights every week, you couldn't be too careful. Then the Public Security Bureau to double-check that no exit visa was needed. 'Do you have your permit to enter Mexico?' they asked gruffly. I argued with them that I would get it automatically on arrival. 'No,' they said firmly. 'From any other country, yes. From Cuba you have to have a special endorsement from the Mexican Embassy, or they won't let you land.'

Now the race was on for the stamp that garnered $10 revenue for the Mexican government, and prevented me from shuttling endlessly between two countries which could have denied me admission. The clerk at the Mexican Embassy was firm – it took two days to issue. He relented in time for a late lunch when all the other diners had gone home (or maybe the restaurant was permanently empty?).

Herberto and his colleague rejoined me over *moros y chrisanos* – black beans, spices, and local rice. They appeared a trifle nervous, guided the conversation to safe subjects, and looked over their shoulders frequently. When they wanted to say something important, they whispered confidentially. Communication wasn't eased by the lack of the English-speaking daughter who'd come to the airport, since my Spanish, even with the Peron government's aid, hadn't become fully fluent. Herberto explained that they got my postcard (sent seven weeks previously) just last week, and had come on the off-chance they might see me, a fortuitous example of parallel convergence of postal/political and flights/visa delays.

As I parted from the two men, trapped in a system not of their choosing, I gestured to them to retain both my suitcases and the flight bag. They knew of families who needed these things more than I did, and I was able to leave and buy replacement items. I stuffed two shirts, a change of underwear, and toilet items into the brown leather shoulder bag I'd acquired in Guyana, taking Cliff's song literally: 'Travelling Light'.

Only one obstacle now stood in my way before departure. I had the ticket, telex and fresh confirmed-booking sticker. I had the Mexican 'Coming from Cuba' permit. My passport was in order. The plane was on time. But I wasn't prepared for the parting shot from the ticket counter at check-in.

The agent looked thoughtfully, first at my ticket, then my passport, then me. 'You'll need to go out to the customs shed,' he said. 'But I'm not exporting anything. I didn't buy anything at all while I was here,' I replied truthfully. 'That's not the point,' he snapped. 'They must check to see that you're bringing out exactly what you brought in to our country. That you didn't leave anything here.'

I froze to the spot. But, under his steely eye, there was nothing for it but to begin the long trek around the check-in desks and out through a wide door to the tarmac, passing the back of the check-in area, where a row of windows ran behind check-in, one for each desk.

How would I explain the missing baggage without getting my friends into trouble? And what about me, when they discovered the discrepancy? They'd marked in my passport the number of pieces in my accompanying baggage on arrival; they were also listed in a box on my airline ticket.

Before I had time to think of a response to the inevitable question, the window next to the desk I'd checked in at was pushed open from inside. A girl's face appeared: she hailed me. I was halfway to customs. 'You've already been checked. No need to do it again,' she said. I jumped, so startled was I, then made my way back inside. When I got there only the agent who originally checked me in was visible. 'Go through to departure lounge now,' he shouted at me.

There was no sign of the girl who turned me back. Maybe she was the angel. Could I count on such protection through Central America and China, I mused as I settled into the Cubana IL18 that bore me aloft to more adventures?

# 16

## Emergency Trouser Repair

### Central America (1974)

With a mere shoulder bag now to accompany me around the world for four more months, bussing through seven Central American countries – MEXICO, GUATEMALA, EL SALVADOR, NICARAGUA, COSTA RICA, HONDURAS and BELIZE – could be accomplished without the complications of luggage.

Allowing two weeks for this jaunt, that would put me back in Mexico City still early enough in 1975 for the South Pacific flight to get me to Australia with plenty of January left, even allowing for brief island stops and a day or two in New Zealand.

This was a critical calculation, because my funds would run out when I reached Australia, as would my one-way ticket. At that point I'd be exactly halfway around the world from my starting point – about as far as you could get from London on a scheduled itinerary.

But it was, after all, the 'lucky country', where you didn't need a visa and casual work was plentiful. I'd get a job there for a couple of months, and save enough to pay for my return passage to London, either by the most direct and cheapest way if the survival option had to be put in place, or, as I fervently hoped, with my long-awaited visits to China and North Vietnam included. I left no margin for error. In late April I would join the BBC staff, and have a regular salary. Money worries would recede after that, I told myself, but there would likely be an acute shortage of that other precious currency time, so I should use what I now had of it to the full.

Thus fortified by what turned out for the most part to be spurious arguments, I spent eleven days on and off local buses, express buses, comfortable buses, bone-jarring buses, day buses, night buses, domestic buses, international buses.

All went relatively well, apart from a bad fever in Belize, and a game of cards which took up the two rows on each side of me and went on interminably through a night in Guatemala when I tried to sleep. But I most remember my narrow escape on New Year's Eve in San Salvador City.

It was immediately clear from the way both the driver and the first six rows of passengers spilt out like a smoothly but suddenly peeled banana, that this bus was not going any further than El Salvador's capital today. Worse: all buses tomorrow were cancelled. So I had to figure out a place to stay until 2nd January. And that wasn't my only problem! Standing up to stretch at the last stop from my cramped seat, I'd put a large rip at a very obvious place in my pants – currently my only pair, since I'd left all my belongings in Cuba.

As if reading my thoughts a fellow passenger across the aisle leaned over with a smile: 'Come and stay in my house, and celebrate New Year with us.' His house was close to the bus station. As we entered, the first thing I spied was his mother-in-law busy at her sewing machine. 'You can have a shower while I sew up your pants,' she indicated. It seemed too good to be true.

The party started about 10 p.m. and was in full swing as midnight approached. Eduardo, my benefactor, had taken to kissing each pretty woman who happened to pass his front door. Every house seemed to have its own party spilling out onto the street, and there was constant to-ing and fro-ing. A sort of Latin version of Scottish 'first-footing', I told myself.

Unfortunately one boyfriend attached to Eduardo's target for a kiss did not take too kindly to this familiarity with his girlfriend. His left arm was wrapped around the woman Eduardo had been attempting to disentangle him from. In his right hand, he held an almost empty yellow whisky bottle. With one smash it was broken and jaggedy – and shaped into a terrifying weapon. With a second resounding smack, it made contact with my benefactor-host's head, and left it bloody and nasty.

Family honour called for a reply, so Eduardo's brother leapt out of the house and repeated the bottle trick on the offender. This time it was a green bottle. More spurts of red.

In a flash the maligned-boyfriend-turned-attacker-turned-victim called in a frenzy to his friend across the street, who rushed headlong into a vicious attack on Eduardo's brother. The party was now heading towards a full-scale fight, no holds barred.

For me on the sidelines, this could all have been purely academic, a reflection on that fabled Latin temperament, perhaps, or more generally, on man's inhumanity to man.

But with one of those twists of fate, those tiny but otherwise seemingly innocuous words or actions, which in a moment turn spectators of others' misfortunes into protagonists or defendants fighting for their survival (real or metaphorical), I distinctly heard in Spanish a growl which seemed to be aimed in my direction.

The growl translated roughly as: 'Get the gringo, he's with them.' I've always tended in such circumstances to believe that discretion truly is the better part of valour. I bolted.

About two hours later, after a backstreets tour with no guide other than the aim of placing distance between myself and broken bottles, I crawled back to the neighbourhood where the mayhem had erupted. Things had quietened down somewhat, so I gingerly approached the house from the rear. In the kitchen Eduardo, his brother and two friends were bandaging each other up, laughing.

'Happy New Year,' they chorused. 'It's a shame you didn't stick around. The party really got going about one o'clock!'

I returned to Mexico on schedule: buses can be a pleasant change from air travel. Dirt cheap; local flavour by the bucketful. And my trousers were now repaired, ready for the assault on the South Pacific.

A colourful group of Indians swarmed around the bus station in Acapulco. No use starting the search here for hideouts of the rich and famous. The number 32 to the favellas obviously took a different route. One of their number stared at me as I passed. Suddenly transfixed by a strange jogging of the memory bank, I remembered the trip to the edge of the jungle at the northern tip of South America, while waiting for the Cuban visa, and the remarkable story I tumbled on.

# 17

# Head Hunters

*Surinam (1974)*

He looked oddly out of place, the small dark man with tribal markings, emerging from the Cessna, surrounded by burly Dutch and lanky Americans. It was an airstrip on the outskirts of Paramaribo, capital of SURINAM, or what had been Dutch Guiana, one of the three colonial Guyanas,

Tsubo was fresh from the deep jungle, headed for Iowa to help put his tribe's language into written form for the first time. It was his first flight. Initially silent, taking in his surroundings, he muttered something which made his companions laugh. 'He said "We used to eat people like you",' they reported to me as I drew close.

Slowly that afternoon by the tarmac the story was told, how the vastly different world of the forbidding jungle with its cannibalistic tribes totally cut off from life outside, and the enterprising altruistic Americans intersected.

If I'd read the story third-hand, the overpowering emotion I felt on encountering it face-to-face might have been lost through the filter of the writer. All too often such stories reach us in the form of Rousseau's noble savage having his benign existence interfered with by rapacious outside interests, their mercenary intent for ever spoiling some imagined praiseworthy innocence of nature.

But the outside forces in this story were a quiet Midwesterner, Ivan Schoen, and his family. I'd met them the previous day. His daughter, now a bright teenager, was a toddler when Ivan read in the newspaper about four white missionaries being killed by Auca Indians in Ecuador.

Somehow this news item touched a raw nerve. He didn't know whether to feel revulsion, pity, sadness or puzzlement, but it goaded him into action. He decided to dedicate his life to reaching out to another group of Indians in the northeast of the South American continent, the Wayana.

'Maybe they'll need medical help,' he thought. But he was a carpenter, not a doctor; so he commenced a gruelling course of study – tropical medicine and linguistics. Then he took a course in survival skills and basic help to primitive peoples, sold his house, loaded up his few worldly possessions, his wife and toddler, and headed for the jungle.

The Wayana had only seen one white man before, a freelance consultant for the petroleum industry, doing some scouting. They killed him.

Tsubo said: 'We thought about killing Mr Schoen, too, the moment we saw him. He didn't know we were watching him. But we waited. After we made contact we found he was a good man: he helped us, taught us to read, cured our diseases, delivered us from the fear of evil spirits. We are glad he came.'

Over the years since that first contact a fruitful partnership had developed. Ivan's daughter Becky grew up in the jungle, learned to use bow and arrow, hunt, and skin meat, while her peers in the US wore party dresses and went to proms. Yet it would be hard to find anyone more well-adjusted.

Tsubo positively beamed when he talked of the changes in his people's lifestyle since the Schoens moved into their village.

'Before, we used to do very destructive things,' he said; 'we killed and boiled our enemies. Now instead of going on raids against neighbouring tribes, we all get together once a year for a friendly conference.

'Now I have the chance to help Americans learn our language and write it down. Then we will be able to educate some of our people. Since we forsook killing and collecting heads, we sleep better at night, and are at peace.'

Tsubo left for Iowa. The Schoens returned to their home in Tsubo's village. Becky's Dutch girlfriend trained as a nurse and decided to stay in Surinam and use her skills there.

The human spirit, I reflected, which at times can stoop so low, can certainly soar sometimes too!

My spirit was soaring as I had now been privileged to cover pretty much all of North, Central and South America, and a good chunk of the Caribbean. I'd been allowed into Cuba, and was now on my way to another cherished dream, Australia: necessary refuelling point, in resource terms, before China could even be thought of.

I was in for a nasty shock!

# 18

## Godzone

*New Zealand (1975)*

Even after a peripatetic existence covering pretty much the whole earth, I would still vouch for NZ ('En-Zed') – or 'God's Own Country', as the locals put it, often shortened to 'Godzone' – a near-perfect paradise in which to be stranded.

And stranded I was. The delights of brief exotic stopovers in TAHITI, FIJI, and THE COOK ISLANDS on the way down could do nothing to dispel the force of the announcement that Australia was changing its visa policy. The previous free-for-all available to Britons was gone. In its place everyone now had to apply for a visa. Requirements: a return ticket; money to support yourself while there; no work to be undertaken for gain. I flopped all three.

As I stepped off the DC8 in Auckland I knew that NEW ZEALAND, now the last legal stop on my ticket, was my only hope. I needed cash, now, to pay for any future expenses, never mind getting back to the UK to start my job at the Beeb. Further travel adventures were fast receding in the light of economic realities.

I needed a job, and I needed it quick. But I didn't know a soul. And I'd made no prior arrangements, thinking Auckland would only be a transit stop en route to Australia. Wait, I did have one contact I'd forgotten about. My Japanese host John Landon's wife's friend had a cousin who taught at a girls' school. I fished out the piece of paper and phoned her number.

She was gone for the main summer holiday (things being slightly upside down in that part of the world), but her daughter answered the phone. 'I just received a letter from Tina Landon about you,' she enthused. Well at least I wasn't calling completely cold!

What followed was a tribute to the legendary hospitality and friendliness of New Zealanders. My remote contact couldn't invite me to stay in her home with any propriety while her mother was gone, but she immediately took me on as a project.

'I'll come and pick you up at the airport in an hour,' she said over the phone, 'and we can have lunch, then I'll show you around.'

In short order we ended up at a friend's house, who had a friend who knew the youth pastor at a Baptist church, where a businessman in that particular suburb (Mount Eden) rented out a block of flats to volunteers at the church. I was driven to meet Roydon and Graeme, and they agreed I could move in with them while looking for work.

I'd always found the Church worldwide to be far and away the best source of accommodation – all the way from monasteries to YMCAs and Salvation Armies. As a network it was superb. In the three happy months I spent in New Zealand I tried to give as much back as I could, by volunteering every time I could.

Finding work didn't prove easy. My first break came when I accompanied Mike from the flat opposite to the docks where casual labour was hired by the day. My first and last day as a stevedore: I don't think I was very good at it.

I tried various employment agencies without success. Eventually I landed just the right job . . . at the Post Office. They were sceptical at first, and wouldn't let me deliver or sort the mail, because they said Maori names would stump me. But in those glorious pre-deregulation days when the Post Office ran the telephone monopoly as well (before PTT was reduced to PT), there was a vacancy in Telephone Billings for a clerk.

Actually it was a sort of disembodied function. I wasn't on the first floor taking incoming orders from customers for new service or changes, or on the second floor passing these to the engineers, or the fourth, sending out the actual bills to customers. I was assigned to the third floor, whose function consisted of taking in bits of paper from the engineers describing what they'd done, and marking them with the prices to send to the fourth floor so that *they* could send them out to the customers.

The Post Office was said to have lost £2 million that year. I wonder what Tom Peters or John Harvey-Jones would have made of their administrative structure.

Looking back on those idyllic three months, I'm very grateful for the employment that earned the funds for my next big journey, for friendly natives, an almost-British clone in the South Seas with a distinctly better climate, and the best lamb and dairy products in the world. It's hard to believe there wasn't even any inflation, and hardly any unemployment. Britain's EC bombshell and the end of this cosy, protected lifestyle hadn't yet struck.

For a time life settled into a very pleasant pattern. When I wasn't at work in the Post Office I was speaking to various school, church and civic groups, or at camps and conferences telling them how my 'angel' got me into Cuba, and announcing China as my next destination. This sometimes drew gasps of disbelief. More often it struck a responsive chord with the audience: why shouldn't an ordinary person dream of making contact with people even in forbidden lands? Even if he didn't have money, or backing from an organisation.

Now that I was heading towards solvency again, AUSTRALIA granted me admission for three days. There are those who say that three months in New Zealand and three days in Australia are the wrong way round, and there are those who say that three days are too long!

But Australia was now only to be the first stop on the way to China – if I could save enough money, and organise the logistics. There was no Chinese Embassy to approach nearer than Hong Kong. At that time there was definitely no tourism. Only a handful of airlines from outside the communist world flew there: Pakistan International from Karachi and Air France from Paris, being two of the original carriers, which somehow maintained service with almost empty planes right through the cultural revolution.

They only had once-weekly schedules and, based on initial enquiries I'd made in London, it was a dickens of a job trying to book a seat. You essentially had to prove you'd received a firm invitation from an official Chinese government body. Without such confirmation, you couldn't start the paperwork trail. And, of course, without an official sponsoring body, there would be no one to book accommodation in China for you, translate, secure a car, arrange meals, and otherwise take care of you in a strait-jacket society which didn't exactly put out the welcome mat for foreigners, and, in fact, was neither used to them, nor accustomed to providing for them.

Travel to China tended to be limited to screened business-men, especially at Canton Trade Fair time (even they had to endure readings from *The Thoughts of Chairman Mao* at the beginning of each negotiating session); politicians and diplomats (the Kissinger-Nixon ice-breaking missions were in their infancy); occasional goodwill sports groups (ping-pong especially); and a motley collection of 'friendship' or 'solidarity' associations of demonstrable Marxist leanings. That was all.

An individual who was not disposed to promote communism, from a Western country, with any connection with a free, unbiased press, or – even worse – religion, and not part of any group which the Chinese wished to woo, was most unlikely to have a chance to visit China officially. Yes, come to think of it, the omens didn't look particularly bright. I consoled myself with the thought that if I were American, Israeli, Taiwanese, or South African, I would have no chance at all.

Once again, as with Cuba, the key was going to be getting closer geographically. The only two recent entrants among airlines providing service were Ethiopian Airlines from Addis to Peking via Bombay, and Iran Air non-stop from Teheran.

The 1973 inauguration of the Ethiopian flights had given rise to the absurd sight of Haile Selassie's entourage joining in toasts with their Chinese hosts to anti-imperialism, liberation and revolution, after which the imperial delegation returned by limousine and the first-class section of their red, yellow and green 707 to fight against revolution in their own country, and put down any uprising which dethroned them from power. I suppose everybody's in favour of revolution, just not the particular one that topples them.

Anyway, Addis, or even Bombay, was a bit out of my way to increase my chances. Iran Air, at first glance, seemed to be as bad; but wait a minute, the Peking flight continued to Tokyo and, unusually, they had rights to pick up passengers in Japan for China. That was a potential way in. But the way out was critical. Without a visa (I'd try in Hong Kong, Manila and other likely places, but would have to assume failure) I'd have to have a plausible onward routing, timed precisely to pass muster as a legitimate connection, but leaving enough time for a worthwhile stay in China, exiting to a country I actually wanted to go to.

I got out the atlas and decided to work backwards. My next main goal was North Vietnam. Other stops were secondary. If I left Peking bound for Karachi, Bombay, or Teheran, I'd be way off course for getting back to Hanoi – too far west to do it on a through ticket. If I tried to fly to Tokyo from Peking I'd have the same problem in reverse – getting to India, Pakistan or Ethiopia to enter China, since if I tried to both go and come from Japan it would never be accepted as a transit.

Only one solution finally offered itself: fly to Hong Kong and Manila from Australia to obtain as much additional information as I could about China visa possibilities; proceed to Tokyo; fly on Iran Air into Peking; continue two days later on the weekly CAAC flight from Peking to Hanoi, spend five hours in Hanoi before flying on the same day to Vientianne, thence via Iran to Europe, picking up missing bits of the jigsaw of countries en route.

This was not an ideal itinerary: at least two, maybe three, consecutive stops without a visa, two nights to explain in China (where would I stay – the lounge? Was there one?), flights on airlines which weren't easy to book, and always, the danger that if one element failed, any alternative solution would destroy the rest of the itinerary.

But it was a workable one. Now, how to achieve it on one ticket? Because perforce in those student-traveller days I always had double goals: one, get to all the places I wanted; two, do it as consecutive stops (at little or no extra charge) on one journey which you'd have to make anyway.

Many times I asked myself: Why am I so determined to get to China? In a way it had become a matter of pride; in other ways sheer stickability. I'd set out to do it, and I would do it. I felt everything leading up to this had come about for a purpose. I'd been given the time off before starting work. I'd been blessed with the hospitality of generous friends in New Zealand. If I turned back now, could I live with myself? Besides, an irregular itinerary was to be expected, in going off the standard routes. I turned the question back on its head; 'Give me five good reasons why I should NOT go to China?'

Now I came up against reality. This was New Zealand. Sheep grazed at the end of the runway at Auckland Airport. It was a backwater in intercontinental aviation terms. Apart from British Airways direct to London and Pan Am to the US there really wasn't much choice other than Qantas or Air New Zealand. How was I to organise the necessary tickets, even if I had worked out the best theory on paper?

Fate came to my rescue in the shape of Anne Boone, an attractive dark-haired beauty – the sort you fall in love with at first sight. But love wasn't on my agenda; nor on hers. Mutual friends, Warren and Glen Brookbanks told me: 'She's just waiting for Mr Right.'

I wasn't Mr Right. In fact, I clearly didn't fit the bill for any of the gregarious, fun-loving and immensely practical Kiwi girls. They might have momentarily envied the apparent ease with which I conquered faraway places, but their potential husband-material had to be much more adept than I ever would be at building houses, sailing yachts, fixing plumbing and other entries in the self-sufficiency stakes. Also they all knew I was bent on returning to Blighty, and they were too attached to their South Seas paradise to think of any drastic move away.

Anne turned up at one of my meetings where, after I'd lectured on my travels to date, I confided that I had a burning desire to visit China. She stayed to chat with me, and we became friendly, agreeing to meet for coffee a few days later. 'I work in Queen Street,' she said, 'right at the bottom.'

When I went to pick her up, I realised it was the British Airways office. She introduced me to her manager. 'I'll need a ticket to London soon,' I told him. 'No problem,' he answered. 'We fly three times a week. It takes about twenty-eight hours.'

Over coffee I picked Anne's brains. I started gently. 'You remember my talk, mentioning China, and so on. And how I went from Jamaica to Mexico via Cuba on a KLM ticket? Well, a direct twenty-eight-hour trip to London was not exactly what I had in mind, as you probably guessed.

'I've looked over the route maps quite thoroughly, and I figure that by paying the full twenty-five percent excess mileage over the normal economy fare I could go: Auckland – Sydney – Port Moresby – Manila – Taipei – Hong Kong – Seoul – Tokyo – Peking – Nanning – Hanoi – Vientianne – Bangkok – Rangoon – Calcutta – Kathmandu – Delhi – Kabul – Teheran – Baghdad – Riyadh – Benghazi – Tripoli – Tunis – Nice – Paris – London. About twenty-eight days.'

Her eyes widened slightly, but she kept her cool, the way all professional airline employees do in front of customers. She was still wearing her uniform, after all, and this was a public place.

'Do you have visas for all these places?'

'Not for all.'

'Any?'

First faint trace of a smile. I shook my head. 'You take care of the ticket, and I'll take care of the visas. Or rather God will, as He seems to have done before.'

'But British Airways doesn't even fly on any of these routes – not until you get to the very last leg of Paris to London. That's only 200 miles out of 14,000 in total.'

'That's why I'll need your help with writing the ticket. Will you do it for me?' She smiled again. 'I'll try. But no promises.'

I was glad I didn't also tell her I still didn't have the money to pay for it. I knew she'd have enough trouble making all the reservations, working out the mileages, and persuading her boss to issue a twenty-five coupon ticket on which only the smallest sector, both in miles and in yield to BA, was on his airline.

But she did beaver away at it for the next week, calling to say it was ready the day before I was due to depart. (A year later I received a postcard from her. She'd met her Mr Right, married and moved onto his sheep farm.)

Now I could concentrate on the real problems – passport and money. I say passport not visas, because there wasn't much I could do about visas till I got to Asia. I had to do something about my one and only passport, which was presently languishing in Wellington, 300 miles away. How it got there is a complicated story. It had been newly issued in South Africa in August 1972, when my old one expired. Travellers, beware when your travel documents run out overseas!

The procedure seemed innocuous at the time! I walked into the British Embassy in Pretoria, filled in the forms, and returned some days later to pick up my new one. When you're on the road constantly – especially now on my almost-a-year-around-the-globe – necessity forces on you passport and visa formalities on the run which might have been easier at base. But this time it would have dire consequences, as I soon found out.

Unfortunately it was this Pretoria-issued passport which had been stolen in the Gulf of Bothnia just six months previously. And the British Embassy in Helsinki had unkindly only issued the replacement one with a six-month validity instead of ten years.

So my next-door neighbour back home, who went to the Costa del Sol every other year, had thirty-two virgin pages and nine years to run on his before he forked out another £40. I'd been through forty-three countries (at about £1 per country cost in passport terms), and now had to go through the pain of renewal.

It was the same gripe all frequent travellers share. Fill up with stamps too quickly, and you have to renew and pay again long before the validity expires. The British solution was to issue a thick ninety-six page 'book', too fat to fit comfortably in a pocket. The Americans allow you to glue in a sheaf of new pages, creating a concertina effect each time you open them up.

The real pain, when you only have one passport, is being without such an essential document for as long as some bureaucrat decides it will take to send it back. Getting round this problem to avoid such pain is an essential step for all frequent travellers, but I hadn't learned this vital lesson yet. In my naïvety I thought two weeks would be enough after posting my old one down to Wellington, to anticipate the arrival of a shiny new one. Wrong!

'I can do it in ten minutes,' averred the pompous voice of the consular officer (was he Second, Third, or even Fourth Secretary? I wondered) on our eleventh or twelfth phone conversation. 'But I have to get clearance from the place of issue of both your temporary passport' (he stressed the word 'temporary' as if it had been a pending question these last five and a half months whether my citizenship might be revoked) 'and the one it replaced.'

'So what's the problem? Helsinki?'

'No, not Helsinki.'

'Pretoria, then?'

'Not exactly Pretoria. Cape Town.'

Cape Town? What had Cape Town to do with it? That's when I found out that, without the slightest thought of any inconvenience to the taxpayers in whose name they functioned, every year at this time the entire South African government migrated from Pretoria to the luscious Cape Coast, and with them the sycophantic diplomatic community.

And during the two weeks when the 'U-haul' removal lorries full of diplomatic bags, red attache cases and boxes marked 'Top Secret' were on the road, you were well advised not to die, request expatriation, contract marriage with an alien, go on a journey overseas, or otherwise require the services of any branch of officialdom.

For what seemed like the millionth time, I explained my predicament to Her Majesty's representative. I *had* to be on tomorrow's plane to Sydney. The following day's was full. The day after that was the only flight to Moresby, which connected to Manila, and so on down the line to the precious Iran Air booking to Peking. If I had to rearrange any segment now, the whole delicately-constructed journey that I'd spent months putting together, would collapse like a house of cards.

He was unfazed. Indeed rather the opposite. He held out no hope. 'If I haven't received a message from Cape Town by now, the likelihood of it coming before you take off in the morning is nil. And I hope it doesn't come tonight, because I'm on call and I'm the one who'll be wakened up. I suggest you postpone your trip.'

I put the phone down in a determined mood. I wouldn't postpone the trip. Anyway, a farewell party had been organised tonight, and Anne would be bringing the ticket round, and expecting payment. Oh yes, money: the other problem. I still didn't have quite enough. Almost, not quite, even after applying all but subsistence from my earnings to the journey. Well, let's hope against hope the clearance comes in tonight, removing one obstacle. The money would sort itself out.

The money did sort itself out first, and in an odd, and totally unexpected, way. Two people slipped envelopes to me during the party. There had been many other envelopes, containing cards from well-wishers for the most part, so I didn't pay particular attention until I opened them.

One was from Hillsborough Baptist Church, where I'd spoken one recent Sunday evening. As usual my topic had been how an unknown individual could have a dream of travelling to help people on the other side of the world – even in 'closed' countries, and see it realised, even against all odds. I'd been placed on the same bill as Loren Cunningham, founder of Youth with a Mission (YWAM), who held the congregation enthralled as he described his dream of waves breaking on a beach, which turned into groups of young people heading overseas. I'd assumed he received an honorarium, but I was glad to be an example of just one of those people. But the church, which had already done so much for me, now enclosed a speaker's fee. The other envelope contained a gift from a camp-conference where I'd been a guest, and the campers had taken a collection specifically towards my travel expenses in getting to China. Now I knew I'd have to get there!

Most amazing of all was a third gift, which I hadn't seen at first. I'd stepped outside to say goodbye to the last person to leave, and as I turned to go back in through the door, an envelope on the window-sill caught my eye. It had 'John' hastily scribbled on the outside, ten carefully folded NZ $10 notes inside, and no indication who it was from.

I was now solvent, and could leave . . . if my passport was renewed. At 2 a.m. the phone rang: it was the consul from Wellington, saying the message had, after all, arrived, and my passport would be ready for collection any time after nine in the morning. 'Collection? Can't you send it up to me? I'm in Auckland 300 miles north. I can't come down to collect!' 'It wouldn't reach you in time. Besides, forwarding costs are your responsibility.' He rang off abruptly.

Surely I couldn't have come so close only to fail at the last post? There were options, but none that would defeat the combined forces of a consulate bureaucracy which wouldn't co-operate with speedy delivery (by, for example, taking the passport to Wellington Airport) and the acute shortage of time.

And then it came to me. Before I left Britain I'd been given one contact name. He worked in an Auckland radio station. When I phoned the station, they told me he'd moved to Wellington. I'd filed away this information, since I'd no prospects of visiting Wellington. Now I pulled open my notebook and leafed through to find the number they'd given. A 7 a.m. call reached this benefactor, who, for a perfect stranger, was delighted to run round to the British High Commission, pick up my passport, and drive it out to the airport.

An hour and twenty minutes later the NZ National Airways Corp. F27 pulled alongside my waiting DC10. I was on my way to China. But I still had no idea if they'd let me in.

# 19

# Postcard from Peking

*China (1975)*

Three days in Sydney, and then stops at all the 'NEW's (BRITAIN, IRELAND, GUINEA), I fetched up in the PHILIPPINES. Whereas I expected all serious China watchers to be in Hong Kong, there was a surprisingly large colony of them in Manila, too. I lost no time contacting those to whom I had some introduction.

They had tried different fronts: research, business, journalism, magazine publishing, but what they all had in common was that none of them had actually been to China, even once. Most were American and spoke passionately of the time when the door to Red China would open, when they presumably were going to burst through like a battering ram. Meantime, they gleaned what they could from outside the door!

My assertion that I was going to travel to Peking, at least briefly, was received with a lot of scepticism. The unspoken, but clear, message they gave me was: 'If we've been here this long and not been able to find a way in, how can you do it? You don't even have any of the resources or contacts we can call upon.'

The most receptive was a diminutive Chinese man who invited me for supper to his modest house and showed me slides of his cousin in Shanghai. When I even tentatively brought up the possibility of visiting his cousin to pass on his greetings or anything tangible he wanted to send, he stopped in his tracks, stiffened, and said: 'Oh no, that wouldn't do. It would cause big trouble for him.'

By contrast the American China watchers were full of bravado. 'It's coming. Our time is coming,' they would say; 'the Chinese can't keep us out for ever.' And behind this front line with their entrepreneurial zeal I could see the Hiltons, Sheratons, Coca-Colas and General Electrics waiting in the wings to pounce. 'If winter comes, can spring be far behind?'

I particularly liked one burly ex-Marine from San Clemente, California. For some reason he took to me, despite what he perceived as my naïvety about being allowed into the country. He would alternately chide and half-encourage me. He'd gesture expansively at the newspaper clippings he'd collected about China, roll his eyes, look me in the eye, then ask somewhat plaintively, 'Do you really think you'll make it?'

The Marine disapproved of my modest lodgings. 'Look at my car,' he pointed, 'it's the best. You may as well be comfortable.' So saying, he reached impulsively into his jacket, found a wad of US dollars, and stuffed them into my shirt pocket before I could protest. 'Use those to buy yourself a good hotel in Hong Kong,' he insisted. At this rate, I might even have some left over at the end of the trip.

At our last meeting before I left for SOUTH KOREA via TAIWAN, he returned to his favourite theme. 'You really think you'll be able to get off the plane and stay there?' he queried, warming over the subject he'd already aired a hundred times. I was puzzled how one insignificant individual like myself could occupy so much of his time and thoughts. Maybe he felt I had some secret strategy, the formula for which would answer all his needs if he could just pry it from me.

He didn't wait for a reply. 'Well, if you do make it, send me a postcard. A postcard from Peking.' This was his parting shot. He turned on his heel and left. David Aikman, *Time* correspondent in Hong Kong and my contact there, was away on assignment, so I flew on to Taipei, then Seoul, then Tokyo. I knew he was itching to get into China, and had hoped for some tips from him. He was the first person the Marine showed my postcard to, after my visit. That encouraged him it could be done.

I had the boarding pass for the Iran Air flight to Peking in my hand and was through to the departure lounge before the fact that I might actually be landing in CHINA in about four hours thwacked my brain. I hurried to the duty-free shop and bought a cheap camera. 'Shame not to have a record of it,' I told myself.

The flight on 'The world's fastest-growing airline' (which under the Ayatollah rapidly became 'The world's fastest-shrinking airline') was uneventful. It was evening, and there was nothing to see. What should only have been about two and a half hours' flying time point-to-point took twice as long due to the political exigencies of avoiding both Koreas. The airliner nosed off from Tokyo Bay, pointed south into the East China Sea, then crossed the Yellow Sea before making landfall near Qingdao.

As the Iranian pilot commenced a gradual descent, the two dozen passengers stirred from slumber. Since most were stretched out across three seats, scarcely any heads were visible over the seat tops, giving the impression of an empty jet.

I couldn't sleep. I was much too excited. The four hours felt like an eternity. I'd been turned back so many times from Cuba I couldn't help wondering if this would be the same – maybe I'd get in eventually, but would this first time see me hustled straight through to Teheran after only forty-five minutes' ground time on Chinese soil? That would cause me to miss a dozen other planned countries and I'd miss North Vietnam, but that wasn't so bad as failing to get into China, after all the preparation, and now that I was on the brink – almost there. Almost, but not quite yet.

If the flight had seemed long, I thought the taxiing would never stop. I craned my neck for any distinctive view. I could only see the huge Douglas firs that looked like giants in the night. Their branches lightly blowing in the wind this way and that took on the appearance of maniacal arms conducting some sort of macabre symphony. The whole effect indeed was of being in a forest clearing, so small was the old Capital Airport.

At last the whine of the engines stopped. The left front door of the 707 opened. Two green-uniformed guards, rifles at the ready, pounced on the first row, darted to the second, and continued methodically back through the plane, stopping everywhere there was a passenger, prodding their shoulder with the rifle saying something I couldn't catch. I was in row seventeen – officially 17A, but I sprawled over B and C as well.

No one moved after being prodded. I strained to pick up what the guards were saying. Suddenly they were at my seat. 'Teheran? Beijing?' the first said, as I felt the edge of the rifle touch my right shoulder. For a split second I thought: 'You can say Teheran, lie down and go to sleep again.' But it was too late. I heard my own lips mouthing 'Beijing', as if listening to another person.

The guard tapped twice on my shoulder, called to his colleague and gestured for me to follow them up to the front. I picked up my shoulder bag and started up the aisle. There was no one sitting behind me. The other twenty-odd Teheran-bound passengers in front looked up curiously at me as I passed them, almost as passers-by instinctively watch when a criminal is apprehended and marched off under police supervision. I was the only passenger to get off.

The scary part began at the foot of the Boeing's steps. I stared across the square of tarmac – we were the only plane in sight, parked as far away as possible from the old-style terminal building, with its stone balcony protruding.

I began the escorted walk diagonally across the parking area, feeling the huge fir trees closing in on me from every side. They were dark and menacing, not the friendly green of daytime. The only other thing I could spot was the long elaborate placard – easily two planes' length – with big Chinese characters proclaiming some strident message. Was it the 'Death to Imperialism' or 'Down with America' that Nixon's aircraft manoeuvred around to avoid having them in the picture? Whatever the message was I didn't expect it was comforting.

There was none of the hustle and bustle you expect from a major international airport: no endless large-pane windows; no scurrying here and there of trucks and vehicles of various sizes; no loud-speaker announcements; no purposeless milling of hordes in transit. Just me, my two guards, and a few lights on at the basement level which we were approaching. In the reflection, I caught a glimpse of the enormous portrait of Mao Tse-tung on the upper level.

The room I was brought into resembled an old customs shed – the counters were of tile, and very low. Customs, strangely, came first. My shoulder bag was emptied and checked over by an officer who looked my age. 'He's grown up totally under Mao,' I thought. He asked if I had a suitcase. I said no, but he sent someone in search of it anyway, perhaps feeling I hadn't understood. We waited, and nothing more was said until it was established to his satisfaction that my suitcase wasn't involuntarily on its way to Iran.

He cleared me to go to the passport counter. As he did, I heard the distinctive sound of the Boeing 707's four Pratt and Whitney powerplants start up. 'It certainly doesn't wait around,' I thought, followed by: 'My doom is now fairly well sealed,' followed in turn by: 'They can't put me back on that plane, at least.'

Passport control again was a single twenty-something male. He had a mixture of not-quite moustache, and not-quite shaven cheeks. 'Visa?' he queried, after flipping through my passport and not finding it.

'Hanoi,' I said. It came out 'Ha-noy'. No response. Slight agitation. He went off to confer. A girl who looked younger came and repeated the question. 'Ha-noy,' I said, mustering all the confidence I could, as if it was a routine matter to be marched off an Iran Air 707 at gunpoint in the middle of the night, expecting to be transferred to the next plane to North Vietnam.

At last the penny dropped. 'Ha-noo-eh,' they said to each other, after transcribing my ticket. The girl went off again, perhaps to check the schedule of the Hanoi flight. She returned, murmured to him, and he said: 'Wait here.'

After a time, another functionary appeared and said: 'Come with me.' The first officer gave him my passport, still devoid of any entry stamp. Maybe they were going to play this by the book – a pure transit – no marking in or out. Or was it something more sinister?

My new escort led me upstairs and through a series of corridors, arriving at length outside the airport restaurant, which was closed for the night. To the right ran another corridor with doors off each side. He unlocked one on the left, showed me in, and departed. It was a hotel room of sorts, Chinese style, two twin beds, with thick serge blankets, a heavily curtained window looking out on more fir trees, an end table with a colourfully-patterned flask filled with hot water. Spartan on the whole, but quite acceptable. I lay down, and within minutes was asleep.

In the morning I wandered down the corridor to the restaurant we'd passed the night before. The doors were open and sounds of noisy eating reached my ears. I walked in, plonked down at a table next to two pilots from Pyongyang, and ordered breakfast. That is I sat there, and in due course a bowl containing a soupy concoction was placed in front of me. There was no menu. The soup was followed much later by two overdone lukewarm fried eggs which had congealed into one flat spreadeagled piece; the hardened yellow yolk trapped for ever in a sea of glutin. Grainy coffee and a hard round bun came with the eggs. As far as I could see, I was the only customer so favoured. The North Koreans just had soup; they didn't speak to me.

I felt elated: I was in China. I was eating my first Chinese breakfast. My spirits grew even more when it appeared that I didn't have to pay – in a curious manner, access to the restaurant seemed to imply entitlement to a meal; a European face, entitlement to 'Western' breakfast, i.e. congealed eggs.

Daylight also laid to rest the demons of the night. The rustle and movement of the tree branches outside was much more friendly now. Though there still wasn't what you would call a crowd, a clutch of people moved around, an occasional turbo prop lumbered in, disgorged, boarded, and took off. A concession or two opened up.

Emboldened by daylight, egg and soup, in roughly that order, I put together plans for the day. Which sights would I take in first? Tiananmen Square? Temple of Heaven? Forbidden City? I doubted I'd get out as far as the Great Wall or Ming Tombs. I'd gleaned enough from the Manila China-watchers to know making contact with an individual citizen, especially one frowned on by the government, would not be as easy as in Romania, Russia, or Cuba, even though I had the beginnings of where to look; but I could greet people in the street, see who responded. I was awash in optimism.

The optimism didn't last long when each bus driver refused to take me into the city, and the few taxi drivers mysteriously melted away when I approached them. I gradually got the message that I was free to wander around the immediate vicinity of the airport grounds and buildings, but no further. My board and lodging were taken care of by the Chinese state airline, but their hospitality clearly didn't extend to tourist trips to monuments, or, worse still perhaps, in their eyes, unfettered roaming around in the capital city.

So, even before lunchtime on my first day, I learned the ground rules of my visit. I decided to put a lid on rueful thoughts, and enjoy what freedom I had. I struck up conversations with all who were polite enough to listen. I went out on the balcony and had a People's Liberation Army sergeant take a picture of me in front of the gigantic Chairman Mao hoarding, with my cheap camera. I traded goodies with the shopkeepers. Even the waitresses in the restaurant overcame their initial reserve, smiled, and occasionally managed a word or two of English, as I became a regular customer.

Aircraft arrivals were a big social event. Usually the loudspeaker burst over the cacophony of Chinese music that seemed to be all-prevalent (sometimes martial, sometimes operatic), to announce the provenance of this particular aircraft. The old-style arrivals board would click and turn over, and a scattering of green uniforms and blue suits would parade out to the balcony to gawk.

Except once. The arrival of the weekly Aeroflot IL62 from Moscow was preceded by a sudden cessation of the music. Some words came over the speaker – maybe a peremptory announce-ment, maybe something totally unrelated. Then an all-pervading silence descended. A few Chinese shuffled around, heads down, eyes averted. A cemetery-like atmosphere began to spread. One floor below, the Russian captain and his co-pilot climbed the stairs, then walked along the narrow corridor leading to the airline offices.

They didn't stop to buy, chat, or linger at any point. As soon as they disappeared behind the door marked 'Aeroflot', the music started again. I don't suppose the Peking run was one of the more popular assignments for Aeroflot pilots. If this was how the Chinese viewed the Russians, how would I be received in North Vietnam arriving from China? It wouldn't be long before I found out.

First, though, I had to send a postcard to the Marine . . . from Peking!

# 20

## Cheap Day Return – Hanoi

*North Vietnam (1975)*

The day of my flight to Hanoi dawned bright and crisp. With eager anticipation I watched the ancient IL18 – so much more like a bulky East European war machine than a lumbering civilian turbo prop – being towed into the same position as the Iran Air Boeing from which I'd disembarked only two nights previously. In the daylight, it didn't seem so far away.

I was anxious to move on, filled with a sense of awe. That I was flying from a country forbidden even to many powerful people who longed to enter it, to a country at war, even to the other side, 'behind enemy lines', as it were. I knew I'd only have four or five hours in Hanoi, but hoped that there I might be able to go into the city and have a look around. If all went well, later that same night I'd be in Vientianne, the Laotian capital I'd failed to get to from northern Laos in 1970.

Surprisingly, nobody bothered to look at my passport. Obviously they regarded the first leg, to Nanning, as a domestic flight. It felt exhilarating to be flying over the Chinese countryside, on my way to a second Chinese city, one that was far more remote to a Westerner.

Even though the IL18 was now well past its 'sell by' date, I'd always felt it was somehow appropriate to make stately, lumbering progress over a swathe of land behind the 'iron' or 'bamboo' curtain in one of these machines, in the livery of Aeroflot, Interflug, or, in this case, CAAC – the Civil Aviation Administration of China. The colour scheme was old, but by the time it would have been due for repainting, the scrapyard would have beckoned, so throughout their working lives all IL18s had a very '50s post-war look.

Shanxi, Henan, Hubei, Hunan and Guangxi provinces spread out below. From my comfortable seat in the fourth row, I scanned the countryside through the big round window. First casualties of the move to jets all over the world were comfortable seats and big round windows. The flight was long. It covered a huge expanse of Chinese territory, well over a thousand miles.

Catering on board was non-existent. This was reflected in the flight timing: depart after breakfast, arrive in time for a late lunch on the ground; better than anything that could be rustled up in an Ilyushin galley, presumably, was the official thinking. Indeed it took years of fielding foreigners' complaints before CAAC abandoned its policy of dispensing in-flight trinkets such as chewing gum and key-rings, in favour of snacks and meals.

At last we came in to land at Nanning. Thirty or so domestic Chinese passengers disembarked, leaving seven of us as 'through' international passengers, entitled to lunch. For all the difficulty of getting into China, it seemed you didn't ever have to spend a penny on food, once you were there!

Lunch was served in a small side dining room at the airport. It was a two-hour affair. It seemed civilised to dispense with the necessary formalities (passport checking/customs etc.) until after we'd eaten. In fact for all the foreboding with which I'd prepared myself before the venture, and all the horror stories that inevitably were the currency of news emanating from 'closed' countries, I found all the Chinese with whom I'd had to deal impeccably honest, scrupulously correct, and punctiliously polite.

It was a gracious custom: a nod of invitation from the doorway, you eased out of your seat where you'd been relaxing after the last course, and walked the few paces to the booth where your passport was stamped, then you reboarded. This must have been how transpacific travel was in the flying boat days. The other six passengers slipped effortlessly through the formalities. It was my turn.

'Visa?' queried the passport man in his blue Mao suit. Unfortunately there was no mark in my passport to help him. I produced my ticket for him to scrutinise, but it only enlightened him in as far as showing that I was due to fly from Hanoi to Vientianne later that day. The coupon to Hanoi had already been lifted in Peking, in exchange for the boarding pass I held in my hand.

A sensation that all was not well crept over me. I tried to explain that I was in transit. It didn't go down quite as readily as in Peking, in this provincial spot, off a flight between two domestic cities, three days after arriving from Tokyo, despite the fact that this was the first legitimate published connection for anybody flying from Tokyo to Hanoi (it would have been quicker and maybe more politically correct but taken six times as many flying hours, to go via Moscow; and of course this route would have been impossible without a visa – never mind missing seeing China, which was the whole point).

The passport man went off to consult his superiors. He hadn't expected this exception to his run-of-the-mill duties. Once a week six or seven people exited China here on their way to North Vietnam; later the same day the entry of another six or seven en route to Peking was processed. That was their only international flight. He obviously had no guidance for a Westerner without the correct notation in his passport.

I had been foolish, figuring that having come so far, there would be no further hiccups. I'd focused ahead, jumping the next hurdle in my mind, that of Hanoi. In theory any official could have denied me embarkation since I didn't have a North Vietnamese visa. My arguments against such restraint were twofold – one, that I had a confirmed flight out a few hours later, which fully met the 'Transit Without a Visa' (TWOV) rules of IATA, the International Air Transport Association; two, the pragmatic thing to do surely was to let me leave the country. What did they plan to do with me otherwise?

In all this reasoning I missed the fact that the Chinese official didn't care a fig about Vietnamese regulations. After all, there'd been intermittent skirmishing between the two countries, soon to blow up into full-scale war. This flight, the only scheduled cross-border link between the two countries, would soon be suspended.

What the Chinese official cared about were his own country's rules. These said that all passengers leaving China by air must have an exit visa. I didn't have an entry visa, for that matter. Ah, there was the rub: he couldn't give me an exit visa until I had a proper entry visa.

Next thing I knew I was being hastily bundled into a car, with the passport man, two of his superiors, another airport official, and two public security officers with guns. I was in the middle in the back, between the two guns. They weren't exactly sticking in my ribs, but it did add a certain edge to the proceedings.

We drove for forty miles, in the direction of the city, through some of the worst slums I'd seen anywhere, then piled out in front of a nondescript building. Inside I was instructed to hand over my passport and wait. If I was being arrested, I figured, they'd have turned out my pockets as well.

Twenty minutes later all was plain. This was the bureau for dealing with foreigners. They'd retrospectively issued me with an entry visa. Now the passport man could take it to the airport and cancel it with an exit visa. How scrutable!

The drive back was more relaxed, less menacing. Everyone felt relieved. A problem had been solved: but when I reached for my cheap camera to take a picture through the car window of the passing urban scenery, four pairs of hands descended on me abruptly enough to force a change of mind.

Back at the airport the exit stamp was duly placed. Then the committee of six who'd shared the ride into town with me surrounded me saying: 'Pay the money,' and came up with an astronomical sum in yuan for visa issuance and transport, presumably. I couldn't say with precise honesty that I didn't have enough to pay, but if I'd given them what they asked, I'd certainly only have pennies to last me all the way to London. 'I can't pay that much,' I said; 'besides, I didn't expect to have to pay,' adding for good measure: 'I'm a student.'

They consulted with each other for a lengthy period. Finally one of the passport man's superiors stepped forward and declared, in a speech-making voice: 'It is a gift from the Chinese people,' and handed me the receipt they'd laboriously filled out in pen. I bowed, thanked them, and filed out to the aircraft hastily before any minds were changed.

The other six passengers were relieved to hear that the plane could now depart, some three hours late. Perhaps they should have checked the passports before lunch, after all. Our flight route followed the river down to Pingziang, where the border was crossed. I'd now been through so many dramas of one sort or another that I was numb to the fact that we'd entered airspace over NORTH VIETNAM.

We flew over Lang Son to port and Thai Nguyen to starboard – at least I assume that's what they were, since they were the only two towns of any size on my map – then circled to land at Hanoi. I couldn't see much of the capital city that had successfully been thumbing its nose at a superpower. It was still daylight, but not for much longer. As we touched down I snapped photos of MiG fighters lined up beside the runway.

I was certainly more conspicuous here, with a war going on, even than in China. The lieutenant handling arrivals simply asked me if my embassy was expecting me. I told him I was due to catch the plane to Laos. 'Gone half an hour ago,' he said. Inevitably he went to see his commanding officer in an inner office. 'Bad news,' he said on his return. 'He says you can't stay. Sorry.' Then he leaned down towards me and whispered confidentially: 'We know what's going on in the world. We listen to the BBC. Don't be disappointed. Come back when the war's over.' (Three weeks later I had a mental picture of him 'liberating' Saigon.)

I had no fight left in me. I meekly acceded. There was only one way I could leave the country: by the same plane I had entered. To China. Once more I boarded the CAAC Ilyushin. Once more I encountered the passport man at Nanning, who by now had run out of ideas as to what category I could fit into. There was no meal this time. Once more I disembarked at Peking's old Capital Airport very late at night, entering China without a visa for the second time in less than a week.

This time the reception was harsher. A higher ranking officer met me as I stepped off the IL18. I couldn't see his uniform, as he was bundled up in an overcoat against the cold. He harangued me for several minutes in Chinese. I knew I was expected to say something in reply. I needed my guardian angel whose help was evident in Cuba. All I could think of to say was: 'Sir, I'm sorry for whatever it is that's bothering you. I'll answer all questions in the morning. Right now I'm dead tired from this long trip. Could I sleep first?'

He gave an abrupt order, turned on his heel and marched off. I was put into a room not unlike the one I had before, but this time the door was locked, and they kept the key. I was told to expect my interrogators next morning.

Sharp at nine they knocked on the door. It's a good thing I was too tired to spend the night quaking with fear, and slept instead, for the door opened to reveal, not a fearsome clone of the colonel or whoever had shouted at me on the tarmac the night before, but an eighteen-year-old boy and nineteen-year-old girl, with passable English.

They were clearly excited at the prospect of a real foreigner with whom they could practise their English. Soon we were drinking tea and chatting together, sharing experiences. The menace was gone from the interrogation. After an hour they took me back down to the basement where I'd first arrived, my baggage had been searched, and the Hanoi flight times checked. This was clearly also a CAAC behind-the-scenes operational area.

The boy and girl took my international ticket, and puzzled over all the stops that could not now be made. Basically they read through all the cities until they came to one that had a flight from Peking – Teheran. In three days' time. When they handed back my ticket it was minus all the coupons in between, and with a new booking for the Iran Air flight affixed exactly one week after I'd arrived – sort of completing the circle.

So I flew to Teheran, where I marched into the Pan Am office and got a refund for the missed sectors. My route from there was Riyadh, SAUDI ARABIA and Benghazi, Libya, but I was diverted to Tripoli. The last stretch of my journey was to be performed by a chocolate-coloured Libyan Arab Airlines Boeing 727, with a complicated arrow pattern on the tail. I hoped it wasn't one of the jets due to be scrapped because of the American embargo on spare parts.

I boarded from the front walk-up steps, through the first-class cabin, and had just ducked under the curtain separating tourist class, when I felt a firm hand placed on my right shoulder. 'Come,' said the uniformed Libyan. He had severely cropped hair, and a razor-thin moustache.

'What now?' I fretted. I couldn't immediately think of any transgression of the laws of the People's Jamhariyah, or anywhere else for that matter, that I was guilty of. I instinctively obeyed. The obliging steward was only offering me a seat in first class, gratis. Grateful, I stretched out, and ruminated on the past nine months.

My travel horizons had certainly broadened. I'd had the good fortune to enter three countries that most people couldn't get to. I'd had adventures galore. But I definitely wanted to go back to China and see more next time. And spend longer in Cuba. Perhaps North Vietnam would be more open once the war was over. And of course there was a raft of new countries I hadn't been to, despite clocking up so many miles.

But would my wings be clipped now that I was committed full time at the BBC? No long summer vacations were in prospect here!

# 21

## Where Eagles Dare

### *Albania (1975)*

I was back from my near-year-long jaunt around the world in time to start my new job at the BBC in mid-April 1975. Since perforce I planned to be around in London a while, first item on the agenda was finding a place to live. A more prudent and better-organised individual might have taken care of this ahead of time, or at least planned to arrive back in the UK with sufficient time in hand. I simply turned up. I had no choice. Travel on the scale I'd undertaken required every ounce of organisation you had. There was none to spare for the domestic issues which consumed ninety-nine percent of a normal existence.

Neil Kern, an old pal from Lincoln, who was in the throes of deciding between a career as an opera singer in Milan or a game warden in the Transvaal, arranged for my first few days to be spent at his parents' in Woodford Green. From there I phoned old contacts, to let them know I was around. 'We thought you were at the other end of the earth,' was the most common reaction. 'So you haven't received my postcard from North Vietnam yet?' I would parry.

George Hider phoned back on the second day from his office at Tower Hill to say he had a friend whom I should go to see that evening – Keith Wynne. 'He might be able to help you.' I followed the directions. 'Two minutes from Victoria Station. Left, left, left again.' After negotiating the scissors-like Grosvenor Gardens, I found I'd crossed some invisible but very real barrier between the central London of the landmarks identifiable to all tourists, and the fashionable 'town' residential addresses of the well-heeled. It was still SW1, but it was Belgravia, part of the huge swathe of prime capital real estate that made the Duke of Westminster Britain's richest man.

I did a quick mental comparison with the flats of friends I'd stayed in around Earls Court and Wimbledon. In front of me were houses, not flats, each one worth a million pounds freehold, except that you couldn't buy the freehold, just lease for various periods between recyclings to Grosvenor Estates. How could Keith help me find a place to stay that I could afford? Would all the places he recommended be as swish as this? I pressed the doorbell somewhat apprehensively.

It turned out Keith had been a lodger with George's family when he first came to London from Cheshire, and now that he was established in a well-paying job (the house was thrown in as a perk) he felt it was time to repay the debt. So I was offered the third floor to myself. 'How much?' I asked. 'I can't charge you rent,' Keith said, 'Ruth will work out how much it costs to keep you, for food etc.' Food too! This was too good to be true. I moved in the next day.

My bedroom overlooked the house of actress Hayley Mills, next door. We only met her when six-year-old Tim Wynne slept outside in the garden by choice one night, then, wakening and finding himself in strange surroundings at 2 a.m., bawled the neighbourhood down. For the most part Julie Andrews, Ted Heath, Lord Boothby, Lady Lucan and the other neighbours kept to themselves . . . although I swear I saw Lord Lucan late one night after his famous disappearance!

From my new pad I could actually walk to Broadcasting House, past Buckingham Palace, through Green Park, up Bond Street. The first three months were occupied largely by training (script writing, news fundamentals, radio production skills, television directing, on-air interviewing), before being turned loose on a variety of broadcasting tasks throughout Britain and Ireland.

Although I put in long hours, the work was fun. It was hard on days off to break the newly formed habit of scanning at least eight newspapers by breakfast time. My travel horizons temporarily contracted. But I was able to take advantage of short breaks, or job-related visits to Europe.

I visited two unique 'countries', whose comfortable living depended on casinos: the tiny principality of MONACO on the Côte d'Azur, and even smaller CAMPIONE, an Italian enclave totally within Switzerland.

CATALONIA allowed the BALEARICS (Ibiza, Menorca and Mallorca) to be covered in a day, out by Iberia, back on Aviaco; and ANDORRA, the secretive Pyrenean tax-free principality, which made a good living by manufacturing poor quality cigarettes which nobody smoked. Tobacco companies bought and dumped them in exchange for the right to participate in Andorra's lucrative duty-free sales to non-residents. It was only two and a half hours' drive up twisty mountain passes from Barcelona.

Another 'country' also straddling France and Spain was EUSKALDUNAK ('people on the same side'). It's better known as the territory of the Basques, who though they have enjoyed home rule since 1980, have yet to achieve full political autonomy. 'Pelota', the world's fastest ball game, played with a goatskin ball thrown hard against a wall, originated here, and recently made it into the Olympics.

Arguably the best-known Basque was Ignatius of Loyola, the nobleman who gave away his fortune and founded the Jesuits.

His personal prayer was:

> Teach us, good Lord, to serve you as you deserve;
> To give and not to count the cost;
> To fight and not to heed the wounds;
> To toil and not to seek for rest;
> To labour and not to ask for any reward;
> Save that of knowing that we do your will.

If one thing stands out in all my years of travelling, it's the selfless people I've met whose lives have exemplified that prayer. Loyola ended up in prison for his pains. 'If the Master has suffered, shall not also the disciple?' But if anyone had told me that my next trip would bring me face to face with a grotesque suppression of all that was good in an entire country – a sort of Dark Ages revisited on Europe – I would have been incredulous.

It started harmlessly enough: an invitation to John Landon's house in Ealing to meet a few friends and reminisce over Japan experiences. I knew John and Tina had something more in store for me, though, the moment I walked through the door. The main topic of the evening was not Japan but a tiny country that was about as different from any other as you could imagine.

Isolated politically since it had a public rift with the Soviet Union and China, its only two allies in the world, it was harshly ruled by a dictatorship that had already run for thirty years, and quashed all forms of dissent. After withdrawing from the Warsaw Pact, it was in a permanent state of almost-war with both its immediate neighbours. There had been a shooting incident with a British vessel in the Mediterranean, in consequence of which the country's gold was held ransom in the coffers of the Bank of England. And the deposed monarch, who went by the delightful name of King Zog, held court in exile in the Ritz Hotel.

The country was Albania, sandwiched between Yugoslavia and Greece. It was the only country in mainland Europe I hadn't been to. This fact alone made it a worthy candidate for a visit. Its intimidating nature, seeming inaccessability, and total lack of diplomatic relations with Britain, merely added to the challenge.

Kevin, a mild-mannered accountant who had worked for BOAC, introduced himself to me: 'I'll be your partner in crime on this one,' he laughed. He brushed off my objections. 'I'm just back from Andorra, no time off now for three more months, and we don't know how to get there. Even if we did, they probably wouldn't let us in. Besides which, winter's the worst time!' 'Aw, come on,' he insisted, 'there's always Christmas!'

Next morning I was on duty in the main BBC newsroom at Broadcasting House. I had the unglamorous but responsible ('Somebody has to do it!') task of copy 'tasting'. This involved processing the huge amounts of teletype pouring in from correspondents, Reuters and other news agencies, selecting which stories to alert senior editors to, and 'spiking' the rest by literally impaling the thermal paper on a six-inch steel spike.

There was danger in miscalculating in either direction. If you passed through stuff later deemed inconsequential you were in trouble. But if something important was found buried on your spike . . . woe betide! Suddenly I did a double-take. There among the cricket scores in the West Indies, a bus crash in Pakistan, and the fifteenth prime minister in as many months in Lebanon, was an item from Tanjung, the Yugoslav press agency, about the execution of a priest in Albania.

Father Stefan Kurti's crime was that he had baptised a baby in the concentration camp he and all other religious officials had been consigned to when Albania declared itself the 'first atheist state in the world' in 1967. At that time they had destroyed or converted to other uses all 2,169 mosques and churches, with the implausible official explanation that after a popular uprising and 'much fiery discussion' the Albanians mobbed all religious representatives saying: 'Give us the keys to your churches.' Kurti was described as a 'brigand, a spy and a robber, in the pay of Rome, Britain and the USA'.

During my lunch break I perused the BBC clippings library to see what else was known about this freakish country. A slim file divulged: two and a half million inhabitants; most backward European country; and details about the megalomaniac ruler, Enver Hoxha. Nothing about how to get there, although one article said there was a flight from an East European capital every other day, and another indicated individual tourism was not allowed. Think positively . . . that surely meant group tourism was in order!

I needed more to go on: a Westerner who'd been there, to verify if it was really as bizarre as it sounded. I drew a blank with my East European contacts, Lindsay Brown and his network, even the originators of printed material about the country. The attitude of everyone I spoke to for information was: 'If you manage to get there, tell us all you can when you get back.'

Then I remembered Rudi, the Swiss adventurer, who always wore a very secretive air and a pair of dark glasses. We'd often shared travel tales and I'd attended one of his lectures in a large auditorium in New Zealand when he caused a minor stir by looking round and saying conspiratorially: 'There's someone in this audience tonight who's recently been in Cuba.' He didn't identify me though, and proceeded with his lecture.

I tracked Rudi down. He was home for once. And, yes, he did know a woman who'd been to Albania. She'd given a New Testament as a gift to her hotel chambermaid, and as a result had been threatened with a firing squad, then deported. Clearly the Albanians meant business about religion.

As well as yielding a good radio interview for the BBC's *Sunday* programme, Rudi's friend Reona gave me the first clue how to go about travelling there myself. The nearest embassy was in Paris, but individual visas were not readily granted, as I suspected. However it was possible to gain entry as part of a small group organised by a friendly left-wing travel agency on the continent.

There were strict conditions. No Americans, of course. But no Russians, Greeks or Yugoslavs either. No journalists. Positively no pastors, priests or missionaries. Only one group visa on a tiny piece of paper was issued, and this was held by the group leader at all times. No wandering off from the group on your own was permitted at any time.

The phone numbers in Paris and Rome proved unreliable. I hated to give up. I was saved by a day's browsing in second-hand bookstores along Charing Cross Road. Tucked away in Collett's between Che Guevara biographies and panegyras to Fidel and Uncle Ho was a shiny red edition of the collected speeches of Enver Hoxha. Inside that volume was a leaflet advertising the British-Albanian Friendship Society, with an address in – of all places – the Isle of Wight.

Success! The man who answered the phone didn't sound Albanian. I didn't think they were numerous on the Isle of Wight. 'We do send five groups a year,' he ventured, 'ten per group. But there's a huge waiting list for next year. Most people prefer the two-week trips in summer, when the weather's good, and they get to tour extensively. That's why we can't fill the December one which stays put on the beach at Durres.'

'Next December?'

'No this December. Matter of fact, it covers Christmas. They don't celebrate it of course; just a normal day to them.'

I booked two places, the rarity value of the destination temporarily obscuring any misgivings about the nature of a Christmas beach holiday in the world's first atheist state, and flew to Ireland on 21st December for an early Christmas with my parents. I almost came a cropper when next morning's Belfast-London Trident was strikebound. It was not the first time I regretted such unavoidably tight connections. BA came to the rescue, ferrying me through Manchester, and with barely minutes to spare I was tucked into the back of a JAT 727 at Terminal 2 in Heathrow awaiting take-off for Belgrade via Zagreb.

Kevin looked as if he was being strangled by his camera gear. I was trying to figure out how to conceal my BBC-issue Uher tape-recorder from unwelcome attention. At least the heavy books

I'd agreed to carry to an Albanian contact in SERBIA would be dropped off in Belgrade. They took up virtually all my hand luggage. My clothes were checked through from Ireland.

Or so I thought. When my suitcase didn't appear in Belgrade, I was pretty miffed. JAT said it was not their fault. So I joined the eight other thrill-seekers at six next morning for the fifty-minute hop to Tirana, capital of ALBANIA, with a bulky Uher, two very bulky books (my contact hadn't turned up, so they had to be saved for the return trip), my research notes on Albania, a just purchased *Time* magazine, and not much else.

From the briefing literature handed out by our guide (who himself hadn't been to Albania) it looked as though everything I had would be confiscated. 'No spies, missionaries or journalists,' the visa regulations helpfully spelled out. What a great practical joke to hand over a passport which read: 'Profession – spy'. On second thoughts, perhaps not! What would they make of the Uher?

I read on: 'Bibles and other religious literature, *whether or not for personal use* are not allowed to be brought in. No pornography.' Then, almost as an afterthought, 'No former Albanian citizens or their children.' What with the ban on any nationality they happened not to like, that about covered it, I suppose.

The moment of truth arrived, as we filed off the aircraft past two armed guards. Rinas Airport was deserted apart from a few MiG fighters, the officials processing us, and the thirteen passengers (I hoped the other four weren't spies or missionaries for their sakes . . . and what was that about having to make up a group of ten? Even we were only nine).

My *Time* magazine was the first to go, but they accepted the Uher as a device for playing 'folk music', and overlooked the books. Kevin and three others were hastily summoned to a separate booth, then pulled through a doorway into another room. Half an hour later they emerged with smiles on their faces, cropped hair, and wearing a new pair of industrial-strength blue jeans, a sort of Albanian generic version of Levi 501s.

As we piled into the sardine-can minibus that, unknown to us, was going to be our virtual home for the next nine days, we could see the white-coated barber laying aside his scissors until the next plane . . . in three days' time. Apparently I'd missed the dress code section in the advance instructions. Kevin's fellow victims had the slightly stupid smile of people in the know. 'We wore flared trousers deliberately. You can't buy jeans like that in the West for one dollar.'

Slowly, with British reserve, the participants identified themselves and their occupations. One morsel at a time, as if not too much could be divulged at once. The two Albanian guides said nothing. Maybe the reason Americans were prohibited was that they feared they'd all have been wearing badges saying 'Hi. My name is Herb,' and pumping everyone's hand. The reluctance to speak made you expect that if pressed, they would admit: 'I'm in rocket science actually,' but once we were all more forthcoming, our stated identities seemed low key enough to satisfy even the Albanians.

If they'd administered a truth serum at the airport I suppose I'd have been forced to admit: 'I am a journalist. I work for radio and television. I'll be writing and broadcasting about this trip. I'll be making a fair but honest eye-witness assessment of your country. I have no political axe to grind, but I am concerned about human rights abuses. I don't believe you have eradicated all religious belief. I'd like to meet ordinary Albanians face to face, and hear their uncensored views. I'd like you to open your country up to tourism, so that others can have this opportunity we are privileged to enjoy.'

In the event I declared, truthfully enough: 'Purpose of journey: tourism', and let it go at that. For a moment I glanced round at my fellow-travellers and imagined a surreal party of missionaries, journalists, Americans, even a spy for good measure, cruising through Albania, upsetting the delicate balance in this workers' state just by being there. A pity the reality was a bland cross-section of the UK, no one to give offence. That is, assuming my Uher, Kevin's cameras and our joint questions didn't get us into trouble.

A wise traveller once told me to overcome the instinctive reaction when overcharged by a taxi driver and think of what you'd be willing to pay during rush hour in pelting rain, when late for an appointment. This was the frame of mind with which I approached the prospect of a week on a two-mile stretch of beach in uncertain weather, with soldiers with rifles stationed at both ends to make sure guests didn't stray too far, when of course what everyone in their right mind wanted to see was the capital, other towns, lots of people, and as much of Albanian life as possible. And enjoy Christmas! Even the beach at Durres was better than nothing, but I couldn't help hankering for more, now that I was there.

A high-up member of Hoxha's ruling party solved this for me very conveniently by dying the day our group flew in. It wasn't clear whether the government blamed even the proximity of foreigners for his decease. Come to think of it, that might have accounted for the taciturnity of the guides on arrival. But what was clear, was that with the funeral due to take place in Durres, and Hoxha delivering a fiery nationalistic speech, somebody thought it would be prudent to remove non-nationals from the scene.

In a centralised non-democracy, this is absurdly simple: you just announce the fact. So as we filed into the lobby of the Adriatik Hotel, billed as our base for just over a week, this was the first communication we received.

'You will get your luggage ready and put it outside your room before breakfast tomorrow. We will be leaving on a tour of Berat, Appollonia, Fier, Gjirokaster, Pogradec, Elbasan and Tirana. You will pay the cost in lek before we leave for the additional optional tours.' A brief protest about the compulsory nature of the optional tours was silenced. And I had expected to go shopping for clothes to tide me over for the next few days. All we saw of Durres was the obligatory Cultural Palace.

The two official guides were models of correctness. They had to be, I suppose, on pain of death. Their names sounded like some of the towns we were to visit, so as we couldn't quite get our tongues around them, we called them Alpha and Mrs T. Alpha was a roly-poly tousle-haired twenty-six-year-old commentator on Radio Tirana, the station that rivalled BBC, Voice of America and Radio Moscow in saturation shortwave coverage of the globe. Diminutive Mrs T., twice Alpha's age, and married with two children, was the less austere of the two; but she could erupt into a fiery temper if provoked, even by something trifling.

I had no choice but to wear the clothes I'd now travelled in for three days, as we set off on what was to be a comprehensive tour of the country. The crazy politics of isolation apart, it offered some delightful vistas. We saw Berat, described as a museum of a thousand windows; white cottages in the valley of Kruja, where women were hard at work washing their clothes by the river; the road sweeping down from the Krabba Pass to Pogradec, where we lunched in a hunting lodge by Lake Ohrid and looked across to Kosovo, the Yugoslav province populated mainly by Albanians.

I don't know if anyone had successfully swum across this border lake in search of freedom, but it certainly wasn't a good idea the other way round. Newspaper reports told of Yusef Balyrakis, a prisoner in Corfu during the Colonels' regime breaking out of his fortified camp, swimming the two miles across the strait, to land exhausted on an Albanian beach, and promptly being arrested for illegal entry.

Later I made a film about disputed territories in Pec and Pristina (Kosovo); Skopje (one of the four MACEDONIAS); and Ioannina (IPIROS). The Greeks laid claim to the southern region of Albania around Gjirokaster, which they called NORTH IPIROS.

Donkeys were plentiful on hillside defiles, carrying provisions to small villages off the main roads. Women in colourful head-dresses swept the pavements with straw brooms. In the small towns, horses and carts vied with bicycles and buses for right of way. It was all very Balkan.

Virtually 100 percent of the land was state owned. All the farms we saw were either collectives or, more usually, showpiece state enterprises like our first stop outside Durres. It specialised in tomatoes, and its 4,000 workers were paid a fixed wage if they fulfilled their 'norm'.

We saw a few individual craftsmen (cobblers, blacksmiths) at work on the road outside Fier; knitting combines, and the inevitable hydro-electric schemes, textile and steel mills dedicated to Mao Tse-tung. But what caught my attention were the young 'volunteer gangs' pressed into service everywhere to build roads, dig ditches, and lay railway tracks. All office workers were apparently required to do manual work one month out of the year, and school leavers a year's 'productive' work before being considered for further education. All the construction units mixed cement by hand.

I asked Alpha what people earned. 'A manual worker earns a wage that isn't much higher than the lowest in the land, nor much lower than the highest in the land.' Clearly Comrade Hoxha with his Mercedes and other indulgences was not included in this comparison! Rent was two per cent of salary; and medical care, such as it was, free.

Albanian workers were frequently told they were living in

paradise. I picked up a copy of the party daily *Zeri i Popullit* where the headline story was the ferocious rate of unemployment and high prices rampant in capitalist countries. Bread and vegetables seemed to be cheap, but a suit cost a month's wages and a television set four months'. I saw one shop in Elbasan besieged when a delivery of Chinese-made toy cars and novelties arrived.

We reached Tirana late on Christmas Eve, to be greeted by statues of Lenin and Stalin. Red stars in shop windows were the only concession to the holiday. In the Hotel Dajti we had big, spare rooms with parquet floors and heavy oak furniture, 1950s Chinese style. There were no signs that much upkeep had been carried out. On a tall shelf stood an ancient wireless with enormous knobs, the sort that wouldn't have heard of the Light Programme but was carefully calibrated with markings for Radio Hilversum and other European frequencies.

I turned the set on, and after a burst of static was surprised to pick up a carol service taking place in Austria. The choirmaster had just finished telling the story of how 'Stille Nacht, Heilige Nacht' had come to be written. When they started singing, the purity of the voices filled the room, and dispelled the cloud of barren statistics and lacklustre existence that Hoxha's Albania had served up in the name of progress. Well, at least they hadn't succeeded in shutting off the airwaves entirely. I wondered who else was listening in Albania on this, the night of the Saviour's birth.

It was unlikely I'd ever find out. Contact with local Albanians was strictly forbidden to our tour group. If I tried tonight, as I'd already attempted on many occasions, to go outside to the street, I'd be guided back to the hotel in minutes. I went down to the lobby, where the two guides were sitting, and asked them if they'd like to join Kevin and me for a cup of Turkish coffee.

To my surprise they agreed. There'd been some bad feeling earlier in the day when a group member had offered some sort of gratuity and was roundly denounced as offensive to the proud Albanian nation. But I suspect that was for show, since the incident took place in a very public area. This time they were relaxed. 'Tell us about Christmas in Britain and Ireland,' said Alpha. Kevin produced his *coup de grâce*, the Christmas cake he'd brought with him, and parcelled out four pieces. For good measure he inscribed Christmas cards to both guides, and presented them with a book. I told them the story of 'Silent Night' and the birth of the Christ child in Bethlehem, and how my family celebrated. They made no response, but were not hostile.

Boxing Day dawned, with more displays of the cult of Enver. Everywhere we went we saw him. His face was on government buildings, and outside blocks of flats. His name was spelt out in stones on mountainsides. His sayings were displayed on banners hung across rooftops. Every town had an Enver Hoxha Street.

We were back to the routine our minders had perfected for ensuring no unofficial contacts were made with the populace. The minibus with us nine, Alpha and Mrs T. would pull up outside a hotel for the midmorning break between sights. Two guards-cum-waiters would station themselves on each side of the bus, so we had no choice but to walk between the bus and them into the hotel. The barman would already be looking out at us from behind his counter. No other customers were in sight. Any locals had been ejected ten minutes before our expected arrival. We would drink our coffees at inflated prices (locals paid 4p a cup), and get back on the bus.

I only once managed to evade this policing, and then for fifteen minutes. Nothing more harmful than slipping into a local birari and joining a group at a table having Turkish coffee. Mrs T. fetched me back to the hotel. I wasn't the only one chafing under these restrictions. The two teachers from Edinburgh were always attempting to get corroboration of anything the guides said, and writing copious notes. The Sheffield man, I was sure, had slipped off once or twice unspotted. And Frank, the tall quiet one who said he was an expatriate . . . you could never take a picture without finding him at a vantage point further on, smack in the middle of your lens.

I was taking pictures both for the BBC and a picture agency in London. So when Kevin and I saw what we took to be a camouflaged airfield in the valley below, he wandered away on a pretence to the edge of the cliff to get a better shot. He was startled to hear somebody on a ledge below him . . . it was Frank! The same thing happened when we passed what our guides told us was a sanatorium, and we surmised to be a prison.

We were allowed back to Durres on 29th December. The paranoia about foreigners had temporarily died down. I suppose with fewer than 200 visitors from the entire Western world in a year – and us the only nine there at the time – a certain amount of watchfulness was to be expected. Early on the morning of the 30th when we were to leave, I walked along the beach a little way. The sun was coming up. I prayed that one day a new sun of openness would rise on Albania, and banish their darkness and isolation; that the God whom the government tried to suppress would be merciful to the longsuffering people.

Out at Rinas Airport there was no barber, no jeans seller, no plane in fact. It simply didn't bother turning up . . . probably too few passengers to make the journey worthwhile. Emergency negotiations were held. We would leave by the overland route next day, but what a panic! Our exit visas were for the 30th by *air*. Changing them to 31st by *land* took most of the rest of the day.

There was one silver lining in this cloud which enveloped our departure. We would now have to transit the northern town of Shkodra, where the atheist museum was located. Information about this museum was scarce in the West, and I longed to bring back a first-hand report of how far the Albanian government was going in its propaganda war against God. It seemed the protocol was to show the museum to delegations from the communist bloc, but not to general Western groups. Maybe now that our itinerary was again revised, we could prevail on the authorities to open it up to us, to fill in time on our last day which was otherwise unplanned. Even if we did succeed in obtaining permission, a further problem would arise if, as suspected, pictures and tape recordings were banned. But one thing at a time.

In the event we did get permission, but only at the last minute when we were virtually at the museum's door. And it was clear there was an embarrassment at the contents of the exhibits. We were made to give undertakings that the visit was at our request, and pictures were banned. Four guards were stationed in each room we entered, one per corner.

'Right,' said Kevin, 'you stage the diversion, and I'll whip out the camera and do a lightning shot before the guards come back.' It seemed easy enough to say yes at the time.

The exhibits were shockingly crude, even with advance knowledge. It was rather like an art gallery where all Holman Hunts and pre-Raphaelites were removed in favour of a solid diet of the highly dubious Robert Maplethorpe. The 'traitorous activity of counter-revolutionary clergy' was roundly condemned. Catholics were spies for Italy, Orthodox for Greece, Muslims for Turkey.

Any church worker was automatically identified with the vilified 'landlord class', subject only to contempt and bitter prejudice.

There was unfeigned smirking at the dereliction all church buildings had been allowed to fall into – those that weren't turned into factories or cinemas. The lovely Byzantine church near Appollonia, once visited by the apostle Paul, was crumbling. Inside, the bishop's chair and sacred paintings were left to rot. Its bell was silent. A crude model of a communion chalice with a microphone inside was meant to validate the claim that all priests were operatives for a foreign power.

Under pressure of the surroundings, Alpha became even more strident. 'We are vigilant against all foreign aggression. Spies have even entered our country in the guise of tourists, with religious literature. The Albanian people are always on their guard, and report this. Here are examples of what we have confiscated.' She pointed to Rudi's friend's New Testament, and booklets not unlike the ones Kevin had given her as a present. Kevin wasn't there to take her look full in the eye – he'd found a way to slip off undetected and snap a few pictures elsewhere while the going was good.

For me the most telling exhibits were recent articles from the controlled Albanian press – reports of speeches by anti-religious officials. 'Festivals are still kept. The fields are deserted at Easter. People wear crosses around their necks and have the sign of the cross tattooed in the palm of their hands. In the northwest a pilgrim march to the ruins of church buildings has been held. Our leaders have determined that all religion is harmful to the progress of the state, so they have forbidden it. Anybody who continues in any religion is an enemy of the state and a traitor. Traitors have to be shot. The stamping out of religion has not yet had the desired effect. According to the party secretary of Puka District, preachers of religion are still around. There are still men and women who confess the Christian faith and meet together late at night to pray. We shall find them and destroy them.'

Why all the stridency if the 'class struggle against religion' announced at the fifth party congress was really only a reflection of a purported reality on the ground – unmask religion and leave only a few old people with one foot in the grave still believing? In fact, despite the torrent of words and 'evidence' to the contrary, the unprecedented drive against belief in God masked an extreme

First country. Isle of Man.
Five years old.

Bicycling to Belfast Airport to
spot planes - the nearest I got
as a teenager to flying.

Peking without a visa.
March 1975.

Traditional dress,
Sapporo, Japan.
Summer 1970.

Gala send-off for longest train
journey in the world. Platform 8,
Victoria Station. October 1979.

The Siberian Seven lived in this basement in the US Embassy in Moscow for two years, hostage to cold war politics.

Trans-Siberian Express. November 1979.

With the panda in China. 1981.

Southernmost (bare ice) runway in the world. Unloading 1940's DC4 after record flight from South America.

Construction of base camp at 80° South.

Thiel Mountains. Building emergency-snow-wall-shelter. Halfway to Pole.

South Pole. January 1988. Flags of all nations, with a peculiarly American flavour.

sensitivity to the one threat left in the country of independent thinking, that wouldn't accept the crude pretensions of the puny Hoxha to omnipotence. Not for the first time the peasants whom the arrogant urban idealogues despised, but in whose name they allegedly acted, knew something their masters didn't. The communists were determined to suppress, with as much ruthlessness as necessary, any denial of their own lordly ambitions. But could they fight against God and win?

As we left the atheist museum I glanced up at the cynical inscription: 'Albanians do not believe in God any longer because God doesn't believe in Albanians any longer.' My briefing notes had referred to a passage from the prophet Isaiah: 'This is a people plundered and looted . . . trapped in pits or hidden away in prisons.' How long before the promise would be fulfilled? 'I will turn the darkness into light before them and make the rough places smooth . . . I will not forsake them.' Meantime Albania waits. And cries.

Real life doesn't have as many fairytale endings as fiction, but it was still hard not to leave Skipiria – the Albanians' name for their country – land of the Eagle and its proud people, downcast at the misery one petty dictator, with grandiose notions, could wreak on his subjects. Our much-utilised minibus trundled north to the frontier at Hani-i-Hotit, where we completed formalities and were disgorged into MONTENEGRO. There were no porters, so all luggage had to be manhauled across no man's land to the Yugoslav post. Once clear of that we hired transport to Titograd, where JAT had thoughtfully put on two Caravelle jets for the internal flight to Belgrade, five minutes apart. The operating philosophy of their airline clearly was 'Double or nothing'.

By tearing across the tarmac at Belgrade like sheet lightning Kevin and I hopped on board a KLM DC9 just leaving for Amsterdam. That got us back to London in the dying hours of the year. I phoned my editor in the TV newsroom. 'Don't bother coming in,' he said. 'It's a slow news night. (pause) You've just landed from *where*? On second thoughts, get down here. You might be the lead item!'

As the New Year dawned I was tapping out the first of many articles on the mysterious and needy land in which I'd spent a weird but fascinating nine days. Mine weren't the only articles, however. The two Edinburgh 'teachers' turned out to be journalists at the *Scotsman* and *Economist*. Front-page items in the Christian press by 'recently returned travellers' indicated at least two of our number had been missionaries, despite the visa restrictions. And the spy? A day or two into the New Year I looked in at the picture agency that had been so excited about my photo trip before I left. Bad news. The pictures were great, they said, but the New York office had gone over their heads and bought substantially the same pictures . . . just yesterday in fact. Frank was the CIA man after all!

The BBC photo library was glad to put the pictures Kevin and I went to such trouble to obtain on file for future use when the country would become newsworthy. They also had a practice – standard among news organisations – of pre-writing obituaries, so that a full instant profile was available when news of an important death came over the wires. In that way the obituary I wrote of Enver Hoxha joined the one I did on Charlie Chaplin before the trip, to be put in a filing cabinet and only see the light of day years after I'd left the Corporation.

For a long time after my trip I buttonholed anyone who would listen to inform them of the plight of this benighted Balkan nation. I tried not to forget what I'd seen when, years later, my fledgling travel business arranged for many tourists to visit, as the reign of Hoxha seemed to continue with no end in sight.

And then, sixteen years on, the revolution rumbling through East Europe finally hit Tirana. Hoxha was gone, and his successor Ramez Alia threw in the towel. Writing this, I've just come back from a return visit to Albania with an enthusiastic group of Christians and aid workers. The atheist museum is closed, I was able to stay with an Albanian family, and the Cultural Palace in Durres was occupied by . . . a new church, composed of ninety-five percent of the under-thirties Hoxha's regime had targeted with the full panoply of totalitarian power as the new atheist generation. God hadn't forsaken Albania after all!

Oh yes, my suitcase? It turned up in Manchester, so JAT was not to blame. When I later interviewed the British Airways CEO about the entry into service of Concorde I congratulated him, then added: 'Now, on a more down to earth level, about my Albania bound suitcase that only made it to Manchester . . .'

I was becoming increasingly earthbound as work piled up at the

BBC, and I began rotating around the different directorates – a spell in Belfast where I was shot at on the Falls Road; television in Southampton; local radio in Bristol; and, increasingly Scotland, where I decided to base myself.

The job did take me to Britain's delightful offshore islands, including SHETLAND, JERSEY, GUERNSEY, ALDERNEY, SARK, HERM, and LUNDY.

Short journeys within Europe, even North Africa, could be achieved on days off. Freddie Laker had DC10s all ready for his revolutionary Skytrain service to New York, but he couldn't operate them until he got final route approvals. So I, and hundreds of backpackers, benefited from cheap flights to places like CORSICA, CORFU, CRETE, mainland GREECE, ISTRIA, and the CANARIES, as he utilised this extra capacity. From Las Palmas it was a short hop to La Ayyoune, capital of the disputed WESTERN SAHARA, and the SAHRAWI REPUBLIC of rival claimants the Polisario.

It was clear to me that, even after extensive travels in Africa, there were still many countries on that continent which I'd yet to visit. But when would I get the chance?

# 22

## Hot Spots

*Angola, Turkish Cyprus (1976–8)*

I took, rather than got, my chance. It was almost a year since the MPLA had seized power in ANGOLA. I pestered my employers for the chance to go there and report what was happening. Little news had filtered out since the takeover. But they had other ideas for me, and felt Africa was the preserve of existing foreign correspondents. 'Why have they not done anything then?' I asked impertinently. 'Probably can't get in,' said my superiors. 'What if I managed to get in and bring back a report?' I countered. 'If they can't, you can't.' Now where had I heard that before?

Angola just also happened to be ideally situated as a turnaround point in an ambitious fill-in-the-spaces-where-you-haven't-been Africa journey. So with two challenges, and as usual no time to apply for visas which would have been turned down anyway, I took two weeks' holiday between assignments and was in MAURITANIA, West Africa, before giving myself any opportunity for second thoughts. Since it was my own time I could amble down the west coast . . . SENEGAL, GAMBIA, and all stops to Ivory Coast, where I took a train inland to UPPER VOLTA, now renamed Bourkina Fasso.

Two things about the train journey were memorable (I don't count the inevitable suffocating overcrowding). First a stationmaster way up the line ordered me off; for my safety, he said. I don't know what the real reason was. It was about 2 a.m. and he offered me the table in his office to sleep on for what was left of the night. I remember watching his pen scratch across the paper in front of him as I dozed off. The second was the commotion halfway through the return journey, as a new passenger boarded. I knew something was unusual when, despite the crush, people actually moved out of the way to let him take a seat, then formed a dense throng around him. A large part of his arm was missing. He'd been attacked by a gorilla only hours before, but recovered sufficiently from the ordeal to talk animatedly about it to the onlookers.

Getting into Angola from the CONGO was not difficult at all. It was getting out that was to prove the problem! Apart from me, everybody on Air Algerie Flight 2738 was part of a trade union delegation. I hitched a ride into Luanda with them; I would have been stuck at the airport otherwise.

The wide 'avenidas' shone in the bright sun. The graffiti of war shouted from all the buildings – a clean-up campaign had been going for the best part of a year, but even UNITA and pro-Savimbi notices were left to peel off in their own time.

I viewed a half-hearted attempt to fill in the holes in the road. Small clusters of workmen were chipping away with picks and shovels, but their progress appeared to be as uneven as the road surface they were working on.

Pot-holes in the roads weren't the only problem the new MPLA regime was faced with. The economy was far from healthy. Glossy posters in travel agents' windows still lured passers-by to take holidays in South Africa, but judging by the lack of customers, there were no takers, for South Africa or anywhere else. The copies of *Newsweek* and *Jeune Afrique* in the bookshops were a month or more out of date.

Banks were in the process of being nationalised. I went into several which had been privately owned. In each of them the tellers shrugged their shoulders when I asked them to change £50 into escudos. 'The bank isn't functioning,' they said, pointing me in the direction of the government-run Banco Nacional de Angola.

There, I queued for two and a half hours, until the beginning of the long midday break. In the end, the only way I could get some local currency was by persuading a cashier to dip into his wallet and do a private exchange.

The shops were very bare. Shortages seemed to be due to a lack of transport to shift produce from the provinces into the city. Every third or fourth vehicle that I saw in Luanda was either military or commandeered for military use. Local buses were crammed full, and for a journey beyond the city limits you needed to have good contacts to arrange a lift well beforehand. The pre-war taxi fleet of 600 had shrunk to almost nil. During all my time in the city centre I never saw a taxi within hailing distance.

Luandans had learned to live with shortages. Every night, queues formed outside the main restaurants and hotels about an hour before they officially opened for dinner. And the meal, when it came, was a drab affair. There was no menu because there was no choice. It was the same in all the hotels. For three nights in a row I was served a watery soup, a main dish of fish and rice, followed by grainy coffee. The variation was fish and potatoes at lunchtime. Only occasionally did a small piece of spam appear as an alternative.

If you didn't like the local beer to drink with your meal, water was the only alternative. Bottled soft drinks were only a memory. I went to stores, cafes, bars, hotels of all stripes – and none of them had any.

Soft-drink advertisements still adorned the streets however. At least, in those places where they weren't entirely obliterated by political slogans: 'The struggle continues . . . Victory is certain . . . To produce is to resist . . . power to the people.'

The Marxists had seized the propaganda initiative: young zealots were out stopping cars and distributing pamphlets to the drivers. The gist of the pamphlets was that the revolution must continue in the attitude of the people. Election posters proclaimed the virtues of candidates standing for posts within the Luanda adminstration. Prominent in the description of each was his loyalty to the MPLA. What struck me was the incredibly young age of the candidates, the average being about eighteen.

Those MPLA officials whom I got a chance to talk to were bursting with pride in their country's new status, as one of the youngest sovereign states in Africa. 'We are just like a child as yet,' one said to me, 'we have to grow up. We make mistakes, like any young child, but we have to learn.'

The same official sternly lectured the clerks at my hotel for their inefficiency, and the bad face of Angola that they were presenting to me, a foreigner. But he couldn't vent his wrath on the telephone system in the same way. After trying all morning to make a call, he gave up, and drove across town to his contact instead.

Amongst the people I met in Luanda, I could discern a wide range of attitudes to the MPLA. The young and idealistic saw in it an ideology which would unite the country. The slum dwellers, the workers and budding trade unionists, the junior civil servants, the urban unemployed, and anybody who had a bad deal under the Portuguese, gave the MPLA their full backing. Of those left who'd prospered under the Portuguese, the intelligentsia for the most part kept their own counsel. For whatever the situation in the rest of the country, Luanda had always been an MPLA stronghold, and they looked firmly in control of the city now.

But if the MPLA controlled Luanda, who controlled the MPLA? Not the Portuguese certainly. They were still getting out: I met several in the banks completing their exit formalities.

Some weren't so lucky. The daily newspaper, *Journal de Angola*, featured prominently a report of a Portuguese national who was being expelled from the country for irregularities in foreign currency dealings. He'd been tried by a people's tribunal, and, the report added significantly, all his goods had been confiscated by the state.

The Portuguese had left their stamp on the MPLA. The ethos of the new rulers owed as much to revolutionary Europe as to emerging nationalist Africa. It was urban and ideological, anti-clerical and trans-tribal, a movement that derived more from left-wing chat in the bookshops and coffee houses of Europe, than the religious, rural, peasant, very tribal roots of Jonas Savimbi's supporters.

So far as I could see, even though the MPLA had the upper hand in government, the various factions weren't at all reconciled, and wouldn't be for some time. Out in the countryside the Benguela Railway, the main commercial artery, was being blown up one section at a time by UNITA or FNLA rebels.

And it was said that a Soviet-style purge was under way in the top leadership. Two veterans of the struggle against the Portuguese, Joaquim Pinto de Andrade, and Daniel Chipenda, were ousted, either for opposing Soviet leanings, or for not fully toeing the line of MPLA leader, Augostinho Neto.

One thing was sure: Cubans were piling in in record numbers. I met them everywhere I went. And I had my work cut out, with my poor Portuguese, not to be taken by the locals for a Spanish-speaking Cuban.

Angola's administration certainly needed help at that stage. A simple matter like my onward flight to Mozambique caused great consternation to all involved. It should have been simple. Two former colonies of Portugal, one in southwest Africa, the other in the southeast, both now independent; their new respective airlines TAAG and LAM having a weekly flight each between the capitals, Luanda and Maputo.

They were in the OAG and ABC guides, had flight numbers, and I'd booked one. But they'd no idea at the airport when or if any flight would operate. I sat there all day. Rats ran across the transit lounge floor. One domestic flight landed. The TAAG staff hurriedly searched it for leftover food, which they immediately filched. It was a far cry from the recent past when South African jumbos refuelled en route to Europe. When the staff packed up and went home I returned to my dismal third-class hotel room.

Next day was Sunday: standing room only in the Methodist church. On the front wall, in bright red paint, were the letters 'MPLA'. Outside, a soldier stood guard with a sub-machine gun. He challenged me as I entered. But it was only to ask if I had a cigarette. Inside, the singing was fiery, but there was palpable fear in the air when you probed beneath the surface. Churches are good places to take the temperature of a revolutionary regime.

As fighting spread, many Christians had joined the exodus of refugees to Zaire. The problem for those who remained was their presumed association with one or other of the rival factions. Loyalty in the countryside had always been along tribal lines. Maybe the future of the Church depended on the outcome of the guerilla war.

In Luanda, the Roman Catholic cathedral was daubed with slogans. The largest was 'Down with imperialism', perhaps implying a connection between the overthrown colonial masters and their religion. Already, leading clerics were in and out of jail.

Finally the local airline decided the only way I'd ever get to Mozambique would be by flying up to Europe with a complement of Portuguese on one-way tickets, then back down again the next night. It was only 8,000 miles more flying than necessary, but I could call in on my friend in Lisbon again.

The plane stopped in Cabinda, a territory that couldn't make up its mind. Cabindan separatists frequently joined UNITA to launch attacks against the Luanda government. The 2,800 square mile enclave was cut off from Angola by Zaire, but Luanda had no intention of letting it go, even when South African commandos also attacked it. For inside Cabinda lay the Malongo oil complex, run by Chevron USA, which produced two-thirds of all Angola's foreign exchange earnings. So the dirt-poor Cabindans looked out from their shanty town at crack Cuban units protecting the Texans whose expertise produced the wealth that kept the MPLA in power.

In the Lisbon office of TAP, they informed me that the new ticket issued by TAAG was good for travel to Maputo via NAMIBIA and South Africa. I opted for that, and a side trip to OVAMBOLAND and WALVIS BAY. There the human side of Angola's tragedy could be seen with full force. Thousands of refugees from the fighting were camped in pitiable conditions under the blazing heat. They were glad to be alive; many had seen family members shot as they were escaping.

MADAGASCAR, MAURITIUS, REUNION, RODRIGUEZ, a quick visit to an ex-BBC colleague now ensconced as News Editor at Radio FEBA, SEYCHELLES, and a side trip to ZIL ELWANNYEN SESEL completed this African break.

I came back to Glasgow to find my Irish-registered Triumph 2000 parked in front of Broadcasting House in Queen Margaret Drive, the subject of intense police scrutiny. It had been immobilised in icy conditions.

For most of the next two weeks I remember sitting on top of any available radiator to get warmth. It was the winter of the 'big freeze'. My most remembered news story was of a travelling salesman stuck in a Scottish blizzard in his car, who kept warm by wrapping himself in ladies' stockings, of which he conveniently had a stash in his boot.

Travels on and off the job during the next couple of years were mostly to 'hot spots', sometimes literal, sometimes metaphorical. A return trip to Cuba let me take in islands and dots I'd missed previously in the Caribbean, including BONAIRE, Montserrat, and NEVIS. I fell asleep on Seven Mile Beach in the CAYMANS, and woke up fully lobsterised. The Bahamasair flight to GRAND TURK and CAICOS, on an HS748 turbo prop they'd managed to configure for fifty-two passengers instead of forty-four, was excruciatingly painful. In consequence, I couldn't move my neck or legs without smarting. Fortunately, the next sector was back to Heathrow via BERMUDA; thence direct to Wales, where Lindsay Brown's mother coated my back in buttermilk, an excellent cure.

I got into trouble completely by accident on a January news trip to frigid Romania. First Edinburgh, then Heathrow, then Zurich airports were shut, so a five-hour air journey to Bucharest took four days, before I finally landed in −23°, and slithered across the snow to the terminal. On a night train to Oradea, to visit Josef Tson, the heating gave out and my left leg stiffened alarmingly. I took refuge in a station waiting room mid-route.

I was staging back through Amman and Cairo for negotiations connected with my fast-growing sideline travel business, and had to go via Istanbul. Tarom, the Romanian airline, always a fund of knowledge, suggested I take the Austrian Airlines flight to Vienna to connect there. Apparently the Turkish Airlines 727 was picking up on the way west but not east. So I got on, found we were flying first to Brussels, then direct from there to TURKEY. It was seven hours late. When I asked for a second soft drink, the flight attendant, who looked like this was her day job, and nights were spent belly-dancing, snapped: 'You've already had one.'

It was at Yesilkoy Airport in Turkey at 3 a.m. that things went badly wrong. Seeing that my ticket read Cyprus after Cairo, a zealous Turkish official thought he'd help me out by missing out unnecessary intermediate legs and getting me directly to my destination, or rather, the part of it they'd recently invaded.

Next thing I knew I was on the 9 a.m. Cyprus THY DC9 via Adana to Ercan, the massive American-financed military airfield in Turkish-occupied Cyprus, or the Republic of Northern Cyprus, to give it the official name it's known by in the one country which recognises it.

I didn't mind this diversion so far. But since you could only fly to Turkey from Ercan, I had to get over to Larnaca on the other side of the island, to continue my journey to Cairo.

I walked. It sounds stupid in retrospect, but I just walked up to the UN barrier on the 'green line' in central Nicosia, and said I wanted to cross. I was greeted with uproarious laughter. 'We don't mind,' said the Turks, 'but the other side will send you back.' 'Not permitted,' said the Greek on duty. I retraced my steps.

'If in doubt, phone Her Majesty's representative,' goes the official recommendation. This time it really did work; but first I had to find a phone. There were none in the streets. Or rather, those there were didn't seem to work. Everybody pointed me up the hill to a pleasant, but not particularly imposing, house.

The door was open: I walked in. I was in a kind of sitting room transformed into an office. It was the residence of Rauf Denktash, self-declared President of NORTHERN CYPRUS. His assistant, a boy of about sixteen with the beginnings of a moustache, greeted me, and dialled the British High Commission office on the other side of the divide.

'Oh,' laughed a fruity voice, 'so it was you we saw just now. Quite amusing. Must say, highly unusual to try to cross *that way* round; gave the Greeks a bit of a shock. Never mind, here's what we'll do. Stay on that side for tonight: quite decent hotels. Come back about nine tomorrow. Hold a white handkerchief above your head, I'll phone the control point as you're crossing. Our building's right on the line, and I'll be able to keep you in sight.'

So I thanked Mr Denktash, who, it turned out, had the only phone in his territory that was connected to 'the other side', and spent a night in Turkish Cyprus. Next morning I took out my best handkerchief, held it aloft as directed, and walked up to the checkpoint I'd been turned back from the night before.

The officer took the phone call, looked up at the window of the High Commission to double check its source, then addressed me. 'This is very irregular,' he said. 'We do not recognise the Turkish occupation. How did you arrive there?' I indicated the visa page, stamped at Ercan.

'We do *not* recognise the Turkish occupation,' he repeated; took a pen and scribbled over every corner of the Turkish stamp. Then for good measure, he wrote 'Not Valid' over his scribbles. I was through the green line. The journey back was without serious mishap, just heavy snow in the Jordanian Desert, a blocked road that prevented me getting to Aqaba, and food poisoning in Cairo. I've never transited that city without incident.

I came back to an ultimatum. A watershed was opening before me.

# 23

## World's Longest Train Ride

### Poland, Beylorussia, Russia (1979)

It was more like a series of ultimatums, some self-induced, others coming from external pressures, and all arriving at the same time. I had to decide whether to allow my sideline travel business to develop into a fully fledged commercial operation, and I had to decide whether to go and live in America. How could I know that a positive decision on both would sharply curtail my world travels for the foreseeable future? It certainly didn't look that way at the time.

The move to Scotland had been a success in journalistic terms. I'd resigned my staff position at the BBC, to get better terms as a freelance, to allow me more choice in what I did, and to give the freedom that comes with being self-employed. Freedom to travel was an important consideration, not only to follow up promises to keep in touch with overseas friends, but also to pursue that goal which still haunted me . . . every country in the world.

I loved Scotland. It was a wonderful place in which to live, and I had numerous friends. With devolution, or modified independence from England seriously in the air, North Sea oil coming on-stream, and the stirrings of greater interest on the part of Europe in its fringes (the EC had just opened a one-person information office in Edinburgh), it was a good time for news. I was on air daily on *Good Morning Scotland*, contributed items to the *Today* programme, national news, *Newsbeat* on Radio 1, much of the Radio 4 output, and BBC World Service, and did regular features for Radio Ulster and Radio New Zealand.

My appointment as correspondent for ABC News in America had come about as a direct result of the International Gathering of the Clans in Edinburgh, which brought thousands of American and Canadian McGregors, Stewarts and MacLeods pouring into Edinburgh in search of their roots.

The politics of 'devolution' – the nearest Scotland was to come since 1707 to having its own parliament again – left New York editors cold. 'Only send us stuff that would make the front page of the *New York Times*,' assignment editor Charlie Arnot impressed on me. But this was different. This involved Americans, and the Alex Hailey fad was good box office. In all the years I worked for ABC, they never quite dispelled the image of entertainment conglomerate buying their way up the news ratings.

Charlie went ape over the merest mention of royal stories. 'Queen at Balmoral? Great! Prince Charles' first visit to a North Sea oil rig? We'll take it.' The rig in question belonging to Occidental was a bonus. Armand Hammer, the feisty octogenarian friend of Stalin, played host. Afterwards he presented me with a glass paperweight containing a microscopic amount of his black gold. The other souvenir was the hard hat worn for a few milliseconds by the Prince . . . I barely got past reception at the BBC before I was mobbed by a clutch of secretaries, each determined to have it.

ABC never fully realised the logistics of being included in an invitation to the favoured few for top level royal events. There were only six seats available on Hammer's helicopter, for example. But to New York everything was instant. Pick up the phone and make it happen. So I warned them about Jubilee Year, when the Queen and Prince Philip would traverse the length of their kingdom providing lots of copy. Charlie duly sent me with them, seemingly everywhere they went . . . except for Ireland, which for some reason ABC said no to, after I'd made extensive preparations.

I was relaxing at home in Dalkeith Road about 9 p.m. the night before the Ulster portion of the royal visit began, enjoying the prospect of a few days off. The phone rang: it was Charlie. 'We'd like you to get over to Belfast and shadow Queen Elizabeth,' he said, scarcely betraying the urgency in his voice. Brushing aside my protestations that I'd previously and laboriously set up all necessary permissions, only to have him neg the assignment, he continued: 'We've a hot lead. The IRA will attempt to shoot Queen Elizabeth. You'll have your tape recorder running beside her at all times. And we'll be the only network to have the sound of the bullet that killed the Queen.'

The last plane from both Glasgow and Edinburgh had departed, and the first one next day was too late since the royal yacht *Britannia* was due in Belfast Harbour before 7 a.m. There was nothing for it but a night drive in the Triumph 2000 and the 2 a.m. Stranraer to Larne ferry, plus talking my way into the necessary credentials on the spot.

When I made it to the first breakfast function, ABC seemed to have mustered as many correspondents as the BBC had on a good day. Peter Jennings, then UK bureau chief, now national evening news presenter, from London; Bettina Gregory from Washington; a clutch of producers from the States; and everybody was arguing about how there weren't enough on-air reporters for hourly features. I was drafted in, and all thoughts of the deadly bullet were forgotten.

In the end there was no attempt on Her Majesty's life; just a bomb scare in the press area which kept us all penned in until the police decided if it was for real. And *my* picture ended up on the front page of the local papers because my former editor recognised me in the enclosure at the royal garden party, and decided to run a sort of 'local boy makes good . . . from the Birches to the USA' story. Odd, since he was a guest, and I was in the press enclosure!

A letter from another American was waiting for me when I got back to Edinburgh. This time it had to do with the travel business, not broadcasting. It contained a proposal from California to send groups of Americans to Europe and the Middle East, using my agency. Would I come and discuss it? Enclosed was a ticket. Before I knew it, that journey was followed by another, then another, and another . . . until I became a regular monthly commuter from Edinburgh to San Francisco, often noting the early blossoms at one end, before returning to shovel accumulated snow from my front door at the other.

The travel business took off with a vengeance, ironically because of an unusual combination of circumstances. First, the American client who started booking groups with me became my business partner, handling all promotion on that side of the Atlantic. Second, our product range suddenly and dramatically expanded, and with it our constituency of potential clients. It's a good thing it happened the way it did, or we'd have been flat broke.

Our first brochure had thirty-two pages of tours that customers could – and *did* – book with any other agency: 20,000 brochures, lots of lookers, no bookers. It was only a footnote that saved us: 'We hope next year to be able to offer a CHINA tour; pricing, dates, itinerary, other details as yet unknown. Please contact us if interested.' The first caller, with a Hoosier accent which I mistook for a Southern drawl, asked if there were nineteen places left on the tour . . . if so he'd take them on the spot. Overnight the business catapulted from brokering cheap tickets for students, fellow journalists and friends to wholesaling tours to new, exotic destinations.

It had all come about from my attempts to go to China again . . . properly this time. After all, I hadn't seen much – even of Peking – in my week there. It seemed natural to put together a group of clients willing to pay, and go as the escort. Fortuitously my China contact, Philip Morrell, was just about to leave his executive position with Thomson, Britain's biggest tour operator, and launch his own company specialising in pioneering China tours. He needed agents to package his tours and sell them widely, especially to America, where no infrastructure was set up.

Philip's girlfriend Elizabeth had studied Chinese at Edinburgh University. I went to see them in Philip's flat in St John's Wood, and agreed a formal agency. It was now becoming clear that I would have to attend to the travel business full time, and relocate to California. My means of emigration was to be highly unusual. The first new product from Philip's stable had never before been attempted: a six-week, 9,333-mile, seven time zone, nine-country train ride from London all the way to Hong Kong, with stops in Siberia, Ulan Bator, and seven Chinese cities.

That's how on Tuesday, 16th October 1979, I heard the stentorian tones of Victoria stationmaster Ron Neill, dressed in tails and topper, announcing over the tannoy: 'The train at platform eight is leaving for Paris, Berlin, Warsaw, Moscow, Irkutsk, Ulan Bator, Peking, Nanking, Canton and Hong Kong.' The early morning bleary-eyed commuters from Bexleyheath and Bexhill were visibly shocked!

There was champagne, a piper in full regalia, and a bevy of VIPs for the official send-off. My own motley crew of guests included representatives of the Duke of Westminster's Grosvenor Estates, the BBC, All Souls – Nash's splendid church next door to Broadcasting House – Arts Centre Group, and assorted friends who had nothing better to do that morning. Plus a former Moscow diplomat whose brains I'd been picking about what to expect en route.

In view of the historic nature of the journey, both the Soviet and Chinese Embassies in London had been invited. The Chinese didn't come in case the Soviets did. The Soviets didn't, in case the Chinese changed their mind! A harbinger, perhaps, of the diplomatic minefield lying ahead. Only one government was represented – the colony of Hong Kong. She apologised for not bringing her entire dragon-dance entourage ('too early') and informed us she'd be flying to Hong Kong in about five weeks' time . . . so she'd arrive before us!

As the train was pulling out, I noticed a familiar face – Ken Andrewartha, whose office was just round the corner. He pushed a large parcel through the compartment window. 'It's for an Orthodox priest whom the authorities exiled to a village in Siberia. Somebody met him about nine months ago, and he asked for this. Maybe you'll be able to deliver it!' My bags were already bulging, as this was meant to be an intercontinental move more than a pleasure trip, but I heaved the parcel onto the seat.

The eighty-minute journey through Kent to Folkestone Harbour gave me time to muse. It was too late to back out now. I was becoming an expat, or was it an exile. At age twenty-nine I'd decided to abandon Britain and Ireland where I'd grown up, been educated, and had all my work experience . . . for what? An uncertain future with an unproven company in an unknown working environment in unfamiliar surroundings. And a fickle industry, to boot. The travel world was noted for its glamorous image – but in reality was it long on purveying dreams, and short on delivering a living wage? I would soon find out. My flat was sold, insurance policy cashed in, and all my worldly possessions not awaiting transit in a warehouse at Southampton docks were reduced to the two suitcases I was carrying.

It was an act of faith, another of the several I'd made in my travels. But this one was an all-or-nothing gamble: I'd burned my boats. This six-week-plus journey wouldn't return me to my starting point, it would bring me more than three-quarters way round the globe, landing me in an entirely new base, depending on a fledgling company to keep myself financially afloat.

We had no office, unless you counted the space on my business partner's kitchen table. And this pioneer London-Hong Kong railway journey (talk about travel exotica!) was going to be our main product. All this while the two communist giants we would be representing were regarded with deep mistrust by our target customers.

My mind drifted from the uncertain future to the hectic recent past. Taking the decision to move continents was one thing. Implementing it was something different entirely.

Selling my Triumph 2000 proved difficult when it refused to engage reverse gear, then later gave up the ghost altogether. I had it towed to the AA pound in Edinburgh, and finally sold it 'as is' to one of the mechanics for six ducks. At least, that's all I was able to buy with the cash he gave me, so I organised a series of farewell dinners (duck à l'orange) for my friends. A pity I didn't realise on the afternoon of the first dinner that there was nowhere to buy fresh duck in Edinburgh, and that the frozen variety would take longer than three hours to defrost!

Appropriate, I suppose, since my closest friends had lived in a flat referred to as 'The Duckery'. Jim Duck, a medical student, and his sister Anne, presided over a mixed student flat near the Meadows. Unfortunately, their phone was listed in the name of their father, a Mallaig GP, Doctor Donald Duck. Really! So every Saturday night as party time was in full swing, invariably the phone calls would begin around midnight: 'Hello, is that Donald Duck? Mickey Mouse here!'

I left packing too late, and had to stay up all night three days in a row before vacating the flat. As it was, the rubbish collection couldn't cope, and I left a giant pyramid of paper in the centre of the empty living room.

The last item of furniture to go was an extremely old, extremely heavy, oak wardrobe that I'd bought at a George Street auction for £5. Somebody finally bought it from me for a pound and agreed to pick it up from the ground floor stairwell if I got it down the two flights of stairs. My brother Tim and I struggled manfully with it, but as we piled out into the taxi in the early hours, it was still sitting at the building entrance as a grand unclaimed prize.

Scotland had been good to me. I would miss it. I'd found part of my family heritage there, as a minor sept of the Gordon clan, and been officially inducted into membership of the Gordons Society on the same day as my BBC colleague, Haig Gordon. I'd been a guest of the Duke of Atholl – the only person in Britain permitted to maintain a private standing army – at the magnificent Blair Castle. The only downside was that my visit coincided with a piping competition which lasted all day.

Speaking of bagpipes, they were also the reason for my inadvertent appearance in a girlie magazine. The BBC sent me to interview a German who'd won a magazine competition to go anywhere in the world to have a wish fulfilled. He chose to come to Scotland to learn to play the bagpipes. The photographer with him took pictures of the interview, and promised to send me a copy of the edition in which they appeared. It was only when I opened the 'plain brown wrapper' that the nature of the publication, which had an innocuous name, dawned on me!

My thoughts turned from Scotland to the trip ahead. I glanced at the tour preparation materials, larded with masses of the most minutely-detailed information.

Remember: Scottish and Irish banknotes are not accepted in the Soviet Union and China . . . Packing for six weeks' travel, when clothing must be suitable for a range of temperatures and social conditions, in one 44lb. suitcase, may seem impossible, but is not . . . The less you have to carry, the less tired you will be . . . You cannot take zlotys out of Poland, roubles from the Soviet Union, tugrics from Mongolia, or yuan from China . . . Remember that you will be eating unfamiliar food, sleeping in bunks, and, at times, will have insufficient exercise.

It's best to take sufficient toiletries for the whole journey, because you won't want to waste sightseeing time searching for toothpaste . . . As Russians wash in running water, take a universal bath plug . . . Loose, uncrushable layers, topped with a warm overcoat, are best . . . hotels are extremely hot, trains and buses warm, and outside temperatures freezing. In the Autumn you will notice that the Chinese leave their hotels unheated when we would normally switch heating on!

. . . Fresh fruit has to be eaten before entering the Soviet Union.

Even with the social atmosphere of a group, train journeys can be boring at times . . . Reckon to lose sleep on the nights you cross frontiers . . . In China you should expect four-berth comportments [I assumed this was a typo] . . . The Tour Escort organises the sharing of accommodation and does his best to satisfy passengers' preferences, not always an easy job! Remembering that guides are responsible for their charges' whereabouts will help you to be tolerant if they are occasionally a bit bossy . . . Punctuality is essential, especially when the train only runs once a week.

It did give rise to some intriguing thoughts: What happened if one person was late and we missed the weekly train to Mongolia? If you didn't consume all fruit before Russia? Were content to settle for three to a compartment (or comportment), or even five? Or became more tired, yet got extra exercise, from hoisting your overweight suitcase full of uncrushable layered clothing, Scottish banknotes and contraband fruit, up through train windows onto the luggage rack? What if your case didn't fit on the rack, as happened nine times out of ten, to our group?

After this litany of potential hazards, it was comforting to read that 'There are ample opportunities for shopping', presumably to make packing decisions at each stop even more acute, and render the mythical 44lb not only impossible but downright unattainable.

The nub of the matter was concealed under a section called: 'What to Expect'. The writer of the guidance notes affirmed: 'Having shown interest in this type of journey, it is reasonable to anticipate that you are the sort of person who has been attracted by the novelty of visiting the remote or recently inaccessible areas which this tour covers. I am sure you do not expect to be whisked by limousine from one Western style luxury hotel to another.'

Travel firms frequently over-hype their itineraries. But somehow this one had the real feel of following in the footsteps of Marco Polo on his amazing quarter century of exploration, trotting wearily through the Gobi, enduring danger and discomfort for a shot at the riches of Cathay.

True, it was only a series of fifteen separate train journeys (including the storied Trans Siberian) connected in a way previously impossible politically – to and through China – the Middle (or 'Central') Kingdom, where half the six weeks would be spent.

But by linking the journey into a seamless whole, travelling slowly (by surface) from place to place, entering China from Siberia via Mongolia, going from west to east overland instead of across the Pacific, penetrating two formerly completely closed countries, forging the first significant Sino-Soviet joint tourism venture, and reopening the rail link from London to Hong Kong that had been dormant for half a century, we had the feeling of being travel pioneers.

Russia, Siberia, Mongolia, and China each had their own mystique, aided by a seemingly impenetrable veil of secrecy. Now we would have a chance to encounter these places close up for ourselves. What an adventure!

The Kent coast came in sight and broke my reverie. After a last brief, blustery view of the chalk cliffs from deck, and two hours on a choppy English Channel it would be surface travel over land mass all the way to Hong Kong.

I dimly remember clambering on and off the ferry, the night-time coach from Gare du Nord to a sterile Sheraton in Montparnasse, another train next day to West Berlin, first sight of the wall at Griebnitzee, then the fearsome East German border guards searching underneath the train with their Alsatians. But I only really wakened up as we crossed into Poland. After all, I'd been up for three nights packing all my worldly belongings ('There are no porters in Mongolia, so passengers should only bring luggage they can carry at all times. Luggage may have to be passed over your head through compartment windows. Bear in mind the cramped space inside some trains.').

It was late Friday afternoon when we pulled into Poznan, after seemingly endless pine forests. The town had an ugly grey appearance. It was hard to know whether to blame this on the season, time of day, communism . . . or all three. A few hours later we disembarked in Warsaw, at what seemed more like a halt than a major terminus.

Saturday was sightseeing: Lazienki Park, with its bronze monument to Chopin, the church where his heart is buried, Marie Curie's laboratory, the amazingly reconstructed eleventh-century old part of the city, which had been virtually obliterated during World

War II, the flat open space of what had been the Jewish ghetto, the exhibits of pictures of the heap of rubble that was Warsaw in 1944.

Somehow everything you saw reminded you either of the appalling suffering of the Poles under the Nazis, or their then domination by the Soviets. But the incredible optimism that led them to rebuild after the war showed itself in other ways too. Our guide pointed out the thirty-storey Palace of Culture, an ugly building in the Soviet 'wedding cake' style of architecture . . . a gift of Stalin to the Polish people, the official line had it. Then she added, mischieviously: 'Did you know that the best view in all of Warsaw is from the top of that building? Why? Because it's the only place in the city from which you can't see the Culture Palace.'

For me the whole spirit of Poland was captured in one tiny incident as we left the Forum Hotel by coach on the Sunday, bound for our train to Moscow. In a side street the driver shrieked to a stop, then leaned out of his window to gesture to following traffic to do likewise. Six cars on the opposite side of the street had already halted. I couldn't immediately work out what was the cause of this holdup, as there was nothing in the road ahead of us.

Suddenly a little girl – she couldn't have been more than seven or eight – stepped off the pavement to the right of us and walked across the road to the open doors of a church. I say walked, but really she processed, in an affectionately innocent way. She carried a posy of flowers. A second girl followed with a Bible, a moment or so later. Then a third, and a fourth, until there was a regular parade. They were clearly going to Sunday school, an unremarkable event in itself, but one charged with symbolism to all the bystanders.

To them, and to the coach driver, it was a mark of respect for Mother Poland, and for an alternative, deeply rooted faith that was probably the only force left capable of challenging the interloping communists. Later I thought of that little girl and the Sunday parade when I saw the first television pictures of Lech Walesa kneeling in the snow praying outside the Gdansk shipworks at the birth of Solidarity. To a nation with a thousand years of history – and faith – two generations of Marxism was a mere blip on the screen of human affairs.

The list of things we were forbidden to take out of Poland

revealed what was in short supply in their centralised economy. 'Footware, woollen goods, children's garments, leather, liquid fuel, tyres and tubes for motor vehicles and sewing machines.' The group must have left all their sewing machines behind, because everyone was allowed through.

Brest-Litovsk, where we entered the USSR, seemed more appropriate as a place to sign treaties than as a railway junction. It was functional, in the Soviet grand style. The customs declaration had us acknowledging our awareness that in addition to objects we listed on our form we had to admit for inspection: 'Printed matter, MSS, films, sound recordings, postage stamps, graphics, live animals and birds, raw foodstuffs of animal origin and slaughtered fowl', seemingly giving equal weight to poultry matters and thought control. Had we been undertaking the journey today, we'd have been completing the documentation to enter the Republic of BYELORUSSIA, then leaving it for Russia. We didn't see much of its capital, Minsk, at 2 a.m.

The train contrived to arrive at Byelorussia Station in Moscow three hours late. It was a bitterly cold October Monday evening. Night was drawing in, and poor Svetlana, who'd been expecting us in the afternoon, was rubbing her gloveless hands together to keep them warm. Svetlana, twenty-three, a graduate of the Foreign Languages Institute, had stringy blonde hair and a lost-sheep expression. She was our official minder from Intourist, the state behemoth that owned all the hotels, buses and campgrounds, and was the monopoly travel arranger.

We were all so anxious to make the most of our time in Moscow that we heaved a collective sigh of relief on finding that we weren't to be billeted out in the French-built Cosmos Hotel, next to the Exhibition of Economic Achievements (a long drive in to Red Square), as we'd feared. Unlike the cosy old city centre Metropole, haunt for *agents provocateurs*, shady foreign businessmen and the party elite, or the third-rate Berlin where I'd stayed previously, the Cosmos was the new location of choice for foreign tourists – a cavernous building where volumes (of tourists *and* dollars) could be amassed yet minimal interaction with locals maintained. The huge, but central, Intourist Hotel seemed the ideal compromise.

The sightseeing got under way immediately after breakfast on Tuesday: Tretyakov Gallery, Kremlin, GUM department store, Space Pavilion. But we couldn't go in to the University, even though the bus trailed us up to Lenin Heights. 'Day off,' the city guide said. You picked up guides like flies: a national one, a regional one, a city one, plus one for each attraction. The supposition was that they were there to check up on each other as much as us. If it was a day off, what were all these students doing carrying books around? We passed the Olympic Stadium (locked), the all-year ski-run (closed), a few interesting-looking churches which people were milling around ('only a few old people still go to church'), and the enormous swimming pool, capable of holding 2,000 (empty). After seeing a dry Taj and Niagara, I fully expected it to be drained.

The requisite double homage to Lenin, visits both to artefacts of his life in the museum, and to his actual body, miraculously preserved from putrefying in the Red Square Mausoleum, was set for Wednesday. A slight problem for me, as I had other plans. I had to separate from the group as inconspicuously as possible to carry out my twin missions. For some time I'd been part of an informal network to help people persecuted for their faith by all-powerful governments. Sometimes my role involved spreading uncensored news, other times bringing into restricted countries medical supplies, requested literature or other help.

This time it was slightly different. I was asked to make contact with a 'friend' in the American Embassy and do what he told me. To protect everybody involved in the circle of help, this friend wouldn't know who I was. Yet we needed to pretend to be related, so the Soviets wouldn't suspect anything untoward. I phoned my contact at home, and he was quickwitted enough to greet this total stranger as a favourite nephew who he was delighted had turned up. 'Come and have lunch with me tomorrow at the Embassy,' he said. 'Bring a friend.'

Since everybody on the tour was American except me, there were several willing volunteers to accompany me. I took Patty, a thirty-three-year-old Californian furniture dealer, who drove a green Jaguar when she wasn't travelling. By the time I'd penetrated Embassy security, reached the eighth floor and been searched two additional times, I realised my contact was of a higher rank than I'd expected.

Colonel Bob was an affable man from South Carolina with a military bearing. 'It'll most likely be hamburgers today. But good fresh salad. Bit of a change from all that stodge in the hotels.'

He seemed to be interrogating my carrier bag closely. Then he rummaged in his closet for a similar bag of his own, and filled it with very heavy books from his shelves, while Patty and I hovered in the doorway. When we finished lunch he nudged both bags with his feet under the table, repositioning them slightly to ensure that when I left I would take his instead of my own.

Patty questioned me in the taxi on the way back. 'That bag switching wouldn't have fooled anybody. What gives?' It was simple enough: the Colonel was able to exploit his diplomatic status to ship in Bibles, hymn books and other innocent paraphernalia banned or severely limited by the ardently atheist Soviet authorities. But if he then tried to pass them on to Soviet citizens he'd have been turfed out of the country immediately. So I was to be the go-between. That night I spent dodging two KGB plainclothes men (giveaway, the shiniest shoes on the block) who were keeping watch on the humble flat of the believers who were to be the recipients of the various books, before they in turn would copy them by hand and further distribute them. I was only able to put my head round their front door for a second, and dump the books on their kitchen table, before disappearing into the night. They thought they'd seen an angel. Odd how totalitarian authorities at once mistreated and ridiculed the lowly individuals who simply adhered to their creed despite severe pressure, and yet feared them enough to marshal against them all the apparatus of a repressive regime, as if they were spies or political enemies.

My other undercover job in Moscow involved returning to the US Embassy under cover of darkness to report for the BBC on a standoff between the superpowers that was being played out in the Embassy basement.

Some time before, two families from Siberia who'd repeatedly been harassed, denied religious freedom and then refused emigration, had travelled the 5,000 miles by train to Moscow from their village to present their case directly to the American Embassy. They'd been sponsored by an American family, but the obstinate refusal by the Soviets to grant them an exit stamp, combined with taking away their internal papers and threatening them with continual fines and imprisonment, in effect held them hostage in no man's land.

The determination by the Soviet militia not to let the families enter the Embassy gates began a drama that would run for several years. The families tried to pass. There was a scuffle. A younger brother was dragged off screaming to detention. The remaining seven bolted through the entrance and sought asylum. The inability or unwillingness of the Americans to guarantee their safe transit from Embassy to airport, and the Soviets' intransigent attitude that the families would have to return to their village to the same non-existence and undoubtedly suffer a vengeful reprisal for their defiance, led to a diplomatic impasse.

In Britain I'd been kept posted on developments, but this was my first chance to meet them face to face. The Vaschenkos and Chimkalovs at first bunkered down in the reception area, then in the canteen, finally in a tiny basement room, where I was to interview them. Despite the tight security of earlier in the day, I found it relatively easy to find my way to the basement without being challenged. The seven were in good spirits. None of us dreamt at that stage that they would spend two more years in that room, or that I would make several repeat visits to them on future trips. Lydia, in her early twenties, had the best English, and acted as spokeswoman.

They were saddened by the lack of response by the US government to solving their case, but philosophical about the little they'd learned of power politics. They had an unquenchable optimism that they'd gain their freedom in time, and a serenity, crowded together there in those cramped quarters, that was hard to credit. They expressed solicitousness about my clothing, 'Not warm enough for October in Moscow,' and offered to lend me père Vaschenko's overcoat (since he wasn't planning on going anywhere in the near future) then laughed at me when I tried it on, and looked a bit ridiculous.

I felt admiration for these simple people who put their lives on the line for wanting no more than all of us in the free world took for granted every day. I promised I would tell their story in their own words. We did the interview in the bathroom, the only place not bugged, and it was broadcast worldwide the following week as I was rolling across the vastness of their homeland. Lydia had to go on hunger strike, almost dying in the process, before the two families eventually got their wish, and settled in the West.

How I got the tape out to London still has to remain a secret. I didn't get any feedback until I reached Hong Kong. My producer said he loved the piece, but wished I'd been a bit tougher in the interview, and less obviously sympathetic. I suppose it looked very different from the comfort of Broadcasting House, just another drama in the changing political scene. Did he want me to play devil's advocate for the Russians, say that their repressions maybe had a good side that eluded me somehow, that perhaps Goliath wasn't a bad giant after all, and David was a bit harsh to cut off his head? Could he have done with a dash of sympathy locked in a nine by ten room with an uncertain future?

I seethed inwardly over my producer's reaction. That maddeningly Western liberal trait of balance, of compromise, of always seeing the other side, however appalling; above all the tendency to regard everything as if it was a potential subject for even-handed debate, an essay with no conclusion, was such a gift to the skilful Soviet purveyors of disinformation. The 'Siberian Seven' as they came to be known, and tens of thousands like them, were shut out of their own society, disenfranchised, denied their basic human rights . . . and the defenders of freedom wrote wordy pro and con articles about the Kremlin and the White House in the *Guardian* or the *Washington Post*.

The writer and Nobel laureate Alexander Solzhenitsyn survived years of barbaric treatment in prison camps in the region these seven had fled from, and I was setting out for. His conclusion was that 'One word of truth would conquer an army of lies.' The lies were plain for all to see around us on our journey. I thought I glimpsed for a moment a fraction of that word of truth in the Vaschenkos, Chimkalovs, and the little girl in Warsaw with her bunch of flowers.

On a personal level, what lay ahead for me in the vastness of SIBERIA? It was an exciting opportunity to see at first hand a region known in popular lore only for salt mines, forced labour camps, freezing weather, and exile. And I still had a couple of assignments.

# 24

# Yurts, Lamaseries and Motorcycles

*Siberia, Kazakhstan, Buryatia, Outer Mongolia (1979)*

Although it was nearly 9 a.m. when our Central Kingdom Express group of twenty-three reached Yaroslavl Station the concourse was still full of assorted drunks and down-at-heel characters just coming awake. The anticipated romance of the Trans Siberian began to pall slightly when, having heaved and shoved ourselves and our baggage into the assigned carriage, we found it wasn't the right carriage after all, and had to start all over again.

We were four to a compartment, taking up one and a half of the nineteen green carriages of the 'Rossia'. This journey would be the longest continuous sector of the whole trip, over a route that was both Imperial Russia's claim to territories all the way to the Pacific Ocean, and a lifeline for the hundreds of communities strung along its length.

It ran mostly through the Siberian Lowlands, yet crossed the magnificent Ural Mountains, joined two continents, skirted KAZAKHSTAN, traversed permafrost, barren steppe, birch and pine taiga, and, at precisely the point we branched off from it, began its long meandering along the mutually hostile border with China. Perhaps that was why the reading matter displayed in the corridors alongside Lenin's speeches featured titles such as 'What Price Chinese Hegemony?' and 'Peking's Policy – Threat to World Peace'.

A total of eighty-four stops were scheduled, from thirty minutes at the big ones like Perm, Kirov, Sverdlov, Omsk, and Krasnoyarsk, to two minutes at Kanfensk-Uralsky, to what seemed barely a whistle at Cheremkhovo. Sometimes the Cyrillic lettering at a hastily glimpsed halt didn't match that on the closely printed timetable posted in our compartment. The Russians on board seized the opportunity at each stop to stock up on food from the kiosks on the platform, even though they were usually clad in pyjamas or track suits, often with bare feet and sandals. The outside temperature gave various readings under zero – none above.

The wood-burning furnace kept temperatures inside the train swelteringly hot, so you always faced a blast of icy air as soon as you ventured out. Since you had to walk the length of seven carriages to get to the dining car, this was a frequent occurrence. It became a practised art each mealtime after completing the transit of one carriage to force open the heavy iron door while the wind tore at your legs and face, then to avoid slipping on the treacherous metal interface between carriages, while leaning your weight against the door of the next unit to open it.

When our group was in the dining car, no Russians were allowed. Meals were heavy four-course affairs. Lots of borscht, blini, potatoes with everything, and, invariably, beetroot salad. Occasionally elk meat, or maybe the hamburger just tasted like it! Pyelmyeni, a kind of ravioli, was outstanding. Since the train ran on Moscow time, but the dining car on local, the intervals between meals seemed to get shorter and shorter. The ultimate time absurdity was arriving into Irkutsk at 03.17 Moscow time after consuming a vast breakfast of spaghetti, eggs, black bread and cucumber.

Tea was always on tap from the samovar in each compartment, at 3p a cup, 2p if you didn't take sugar; that is, assuming you remained on good terms with the dragon ladies who dispensed it and kept order generally in the carriage. They brooked no mischief in their charges, and were known to strike from time to time.

I had to really crane to see the obelisk marking the boundary between Europe and Asia on the third day. In general, outside viewing interests were a steady procession of smallholdings and dirt road communities with weatherbeaten houses in need of paint. Villages with wooden houses, wells and outside lavatories. Sometimes a shack near the railway would lean at a crazy angle, like a Saturday night drunk. Women carried out a lot of the signalling duties, and did much of the track maintenance.

By night you often fell asleep to the accompaniment of freight trains thundering past on average every five minutes. The Trans Siberian was a busy artery of commerce, connecting the capital to the resources of its hinterland. We were spared much of the blight – the new factories, hydroelectric projects, and mines were mostly to our immediate north. On the second night a rare sunset cast a pink glow all along the telegraph wires, silhouetting them against a lilac sky, which was looking down benignly on the Dr Zhivago landscape. One British wag whom I later booked on the CKE said it was no different than going to Inverness from Clapham Junction by British Rail, except that more people spoke English. I clung to the romance.

True, for Siberia to live up to its billing as a land of legend and adventure, you had to use a good deal of imagination. Those inhabitants of the one-room wooden houses were probably descendants of the privileged elite brought there on foot, in chains, or maybe even on a train like ours, to eke out their lives in a harsh exile. It was hard to visualise the Decembrists, until we noticed the finely detailed filigree, individual touches in each wooden home in Irkutsk, as if they were determined to render as asthetic as possible their place of isolation.

The modern move-in Siberians were different. At least the ones we saw petitioning the dining car for alcohol to purchase, or returning to work after a rare break in the capital. They were exiles of choice – if you could call economic necessity a choice – lured by the doubling of wages offered as compensation for the diminished social environment.

The twenty-seven-year-old priest I had to deliver Ken Andrewartha's parcel to was a real exile. He'd clearly angered the government by allowing too many young people to come to his church, and thus spoil their propaganda statistics. So the supine church authorities connived at his reassignment to a village far from students, intellectuals, journalists, and especially foreigners. So how was I supposed to reach him?

Meantime we had a relief from the train on the fourth night, Saturday. In a hastily arranged concession, we were allowed to disembark at Novosibirsk, something hitherto impossible, and visit Akademgorosk, the collection of research institutes of which the Soviets were very proud. We heard later that there'd been a chemical explosion in one of the labs, releasing deadly toxins into the surrounding area. It had not been reported. Perhaps it was better to be ignorant at the time.

I had the address of one of the many churches that met in the woods all over the Soviet Union, away from prying eyes in the cities, this one about fifteen miles outside Novosibirsk. Since the city itself was not on any Westerner's itinerary, it was a fair bet that this church would have had no foreigners visiting recently. I resolved to remedy that and caught a mixture of buses, taxis and lifts. When I got to within about three miles it was easy to find my way by following the stream of humanity walking, four, sometimes six abreast, off the main road across a series of fields. It was clear they regularly walked this route each Sunday, some of them all the way from the city.

They were a little bit too pleased to see me, not having had a British visitor for ten years or more. They ushered me to the front, then fell into a hush, obviously expecting a sermon. A translator was hastily laid on, but he only knew German. I don't remember what I said to them, as I hastily borrowed whole sentences from Brecht's *Leben des Galilei*, Goethe, and other A-level texts; but I do recall seeing once again the same luminous appearance on the faces in the congregation as with the Warsaw girl.

Far from withering out and dying a natural death, as Marx had predicted from his eyrie in the British Museum, the faith of Mother Poland and Mother Russia was alive and well. But to find it, of course, you had to do a bit of probing. Meantime the local guide was telling the other members of my group that people didn't go to church any more.

The group, concerned about toilets on the train, were now concerned about bathrooms in the hotel. Despite the clear hints in the preparatory notes, most had not brought a universal plug, so after three days of not showering, could not now take a bath. In my room it didn't matter much, as both the hot and cold water taps ran cold.

Two further nights on the showerless train brought us to Irkutsk, fur grading capital of the world. Here we saw the graves of the exiled Decembrists outside Znamensky Monastery, and learned that the growing season lasted precisely seventy-two days. We were entertained by a tribal dancer from the Buryiat region, at that time not autonomous, but soon to join the dozens of other areas seeking to shed the Soviet yoke. But it was Lake Baikal, forty miles distant, 400 miles long and fifty miles wide, deepest freshwater lake in the world, that we wanted to see, and that formed a pleasant day's excursion.

First there had to be a boring talk at the Limnological Institute. But then came an unexpected payoff: the village by the shores of the lake that was selected for our picnic stop, Listvyanka, was where the twenty-seven-year-old Moscow priest had ended up. So the left hand of the government, in banning him there, didn't take into account the right hand (tourist) propensity to arrange visits by foreigners. He wasn't in when I dropped by. But he must have been a bit nonplussed on his return to find the commentaries he'd requested nine months earlier waiting in his mailbox.

Strictly speaking, we now left the Trans Siberian and boarded the Trans Mongolian, though the lines only diverged at Ulan Ude, capital of *Buryatia*. Naushki, Erlian, and points south to Kowloon, instead of Chita, Skovorodino, and points east to Vladivostok. Before the London-Hong Kong through link had been abandoned pre-war it would have been the Trans Manchurian, anyway. So much for historical accuracy. The scenery had ceased to provide the stimulation of the earlier part of the journey, so most of the group turned inward. There was more card playing, social visiting between compartments, napping, even leaning precipitously out of carriage windows to clean off some of their accumulated grime since the job description of the dragon ladies didn't seem to stretch to this.

Since London I'd been sharing hotel rooms and train compartments with Brian, the tour escort: a jovial character who could always be relied upon for a Buddy Holly impression at the request of a Soviet bartender, or one of an endless stream of horror stories from previous expeditions. Except for the night in Moscow when I was trying to drop the KGB tail and arrived back to find Vince in my room instead. He, Rosemary, and daughter Melanie had flown in to join the tour late.

Brian had looked at the different last names, put the females in one room, and paired Vince with me, allowing himself escort's privilege of the only single room. It only lasted one night. They'd arrived after the others had retired. Vince, an affable tanned San Diegan, greeted me not at all unkindly when I rolled in, but the look on his face told me he'd prefer six weeks of sharing with Rosemary.

The drawback of being billeted with the escort was that there was nearly always a crowd of people hovering, waiting for the latest nuance of change in the arrangements, for any tidbit of informed speculation as to what lay ahead. I left Brian telling a dozen fellow travellers his favourite story of how he was despatched by a previous employer to Italy by plane to tell a waiting group of 200 – or was it 300? – Britons waiting to join their luxury cruise that the ship was still in dry dock and there'd be no cruise. 'If you can do that,' he said, 'you can do anything.' The way he told it, the tragedy dissolved into farce, and actually had a happy ending. He'd been a Methodist lay preacher before turning to tour escorting. Maybe there was some connection between the qualities needed for both jobs.

I pushed out of the compartment past the man from Whittier, Orange County, home of Richard Milhaus Nixon. 'I know the man. I've written a book about him.' Past the young widow, also from California, whose children were engrossed in a trip-related homework project. Past the clutch of merry divorcees, also from California, and the New York retired businessman whose vocation he now saw for himself was on the stage (he occasionally sang us musical numbers to prove it).

I was in search of Svetlana, who'd gradually released her grip on us, the further we got from Moscow, and anyway didn't have much to do when we were in motion except supervise payment in the dining car. I trundled through eleven carriages and found her curled up in a corner of what looked like a cross between the furnace room and the cupboard where the Dragon ladies alternately stacked linen and had their own tea break. Although our soft-class accommodations were far from commodious, they were certainly palatial compared with hers. It seemed she shared them with about a dozen others; whether passengers, staff, or friends I couldn't tell.

She was about to leave us at the Soviet/Mongolian border at Naushki. Since this was a continuing through train, and there didn't seem to be many locals about now that we'd parted from the main Siberian line, it was anybody's guess how she'd get back home again. Being an Intourist guide undoubtedly was the dream of many twenty-two-year-old girls in their last year at the Institute for Foreign Languages, for the status, contact with foreigners, escape from everyday rigours. It wasn't the automatic ticket to marriage with a Westerner that many supposed; too many difficulties in the way to be practical for all but a few very determined ones. And, judging by the en route accommodation, it wasn't exactly a gravy train while in the job, either. But it certainly beat being third seamstress at the Number 2 Embroidery Works at Mineralny Vodka, or assistant crane operator at the Lenin Heavy Industrial plant.

The other assorted baboushkas melted away, shy at the intrusion of a foreigner. I presented Svetlana with some small thank-you gifts, and a Mickey Mouse carrier bag to put them in. A couple of hours later, as the train pulled away from its final stop in the USSR, the bag made it easy to recognise her standing in the middle of the throng on the platform. Actually it would have been easy without the bag – she was the only female. About 400 troops were lined up awaiting transport to the Mongolian frontier, probably in less salubrious conditions than those in which we said farewell to Russia. It was a rather ominous sign that troop trains now replaced freight movements on the line. From time to time tanks on flatbedded cars passed. The railway station waiting room we'd just left looked for all the world like a barracks. The smell of empty beer bottles, stale cigarette ash, and unlaundered military uniforms still lingered.

It was November already. With a new country about to be experienced, I pulled out all my briefing matter on the subject. The fact that they were letting us in showed that they were trying to encourage tourism. But with a name like OUTER MONGOLIA they had a long way to go. It sounded like they were only just beaten to last place in the country naming competition by 'Weeping and Gnashing of Teeth'. There was an INNER MONGOLIA, capital Hohot, but it was completely absorbed as a province of China.

That came in handy when a group of Christian Scientists later paid our agency a large sum of money to get them to Mongolia and China. After three months with no reply from Ulan Bator to any of my telexes, the only alternatives seemed to be either to go to Ulan Bator in a probably futile attempt at confirmation, or to give their money back. I tried one last tack: 'Would Inner Mongolia be all right?' Amazingly they said yes. It's a good thing not everybody's a country connoisseur.

One of the many problems with Mongolia as a tourist destination was an almost complete lack of information. The US Department of State *Background Notes*, normally so helpful about the world outside Washington, declared blankly: 'The US Government does not recognise the Mongolian People's Republic and does not maintain diplomatic relations with it.' There wasn't much to add to this.

Visa procurement for our visit, and that of groups we subsequently sent to Ulan Bator, was an exercise in brinkmanship, requiring en route issuance. This was where you really did need to produce the tickets before you'd be granted a visa; you needed more than to produce them, you needed to have them to travel to get the visa. It's a good thing nobody thought of making it a requirement to have a visa before they issued the tickets. Come to think of it, where would you buy Mongolian Railway tickets in London? In time our agency began to be looked to as a sort of unofficial representative of exotic destinations like this in North America, and even we sometimes found leaning on the Chinese, the Soviets, or the Romanians to buy them for us was quicker than waiting for a reply from Ulan Bator.

Of course all the useless turgid information put out by bureaucrats was readily available: mind-numbing statistics and pronouncements that left you totally unenlightened, but doubtless provided a rich vein to mine for Ph.D. students specialising in the economies of little-known northern Asian communist countries.

'The sixth five-year (1976–80) National Economic and Cultural Development Plan calls for closer integration of Mongolian and Soviet economies under the direction of the Mongolian-Soviet Intergovernmental Commission for Economic, Scientific, and Technological Co-operation. The plan sets a target for an average annual grain harvest of 524,000 tons and an annual vegetable production of 93,000 tons . . . molybdenum mining has begun . . . trucks have largely replaced camels on domestic freight routes', and so on *ad nauseam*.

In fact it always seems relatively easy to get the statistics on a country before you go there. I knew, for example, that the railway line we travelled on was constructed in 1955, that the official government tourist body, which went by the unlikely name of Zuulchin or Juulchin (the first letter had alternate spellings of Z or J, but the pronunciation sounded more like an X), was founded in 1954, that the mean average temperature in Ulan Bator was 3° centigrade below zero (lower in the outskirts), that the frontier with

China was 4670 km long, but that with the USSR only 3000 km. I knew the latitude and longitude, highest and lowest points. But what could that tell me about what to expect in people, ambience, experience?

Brian, the escort, put his head through the door of my compartment. He was able to furnish some illumination. He had sat in on an early meeting in London with the Mongolians discussing proposed tourism from the West. He said that the meeting was characterised by a lot of throat clearing and spitting, with no readable facial expressions that could indicate how the negotiations were going. In fact he left the meeting rather down, feeling that the Mongolians' answer had been no. Afterwards he found out that the shaking of the head from side to side had indeed been meant to signify agreement.

It seems that this particular meeting yielded a napkin-sized scrap of paper with notations of optional excursion costs for the two tours it was possible to take outside the capital. This paper clearly found its way into the top right-hand drawer of the Operations Desk in Philip Morrell's London office, and for a long time served as the official tariff in the Western world for tours to Mongolia. I know this because every time I would phone Lesek, Philip's Polish Operations Manager, to enquire about the most arcane point of Mongolian tourism, he would reach into the drawer and quote from its scribbles.

The real Mongolia that I eventually experienced was in two parts: the countryside, mostly Gobi Desert, from the train window, and the more highly urbanised than expected Ulan Bator, whose spelling now became transformed into Ulaanbaatar. Or maybe there were a few more a's . . . I don't remember. The Gobi was picture-postcard camels, distant horsemen, brown vistas, lots of emptiness.

Town was motorbikes rather than tents, Hotel Ulan Bator B (Hotel Ulan Bator A was full of East Germans), a disco populated by Czech, North Korean and Hungarian engineers who fought over the chance to dance with visiting Americans, a post office whose stock of philately was almost instantly depleted by our group's bulk purchases, a hideous hilltop monument to hero Sukhe Bator and the last functioning lamasery in that part of the world with a half dozen monks in brightly coloured dels chanting, while others blew long horns and banged cymbals together.

There was some mixup with our onward train reservations. Despite the allegedly seamless nature of the journey, we'd clearly reached the coupling part between the Soviet and Chinese sectors, and were dependent now on new suppliers. Basically the entire journey from Berlin to the Gobi had in reality been carried out by agencies of the Soviets or their satellites. The Russian train into Mongolia was the last of the preceding arrangements. Soon it would be China's turn to take over. In the meantime we had this slight problem – getting out of Mongolia.

I never quite found out if the train we were allegedly booked on didn't exist, or had sold too many berths relative to the number available. Or if the Mongolians, now that they'd bitten the bullet of receiving dreaded Western tourists, decided they liked it – or at least the revenue it brought – and were keen for us to extend our stay. I suggested flying down to Peking. It would have broken the spirit of the overland train journey, but what fun to travel by Mongol Air, on a rickety pre-war IL14. Alas, there wasn't a plane scheduled for almost a week. It was probably busy undergoing maintenance in a friendly socialist state.

Somehow the problem resolved itself. I think in the end we undertook to forgo the excursions and fermented mare's milk tastings and leave a day earlier. We left Mongolia without even coming close to the horrors of cuisine – yak butter, goat's cheese, unrecognisable bits of camel – that dire warnings had been issued against. The food, in fact was unremarkable, which may have made it edible. Coffee which left copious amounts of sludge in the cup when the liquid was drained off, and thick cuts of stalish bread, otherwise fairly routine Russian tourist fare, was the hotel standard, and the uncertainty about train movements saved us from the 'dining toilet tents' threatened in the brochure.

In fact the Chinese phase of the journey had now begun. The train carrying us from Ulan Bator to Erlian was the first of eight Chinese trains we would experience in the following three weeks. It had delicate curtains, a reading lamp on the compartment table, and was spotlessly clean. It was tempting to make unfavourable comparisons with the other communist giant which we had just left. The wailing Chinese music in the background did get to you a bit, softening you up for group announcements. The loudspeaker which piped both into the compartment couldn't be turned off.

The Mongolian experience ended in a mixture of farce and

tragedy – tragedy for those ill prepared, farce when you could step back and have a good laugh at the whole thing six months after the journey was over. Unlike Svetlana, the guide here bade farewell to us at Ulan Bator station. That of course had us travelling without a minder across the bleak topography of flat sand and dunes of the southern Gobi. Not that there was any real opportunity to do anything subversive from the speeding Chinese train. However the Mongolian customs guards were taking no chances. They had a crafty plan worked out. On their side of the border they came on board in force. We were confined to our compartments until they reached each individual one, so that there was to be no opportunity to benefit from seeing what happened to anyone else, then taking preventative measures.

The routine went something like this, apparently employing the only three words of English necessary for the customs people to do an efficient job:

Customs officer: 'De-klar-acc-ion?'

Passenger hands over form, much scrutinising, head nodding, spitting, form stamped and retained. Then the sly bit, using the other two words learnt.

Customs officer: 'Cam-eera. Feelm?'

Passenger meekly hands up camera for inspection, and if inordinately trusting of authority figures, or easily intimidated at borders, blue and silver lead-free pouch containing yellow 35mm Kodak rolls as well.

Customs officer takes camera, opens it, unravels film inside to expose it, does the same to any others he's given, proceeds to next compartment for repeat performance.

Passenger (tragedy) mutters curses under breath, the beauty of the trick being that there was no one to complain to, since we were actually leaving the country. Passenger (farce) grimaces, and when the officer has moved on, pulls film rolls from shoes and other hiding places, explaining how he'd just inserted a few hours before a new blank film in the camera he offered up as a sacrifice.

I fell somewhere between these two extremes. I managed to save my film from confiscation, but after it was developed, wondered why I'd bothered. I knew that the faint dots on the horizon were camels, but I don't think anyone else would have!

# 25

## The Central Kingdom

*Inner Mongolia, China (1979)*

By contrast with Mongolia, the entry to China, at Erlian, even though it took place in the early hours, couldn't have been more warm, from the 'Welcome foreign friends' banner, to the singing group, steaming cups of tea, and apparent desire to make us feel that we were honoured guests. This was where the train had to be lifted up on a mechanical hoist while the bogies were changed to fit the narrower gauge rails for the next part of the trip. Together with immigration formalities, it took four hours. An eight-course banquet helped pass the time.

Here we were in what had been the most mysterious large nation in the post-war period. Not long ago they'd been torturing intellectuals, insulting British ambassadors, imprisoning religious workers, turning their backs on their former Soviet allies, and generally acting inscrutably to the Western mind. Was this a breakthrough in openness, or was it a calculated show? I determined to find out, as much as any one person could.

Of course if I'd been no more than a country collector, I'd have been satisfied with my week of semi-house arrest at Peking Airport in early 1975. But I couldn't see how anybody could other than technically claim to have been in China based on that alone. In any case, the five Mongolian days (three Outer, two Inner) required spending these three weeks in China. There was so much to see and do, if we really were able to get out among the people. This most populous nation, a sort of Rip Van Winkle stirring from long slumber, about to face a cautious and largely fearful world, would both encounter, and cause, some surprises.

The fear factor was not just in the West's outlook towards China. Throughout Russia our guides continually asked us: 'Why are you going to China?' with a quizzical expression of genuine puzzlement. Now our first Chinese guides in Datong were at it: 'Why do the Russians hate us? What did they say to you about us?' Deep down, I suppose, nations, no less than people, like to be loved.

Looking back at those three weeks in China, the entire second half of the Central Kingdom Express, a host of impressions comes flooding back. The sightseeing, though intense, extensive and memorable, was overshadowed by the sheer fact of being there at that time in history – the first faint stirrings to the general outside world, the early buds on the plant, before even the leaves appeared.

We saw grottoes, caves, Buddhist temples, winter and summer palaces, the huge Nanking Bridge over the Yangtse River, Chairman Mao's birthplace at Shao Shan, an immaculately preserved 2,000-year-old cadaver, the Great Wall, Forbidden City, Ming Tombs, Temple of Heaven, the world's last steam engine factory, carpet factories, porcelain factories, agricultural communes, endless museums, circuses with performing yaks (which seemed enormous when you were given a front row seat), opera (Chinese style of course), folklore performances, acrobatic displays and concerts. We had banquets – ten-course ones and sixteen-course ones – and Peking Duck at the Sick Duck Restaurant: so called because it was next to the hospital; I wonder what Jim Duck, now a GP in Dumfries, would have made of that. In short we were kept busy and given our money's worth from morning to night.

But it wasn't what we did or didn't do. It wasn't which items we selected from the gigantic à la carte menu on offer. There were times when I heartily wished not to set eyes on another monument to Sun Yat Sen, or any more reminders of Mings or Dowager Empresses, when one park or temple or museum began to look like any other. There was, to be frank, sightseeing overload, way too much for one tourist to handle.

People began reacting in strange ways. A lot of the group started skipping tours. This was frowned on by the Chinese. People became tired, succumbed to illnesses, showed signs of tetchiness, irascibility. There were fallings out within the group, some later repaired, others not. If a particular request was not met, an injustice or slight imagined, there was a period of sulking.

Anything, however seemingly harmless, was fodder for complaint – room allocations, sharing arrangements on the trains (we had to sleep four to a compartment), hotel assignments being a long way from the centre of town. Dreams of stepping out of the Peace Hotel onto the Bund in Shanghai, or the Peking Hotel in Peking, had clashed with the reality of an arbitrary Chinese allocation to the far suburbs, prompting suspicions of the tour organiser having cut corners and paid less. Even the food. When you start getting complaints about having to eat lots of delicious and varied Chinese dishes over three whole weeks, then you know something is fundamentally amiss.

One evening the whole group seemed to be mad, either with each other, the Chinese hosts, or with Brian or me, as proxies for the tour organisers. The meal was one of those eight-to-a-table affairs, with communal dishes being placed by the waiters on a sort of large lazy Susan, which could be slowly rotated in either direction for everyone to have a turn helping themselves onto their individual plates. Suddenly one diner decided he couldn't wait for the slow rotation, and gave the lazy Susan a mighty spin, calculated to ensure that it flew past the intervening four diners and came to rest in front of him. Before he finished helping himself, however, someone else had the same idea, and off went the assorted chow meins, sweet and sours, and mixed vegetables in a frenzy of spinning. How rude, uncouth and spoilt we must have seemed to the Chinese.

One of the protests I led was against the refusal by the Nanchang Hotel staff to turn on the heating. It was 16th November, barely above freezing for a brief period at midday. Every year the committee responsible began heating the hotel on 19th November. They were sorry, they could not make an exception in our case, even though we were, of course, 'honoured foreign friends', and we would just have to accept it. My protest failed. We all got miserably sick, and snuffled the rest of the way to Canton. Perhaps it wouldn't have been so bad if they hadn't also fiendishly gone into our rooms every time we were out on an excursion, and opened wide our windows.

But at the end of the day, even though this was the hardest

part of the trip ('normal psychological behaviour when twenty humans who haven't chosen each other are closeted together for six weeks,' said the director of a French Antarctic base to me when I told him of all our fights and misunderstandings: 'You should see the men after they've spent a full year together in the harsh, unforgiving white continent'), the main memories are not of the difficulties or the petty fallings out, nor of the actual sights. More a cacophony of sounds and images, when the dam finally burst open and the torrent of encounters rushed out, preconceived expectations clashing head-on with the reality all around of a living, breathing society with strange ways, that we were among the first to experience eyeball to eyeball.

There were the sheer crowds. To have the population density recited to you was one thing. To see rows ten deep on the pavements, quite another. In many of the out of the way places we went, and even in the larger city centres, admiring crowds formed around any of our group the moment they set foot outside. The din of the horns of buses like ours – often being the only four-wheel vehicle attempting to establish right of way against untold numbers of bicycles. The stately old hotel rooms, antimacassars, writing desks, pens with nibs, inkwells, Thermoses, seersucker bed drapes, no locks on the doors, people running after you to return discarded items, the genuine astonishment of the man in the street at our presence, yet their uncomplicated naturalness of response to us, opening up to us their lives unadorned. And everywhere children and babies, kindergarteners roped together in a crocodile, toddlers in their snap-open pants.

It's impossible to describe fully what it's like to be somewhere before the Hiltons, Sonys and Coca Colas arrive, to be the 'first' tourists. You're so busy trying to take in this mammoth onslaught on all the senses, you scarcely pause to wonder what they are thinking about you. This was put in perspective for me by a thoughtful twenty-two-year-old foreign languages student in Shanghai, who'd been observing our group closely, and claimed to have encountered one other package-tour bus load of Americans. After engaging me in English conversation practice for a few minutes, he broached what was obviously concerning him: 'Are all Americans old? Are they all fat? Are they all rich?'

Two personal encounters on the tour stood out for me. China's Western missionaries had all been expelled by 1950, leaving fewer than a million Christians out of a population of a billion. For them hard times were the norm, in the face of a bitterly anti-religious and ruthlessly centralising government. Horror stories of suffering in the cultural Revolution had been smuggled out, when Mao unleashed his youthful Red Guards to wreak havoc. China had a long history of Christianity, going back to the Nestorians in the ninth century, still commemorated in Xian. But now the Catholics had been forced to renounce Rome, and there had been only one tiny Protestant church building in the entire country open for public services, attended mainly by foreigners. Would the new stirrings of openness be extended to the Church? And what stories of heroism and endurance would individual believers have, when they began to emerge from hiding?

Immediately on arrival in China I'd put in a request for an appointment with a particular professor at Nanking University. The word was that the long-closed Theological Faculty was about to be reopened, and I judged he'd be the deputy principal. This was a potentially safe level. The principal as figurehead would have to carry the government's banner overseas and at home. To meet someone without a title or position of authority would have been against protocol; he neatly fell between these two categories. I hoped my contact would be free to talk openly to me, though I guessed not. But at least the last seven years of intense travelling in difficult places gave me a slight edge interpreting when people talked in riddles.

To my dismay the senior national guide insisted on accompanying me 'to translate and help', once the word came, unexpectedly, that my request had been approved. No need: he spoke English. But the notion of control does not easily give way. We sat as an uneasy threesome once the preliminaries were out of the way, and tea served and consumed. He probably knew who she was better than I did.

(A full year after our return Vince, the San Diegan, was casually showing slides of his trip to a group of friends, including a CIA man whose field of expertise lay in China. At one point he called out to Vince: 'Hold that one. Let me get a closer look. Yes. She's known to us.' His tone implied foe rather than friend. The slide was focused on the guide who now sat in on our conversation.)

Then the professor, an enormously dignified, small man, launched into his story. At no stage did his voice rise above normal or did he become agitated. His narrative was all the more powerful for that:

'My rehabilitation is complete now. I did manual work for ten years. I was thankful the Red Guards did not kill me, as they did so many others, even in their own families. They approached me in my study. I had about a thousand books and texts. They told me to pick which three I wanted to keep. The rest would be destroyed.'

His story continued. Like many survivors, he refused to be drawn into greater detail about the past. I sensed there was a lot more suffering than he felt comfortable talking about. It was over now. He talked excitedly about the future, new classes, new students. He showed me a partial translation he'd been doing, of a religious text. In front of the 'guide' he couldn't admit to a shortage of texts. And of course literature available in Mandarin from elsewhere, especially Taiwan, was politically impossible.

That was where the riddles began. He told me that of course they couldn't use foreign texts that had 'errors'. I seized my chance. I'd brought from London some books I knew he would value, but now knew there would not be a private moment to pass them on. So I continued his line of reasoning. 'Maybe it would help you to compare and contrast the mistakes in the foreign editions, with your own work. I have some examples that you could perhaps use, purely for your own research.' 'Thank you,' he said.

Afterwards the guide said to me, 'It was very strange to me to sit in that meeting with you two. Normally I have to explain the Chinese person and ways to the foreigner. I am Chinese and he is Chinese, and you are the outsider. Yet you seemed to have a rapport with him, something I didn't share. Yet you'd never met before. How can that be?'

The second encounter was in Canton. A second church building had just opened a few weeks before our arrival. David Adeney, an Englishman living in Berkeley who'd been a lecturer in China before his expulsion thirty years ago, had a keen interest in this church, and had given me a set of questions to ask about it. The questions were in English. I eventually found my way through the back streels to the church, this time without the guide. The closer to Hong Kong, the less heavy seemed the hand of control. It was locked. I went to the house next door, and with the aid of pantomiming explained my desire to be shown around the church.

The lady fetched a key, let me in, and we made our way to the small wooden dais and platform area. It was laid out free church style, very plain. Joint suffering under communism had at least broken the back of denominational rivalry. She sat down at the piano. So far, not a word of English. An excited flow of Cantonese spilled from her lips, but I didn't understand a word.

How to ask the questions? I had a guide interpreter when I didn't need one; now that I didn't have one I could have used one. She looked at me, wondering what was next. I ploughed ahead with the first question in English. About all she would have understood was the interrogative in the voice. I felt stupid. She grabbed a scrap of paper and started scribbling Chinese characters on it. 'Oh, she's trying to tell me something as well,' I thought, not realising at first what was going on.

Second question in English. More scribbles: four more, the same. She handed me the paper. 'Well, at least I'll have a message to take back to David in Berkeley,' I thought. 'And he can translate it for me.' It was frustrating not being able to communicate. Here was someone who'd had their church snatched from them, been in the wilderness for two decades or more, and now had a terrific story to tell. The light in her eyes shone as first she talked, then scribbled.

She caught hold of my sleeve and drew me towards the piano. Opening the lid, she selected a piece of music and started playing, accompanying herself as she sang in Cantonese. I recognised the tune, 'Silent Night'. I picked up the words in English. We sang together – same tune, different languages:

> Silent night, Holy night.
> All is calm, all is bright . . .
> Christ the Saviour is born,
> Christ the Saviour is born.

It certainly looked as if all of China was being born anew, in front of our very eyes, as witnesses. I felt as if I'd seen the light that shone in a great darkness, and the darkness was not able to overcome it.

Later in Berkeley, when I passed over the woman's writings to David, he was amazed. 'How did you communicate the questions to her?' he quizzed. 'She's given me all the answers I wanted.'

I smiled.

\*          \*          \*

So fast was the pace of change now that the 'Bamboo Curtain' had indeed opened a crack, it was no longer necessary to disembark and walk over the bridge on the Chinese/Hong Kong border. Instead, our clearance was effortlessly seen to in a few minutes at an upgraded Canton Station, and we plied straight through to Kowloon in what could have easily been a Boston-New York commuter train in 1hr 50 min.

From Hong Kong I could have flown to San Francisco non-stop. Instead I took the long way round: BOUGAINVILLE, the SOLOMONS, NEW HEBRIDES (now Vanuatu), NEW CALEDONIA, NIUE, Fiji, both SAMOAS, filling in all the dots I could in a reasonably straight line east and southeast from the Philippines and Taiwan. This long migration route might be the last travelling I'd do for some time, so I wanted to up my island count while I had the opportunity of crossing the Pacific. In Pago Pago (so musical when you sound the 'n' it doesn't have) I stayed at the Rainmaker Hotel, then flew via HAWAII to Oakland, across the Bay from San Francisco.

My business partner had secured premises that allowed us finally to move from his kitchen table – a cupboard (at least that's how small it felt) above his other business, the Logos Bookstore on Telegraph Avenue, almost directly opposite the main entrance to the University in Berkeley, and round the corner from the notorious Peoples' Park. The added colour of the environment came free.

To those whose task it is to draw up definitive lists of countries, I've often thought of making a plea for Berkeley to be added, or at least Telegraph Avenue. Based on criteria such as own language, peculiar culture, noticeably different natives, tolls extracted to enter, rejection of the authority of other powers over it, and uniqueness in the world, it's hard to think of a single street anywhere that better qualifies as a unique and different territory.

True, nobody actually put up a sign that first day: 'Leaving the USA. Entering Berkeley', but the pointers were all there that I'd inadvertently located my new business in a country I'd not been aware of before.

The first person I met asked me for spare change for breakfast, the second was dressed as the Pied Piper, and people actually were following him down the street. The third was carrying a placard warning against microbes as the source of all evil. I had to pick my way over the recumbent bodies of the fourth and fifth, as they had chosen the awning of the bookstore to sleep in. Round the corner, plots on the moon were available for sale or on a long lease. But what really caught my eye was a man seemingly shouting from the top of the telegraph pole across the street. Apparently a friend of his had shinned up a pole on my side of the street, out of my line of sight, and they were having a loud discussion about eighteenth-century poetry.

'Welcome to Bezerkeley,' said Bob, my business partner. 'Are you glad you came?'

# 26

## Strawberry Jam and the Corpse

*Central Asia (1980)*

So began five years when my life, business and travel patterns were increasingly involved with the two giants of the communist world, China and the USSR; first from Berkeley, then the climatically more benign La Jolla (La-Hoya), California. It seemed odd that I'd relocated from Europe to one of the superpowers, only to represent, in a sense, its two most feared enemies. My passion for travel was still very much to the fore, but economic reality told me that I needed to tend to the newly enlarged travel business, and make it a success.

We were fortunate in having the Central Kingdom Express – the London to Hong Kong railway journey I'd just completed – as an exclusive product, joining Russia and China in one trip. That meant of course that we sold lots of tours to each country separately, and our eyes were on new variants, side trips and access to other closed areas: the Silk Route, Central Asian Republics, North Vietnam, North Korea, Tibet . . . eventually new border crossing points to China from Pakistan, Nepal, Kazakhstan. I had a hunch that my new full-time vocation, specialising in rather esoteric destinations, might be just right for opening doors for personal travel, especially to the now dwindling number (as I thought) of countries I had yet to visit.

My first contact with the Soviet Consulate in San Francisco came on my second day in Berkeley. I had to process a visa for one of our passengers. Not knowing the elaborate system of double interlocking gates, and the camera mounted on the entrance, I wondered why it was taking them so long to let me in. (Later I learned to stand well back, show a good left, then right, profile to the camera, smile, and wait nonchalantly.)

Once inside, everything was businesslike, and we agreed a form letter which would allow them to process our clients with a minimum of fuss.

That same evening, at his home in Orinda, my partner had a visit from the district head of the FBI. 'Do you know Mr John Todd, car licence plate number . . .?' he reeled off, followed by: 'What was he doing at the Soviet Consulate at 11.37 this morning?' I think Bob assured him that my business was genuine, but it was a scary initiation into cold war realpolitik for a new migrant.

Apparently the FBI had installed a camera at the entrance to Green Street, so that all vehicles approaching the consulate were routinely photographed. The licence numbers would then quickly be fed into the Department of Motor Vehicles computer, and the registered owners (in this case my business) questioned. All this in the land of the free! We were able to prove this was the case when Karin, Finnair's new sales rep., had the same experience. Her parents in Kansas got the visit, since she hadn't yet registered her Mazda in California.

Entertaining visiting executives from Intourist quickly became one of our company's duties. Their movements were severely curtailed by the State Department – in theory paralleling the treatment in the Soviet Union of US diplomats. Seattle was off-limits because of Boeing. In the Los Angeles area Disneyland was in, but anywhere near defence contractors out. San Francisco was all right, but they weren't permitted beyond a certain radius.

An insurance adjuster friend put me on to an ancient but adorable red Jaguar XJ6 (one careful lady owner, guaranteed low mileage, low, low price) and that became the backbone – indeed sole member – of our fleet for driving out-of-town guests around. Visiting Russians enjoyed the elegant upholstery and wood panelling as they were being ferried around, relaxing to their choice of music. When it was my turn at the radio dial, I always tuned to KGB Radio to observe the response when the call letters were announced. Since the Cyrillic adumbration was of course different, it didn't quite have the hoped-for impact.

'Private' facilities at Antarctic camp.

Every year the North Magnetic Pole moves. This was the precise location in April 1988 (77° 41'N 103° W).

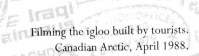

Filming the igloo built by tourists.
Canadian Arctic, April 1988.

A helping hand through the surf to land on Danger Island, May 1991.

Drying off, Danger Island, on the 'forbidden' Archipelago.

All aboard the private Lear Jet for Midway, March 1992.

I had to unload the catering to find a seat.

N A F MIDWAY ISLAND

Last 'country' in the race. Success!

Presentation of TCC special award for exceeding 300 countries, Los Angeles, January 1989.

£70 'standby' flight (subsonic) on Concorde, June 1989, London to Cornwall.

However, any time a routine Highway Patrol vehicle hove into view, they immediately dropped the 'at ease' pose, and adopted a sufficiently stiff, official demeanour, presumably ready to be questioned. Every few miles they interrogated me to make sure I wasn't taking them beyond the allowed limits into some unspecified retribution.

I allowed myself some mild fun with neophyte travellers. 'The 76 sign at Union gas stations? Yes, that's the enhanced speed limit.' And, borrowing from Gerard Hoffnung's advice to foreigners in England: 'Ignore all left and right signs. These are merely political slogans.' The quips about zebra parking places being provided everywhere, trying the famous echo in the British Museum Reading Room, and obliging fellow passengers by shaking hands with them immediately on entering a railway carriage, of course didn't translate to America.

Ultimately the combination of the Russians and the FBI was fatal for my Jaguar – or maybe gave it a new lease of life, depending how you looked at it. One day I got a telex message from the avuncular Eugene Korolkov, head of the New York Intourist office, to say that he and Mrs Rodionova, from the department in Moscow that handled our affairs, would be in San Francisco a few days hence. Could I pick them up at the downtown Hilton and take them to lunch? Since Mr Korolkov had been kind enough to give up a day off and sit waiting in an empty office in the Rockefeller Center for me, on one of my business trips to New York, when I didn't turn up, assuming he wouldn't be there, I figured I owed him a lunch.

I was surprised when a third, unannounced staff member, and the Consul himself, stepped over to the car and indicated they'd be able to dine with us, following the Jaguar in their Embassy-issued vehicle. I assumed casually, without giving it too much thought, that somebody from the FBI would be following the Russians, harmless as the situation was, just the same as we'd automatically have had a KGB tail in Moscow. What I hadn't bargained for was the Consul saying: 'I have something for you. I'll give it to you at lunch.'

I chose Pier 39, and the two cars pulled into the underground garage side by side. 'Let's do the transfer now,' said the Consul. It was a huge box of brochures on various tourist areas of the USSR, the type we sent to clients as part of our information package once they signed up. He opened up his boot, and I mine, and the box thudded into its new home. Thoughts of the FBI and the potentially suspicious nature of such a parking lot transfer to anyone who watched spy movies, or read Le Carré, or was professionally engaged in the 'trade' were far from my mind. In the next two hours the only mental calculations I managed were of whether the credit limit on my card would be enough, as the Consul urged on our Intourist guests the best that the menu had to offer, while I picked up the tab.

It was a strange feeling to have the tables turned. Instead of Westerners complaining about rubber chicken and surliness on Aeroflot, it was the overbooking of the United flight from New York that was being discussed. I wanted to ask if they'd been offered denied boarding compensation, but bit my tongue, remembering the previous visitor who'd benefited from this instant $400 windfall.

Since it was Mrs Rodionova's first visit to the city, I invited her to select her sightseeing choice. Dangerous, because when I'd done that before for a Georgian, he wanted to see the Golden Gate Bridge in fog. It was foggy, so foggy that he couldn't see the bridge through it when I drove him there. He was ecstatic. 'I have seen the Golden Gate Bridge,' he said, even though he hadn't. Mrs R. opted for Lombard Street. 'I want to see the crookedest street in the world,' she intoned. The Consul thanked me for my largesse, and drove off with his colleague, FBI doubtless hot on their tail. I set off with Mr K. and Mrs R. for a zig-zag ride down Lombard Street.

Halfway down I knew something was badly wrong. The Jag. made a series of rattling sounds, then sputtered, and would have given up the ghost altogether had it not been for the built-in propulsion afforded by the steep gradient. Still admiring the crazy angles of the houses on each side, we coasted round the last of the series of s-bends to the bottom of Lombard Street, where we finally ran out of steam and came to an abrupt stop. The head of Intourist in North America found himself in the undignified position of joining me to push us clear of traffic.

With no glimmer of life from the engine, I surveyed our options. The two Russians were due to be star turns at a seminar for travel agents we were sponsoring at Berkeley in an hour's time, so they had to get there, while I stayed with the car and awaited a tow. I furnished them with an umbrella, several quarters, and directions to the nearest BART transit station. Bob would pick them up at the other end. There were hurried quizzical looks. Did the BART line at any stage run outside the twenty-five-mile limit they were subjected to? In fact was BART covered under the regulations? They swallowed their reserve and hurried off.

It was only when the estimate for repair came to more than I paid for the car, and the description of the extensive damage was being solemnly detailed to me by the dealership, that I began to form the idea of sabotage during our $100-a-plate lunch. Of course, it could also have been because I'd omitted to put oil into it for a considerable period of time. Either way, I was left with a worthless asset. I decided to sell for what I could get. The ad. ran while the car languished at the dealership awaiting my decision on repairs, more precisely whether I could afford them. I was surprised by the response: over a hundred willing buyers. Did they know something I didn't?

One man was particularly persistent, and appeared at the dealer's, cash in hand, ready to buy on the spot. I sensed something was wrong in my calculations of worthlessness, but couldn't put my finger on it. I stalled him, and played for time, trying to get the interested parties to up their bids against each other. Finally the persistent man saw that I was going to be able to achieve more than he was willing to offer, so he said: 'Look, since I'm not going to get it I'll give you one piece of advice. Don't sell it. The body's in excellent condition. The smashed engine doesn't matter at all. Put a Chevy 350 small block motor in it, and it'll run a treat. You'll never have a problem again.'

I took his advice, and after the tender ministrations of a former racing car driver named Bogie, my Jagrolet was born. It was fun afterwards to see the expressions on the faces of attendants at service stations when I pulled in for petrol, and they lifted the lid to do an oil check. I did get stopped once for speeding while the speedometer was being recalibrated. The Berkeley cop said: 'Do you know what speed you were doing?' And I answered truthfully: 'No. My instrument reads zero all the time.' He let me off, after asking if I'd brought the car across the ocean with me (mysteriously changing steering wheel side in transit?).

At that time in America there were about 30,000 travel agencies. Only a handful (fewer than one per state) were fully accredited by Intourist, so the others had to deal with one which was. As Intourist circulated a manual with our company prominently listed as one of the authorised agencies, we started to develop a good wholesale business with other agencies bringing us their clients.

To keep up to date on all aspects of USSR tourism meant, as well as entertaining Intourist reps, attending trade shows and conferences in Russia, and trying to get to all fifteen constituent republics of the USSR to experience what they were like to visit at first hand. This tied in very well with my avowed intention to go everywhere on earth it was possible to go. The only slight obstacle lay in the United States Department of Justice, Immigration and Naturalisation Service branch, who were overseeing my application for permanent residence in the US.

It wasn't that I thought in terms of permanent anything. Just that they really only had two categories for 'aliens', as they so fetchingly referred to non-Americans: ninety-day visitors with possible extension for another ninety, and permanent residents. There were other categories for inter-company transferees, artistes of international renown, clergy, sportspeople etc. But as I didn't seem to fit any of them, and you don't have much of a life in the US without a social security number, I plumped for the legal application process.

I wish I hadn't. The first communication I got was from one of those bureaucrats who'd managed to swallow a dictionary, then turn all the words inside out: 'Your case is proceeding normally,' he said. 'Do not leave the United States during the pendency of your application.' I'd never seen 'pending' turned into a noun before, but that wasn't the point. Their archaic procedures may have been suitable in the days of huddled masses yearning to be free of whatever they were fleeing from, and happy to dwell on the shores of the promised land (or incarcerated on Ellis Island), while waiting for a disposition of their case. After all, the traffic was almost all one way then. But what about someone whose business required him to travel overseas and return?

Apparently there was no such category. As an applicant for permanent residence you *could* leave, but your papers would thereupon be tossed out, and you'd find yourself at best starting the whole lengthy process all over again at a later date, at worst meeting unfriendly scrutiny when you next showed up at Kennedy Airport. An acquaintance of mine, the Air India manager for the West Coast, found himself booted out when he tried to return to his home in the US. Something about the reclassification of places divided between pre-partition India and subsequent Pakistan.

The point was you had some sort of tentative status – and were protected by due process – whilst on the territory of the US, but the moment you left you lost both, went to the back of a lengthy and growing queue, and had no recourse against an arbitrary decision of an overseas embassy or port of entry immigration officer to not let you in. Fatal, if your home and base were there. Also, since American immigration law placed so much emphasis on 'intention', they had you in a catch-22 situation if you left, having applied, as it were, to stay. You could only get in again on a tourist or business ninety-day visa by emphatically stating you did not intend to stay more than ninety days. Yet you had already declared the opposite. One or other statement, for ever assigned to you in the records of the Immigration and Naturalisation Service, could later get you into big trouble.

It wouldn't have been so bad if the application only took the three months or so it was supposed to. Mine took three years. Other British friends gave up early in the process, each employing their own techniques to beat a very rigid, inflexible, and cumbersomely slow system. One continued to come and go two or three times a year, entering anew as a 'tourist' each time. Another simply transcribed his telephone number to act as his social security identification. Yet another put his trust in a highly unusual form of insurance: 'Every year I slightly overpay my taxes,' he said. 'They won't come after me.' When an immigration lottery was announced for 'illegals', tens of thousands of Irish long-term residents of New York jammed the mail boxes with multiple entries.

To avoid trusting any such hare-brained schemes and getting on the wrong side of the law, there was but one solution. Quaintly called a 'parole', it let you, in the event of a dire emergency, go through a speeded up process of having your alien registration card (called a 'green card' even though it's blue) issued, so that you could travel, only to have it taken away from you immediately you returned.

This was certainly an emergency. We had a tourist group of Americans and Britons scheduled to leave London for the Central Asian Republics. It included a number of Persian and Turkic specialists, and I'd asked Michael Bourdeaux, founder and director of Keston College – a prominent Soviet research institute

– and co-winner with Mother Theresa and other luminaries of the Templeton Prize, to lead it.

The phone call was from Michael. He was in Kent, I in California. Departure was set for Saturday; today was Tuesday. The passenger list was long since closed. Full payment had been wired to the Russians, all documentation telexed, visas issued. What was up?

Plenty. He'd had a call from the Foreign Office in London. Did he know that, according to the US State Department, one of our passengers, a Ukrainian exile, was planning to smuggle out a corpse? It sounded like big trouble. Could I look into it? I brushed aside his anxiety. Wild rumours were unfortunately the currency of US/Soviet commerce. Anyway, even though I didn't personally know Karl, the passenger concerned, he'd booked on the recommendation of thoroughly reliable mutual friends, and I couldn't begin to believe that he was about to attempt anything foolish.

It was the next part of the phone call that was disconcerting. The Soviet Embassy in London had contacted Michael to say they'd made a mistake in his visa. Could he return it to them for correction? On this I smelled real trouble. This was not about mythical bodies being purportedly smuggled in and out of countries. This was the Soviet government flexing their muscle. Michael was a known authority on human rights in the USSR, and when he was quoted in the press his comments weren't always flattering to Moscow. That they were always rigorously researched, accurate, fair, and usually nothing more than a plea for the Soviets to live up to their international obligations, mattered not a whit to the Kremlin. Anybody who didn't toe their line was 'anti-Soviet'.

Our privileged position as a tour operator meant that we usually got much quicker visa approvals than an individual would have been able to on their own. We'd never yet had a single visa denial. And we never did – in the US. But this time, after passing the London screening, somebody in Moscow, double-checking visas issued against the 'banned' or 'outspoken' list, had clearly decided to override the decision to let Michael in. They were just going about it in a very sneaky way.

I booked a flight to London for the next day to sort things out. The reason I wasn't accompanying the group or seeing it off in the first place was the absurd American immigration rules. Now that almost certainly the Soviet plan was to render the group leaderless, what to do? We had no one standing by to replace him, and it was too late to apply for anyone else through normal channels. Lorna, his wife? Maybe she could go without him? But I had better get over at least to London, perhaps also Moscow, to smooth things over. How on earth to secure both a Soviet visa for myself, which usually took two weeks, and a 'parole' to leave the US, which seemed virtually impossible?

In San Francisco you could only get in to see anyone other than a gatekeeper in the Immigration and Naturalisation Service by joining a long snaking queue outside the Sansome Street building before 6 a.m. Only the first through the door when it opened had any chance of securing a number for an appointment with an officer later that day. For everybody else it was: 'Come back tomorrow.'

The officer smiled when I told him of my dilemma. 'What's the point of me giving you a parole?' he asked laconically. 'You'll never get a visa for the Soviet Union in one day.' Whether against his better judgment or not, he prepared the necessary papers anyway. In Green Street you couldn't just walk in and ask for a visa. You had to provide evidence of the telexed confirmation number from Moscow, showing you'd paid for your arrangements in advance. The fact that we had paid for Michael's place and it was now going begging was of no relevance to them.

Since the visas for this group had all been processed in London, there was no record in San Francisco. Intourist was nothing if not bureaucratic. A European department organised all our London bookings; the North American department only handled bookings we initiated direct from California. Of course this came in useful in times of tension (Olympic boycotts, Afghanistan, martial law in Poland, the shooting down of Korean Air 007), when other American travel firms got blindsided by go-slows or tit-for-tat measures by the Soviet Embassy in Washington, and we were able to quietly have things processed in London.

Now, too it was a salvation, for Green Street decided they could give me a two-day visa, good for Moscow only, for business discussions with Intourist chiefs. Not exactly what I needed, since to go anywhere in the Soviet Union your visa had to specify each pre-arranged and prepaid city. But it would get me in, at least, if necessary, and I could take it from there.

My jubilation at mini-victories over the red tape of two superpowers was short lived, alas. By the time I reached London the Soviets had also pulled Lorna's visa. They were really playing hardball! I vividly remember leaning across the desk of the Intourist chief in Regent Street on the Friday afternoon at five o'clock, shouting and railing down his phone to the Embassy, occasionally banging my fist for emphasis. I knew it was to no avail. The time change meant that the people we needed to reach in Moscow had long since taken off for their weekend dachas. London had acted on instructions from above. There would be no change of heart.

'You should choose your leaders more carefully,' was the Russians' parting shot to me. Their notion of partnership still fell far short of even modest concessions to freedom of choice. In their eyes, the hand of central control, approval and disapproval of every activity or participant, should reach, even by proxy, into the affairs of commercial companies doing business with them. For me, encouraging travel to Russia or anywhere, was a two-way contribution to understanding. For many of them, promoting travel to the USSR was promoting its government's aims.

Well, I was having none of it. I stormed out of the premises, and went to my brother's flat to plot strategy. Overnight a cool head produced more dividends than fuming. I packed a small bag and headed to Gatwick Airport for the 9 a.m. check-in on the Saturday. I assembled all our group, and took Karl aside. 'What's this I hear about you and a smuggled corpse?' I asked, as nonchalantly as possible. He smiled. 'Oh that! I have a crazy uncle who fled from the communists. He's been going bananas ever since he heard about this trip. He felt I'd get in trouble. I think calling the State Department was his way of trying to get me not to go. But don't worry. I'm not going to do anything illegal.'

So the State Department told the UK Foreign Office. Ten to one the KGB were in on this non-event of the smuggled corpse too. I collected everybody's passports and separate buff two-page visa inserts, went to the desk and said: 'Fifteen tickets, fifteen visas, fifteen passports,' holding them up so they could be seen and counted. I didn't feel it was up to me to volunteer the information that one of the visas was just for two days and Moscow only, and that the name on it (mine) did not match the Mrs Bourdeaux on the appropriate ticket. The agent tore off the fifteen flight coupons, and handed me fifteen pre-prepared boarding passes, one of which had the name Bourdeaux clearly visible on it.

It hardly seems credible in these post-hijacking and post-Lockerbie bombing days that up till the early '80s at least you could often get onto a plane using someone else's name. It was much harder to board an international flight of course, if identities were checked against passports, but even then charter flights and group check-ins were often not as strict. So I travelled to Moscow by Aeroflot Tupolev 154 as Mrs Bourdeaux. I had no trouble getting through immigration. Then I simply turned to the Intourist guide and said: 'Look. Another mistake. They've only filled in the first two days of my visa. How am I supposed to lead the group around Asia for two weeks? Can you get it sorted out?' She did, and I relaxed again. At least now if anything untoward happened, I'd be on hand. I determined to keep a special eye on Karl.

The trip passed unremarkably at first. My company had a standard itinerary which we called 'The Golden Road to Samarkand'. It focused almost entirely on UZBEKISTAN, but there were easy side trips to the old, old city of Pendjikent, destroyed by marauding Arabs in the ninth century (modern IADZHISTAN, ancient Sogdia); the Maiden's Fortress at Mary (TURKMENISTAN); Chimkent and Turkestan (Kazakhstan); even the garden city of Bishek, which the colonising Soviets renamed Frunzein honour of a Russian general (KIRGIZIA). In those days it was like going from one state to another in the US. There were no political borders to cross.

If your interest stretched to great states of the past, in the foothills of the Kopetdag Mountains around Ashkabad, you could see the ruins of Nisa, capital of the once mighty Parthian state. Or my favourite – the fifty-minute flight by Antonov 24 to Urgench, followed by a pleasant drive through peach and pear orchards and vineyards to Khorezm Oasis, surrounded by cork elms. There laid out in front of you was an open-air museum, the capital of the Khiva Khanate, which dated back more than 2,000 years.

Intourist offered excursions to deep karst caves, the purported dwelling place of Neanderthal man, Karakul sheep-breeding museums, factories producing twenty-four varieties of tea, exporters of cinema equipment to India and Mongolia, even to the dreadful modern architecture in Tashkent that replaced the buildings destroyed in the 1966 earthquake. You were spoiled for choice, some of it impossibly exotic.

I wanted to slip over the border into neighbouring Afghanistan, a mere fifty miles off, but couldn't. The nearest we came was when our rooms in Tashkent were requisitioned for a huge party of Afghanis, who swept into the lobby in flowing white robes, each wearing a red Lenin badge. At Tashkent Airport we waited a full hour for air traffic clearance for our passenger lluyshin 62, while I counted at least seventy heavy military transports heading off in the direction of Kabul. The unlucky were bombed, the lucky got a tour and a Lenin badge.

But in naming our tour we homed in on Samarkand: 'Eden of the ancient Orient', the city of which Alexander the Great said, after capturing it: 'Everything I have heard about the beauty of this city is true, except that it is more beautiful than I could imagine.' Alexander was only one of a host of conquerors, but the one who left the biggest mark was Tamerlane, the self-styled heir of Genghis Khan, who wasn't above reducing any rival city to rubble, and building pyramids with the skulls of his enemies.

Samarkand was truly breathtaking: the turquoise and gold of Registan Square, Bibi-Khanym Mosque, the Gur-Emir mausoleum. In our group we had a lady who claimed descent from Copernicus. She was delighted when the inscription on the remains of the fifteenth-century observatory set up by Tamerlane's grandson, Ulug Bek, paid tribute to her ancestor, among other noted astronomers.

By way of backdrop there were the 'colourful markets' as promised in the tourist brochures. Only no brochure could do justice to the sheer vividness of the swatches of colour that blinded you at every turn. Not only did the wares for sale encompass melons, raisins, pomegranates, spices of every variety, live goats and lambs; the sellers would dazzle you with their orange chequerboard wraps over turquoise pantaloons or pink polka-dot dresses, and the quilted coats that served every climatic requirement across mountain, plain and steppe to the Chinese coast.

If the precise origins of the famous Silk Route were on a trail now lost high up in the Tien Shan Mountains, Samarkand was about as close a glimpse as you got of this longest overland trade route of the ancient world – the shortest and safest way from China to Marco Polo's Europe for a good seventeen centuries. If the stories are right, it came about by accident, when a Chinese general, in Fergana, Samarkand's neighbour, to buy horses, found the horses less than their reputation, but the Fergana merchants willing to pay a good price for Chinese siik. The Emperor Wu-ti was thereupon prevailed on to lift the long-standing export ban, and two-way trade started in earnest. Until the sea routes gradually took over, the position of Samarkand placed it squarely at the crossroads of such trade.

Undoubtedly with an eye to capturing the profits from this East-West commerce, Tamerlane saw to it that no nearby city could rival his. He was clearly something of a megalomaniac. Legend has it that his tomb had inscribed on it: 'If I am roused the earth will tremble.' And that's exactly what happened, five and a half centuries later. On the night of 22nd June 1941, as a Soviet scientist prepared to exhume his body, news came that Hitler had invaded Russia.

The earth-shattering event for our group happened in Gorky Street, about 200 yards from the entrance to the Hotel Samarkand. We'd just finished a shashlik lunch – skewered lamb with carrot and zucchini strips and some interesting spices, on a bed of rather greasy rice, washed down with a sour yoghurty drink – and had half an hour free before the departure of the afternoon sightseeing bus. I was lounging in the lobby; a few others, including Karl, had gone outside to take pictures in the market place.

Suddenly I heard a distinct commotion. The shouting and raised voices had English mixed amongst them. By tour-leader reflex I knew they involved my passengers, and I bolted to the door. What I saw was Stuart and Fred bodily carrying a wrinkled and protesting nut seller through the entrance to the hotel, each with a firm grip on his shoulders.

'We performed a citizen's arrest,' they declared proudly. 'He was a witness.' 'Witness to what?' I asked. At this point Karl arrived, minus his glasses and looking a bit rumpled. Stuart took up the story: 'A ruffian came out of nowhere and bashed Karl, knocking his glasses off. Before we could react, he ran off, but we picked up this man who saw everything. He can identify him when we get an interpreter.'

Everyone was a bit breathless, talking very animatedly. By now the hubbub had attracted attention from many quarters, and a crowd was forming in the lobby. I yelled at the desk clerk to fetch the manager in a hurry. I was conscious of five or six men closing in on the gathering, and attempting to take control. 'Come downstairs,' they invited, 'we'll get it sorted out.'

They were local KGB. Ten minutes ago they'd been cloakroom

attendants, hall porters, barmen, loungers. They swarmed in as one. We found ourselves in a smoky basement. Then everybody proceeded to act as if they were in a '50s black and white movie. The Russians only needed trenchcoats over their cheap suits to be apt for dropping straight into *The Third Man*. Out came the pungent East European cigarettes. A bottle of Stolichnaya was opened and poured. The mood altered between confrontational, inquisitional and palliative. Mostly it was a thoroughly professional exercise in damage containment.

Yes, there would be an enquiry. No, the old nut seller had no idea who the attacker was. He was let go. This was the sort of thing that never happened. Just look at the book for visitors' remarks, and see how many positive comments there were! Karl, I noticed, was a special target to be plied with vodka. Keep them quiet, promise them anything, neutralise the troublemakers, ply them with alcohol, humour them till they get on the plane to the next city – then you need no longer worry. This seemed to be their strategy.

When the smooth operator who was the Uzbeck head of Intourist arrived after a hasty summons, he launched into an oily speech about the benefits of tourism, implying Karl's beating up, in broad daylight, might never have happened. My patience wore thin. I pushed up close to him and looked him straight in the eye. 'Leave my tourists alone for the rest of this trip or else!' I shouted in his face. It was a hollow threat, but it surprised him. I turned and left. Nothing more was to be accomplished.

'What now?' I thought. Was this the outcome of the rumour regarding Karl that had been circulating around at least three intelligence communities? Or was it a fluke? Perhaps an attempt at compromise? A girl in my room? There was, actually. But it was only Tanya, our long-suffering guide, who was looking for me to tell me that she'd sent the rest of the group ahead on the excursion, and was now arranging transport for those of us who stayed to sort out the altercation. It was an Uzbeck police car, flashing sirens and all, which delivered us to the mosque just as afternoon prayers were beginning. Karl really wasn't badly hurt. He was already beginning to laugh about the whole affair.

What put things in perspective for me was our next stop, Bukhara. Ron and Howard, our two Persian experts, were determined to visit the old Jewish quarter. After the Samarkand incident I decided to accompany them. We left the new wide streets of the Soviets behind, and headed for the tiny adobe back-to-back buildings still remaining out of the path of the bulldozer. It looked like the Jewish quarter, with all its history, would soon be obliterated.

Ron grabbed my arm. Ahead of us was a door with a Star of David clearly painted on the outside. We walked up and knocked. No answer. Right at this moment a burly Muslim, with the trademark square Uzbek hat, rode past on his bicycle. His command was peremptory: 'Stay there.' He rode off round the corner. We froze. Was this the start of a new incident? The door opened and a slightly mystified Jewish resident emerged.

Suddenly the Muslim reappeared. He hopped off his bicycle. In his arms was the big round flat bread that was everyday fodder. He came up and embraced us in turn. 'You Christian. He Jew (jerking his head to our new acquaintance). I Muslim. This is bread. Bread is life. We all share it.' Slowly he broke off a piece each for us, and we munched together. Then he hopped on his bike and rode off.

It all happened in an instant – almost as quick as the lightning attack on Karl. Yet standing there, in that exotic corner of one of the harshest atheist empires the modern world has known, surveying representatives of religions that each suffered in their own way at the hands of the Soviets, it was like an epiphany.

The beautiful mosques may have been splendidly restored – but for tourists, not worshippers. Samarkand only had two functioning mosques for half a million people. 'We set out to find the Baptist church,' said Howard, 'but in Moscow they said there wasn't one in Bukhara any longer.' 'Come,' said our new Jewish friend, 'I'll take you there. This is the night of their prayer service.'

Leningrad was our exit point on this trip, and when we reached the arrivals lounge at Pulkovo Airport after our flight back from Central Asia I heaved a sigh of relief. Until I counted: fourteen. Karl was missing. Out on the tarmac he was having a heated argument with the stewardess from our plane. Apparently the crew stored the packs of butter and jam (which go with the hunks of bread and rubber chicken on flights of more than four hours' duration) up on the overhead compartments near the front of the aircraft. Karl had placed his overcoat there. On disembarking, he found it was smeared with strawberry jam which had worked loose from its container.

Ah well, at least it wasn't a corpse.

# 27

# Winter in the Summer Palace

*Pre-CIS republics, Sri Lanka, Maldives (1980–1)*

Despite the US immigration difficulties I still had to find a way of getting back to the USSR and China to keep up our business links . . . and to maximise my country count. It was clear that I had to achieve as much as possible in a couple of big journeys, rather than a series of little ones. Fortunately the Russians and the Chinese tended to hold their major travel trade conventions, or invite you for discussions, in the dead of winter. It was cheaper, and there were fewer paying tourists about, so rooms were available.

This in turn led me to the discovery that travel agents will take their personal trips in *any* kind of weather, and will go somewhere totally out of season, if only the price is right. So our wholesale division started publicising our Russian and Chinese trips by inviting agents on familiarisation trips . . . popularly known as 'fams', also in the winter, and sometimes timed to coincide with our business visits or trade show attendance.

All this rather turned the year upside down. You'd think at first that a travel company would be busiest in summer, or conversely that your best time for travelling some more and going to new countries, would be in summer. In our case we had most paying passengers actually travelling in autumn or spring. Few were families tied to school dates. Most were retired or financially independent, and specifically liked to avoid crowded peak times. In China and on the Silk Route it could be unbearably hot between

June and August. As word spread, more and more tourists opted for May and October, which soon became the months of peak demand for China.

Just about everywhere on our tours (we hadn't yet branched out into the southern hemisphere which would have solved that nicely) it was cold from November to March, and in some locations (Siberia, Peking) it was unbearably cold. So we put our heads together with Intourist and Luxingshe, the Chinese tourism body (through Philip's London office) and secured ground prices low enough to attract agents, then negotiated as many free or reduced rate tickets as we could with airlines, and offered a week in Russia or China starting at $399. Airfare, hotels, meals, sightseeing included!

Pan Am sponsored a series of road shows around the West Coast where we were given a table to exhibit our tours. They made forty tickets available from the West Coast to Hong Kong, from where we could enter China on CAAC, flag carrier of the People's Republic. Finnair co-operated with us to Moscow via Helsinki. Singapore Airlines and Korean Air helped with tickets for our own staff travel, but not for our large groups.

Usually arrangements like this depended on the airline's commercial relationship with you, in other words how good a customer you were of theirs, buying seats for your passengers at full prices. Sometimes it was a matter of serendipity, as with LOT Polish Airlines. They were a virtually unknown quantity in the West, since their only gateway was New York, and they were perceived as being limited to the ethnic market of returnees. Their US sales manager was doing a presentation in San Francisco. I asked him if he'd like to offer us a hundred or so free tickets to get acquainted. A week later he phoned me back to say he was very sorry . . . the best he could do was a ninety percent discount. Was that all right?

Putting this all together, I applied for, and got, two more 'paroles', one for the winter of 1980–81, one for the following year. All through the rest of the year, when my nose was to the grindstone in the business, designing and negotiating the tours, marketing and exhibiting around the US, holding the fort while my business partner or key staff were away, I had to plot very carefully indeed to make sure all necessary travel could be accomplished in one six- or seven-week period, since once I was back in, I knew I might not get out again for a long time.

In both cases I left in mid-November and returned mid-January to include Christmas in Ireland, business visits to Britain, and as many new places as other commitments allowed. Neither of the two normal approaches was open to me – either making the Russia journey across the Atlantic as a round trip, then flying separately to China across the Pacific and back (two separate exits from the US); or continuing in a straight line around the world, which involved bits in between not served by the airlines whose tickets I had; and in any event the dates for each portion of the trip didn't fall in straight line sequence. The hard bit was getting between Russia and China or vice versa, when fellow travellers returned the way they came, and I had to position myself to rendezvous with the next group, often a continent away.

On the face of it, there wasn't much direct opportunity to visit new countries. Yet ground was being broken. At China's first International Travel Trade Conference, the first ever non-governmental congress allowed to be held in the Great Hall of the People, I hosted eighty-six VIPs from the US and Europe.

'Mastermind' Magnus Magnusson was MC. I'd worked with him on *Good Morning Scotland*, and admired his cool precision. When you visited him at home in Torrance, outside Glasgow, you immediately sensed the reason he looked so confident about the answers to difficult questions. Instead of watching television, the whole family would be sprawled out on the floor doing crosswords and puzzles or playing Scrabble.

Daughter Sally, in her last year at Edinburgh University, came to a seminar I spoke at on careers in the media. I think she'd made up her mind before seeking my advice, though. By the time I left Scotland she was a budding wordsmith at the *Scotsman*, en route to morning television. Her book on that favourite son of Scotland, Eric Liddell, always reminded me of the view from my flat's window towards Arthur's Seat, which was captured in Puttnam's movie *Chariots of Fire*.

Magnus reminded me that I'd promised to contribute notes from China to an archaeological review he edited. It had slipped my mind. He chaired the conference with aplomb. There was some rather harsh criticism from hardened travel professionals about the difficulty of booking internal flights, the lack of choice, the control exercised by Luxingshe over what you could see, where you could go, and where you would stay. But such carping missed the point entirely. It was only a few short years since they'd been teaching the population to chant: 'Down with imperialism. Death to America.' To be sitting here even discussing tourism was nothing short of a miracle.

There was a new openness as never before on the part of the Chinese. SHENZHEN Special Economic Zone (whose population would have boomed from 20,000 to over a million by the time I visited) was still a gleam in the planner's eye. The joint venture with Cathay Pacific which would produce Dragon Air, visa-free flights to HAINAN ISLAND and myriad other new destinations I'd go to in future was still some way off. But change was in the air, and it was a privilege to be present during the birth pangs; it wouldn't be long before these contacts provided a way into TIBET, and smoothed the way for tours to NORTH KOREA, I reflected.

Each step forward came at a price. Marshalling the eighty-six guests onto a specially chartered Chinese Boeing 707 was relatively easy, until only eighty-five coupons were surrendered against eighty-six boarding passes. The Chinese kept the plane on the ground for two hours while everybody turned out their pockets until the missing flight coupon was found in the pocket of a travel magazine editor.

The Great Wall was to be done by train due to the icy conditions. The problem was that the bus from the hotel almost couldn't make it to the railway station. As their out-of-Peking visit, our particular group of delegates was assigned to Chengde, which so far as I could see, couldn't be pronounced without spitting – maybe to distinguish it from Chengdu in the warmer south.

Chengde was the site of the summer palace of the emperors, and rightly so. I wasn't surprised to find that no foreign tourists had ever visited it in winter before; and I certainly wouldn't be surprised to find that we were the last. I have never been so cold in my life. Except maybe on the Loop in Chicago, or for the bulk of the year in Edinburgh. But for a pleasure visit, a continent of travel away, Chengde takes the prize.

I remember it well for one other reason. In the corridor leading to our cold rooms a calligrapher practised his art at a small table. On our second afternoon there (Murphy's Law of Tourism: the least desirable places will always be allocated maximum time) I was about to pass this gentle artist when I noticed a crowd gathered around his table. They weren't admiring his art. Stretched out full length on the table was one of the oldest members of my group, the one whose wife told me he might not be able to go because of his hernia.

He'd tripped on the ice and broken one ankle, or possibly both. Due to an acute shortage of wheelchairs in that part of China, I ended up carrying him on my back for the remainder of the journey, until he was safely on board Pan Am in Hong Kong. There were no other mishaps even though, or perhaps because, we had the same guide as on the CKE. An amazing coincidence!

One of our guests was the South Korean owner of a San Francisco travel agency, Peter Jhun. To the Chinese who'd only encountered North Koreans before, he was a star turn. Especially when, feeling the cold in Chengde, he went to a department store to purchase long underwear. Perhaps because of scarcity of product, or maybe language problems, the pair he ended up with were quite definitely ladies' and a rather wild shade of mauve. He wore them anyway.

Peter may not have been able to make himself understood while speaking, but his written Mandarin, learned in school, was great. I vividly remember one taxi ride we took together where he and the driver continually scribbled notes to each other, back and forth until they understood each other without a word being said.

The Canton-Hong Kong flight was on an ageing and noisy British Trident. You could spot many examples of this former mainstay of BEA's European services fleet gradually rusting at the perimeter of various UK airports. Their only participation now in British commercial aviation was to act as practice for fire brigades.

This one was still alive and well, or at least still in flying condition. Peter and I were last to board, and were just about to head through the curtain dividing the galley area from the main cabin when the two young Chinese stewardesses grabbed us by the shoulders to prevent us going any further. 'What have I done now?' I thought involuntarily. 'You are from America?' they asked touchingly. 'Please teach us to dance.' So, for the short eighteen-minute hop, we promenaded and waltzed: 'Left, two three; right, two three; turn, two three,' between the door and the tea dispenser. Yes, China was changing, before our eyes.

Stopovers in SRI LANKA, where a lobster and steak dinner was

$4, and you were expected to hire your own personal policeman to guard your section of beach, at $2 for the whole day; and the MALDIVES, where you could find a whole island to yourself, revived flagging spirits, and set me up for the Russian part of the journey.

Strictly speaking, only the meetings in Moscow, and the fams I hosted in Leningrad were 'Russian'. I made full use of Intourist's offer to assist me in travelling anywhere within the USSR that was open, or potentially open, to tourism.

I liked sunny Baku, capital of AZERBAIJAN, but the statue to the twenty-six Baku commissars left me cold, and I wondered how long it would be before the effluent from the oil drilling in the Caspian Sea would kill off all the sturgeon, or seriously impair swimmers. I loved Tbilisi in GEORGIA, and could see at once that the people there considered themselves of very different stock from those in Moscow. If you checked the male population against a picture of Stalin, most would have resembled him. I spent a delightful evening and early morning in Sukumhi, now part of ABKHAZIA, enjoying the fresh breezes from the Black Sea. It would have been longer, but Intourist sent me to Domodedovo Airport instead of Vnukovo, so I missed my scheduled flight.

Lodging in the shadow of Mount Ararat, in Yerevan, ARMENIA's capital, I thought of the two expeditions mounted by my friend Mark Albrecht to find Noah's Ark. The second one almost succeeded, he said, if the area hadn't been so sensitive to NATO, the Turks (who weren't convinced of the value of the search, and from whom permission was necessary), and the Soviets (whose territory you might inadvertently find yourself on, not having warned them). I was sad that I didn't have time to get out to see Lake Sevan in the east, and Echmiadzin, the site of the ancient Armenian patriarchate.

There were a multitude of other territories with their own claim to self-determination within the boundaries of the one monolithic Soviet state. As I roamed through them it never occurred to me that the main fifteen recognised ones, never mind another score of autonomous areas, would in less than a decade break loose and proclaim their independence in varying degrees:

KARELIA (Petrosawodsk), the timber region forcibly annexed from Finland in 1940; TATARSTAN (Kazan), home to descendants of the Bolgar state conquered by Genghis Khan's Golden

Horde; NORTH OSETTIA, part of a proud, ancient civilisation calling itself 'the Iron people', outward looking and absorbed into Russia, while the southern half remained in the Gruzian empire; DAGESTAN, a mixture of several distinct agrarian peoples; MORDOVIA (Saramsk), a small nation suffering from having been dispersed throughout the entire USSR.

BASKORTOSTAN (Uda), a nation of cowherds who suddenly found themselves catapulted into the twentieth century; CHECHEN-INGUSETIA (Grodny), territory of the original inhabitants of North Caucasus, still closely tied to the soil; and TUVA (Kyzl), a land of Buddhist hunters and horse breeders, whose throat singing was world-renowned. Even CRIMEA would show separatist leanings from Ukraine, and enclaves like NAKICHEVAN and NAGORNO-KARABAKH would lead to bloodshed.

The three Baltic republics were so much easier to get to from Europe than the Asian ones. I'd been to Lithuania, and you could take a twenty-four cruise to ESTHONIA from Helsinki without a visa. Somehow, though, I missed Latvia, and it still remained a blank space on my country list. The port of Kaliningrad was a closed city, so you couldn't get on a train or plane bound for there without a special permit, but it was easy enough to hire a car and driver from the Hotel Lietuva in Vilnius and motor into the surrounding territory of what was the former EAST PRUSSIA.

All in all I felt fairly pleased with myself to have made the most of my opportunities of discovering countries within a country. Some observers scoffed, saying the USSR was one country. Yet the UN accorded a seat to Byelorussia, and there was a fairly general recognition that the Baltics and the Central Asian republics at least really had their own identities. In ten years, the political map would be redrawn out of all recognition. I'm glad I got there when I did.

# 28

# Reunited by Uncle Ho

*Vietnam, Pakistan, Latvia (1981–2)*

The following winter was more of the same – Russia and China, trade conferences and ram trips, more closed cities opening up, few new countries as such. But I did have a rare opportunity to revisit VIETNAM in the company of a returning boat person. She'd married an Australian and was bringing her husband to see her parents in Cholon for the first time since she fled on the high seas. In terms of counting countries it was a moot point whether I should consider it a new one. I'd been to the SOUTH VIETNAM of General Thieu, and North Viet Nam when it was fighting both the Thieu republic and the USA in 1975, although my stay there was briefer than I'd planned. This was the new post-war united Viet Nam, but very definitely under the control of Hanoi. Would the differences between south and north still be apparent?

I carefully planned my route to get maximum value from my LOT Polish ninety percent discount tickets. I had a concertina of them, since Warsaw had to be included almost no matter where you were going. The itinerary read something like:

| | |
|---|---|
| New York-London | (via Warsaw) |
| London-Moscow | (via Warsaw) |
| Moscow-London | (via Warsaw) |
| London-Damascus | (via Warsaw) |
| Damascus-Bangkok | (via Dubai) |
| Bangkok-New York | (via Warsaw) |

From Moscow the Aeroflot internal flights were arranged by Intourist. From Bangkok Singapore Airlines took me to Hong Kong, thence by CAAC to China. On arriving back into Bangkok the former Thai policeman who arranged my Vietnam visit met me with my documentation and put me on the weekly Air France 747 that went into Saigon virtually empty of passengers. The nine of us were all asked to sit in the front four rows.

It was eerie looking back from first class to find forty rows of economy seating completely empty. Even more eerie to land at Tan Son Nhut and taxi past what seemed like a colossal junk yard of every imaginable type of military plane, interspersed with vast empty hangars. This was where it took a full hour to get airborne amongst the ceaseless air traffic when I flew to Cambodia in 1975. Clearly somebody had left in a hurry.

My fellow passengers were a mixed lot – no Americans of course. It would be eleven years before the US would lift the travel restrictions imposed on its own people. The others were all interested in trade: a man from Belfast whose company had a contract to build a new power plant; three Japanese who had no contract, but were coming speculatively to try their luck at getting orders: their suitcases appeared to be full of various kinds of samples. (Judging by the Hondas and Suzukis already about, the commercial prizes went to the swift and aggressive, so they stood a good chance. Everywhere I went I bumped into them, offering their wares like dirty postcards from an overcoat to any passer-by who could be importuned), two French businessmen; May-Lai the boat person; and Peter, the Aussie.

The Air France 747, only Western aircraft of the week, didn't leave empty. It was packed to the gunwales with Orderly Departure Programme migrants, the waiting list for which stretched for years into the future. You saw the huge snaking line as soon as you emerged, waiting for this week's remittances and parcels from the outside world, but single file and orderly, in a communist-imposed sort of way. You knew the lines were bigger outside the office downtown which processed the emigration requests.

At first glance, Saigon in its new incarnation as Ho Chi Minh City hadn't changed much. There were still tea dances at the hotels, you could obtain absolutely anything on the black market; there were even 'ladies of the night' cruising the main streets. If the Americans were responsible for all the country's evil, then it had certainly proved enduring when they left.

The central hotels, the Rex, Continental, Majestic, Caravelle, were open for business, as they had been for the afternoon US military briefings ('five o'clock follies'), and Graham Greene's 'Quiet American'. The baguettes and café au lait surpassed anything else east of the Seine. The inhabitants seemed to always be on the move: pedal rickshaw ('cyclo') operators, vendors hawking wares as they strolled along pavements, demure schoolgirls in white *ao dais* cycling home as if a movement in a symphony.

But the pulse was muted, quiet even. This was no longer the free-wheeling, swashbuckling mercantile Asian country, with a market, for all sorts of goods and services, of tens of thousands of GIs. Gone was the noisy pollution of army trucks and jeeps. Economic decline had set in. Disastrous agricultural collectivisation, and the brain drain, whether by migration or through re-education camps, had taken a toll.

The former middle class hacked out the best living they could, thankful not to be incarcerated. Anybody associated with Americans or the pre-1975 regime kept their heads very low. Amerasian children survived selling trinkets on the streets. Worse, there was a palpable air of fear and distrust. The barman in the hotel always abruptly broke off conversation with me if someone new entered. Shopkeepers looked over their shoulders, conscious of being watched.

It was hard to determine if tourism was on offer, or an 'in your face' brand of history lesson. There was the Museum of American War Crimes, provocatively housed in the former US Information Building, documenting the My Lai massacre and other atrocities. Captured B52s and the detritus of war were cockily displayed the way old aeroplanes used to be sited in children's playgrounds. Each orphanage I was taken to was a set piece in the universal story of the bad Americans, in this case the ones who killed daddy and mummy.

Then there was Cuu Chi, about twenty miles out of town, the underground network of burrows where the pint-sized Vietcong plotted, ate, slept, and hid during the conflict. I suppose I was lucky to get a preview of this potential big draw, a decade before 'real' tourists. As it was I gave my hosts the wrong advice altogether. 'Stop focusing on the war,' I said, almost in exasperation. 'People have had enough. Show them something different.'

The tunnels have in fact been so successful since being opened to foreigners, I wouldn't be surprised to see a sanitised version crop up in a theme park soon. These, of course, were the real McCoy. The only mistake the Vietnamese tourist authorities made was sticking with the original dimensions. It wasn't long before the tunnels had to be widened to allow for the bigger bulk of Westerners.

May-Lai invited me to visit her family. They told me matter-of-factly about the confiscation of their factory by the communists. Being pragmatic Chinese, they were able to work out some sort of arrangement to keep on running it as managers, not owners. Others suffered more harshly. One evening I met a former Associated Press stringer. In the shambles of the helicopter evacuation on 30th April 1975 from the US Embassy roof (since turned into administrative offices for the state petrochemical company) he'd been left behind. He showed no traces of bitterness, just resignation. Both his sons were in prison. He asked to be remembered to his former American colleagues.

Each person deals with reversals of fortune in their own way. Amongst the most intriguing people I met in this visit to the vanquished south was Madame Dai, the former Deputy Speaker in the National Assembly. What accommodation she had to go through with the new leaders may never be known, but she managed to turn the library of her former law office into an excellent restaurant, certainly the best in Saigon at the time.

My main aim in accepting the invitation to Saigon had been to make contact with tourism officials in the north. This had not been possible before. Although it was slightly premature, I wanted to talk to them about future tourism from the US. I put in a request for a meeting as soon as I arrived. I must have kept my nose clean because a day before my scheduled departure on Air France, with 376 migrants, I received word to attend at the immigration office where a visa for Hanoi would be waiting.

It took a full day to exchange the Saigon-Bangkok ticket, and two days to fly up north. One of those days was spent entirely at the airport . . . waiting. Hang Kong Vietnam, as the national airline styled itself, seemed to rely for jets on one rather untrustworthy Tupolev 134. I thought one jet flight three days a week between the capital and the city that accounted for almost half the country's external trade was a rather inadequate frequency. Perhaps the off days gave them a chance to catch up with maintenance.

Eventually it was clear that there would be no transport by air between the two principal cities of Vietnam, even if it was officially an 'on' day. It turned out to be a bonus, from several points of view. First, the next day's replacement was an Antonov 24, with a high wing structure that allowed much better views of the ground; it also flew lower. Because its range was less, it couldn't make the journey in one hop, so I had an unexpected stopover in Danang thrown in, with a glimpse of stately Hue. Best of all, had I been on the jet, I would have landed at the newly constructed airport in Hanoi. As it was the Antonov put down at exactly the same spot where I'd last tried to see Hanoi, and been sent packing back on my Chinese llyushin 18 to Nanning. I'd come full circle.

This time the welcome mat was out. The director of tourism and three of his colleagues were to meet me the following day. Meantime they'd put a car at my disposal to see around. (I got the bill for the car before I left.) The hotel, the Thang Loi, was draughty and offered few amenities. It was a sort of concrete-on-stilts attempt to copy all that was wrong with 1960s high-rise council flats in Glasgow. The only Hilton in town was the notorious Hoa Lo prison.

But everything that was lacking in convenience was more than made up for in experience and atmosphere. My principal guide was a young, happy-go-lucky type who never managed to be quite clean-shaven. Outside the official programme I most enjoyed outings such as a visit to the circus with him and some of his friends. Their uninhibited enjoyment of the clowning took me aback. I suppose I'd expected a stern people, dedicated to imposing their vision of society on their wayward southern compatriots. I remember their laughter rippling through the pitch-black night when the performance was over.

The meeting with Hanoi's top tourism officials turned out to be a minor banquet, with me as the guest of honour, and food that I compared unfavourably with the fried rat and live snails I'd had once in the jungle. They must have been used to catering for French tastes! Since it was (absurdly) a criminal act under American law to promote travel to Vietnam, a good deal of our discussions were taken up with how long this state of affairs would last, and how it could be circumvented. The Americans had a 'Trading with the Enemy' act. I hope they didn't have a 'Talking to the Enemy' one as well!

It was not unlike the situation with China a few years before. The Chinese wouldn't refuse to give a visa to an American, but he had to be in a group of another nationality. That's why the first 'American' tours to China in the 1970s were actually our British ones, and Lars Eric Lindblad's Swedish ones. We correctly sensed that this was the thin end of the wedge, and soon were able to operate groups consisting entirely of Americans. Lindblad wasn't so lucky with Vietnam. When he operated tours there in defiance of the ban, the government succeeded in shutting down his company.

My own discussions with the Vietnam tourist authorities produced no definitive agreements, but a door had been opened. I could see my company offering tours to Vietnam, but even if there were no 'Trading with the Enemy' act I couldn't see Americans rushing to buy them yet. There were always a few adventurous ones, but on the whole they fairly slavishly followed mass trends. You had to be in early, as we were with China; but not too early. When I returned from Vietnam I talked to many influential people about my trip, but I got the clear sense that the scars were too recent. The wound would need time to heal.

When the travel ban was eventually lifted, a decade later, it was amusing to see the spate of articles appearing from travellers claiming to be 'the first' into Vietnam. What they meant was first to buy an American package run legally by an American company. And if it was a cruise ship to sanitise the experience a little, so much the better!

Sunday was church day for me, but the government had other plans. They sent a car to interrupt the church service and ferry me to a private tour of the Ho Chi Minh mausoleum. I don't know if they were making a statement about Church–state relations or not. I knew the likelihood of Western visitors to the Protestant church in Hanoi would have been remote for some time. There had been talk of wholesale arrests, and a great deal of harassment. I wanted to interview the pastor privately. I had done that in the south, and talked to the enthusiastic worshippers in the Catholic Cathedral in Saigon. Here, clearly, it was going to be more difficult.

In the end we reached a compromise, which wasn't entirely satisfying, but the best that could be achieved at that time, in that place, given the communist paranoia about controlling foreigners and their interaction with sensitive locals. The guide picked up four friends – two more than at the circus. The number grew each time.

There was a shortage of cars, never mind petrol, so when a foreign tourist was picking up the bill (they charged per car, not per person) it seemed logical to make maximum use of the space.

The six of us piled into the front row at church. 'To translate for you,' he said, but once I saw the passage in the Bible it was easier for me to recollect the English equivalent than it was for a Marxist indoctrinated atheist to attempt to get his mouth round some of the unfamiliar phrases and concepts in a foreign language. I had the impression that the pastor, after observing our unseemly entrance, altered his sermon somewhat to an evangelistic address more suitable for my five companions as not being part of his normal congregation.

Halfway through I was given the unmistakable nudge that time was up, and we'd have to leave. Although I'd no chance to speak personally to any of the congregation, I fervently hoped that maybe just being there said something to the faithful, whose lot could not have been easy. I was summoned by the secular power from the seat of heavenly religion to the earthly shrine they had erected in their own image.

I am not easily impressed by glass sarcophagi, and Uncle Ho, propped in his last resting place, was no exception. What was impressive was the panoply surrounding it. I was the only living soul crossing an expanse the size of Red Square or Tiananmen, guards posted at each corner, the timing of my entry and exit planned and synchronised by the guide in consultation with militia at the entrance.

There was one guard, stiffly at attention, but no warden, no ticket collectors, nothing tacky. And his modest house close by: the two rooms inside which the orders were drafted which led to the deaths of more than 50,000 American soldiers, perhaps ten times as many Vietnamese, and a tenth of the entire civilian population. 'Oh Lord, let there be peace on earth. And let it begin with me!'

Before I left I had a chance to see what is perhaps one of the truly great sights anywhere in the world. Ha Long Bay can literally be described as a karst formation: a panorama of 3,000 limestone islands pushed up from the sea bed underneath. Figuratively, the thrashing of a dragon's tail gouged out valleys and troughs, which filled with turquoise water.

Each island, each rock, had a different shape: the stakes which sank Kublai Khan's ships, the fisherman's daughter, the bear.

When you began your effortless glide past in a silent sampan, and fixed your gaze on these incredible formations in the beautiful misty light, it was difficult not to surrender, just for a magic moment, to their charm, and believe them real. I had not expected, amidst the scene of the biggest visitation of wrath in my lifetime, to experience such an idyll of tranquility.

Route 5, the main highway between Hanoi and Haiphong, was something else. Two lanes at best, jammed with traffic, the sixty-seven miles took three and a half hours. We had to wait our turn on the one-way river bridge crossings. The numerous potholes spoke volumes about how badly the war had damaged the country's infrastructure. It was a bone-jarring journey. Everywhere I got out to stretch my legs children giggled and pointed: 'Lien-Xo. Lien-Xo!' The only foreigners they'd seen were Russians, so I had to learn to say in Vietnamese: 'I am not Russian.'

I'm told Vietnam has made big strides in developing its tourism since I made my trips there in 1975 and 1981. Undoubtedly Vung Tau will become a beach complex for foreign tourists. When I spent the weekend there, it had retained its function as a rest and recreation base for off-duty Russians from Cam Ran Bay.

It was a beautiful seaside setting, but there was not a thing to do at nights. We rooted around to see what politically apt videos the Russians had in their recreation room. The Vietnamese guide settled on *Raid on Entebbe*, and together, Irish, Australian, returned boat person from the south, and servant of the new northern order, we watched as Idi Amin was outsmarted by the Israelis. Now where did they get the video from?

Somebody also told me they now have a visitor's book at Cuu Chi. Predictably some wag wrote as one of the first entries: 'Hi. We're back,' signing himself simply 'USA'.

I hope this invasion of Americans is kinder to Vietnam than the last one.

Predictably, no Tupolev was waiting to ferry me out of the newly reconstructed Vietnam, and the Laotian airline was no more efficient than ten years back when I'd waited and waited for the DC3 at Ban Houei Sai. But a Thai Domestic plane via Vientianne came to my rescue, and I got to Bangkok in time to spend Christmas checking in on the admirable social work Andrew Way and colleagues at OMF, whom I'd met in 1970, were doing with Cambodian refugees who swamped the camps on the border.

I also arrived to the shocking news of martial law in Poland, the suppression of Solidarity, and the grim Moscow-inspired *diktats* of Jaruzelski, the general with sunglasses. Just when the tide seemed to be swinging in favour of liberalisation. Would the tiger never change his stripes? I had two other immediate causes for concern. I'd left a hundred hardback guidebooks I'd just purchased as gifts for our clients in Warsaw at my transit stop: and LOT was grounded. My tickets exclusively on Polish Airlines from Bangkok to Bombay, Dubai, Damascus, London and onward to New York were now worthless pieces of paper.

Ironically, Aeroflot was the only carrier which would honour them, but only when I upgraded my payment to the (for Aeroflot) then standard discount of fifty percent. Half off full fare, but a fivefold increase for me. I flew via Myanmar into Dakha, capital of BANGLADESH, for a night stop, before connecting on the curiously named Bangladesh Biman into Calcutta whence Aeroflot was going to wing me overnight to Moscow (as if I hadn't spent enough time there lately), then, after two hours at Sheremetyevo, non-stop to London. Or so I thought.

There was a curiously recognisable appearance to the cluster of passengers hanging around the check-in desk at Dum Dum Airport (why are the names of foreign airfields always so impossibly lyrical, exotic, ponderous, or downright silly?) for the weekly flight to Russia. Starting with UAA via Egypt to East Asia, continuing with numerous student charters, branching out to Laker's backpackers, and the rump of Virgin's passengers when you take away upper and mid classes; later Capital and People Express in the US, and an infinite number of second and third world carriers – I'd seen, and would see again and again, those faces.

These were the people who scanned the bucket shop ads in the *Evening Standard*, or the *New York Times*, and bought the cheapest priced air ticket. It didn't matter if there were fifteen stops en route. It didn't matter if there was only one flight every other week. It didn't matter if the plane wouldn't have passed CAA or FAA tests.

And the reason I so often found myself in their company was certainly not just that my purpose was to visit or transit these inconvenient midway stops. More a growing feeling that real travellers usually don't fly business class, hermetically sealed off from the serendipitous, and sometimes alarming, world around them that they purportedly are going to see. The other reason was that, even with just fifty percent off, you could go to twice as many places.

I don't think a single passenger was bound for Moscow. Two-thirds were Indians and Bengalis, the rest preponderantly British. All but a few were headed to the UK. As the night wore on, and the delay on the incoming aircraft extended to five hours, I began to wonder what would happen to our London connection. What I should have reflected on, but didn't, was that it was 90° and steaming in India, -4° and freezing in Russia.

Just as the Tupolev 154 eventually landed and we began to be hustled through to the departure lounge, we were joined by one extra passenger. He was the ultimate hippy, come to find himself in the East. Somehow his search had not been entirely fruitful, for he now stood handcuffed to a plainclothes officer, presumably about to be deported. Unkindly I hoped he wouldn't be assigned a seat next to mine.

He wasn't. He got the seat in front. I wondered if they were planning to keep the cuffs on for the whole flight, but the officer released him as soon as the engines warmed up, and left. First stop, strangely, was Karachi, PAKISTAN. It was appallingly bad luck for the Hindus on board – the majority – especially if they were hungry. The catering for the next leg of the flight was done by PIA. They only offered beef. Sixty-eight uneaten dinners were sent back in their foil trays. Tashkent was the next refuelling point.

It was there that the trouble started. The hippy vanished. I'd encountered in my years of travelling in the communist bloc many cases of defections out of the USSR or its allies. This was my first experience of a reverse case. I have to admit I did discover that he wasn't in his seat in front of me when we reboarded, but the knowledge didn't trouble me. 'Maybe he's moved seat,' I thought. Anyway, a unique feature about Tupolev 154 seats is that they can be folded down fully when unoccupied, allowing tall passengers like me to stretch their legs. Perhaps they should have kept him handcuffed to the seat.

Clearly I wasn't the only one to notice, for a major alert began. Why these things are always fated to take place at 3 a.m. I'll never figure out. It took another two hours for everyone to troop off, identify their luggage, and wait for the all-clear to reboard. There was now no chance of making the London flight.

I was asleep when the announcement of our imminent landing was piped through the cabin. I cocked one bleary eye open and peered through the oval window at the snowy runway we were about to set down on. Comatose as I was, I knew this wasn't Sheremetyevo. In fact it was Riga, capital of LATVIA, the one Baltic state I'd missed visiting. Moscow was snowed in. The pilots had diverted. They went off to a hotel to sleep. We were unceremoniously stranded in the departure lounge (no visas, no rooms) for the rest of the day. Technically our aircraft was impounded with its cargo (us) only intending to transit the USSR. We were there, but weren't supposed to be.

It's a good thing they worked out some rescue plan whereby we got up to Moscow by nightfall. The food in the buffet had run out, and there were fist fights when new limited supplies were brought out to feed us, but there wasn't enough to go round. We were totally in the hands of an airline which was not known by any such slogan as: 'We care for you'.

Moscow, which had at first seemed our salvation, now turned into the next nightmare. We weren't the only ones to be trapped by the weather, so the transit lounge was full of passengers sleeping on the floor. This unequivocally meant the few rooms in the transit hotel were already full. In those days unless you had an advance visa, they wouldn't let you proceed into town even to sleep for the night.

After a night on the hard floor, and no change in the weather, the transit hotel began to sound good. It took a full day's lobbying, complicated permissions and luggage retrieval and searching, but about a dozen of us made it to the hotel, only to be told once inside, as I suspected, that no rooms were free. We joined other hopefuls on the lobby couches.

Sensing no comfort here, I decided to return to the airport, and at least be nearer to the action, in case of any early break in the weather. That's when I received a rude shock. A busload of passengers was being boarded at the entrance to the hotel. I decided to join them. A security guard was calling out names, checking people off against his list.

He was emphatic that if I was not on his list, I couldn't go. He pointed to other hopefuls, milling around reception. No English was spoken, but I could decipher the Cyrillic letters on his clip-board. To my horror I saw that they were instituting their version of an 'Orderly Departure Programme'. Passengers were allowed out of the hotel strictly according to the day they arrived, or how long they'd been stuck. His list covered four days ago.

I waited until the bus door was closing, then made a run for it; I squeezed through the door with seconds to spare. It felt like escaping from prison. At the airport I toured all departure gates, asking to be put down on every standby list. I wanted to be on the first plane out. It was to Brussels, from where a properly filled out FIM (flight interrupt manifest) gained us seats on Sabena for the last leg to London. When we landed in Belgium the entire cabin cheered. We felt as if we'd been through the wars . . . but it was just a scheduled flight in wintry conditions, on an airline that limited your choices. It's often true that you get what you pay for!

It was time to take stock, for me and the world. Solidarity would rise again, but it didn't look like it then. Latvia, where I'd just been in enforced bond, would go through a bloody struggle, along with the other Baltic nations, before gaining its freedom. A day would come when I'd sit across a table in Zurich with one of their Central Bankers, in his thirties, with a Wharton MBA Finance degree, discussing the upcoming flotation of their privatised airline on the US stockmarket.

There would be bloodletting and splintering apart in the former Soviet Union and Yugoslavia. The number of new and emerging 'countries' would exponentially increase. The iron grip of commun-ism would loosen. Petty dictators would stumble. Others would rise in their place. Some newly independent nations would find that freedom held just as many terrors, maybe more; and the old safety nets of lifetime employment, cheap housing and subsidised food, were gone for ever.

Aeroflot and CAAC would break apart into dozens of different carriers, with safety even more questionable than before. Whole carriers like Interflug, and countries (East Germany) would dis-appear. World change at a dizzying pace lay ahead. There was no way of foreseeing that, of course. The West was about to embark on its own freewheeling decade of expansionism, debt financing, and living like there was no tomorrow, incipient graduates devoting more attention to acquiring a well-paid job than satisfying wander-lust curiosity around the world.

I reflected that I'd been privileged to see a great deal of the old order, at first hand, before it changed radically. Back in California I was a frequent speaker at Rotary Clubs, schools, churches, banquets and trade shows. I told everybody, especially the young: 'Go while you have the chance. As soon as you're married, mortgaged and committed to responsibilities it'll be harder. Nothing wrong with those commitments; just that the younger you are, the fewer preconceptions, the more openness you can potentially bring to travel overseas. And you might encounter people and situations which will change your life, and the way you look at things, for ever.'

My personal situation was about to change radically in three ways. First, my ability to travel. 'No more paroles,' said Alan Klein, my Jewish immigration lawyer, whose sole English-speaking client I was. 'You've had too many already. You'll just have to suffer in paradise for a while.' Three years of venturing no further than Hawaii lay ahead.

Second, the calculation of how far along I was in my personal race to get to every territory in the world. A brochure landed on my desk, advertising the Travelers' Century Club of California, to join which you had to have been to a hundred countries. Their definition of 'country' was quite broad, though in the light of what later happened to Yugoslavia and the USSR, not unreasonable. Still, they didn't count some of the places I'd been to, and counted others I never thought of as countries.

They came up with a total of 308. At 150 you reached silver status, 200 gold. I was apparently qualified not only to come straight in as a gold member, but, with 221 from their list, to be included in the top ten travellers of all time, according to the wife of the club's founder, Mrs Roe Davidson. I must have been the only person who joined, *not* expecting to be able to add to his total in the foreseeable future.

The third change was marriage. And it came about in a highly unusual way.

# 29

# Penal Colonies to Ice Caps

*Galapagos, Islands of Oz, Greenland, Faroes (1985)*

Processing visa applications is a very boring job, even at the best of times. When it's August 1983 and your staff are all vacationing while you're barely halfway through your self-imposed stay-put sentence (like being under house arrest, only the house is the USA) it's pretty terrible. One of the consolations is that you get to laugh at the solemn poses people strike in the passport pictures they submit.

After being used to sixty, seventy, and eighty year olds, you also notice immediately three young women in their twenties. 'Whoa,' I thought to myself. 'This is unusual.' I dialled our tour leader, Charlie Spicer, in Greenwood, Indiana, to get more details. Charlie was leading his seventh or eighth tour for us: Korean Airlines to Hong Kong via Seoul, train through China and Mongolia to Siberia, Aeroflot to Moscow, then back to the US via London.

Charlie and I went back a long way. I first met him in the late 1970s when the Wesleyan Methodists had asked him to 'take some things in for the church in China'. 'What's in the suitcases?' I asked as casually as I could, when I saw him tagging eight cases for Shanghai. 'Stained glass windows,' he replied, with not a hint of sarcasm. I signed him up immediately to lead our numerous church groups who didn't want the Holy Land trips we had, but did want the China trips it was very hard to get. Anybody who could collapse and transport church infrastructure on CAAC could surely cope with the rigours of early-days China tourism.

His first job for us, five years back, even before I boarded the Central Kingdom Express, was a baptism of fire. Relations with China were very delicate. One slip-up might have caused irreparable damage to tourism prospects. Due either to bungling or the control factor, or both, three groups were combined into one, a church group of ours, an interline group of airline employees at reduced rates, and a general purpose group.

Each had been promised exclusivity for their group, a concept the Chinese were not very big on at the time. Each group had its own designated leader, plus the person who recruited most of the group filled that role for some passengers. So when you added all the Chinese guides, it wasn't exactly clear at times who was giving the orders.

The general group objected to the hymn singing in the back of the coach. The Christians objected to the smoking of the interliners. The interliners objected to everything. Everybody except the interliners objected to them paying less but taking up seats on their full-price bus. The leaders fought over jurisdiction. The Chinese were bemused.

Amazingly, it worked out well in the end. The interliners and their leader gave a donation to missionary work. The Christians got their own bus next time. The general-interests enjoyed the tour. And Charlie kept the peace with an elaborately devised code. The one bit I remember was 'Bible (bread of life) = bread'. So everybody in his sub-group went around saying: 'Did you bring the bread?' or 'I have two loaves with me and one back in the hotel.'

I reminded Charlie of these incidents from the early days, and he laughed. He'd been an insurance salesman, and was now development director of an educational trust for Asian nationals in situ, later broadened to the whole third world. Without him it was highly unlikely that in as huge a country as America our California company would have recruited so many Midwest participants for our tours.

He explained that one of the local businessmen who'd signed up couldn't now go. He was transferring his place to his daughter, Shelly, and she was bringing two friends. 'You'd like Shelly,' he said mischievously. Charlie's wife Phyllis, who was going along on the tour, determined to play matchmaker.

Thanks to Uncle Sam I couldn't go on the tour myself. But I did make sure I talked to Shelly on the phone to confirm her booking, and suggest she and her friends come out earlier, in case they'd like to be shown around Los Angeles before departure for the Orient. She responded by changing her flight to a *later* one, only just giving enough time for the connection, and barely enough time for me to make an impression as I checked them in. Clearly she'd be a tough nut to crack.

But the combined resources of Charlie, Phyllis and Luxingshe (who baked a cake for her birthday in Peking) at least broke the ice. Charlie saw to it that she was in his room when I telephoned, so that I could chat to her. Eventually she agreed that I could come and see her slides a couple of weeks after she returned. Then, after a hectic long-distance courtship (mostly using passes on now defunct Republic Airlines) we were married the following summer.

Apart from having my future wife as a participant, the tour itself was noteworthy because the destination was Russia via China, and Korean Airlines was the main carrier. It departed three days after the Soviets shot down KE007 over Sakhalin. We had not a single cancellation, but I remember doing a lot of reassuring to prospective travellers over the telephone.

The West's reaction against the Soviets – initiating a boycott of Russia by ninety-five percent of the foreign airlines serving Moscow – threatened to inflame things. How would we get them out of the USSR? It was more luck than judgment (and more parsimoniousness than luck) that saved us. British Airways, KLM, Lufthansa, Swissair, all suspended service. Most other airlines did as well. Unusually, we'd selected Air India's Moscow-Birmingham flight, mainly because the price was so advantageous.

Air India of course had no real reason to be flying that route. They just happened to have reciprocal rights with Aeroflot for Delhi-Moscow, added an Amritsar-Delhi semi-domestic sector, and so were able to carry Punjabis on a through service to the English Midlands to top up the otherwise thin traffic on the purely Moscow leg.

I telephoned Air India's operations centre every day, and they reassured me they were operating as normal, despite the boycott. Then on the eve of the flight I got a surprise telex: 'Re Moscow-Birmingham. Regret to inform you tomorrow's flight cancelled. This is not, repeat not, connected in any way to the boycott. Due to the boycott regret we are unable to protect you on any other carrier.'

It was cold comfort to know the hiccup wasn't because of the same reason no other airline was flying. The problem was real. In a case like this the special tour tickets as issued would have limited transferability to any other airline. Also, about the only other airlines flying out of Moscow were the East bloc carriers, who would take advantage of the open market in the West to sell you a return ticket from London to Moscow for, say, £80, but would use the capitalist-gouging tariff so beloved of communists to quote £300 for a one-way ticket originating in Moscow.

I needn't have worried. Air France accepted the Air India tickets and brought our group back via Paris. It seems the 'perfidious frogs' may have all along been quietly breaking the boycott.

The romance took place in a whirlwind: it had to because of the cost of flying to see each other. Since our company's business was largely international, I didn't qualify for any discounts on domestic tickets. After we were engaged, Shelly came to visit me on alternate weekends. She put these tickets on her credit card, not mine. However, she didn't pay them off until after the marriage, using funds from our joint account. I suppose that was fair!

Also of whirlwind proportions was the international travel I launched on when my green card was ultimately issued. There were two reasons. First, China and Russia were finally peaking for us as primary products. We had pioneered there, but now that access was easier, new travel companies were popping out of the woodwork every day with cheaper tours. China travel packages no longer had quite the rarity value of six years before, and while I applauded the opening up that allowed many more people to experience the country, it also meant less business was funnelled through us. In addition, former passengers told us they wanted to travel with us again – could we put together tours to other exotic places?

The other reason? I was determined to make up for lost time in my personal race to reach *every* country on earth. The Travelers' Century Club (TCC) list gave a form and focus to my plans. There's no doubt it was arbitrary in its way, but so were those of the *Statesman's Year Book*, *Guinness Book of Records* (who changed their methodology every few years), *Guinness Book of Answers*, American Radio Relay League, Club International des Grands Voyageurs, US State Department's *Status of The World's Nations*, and probably of everybody else who kept lists too. Even the United

Nations, while including St Kitts, left out Taiwan, Yugoslavia, and Switzerland.

According to the TCC list, I had eighty-six of their entries still to go. Their numbers changed each year, as entities were added or deleted. Nobody had yet been to all of them. With most of today's independent countries being post-war creations, this meant that probably nobody on earth had been to every single territory which now existed. I got out a map and plotted. To thoroughly research destinations for inclusion in the glossy brochure my company, Voyages of Discovery, was planning next year would mean extensive travel. While I was at it, I decided to add a few side trips, and see how many new places I could get to.

My diary records that in three periods (April-August 1985; December-January 1985–6; May-November 1986) totalling fourteen months, I made eleven lengthy overseas trips – average duration 26.3 days. I covered over a quarter of a million air miles, plus lots of surface ones. Nothing remarkable, of course, to a modern travelling executive, in terms of sheer mileage, or nights on the road. But I did cross 342 borders in that time, many of them requiring considerable advance planning and paperwork, others a degree of finesse, especially if unanticipated or last-minute decisions. And the travel was not all, by any means, in the comfort zone.

Re-reading extracts from my diary of the time leaves me slightly breathless, even today. I see that on a fam in April 1985 we 'lost' two travel agents holding Yugoslav passports on the Hussein/Allenby bridge crossing from Jordan to ISRAEL, when Israeli immigration turned them back across no man's land. We got them back five days later! GAZA, the WEST BANK, and GOLAN counted as three more territories for the Guinness book, but not TCC.

In May, a five-day cruise to the GALAPAGOS not only counted as a new destination for my country count; it also later became very popular with our company's passengers. I noted the differences between travelling as a bachelor, and having a wife with you. Women seemed more forthcoming! On the first day a female Swedish passenger stripped to the buff in front of us. Next day a young New Yorker slipped on deck, landing on her backside. Shelly asked her later that afternoon how she was. Quite unabashed, she pulled down her shorts, and said: 'Would you like to see my bruise?'

It was the captain's last cruise. Imagine the purser's surprise when he opened the safe deposit boxes on the last day to find all the passengers' stored valuables had gone missing . . . after the skipper had left! Maybe Ecuadorean standard rates of pay were too low, and you had to be creative about tips! Oh yes, I almost forgot . . . it was also enchanting to wade ashore amongst elephant seals, play 'race the giant tortoise' when you always won, and observe a red-footed booby nest a few inches from your camera. Equal, in wildlife terms, to Aldabra, South Georgia, and the sub-Antarctic islands in general.

June saw me joining a group of travel executives on an official government-paid six-week tour of Australia. This came about because the Aussies felt we were giving too much weight to New Zealand in our proposed brochure, and wanted to prove how superior they were. The timing coincided with their attempt to put Australia on the world tourism map in a big way by a massive – and highly successful – advertising campaign in America and Europe.

Short of a personal invitation to 'throw another shrimp on the barbie' by Paul (Crocodile Dundee) Hogan himself, everything was done to make us feel like VIPs: flights on Ansett or TAA to Darwin, Alice Springs, Ayers Rock, the Barrier Reef; a charter flight to the delightful parade of hundreds of tiny penguins up the beach at Philip Island, south of Melbourne; private viewing of the America's Cup in Fremantle; and of course the chance to cuddle a koala in Brisbane, and hope it had heeded nature's call before it was your turn.

It was a well organised programme, with only a hint of the chip on the shoulder that sometimes creeps into Australia's relationship with the rest of the world: the new boy on the block wanting respect; the adolescent yearning to be treated as an adult; the former dominion craving equality. 'If I call you a pommie bastard,' one of our hosts explained to me, 'I don't mean anything bad by it. We call everybody bastards, and all poms are pommie bastards. But if I wanted to say something bad about you, I'd call you a real pommie bastard.'

That kind of linguistic nicety gave you a clue that another language was involved here. The man due to drive us to Captain Cook's museum in far north Queensland was feeding his 'chucks' (chickens) when he saw our plane overhead, and made a scramble for the runway. I knew that 'physios' worked in hospitals, but didn't fathom at first that 'journos' wrote for newspapers.

Frankness was a national art, closely followed by crudity. The television news reported a couple of grisly killings. The correspondent repeatedly stepped over the bodies as he delivered his live report, and at one stage got one of them tangled up in his microphone cable.

We had some trouble selling Australia as a destination to certain Americans who felt it was not exotic enough – sort of like a fifty-first state. But they were used to our very off-the-beaten-path destinations, and it wasn't a fair comparison. It worked the other way, too. Vince, who travelled on the Central Kingdom with us, picked Australia the following year. 'What a relief after China,' he said. 'Everything worked. Nothing was a hassle. It was too easy, and too good to be true.'

From a country-count point of view, Australia was excellent. The Qantas transpacific flights gave the chance to stop at Tahiti, for a side trip to the MARQUESAS. The rim of Australia itself provided opportunities for trips to the CORAL SEA ISLANDS, TASMANIA, and, courtesy of the Department of Territories 3,365 mile round trip monthly call, COCOS ISLAND. This was the coconut-palm lined former private fiefdom of one family, the Clunies-Ross. A few hundred Malays now worked the copra there. Once the long distance piston-engined DC6s were retired from service, Cocos was no longer needed as a colourful refuelling point.

The first of my two CHRISTMAS ISLANDS, the Indian Ocean volcanic phosphate-mining one, a mere 190 miles south of Java, was a stopover on the way back to Perth. I picked up my permit to enter these two territories in George Street in the afternoon, took off shortly after midnight, landed in darkness at Cocos, and had about two hours in the eerie half light of dawn at Christmas, arriving back in Perth about 11 a.m.

Probably my favourite territory in that part of the world, and maybe anywhere, was five miles long by three miles wide NORFOLK ISLAND, 700 miles northwest of Auckland. Peaceful. Scenic. Shady lanes, little stone cottages and gardens. England in the Pacific (maybe Scotland rather?). With one big exception – the beautiful balmy Pacific clime. Towering basalt cliffs. Flowering frangipani, fragrant bougainvillea, tropical fruits in abundance, passion fruit for breakfast, custard apples and macadamia nuts for dessert, and everywhere the majestic backdrop of the lofty pines.

The past was evoked in the names of landmarks: Slaughter Bay, Bloody Bridge, Headstone Point. Tranquil now, it had been a brutal penal colony, and descendants of the *Bounty* mutineers found their way here. The 'capital' was the pleasant one-street town of Burnt Pine. No high-rise buildings, no traffic lights (no traffic, mostly), no pollution, no crime. No inoculations or visas needed.

Giving Norfolk a close run was the even smaller LORD HOWE, 440 miles east of New South Wales. I reached it by Beechcraft six-seater from Brisbane. But there was only the pilot and me, so he invited me to sit in the co-pilot's seat. The beauty of the approach, on a calm tropical day, will linger long in my memory: Ball's Pyramid, 1,800 feet of rock jutting sheer out of the Tasman Sea to the south; and ahead, a perfectly composed green landscape of rainforest and manicured squares of pasture, surrounded by story-book white sandy beaches and the world's southernmost coral reef. Sunset over the ocean was still to come. I think I could settle on either of these idyllic timewarps . . . but it would be a long commute to work in Europe or America.

I'd always wanted to go to GREENLAND, a feeling reinforced every time I crossed the Atlantic on a clear day and the voice from the cockpit pointed out the awe-inspiring mounds of white ice cap beneath us. As a schoolboy interested in aviation I loved reading in the Loftleider (Icelandic Airlines) timetable of the one-day tours from Keflavik, the military airfield that served as Reykjavik's international civil airport, to Narssarssuaq or Kulusuk in East Greenland. But you had to get to Keflavik first. My chance for Greenland finally came when Dominic Capezza invited me to sample one of his tours to Disko Bay in July 1985. His tour wasn't one day, though: it was two weeks.

It wasn't so much the purple prose in his tour literature that attracted me: 'Greenland offers an incomparable experience in a boundless wilderness, under a sun that does not set, on a sea with incredible icebergs, gigantic mountains, and deep fjords.' More the rider attached by the Danish authorities: 'Greenland is for the intrepid. A few hours by air take passengers to remote Arctic regions where nature remains very much at odds with intruding civilisation. The climate is Arctic and has considerable influence on travel. Sudden changes in weather conditions may often result in unforeseen difficulties and variable delays.'

Dominic described himself as a cruise line Executive Vice President. In fact he ran Greenland Cruises from his Manhattan apartment, and the ship was the regular government coastal trader, which gave priority to locals. He wanted us to add his tour to the roster of those we actively promoted, and suggested I go as his guest, with Shelly paying for her place, on the least booked of his three departures – 26th July. 'How many passengers do you actually have booked, Dominic?' I asked. 'Only three firm so far,' he said. 'Don't panic. There'll be more as we get closer to departure.'

There were. Two more! A German-American couple who were expecting a real honest-to-goodness cruise, white-coated waiters, deck stewards and all. Unfortunately they signed up after all the documentation was painstakingly and laboriously forwarded to the remote outposts where we were headed. Consequently nearly all my time was taken up trying to find two extra beds in small hotels, and two extra seats on planes that were already more or less on a 'first to turn up' system. Usually that meant Shelly and me giving up our prebooked places to this couple, then fending as best we could.

Montreal, that successful mix of French chic, North American efficiency, and Canadian charm, was the starting point. I haven't yet seen *Quebec* on anybody's list of separate countries, but it might soon be! From there by Nordair combi 737 (half the seats removed for essential freight) to Frobisher Bay on BAFFIN ISLAND, for a dinner of whale delicacies and overnight at the Navigator Inn. That was where the West Virginian in my group announced loudly: 'Well, I've certainly stayed in better hotels than this.'

A Dash 7 of Grønlandsfly, the national carrier, ferried us the 448 miles across the Davis Strait to Godthaab or Nuuk, the capital, founded by the missionary Hans Egede in 1728. Each town confusingly had two names. We were now in Kalaallit Nunaat (Land of the People). A strange name, if you stop to think about it. The following day there was a pleasant motor launch trip up the fjord to a sort of alpine lodge where we admired the spectacular ice-covered peaks and ate a picnic of what were described as Greenlandic specialities.

Monday the 29th saw us airborne, and well beyond the Arctic

Circle by breakfast time. We landed in Ilulissat or Jacobshavn at 9 a.m. and had to kill time till the ship's departure at 9 p.m. The brochure promised that we would be 'day guests' at the Hvide Falk Hotel, whatever that meant. In a sense it was true. Since we'd return there to eat, we dumped all our luggage in the entrance hall, fighting for space with representatives of the colourful 'Inuit life' we were to get an insight into on this trip.

However, once we'd walked around the town in about an hour, taking in shops, bank, post office, and tourist bureau, there wasn't a great deal to do until the dining room opened. 'The town has 3,500 inhabitants who are vastly outnumbered by their dogs,' said the leaflet from the tourist bureau. We would see a lot more of Jacobshavn. Five more days were scheduled on the way back from the 'cruise'. Actual on-water time only accounted for about three days of the two weeks. *Help*! Why didn't I opt for the one-day excursion from Iceland? I'd have been home by now.

The first problem with the m.v. *Disko* came on boarding. I let the German couple take our cabin, while I hung around to see what could be worked out for us to sleep in. But their large Samsonites wouldn't fit round the corner of the deck, nor down to their corridor. They didn't discover this at first, because they were somehow under the impression that I was going to be portering their cases for them. I wish somebody'd given them even the Central Kingdom notes about hoisting your own baggage up through the windows of Mongolian trains, to prepare them. Too late now!

The second problem became apparent at meal times. There was a cafeteria on board, but it required cash payment, so I had to stand at the counter as each passenger ordered, monitor that they weren't overspending Dominic's allotment, then settle each bill. Third problem was what to do at the two stops – Umanak and Upernavik, the latter our northernmost point, 72°.47′N. Dominic's notes read something like: 'Bill, the local schoolmaster will meet you and take you on a tour.' When Bill didn't show up, it was improvisation time all round. Compared with these tiny settlements, Jacobshavn took on New York dimensions – well, at least Cincinnati.

At Upernavik the *Disko* turned round and retraced her steps. Sightseeing now was watching local passengers get on and off. One stocky Inuit lady with an incipient beard clambered on with what looked like a year's supply of fish attached to her person. The moment she was on board she produced a sort of machete, hiked one of the fish towards her face, and scythed off the approximately one-third of it she didn't manage to cram into her mouth.

She turned, with a lot of fishy bits still sticking to her cheeks, to see me staring at her. She looked mean, and not very pleased to be watched. The machete looked as if it would serve for purposes other than cutlery with equally devastating results. I stopped surveying the panorama of local life for a while after that.

Back in Jacobshavn I tried to arrange a tour of the main fish processing factory, but without a competent guide my five charges just sort of hung around, looking like spare tyres. The alternatives were hiking to the Inuit cemetery, hiking along the fjord, hiking into town, or more boat trips. Jacobshavn was a good vantage point for one of nature's great wonders, the forcing out to sea of millennia-old ice at the rate of twenty-two feet per day. Every year eight square miles of ice broke off into Disko Bay, and went in search of another *Titanic*.

The movement of the ice was impressive. It sparkled and shimmered in the midnight sun. Vistas of snow-capped mountains, deep blue sea, and meadows blooming in the brief, but intense, Arctic summer blended into each other until they merged into a vast and seemingly limitless horizon. The awesome scenery lulled you into a stillness. Every day was the same.

That was problem number four: the passengers wanted action. They wanted the optional helicopter flight right onto the ice cap. This required twenty-nine paying passengers. Even counting Shelly and myself, we were twenty-two too few. The Germans pressed for it. There was only one thing to do: advertise in the local trading post. Amazingly, it worked. Only tourists had taken the flight before, and there was a pent-up demand from locals, thirty-one locals, to be precise. Meaning they could have done it themselves any time, but didn't think of it until somebody else offered, then wanted all their places.

My local arranger, the Mrs Fixit of Jacobshavn, pared down her list so that my five passengers could indeed go, but thoughtfully included herself on the manifest, leaving no room for me. I sighed resignedly and went back to contemplating the icefjord from below, rather than above.

When it became clear that there were unlikely to be two additional seats available on the critical leg from Sondre Stromfjord back to Nuuk to connect the Germans and the other three back to

Canada, I threw in the towel, handed them our confirmed tickets, and booked two seats for Shelly and myself to Copenhagen on SAS. We didn't feature Dominic's tour the following year. I'm glad I saw Greenland; but I wish I'd taken the one-day version.

From Denmark I determined to make one stop on the way back home – THE FAROES. My Orkney friend Tim Steer had regaled me with stories of how he jumped on the boat in Stromness each summer for a visit to Torshavn, the Faeroes' capital, where the brightly-coloured houses surrounded a delightful natural harbour.

We didn't get to Torshavn, though it wasn't for want of trying. Maersk Air flew us to Bergen, then right over the top of the Faroes, but all that could be seen underneath us was unbroken cloud. We returned to Bergen; then back to Copenhagen. Same ritual next day. The third day the weather still looked pretty vicious, but the delay was only measured in hours, not a whole day. The 737 screamed through dense cloud, and at the last second the runway at Vagar appeared out of nowhere and rushed up to meet us. Rain was lying in deep puddles all over the tarmac.

On the ground alongside our arriving Danish jet was the Icelandic Fokker F27 that was to have taken us out of the Faroes after our three days there. It was a dilemma, for Torshavn was a couple of hours away from Vagar . . . by *boat*. We boarded the plane, and left a more detailed examination of the Faroes till another time, not wishing to tempt fate further.

Most of our fellow passengers were attending a four-day conference in Torshavn. I assume they somehow managed to slim the agenda down by seventy-five percent. I've often had my travel plans altered by weather, but I wonder what it would be like to live year round in a community subject to such disruption on a regular basis?

Country-collecting travellers who pay attention to the TCC list are sometimes justly accused of only touching down at a sequence of airports, and not bothering to see countries properly. They don't always plan it that way, as my Faroes trip showed.

It had been a good spring and summer of travel – a dozen new territories visited. I would have the busy autumn to get caught up in the office. But I'd need to get my skates on before the end of the year if I was to make a dent in the seventy-four countries out there still waiting to be visited.

# 30

## Daggers, Skirts and Potent Leaves

*Yemen, Aden, Djibouti, Comores (1985)*

Funny how, when you'd made eleven trips to the African continent, visiting country after country, there were still so many to go. It was a big place! Shelly arrived home one day to see me sprawled out on the floor of our La Jolla home poring over the largest map of Africa I could find, making notations of flight connections from the *OAG* on a separate pad, then surveying side trip possibilities on the map.

She joined my deliberations. She was enthusiastic about culture, history, traditions, local colour, people contact; the chance to do something worthwhile, and learn about a place. Merely notching up another destination, hopping from island to island, and visiting sparsely-inhabited places, didn't excite her. Tropical spots weren't her first choice, whereas I felt duty bound to make up for a lifetime (or at least twenty-plus years) of deprivation, and expose my body to all the sun rays it could take. Which just goes to show, just as no married couple is truly compatible, neither are any two travellers.

We settled on a complex itinerary to suit our multi-purpose goals. We would try to tie Africa in with Arabia and Indian Ocean islands. Yemen, after centuries of isolation, was opening the door a crack to the possibility of tourism, and sounded like exactly the sort of destination we could recommend to experienced travellers. It would need to be checked out at first hand.

I had a lead – a very slim one, admittedly – from a French government official, that a supply vessel occasionally serviced the French Antarctic from Reunion. Since the less accessible Antarctic was notoriously difficult to get to, every possibility was worth checking out. There were other potential destinations for our company. And there were the homelands, or 'Bantustans' created by South Africa, nominally independent, but not recognised by any other country. I'd been asked to tour all of them, and write an article.

Then there was Stottler Starr, an executive with Campus Crusade, a large Christian movement. He'd been on the 'strawberry jam and corpse' Uzbekistan tour, and phoned to tell us that his boss, Bill Bright, was planning a worldwide gathering in the style of EXPO 80, to be called 'Explo 85'. While the biggest events would be in London, the African regional one would be held in Kenya, and they'd all be linked by satellite. He thought it would be an incredible experience for us to participate in. I thought back thirteen and a half years, when I was turned back at the Burundi border. Perhaps I could get in this time, from Nairobi.

So, like Topsy, the journey grew and grew, until it reached immense proportions, encompassing Christmas, and a big chunk of December and January. This was a good time to be away from the office, as things were quietest in our business from late November Thanksgiving to mid-January. How fortunate that it was also the most propitious season for hard-to-get-to places like the Antarctic, and reverse season in the southern hemisphere.

DJIBOUTI, the tiny French former colony by the Red Sea, once known as the Territory of the Afars and Issas, was our first base. Anybody who wants to get a fast-disappearing glimpse of what colonial Africa was like under the French, should go to Djibouti before it, too, changes beyond recognition. Nominally independent, it didn't look as if anything of substance had changed from the old days.

You walked off the plane into all the local colour you could handle. The rusty black taxi ride in the pitch dark night up the hill to an impossibly Somerset Maugham hostelry with wicker everywhere, and a talking parrot. The swimming pool was filled with the vilest water imaginable – nobody swam in it. Shelly wakened during the night to find herself staring into the face of a green iguana, which slithered away on the double.

Djibouti was a terrific crossroads. From it we were able to reach Hargeisa, in SOMALILAND, the northern, 'British' bit of SOMALIA; Aden, DEMOCRATIC Yemen (where we were fortunate to leave just before a bloody insurrection started); and Sanaa, capital of the Arab Republic of YEMEN. Of course the planes were usually more full with supplies of qat than with passengers. Qat was the mildly narcotic leaf, with an effect like marijuana, so beloved of the men in that part of the world.

The local airline was called Air Djibouti, with new nationalistic fervour, but everybody, including the signs at the airport, referred to it as Red Sea Airlines. The plane – for they had but one jet, borrowed from Sobelair, the second-line Belgian carrier – was fine on the ground, but in the air it had a nasty tendency to bank at alarming angles, and execute jet fighter attack emulations when taking off or landing, sending the African passengers into paroxysms of screaming. I put this down to the air force trained Belgian pilot enjoying the freedom of relatively unregulated skies on a three-month contract absence from Europe's crowded skies. I hope it wasn't qat.

Another reason for choosing Djibouti was the simplicity of their visa regime. Nothing was necessary in advance. Simply have $25 ready every time you re-enter, and yet another fresh passport page. No discount for multiple entries in the same week. They got to know us quite well as we went in and out.

Every night an Air France 747 roared in, bearing matrons fresh from Paris salons and arrivistes from the Riviera, en route to playgrounds in the Indian Ocean. Usually they'd spent eight uncomfortable hours scrunched up inside the jumbo. It was wonderful to see passengers emerge with not a wrinkle in their clothing, stroll up to the one cracked piece of glass that served as a mirror in the small dirt-floor transit hall, preen, make ever so minor adjustments to their impeccable grooming, and allow a flicker of a self-satisfied smile to cross their pouting lips . . . and that was just the men!

The grinding poverty, and the horrendous refugee problems in the OGADEN, Somalia, and TIGRE, appalled us. We tried to take the train into Dire Dawa in Ethiopia, but were turned back at the border. 'No white faces,' said the railway official enigmatically. He wasn't hostile. Since there was a state of virtually undeclared war in most of these places anyhow, the normal infrastructure had broken down. Travel was best accomplished under the aegis of aid agencies.

How often in past history the Church has been maligned for interfering with the secular power. Equally, in modern history the Church or allied humanitarian efforts are often all that stand between a nation and chaos. The Horn of Africa was a volatile enough region before the superpowers decided to aid proxies in the continual fighting, then abruptly change sides.

The Hargeisa flight was low enough to make out what looked like an infinitely long line of ants snaking along the sand beneath. In fact it was a human convoy: the dispossessed, searching vainly for the promise over the next hill – of food, shelter, comfort, a life for their children, even . . . not a better life, just life, not death.

American farmers would soon be deciding how much abundance to plant this year; Europe would heap up more of its excess agricultural products in barns and warehouses. Worst of all, the emergency aid that could save the lives of these people, and their fellows, would be sent, and received, but only a tiny percentage of it would make it past the obstacles of poor infrastructure, fighting, graft, and almost total lack of care on the part of the petty tyrants who were bleeding Africa to a slow, agonising decline and death.

I'm sure there must be times when God looks down on the ant-like populace crawling below, sees what one section of the humanity stamped with His image is doing to others, stamped indelibly in the same divine image . . . and weeps.

Entering YEMEN was certainly stepping back in time: 1,300 years or so, to be precise. It was as if somebody had hidden this corner of ancient Araby for over a millennium in the backwaters of history, and it was just now awakening from slumber, to reveal a 1,000-year-old university where logarithms were invented, twelve-storey buildings dating back 2,000 years, complete with stained glass, lattice and intricate stone carvings, and the world's oldest dam, constructed 2,700 years ago near the temple of the moon god in the Queen of Sheba's capital.

This was a magic carpet ride . . . for real. The feel, the smell, the sound, the very texture of ancient Arabia. The land of Aladdin and Ali Baba. Men wore jambias (curved daggers with rhino horn handles) in exquisitely carved silver sheaths, which rested easily on their front pleated skirts. Minor criminals, not deserving to have their hands chopped off, were deprived of their jambias for a while – a terrible disgrace to their manhood. What women you saw were covered in black, but at least the fabric of the veil was thin enough for them to see where they were going.

This elbow of land along the Red Sea was in ancient times 'Arabia felix', (happy Arabia), a wealthy nation on the spice trade route. Although briefly occupied by Abyssinians, Persians and Turks, it was never colonised by a Western power. In the souks, probably just as for hundreds of years, you could find vividly coloured fabrics, sandalwood, intricate carvings, silver jewelry, coriander and a thousand other spices I'd never encountered elsewhere. It was common to pass a confined space, look up and see a merchant squatting cross-legged on top of a sack of grain, which formed the apex of a dozen other sacks containing his wares.

It was also common to see a blank space on top of the sack of grain for about three hours every afternoon. The merchant was off indulging in an ancient ritual: the afternoon chew, a sort of combined siesta, Muslim version of cocktail hour, and '60s-style group soft drug experience. I tried to do any shopping in the morning. When he returned to his sack of grain in the evening, he was always a little bit over-excited and excitable. And there was that jambia to think about.

The government press release, as well as inviting you to: 'revel in the sand and surf of Red Sea beaches,' (how exactly do you revel in surf?) promised that 'You'll dine in a mufraj or even spread your bedroll in a funduk if you've a mind to.' It sounded at first like Kenneth Williams on *Round the Horne* with his wurzels and sprogetts, but that was only because I didn't know what a funduk was, I suppose. They do say that travel broadens the mind! I consulted *Yemen: Land of Hidden Beauty* sent to me by someone called Ruthie Roberts. It expounded on the delights in store:

> The mufraj experience is totally delightful, even sensual. You'll be ushered into the funduk like an intimate member of the family. Climbing the steep and winding stairway, you enter the bright and sunny mufraj at the top of the house. [I still wasn't sure what a mufraj was, but at least now I knew it was nice, and had a rough idea of its location.]
>
> You'll remove your shoes and recline on the printed cushions of the mufraj, in Arabic, place for obtaining relief. [Ah, so it's a relief mufraj, or a mufraj is a relief. What a relief!]
>
> After drinking cups of steaming kisher, [?] you'll be served a typical Yemenese meal. Perhaps shafud. [Good. Now I know what to order when a new trendy Yemenese restaurant opens in Kensington. Actually I did manage to get some shafud in Sanaa. It's a lentil, garlic, barley, buttermilk and onion stew.]
>
> And ground lamb. And always the madiid – a frothy gruel of yogurt, butter fat and green onions, which locals insist on calling 'spice papers'. [Of course, mustn't forget the madiid, must we? With plenty of spice papers!]
>
> No utensils are needed. Quickly you learn to tear off a piece of the fresh grilled bread and dip into the vegetables and meats. [How flatteringly confident they are of our ability to pick up new culinary habits!]
>
> Surprisingly, the hand and finger combination becomes a deft utensil for scooping up servings of rice. [Naturally, they're much too polite to tell you that you'll be thrown out of the mufraj if you use the wrong hand!]
>
> After lunch no one is in a hurry to leave. You are told to relax . . . enjoy the view. And of course, given liberal opportunities to join in the afternoon chew. [The afternoon chew. For better or worse, that was what Yemen ran on. I once saw four passengers left behind on Red Sea Airlines, because the pilot didn't dare take off without the heavy bundles of qat which anxious merchants were waiting for at the other end. He knew whom he could afford to offend, and whom not.]

Actually, I never went to a mufraj, or put my bedroll in a funduk. I didn't sample any madiid, and – as far as I know – didn't drink any kisher. We stayed at the new Sheraton. It was a long way out of town, but you could get a confirmed reservation before leaving home. Diminutive Indian migrant workers from Madras, black as coal, served us porridge in the mornings, piping hot Assam tea in the afternoons (in best Raj tradition), and a straightforward Western menu in the evenings. I noticed that the Yemeni businessmen who dined in the Sheraton didn't exactly plead with the waiters to go heavy on the spice papers. And they didn't eat with their hands either. But where would the tourist industry be without splashes of local colour?

Leaving Yemen was the hardest part. 'Be at the airport three hours before departure,' said the Yemenia agent. Since the hotel was more than an hour's journey away, and the Ethiopian Airlines 707, the only flight of the week, left at 6 a.m., this clearly called for an early start. I'm always tempted to take turning-up times like this with a large grain of salt, especially with the first or last service of the day. But the reason I know the Yemenis really meant it was that we arrived at the somnolent airport at a quarter past three in the morning to find the counters deserted.

I relaxed, assuming they were tardy in coming to open up, snatching a little extra shuteye, perhaps, after a longer than usual time on the qat yesterday. Not so. By four I began to get apprehensive; by five I tried to find someone to help. The policeman guarding the doorway to immigration and the departure lounge wouldn't let me pass, and couldn't deal with any enquiries. The airport was so constructed that you couldn't see what was going on airside. There was just a large brick wall.

A brick wall was all I was getting as I attempted to raise somebody, anybody, to check us in. Finally a deputy manager of the Saudi Arabian airline hove into view. He gave me the distinct impression that his airline really ran things by proxy around here (they did give technical help to Yemenia) and that Ethiopian was the worst airline to choose. 'They are *communists*,' he spat. They were no good. Now, would I like to buy a ticket on his airline to Jeddah or Riyadh, and from there to wherever I was going?

I wanted to tell him that when I'd been in transit in Jeddah not long before, I was marshalled into a room, and not allowed to wander freely even in the airport. So all I saw of Saudi Arabia was the futuristic architecture of the terminal building. Also, on take off, we went through the worst airborne storm I'd ever encountered. The flight attendants were white-knuckled with fear;

crockery was unleashed from the galley; nobody attempted to move from their seats.

Of course that wasn't his fault, but then again, he wouldn't exactly have won any Norman Vincent Peale award for winning friends and influencing people, or the customer service award of the year for the Yemeni civil aviation personality who did the most to make a passenger feel relaxed.

It was twenty to six. Either this was an elaborate hoax, and there was no Ethiopian flight at all, or it was late; in either case not much could be done. Or, and it was a big 'or' – the plane was out there, about to take off, and we would be left behind. Bang would go another carefully crafted, indeed agonised-over, itinerary, gently delivering us to Nairobi through Addis Ababa.

At ten past six the Ethiopian Airlines station manager emerged from the other side of the wall, and walked straight into the path of my pent-up wrath, which had been building for three hours anyway, and given an extra stoking by the anti-customer service award contender from Saudia. It was a pity, because he was a very nice man, and I came to realise afterwards that it really wasn't his fault. I suppose there's a lesson there, somewhere. 'A person who controls his tongue is better than he who takes a city.' When you can't control your anger, at least direct it to the correct target.

Shelly smiled as the Ethiopian, the Saudi, and the Irishman locked horns in a three-way verbal tussle. I demanded an explanation and a flight out. I didn't get the second, and only got the first in the station manager's car afterwards on the way into town to pick up his seven-year-old daughter at his house and drive her to school. He was very apologetic. The airline wasn't liked here, he explained. They were made to adhere to the rules with extra stringency.

We were the only passengers that day, but if he hadn't closed his paperwork precisely at 3 a.m. and taken it to the authorities, they would have interfered with his take-off time, and that would have got him into trouble with his head office. It seemed churlish not to accept this plausible explanation, so we became friends, stayed for another three days, and went to a travel agent in the souk well before noon to work out an alternative means of exit.

This involved joining the impeccably groomed French down to Reunion, where we had no luck at all with information on the Antarctic. (Seven years and three weeks later, on board a chartered icebreaker from Vladivostok, Siberia, with a group of Australians, I sighted the vessel my contact had described anchored off Kerguelen. But of course it was too late. I was already there. And technically I'd reached the French Antarctic five years, five days earlier. But that's another story.)

We stayed at the Meridien Hotel, so beloved of French air crews. Reunion is a very chic French dot in the Indian Ocean, just north of the Tropic of Capricorn. It's much more monocultural than the British/Indian/French/Creole Mauritius next door. The sun beats down mercilessly, and it's a popular winter escape for wealthy French. The French seem to bring topless sunbathing with them wherever they go, but it still takes you aback to see the attendants who serve you on the five-hour flight down, breeze into the Meridien lobby in their uniforms, then hop straight out to the pool and disrobe.

We did persuade Reunion Air Services to take us on a long flight by HS748 direct to Dzaoudzi, MAYOTTE, French Comoro Islands, where we transferred to the twice-weekly and rather smelly F27 prop-jet service of Air Comores to the islands of Moheli, Anjouan, and Grand Comore (Moroni). The French Comores, off the east coast of Africa, about equidistant from Malagasy and Tanzania, are famous for little apart from their sunsets, tame lemurs, navy base, and the lack of coups (twenty-three at last count) which afflict their geographically close, but politically separated, independent COMORO neighbours.

On the original pre-Yemenia vendetta against Ethiopia itinerary, we would have had a couple of days to spend in the Comores. This way, it was a bit more rushed, but we did have six hours for a drive around the island, and a visit to expatriate staff at the fairly primitive hospital, peering in, en route, at the tiny one-man shops where people worked their various trades by natural light. As dusk came on, there was little electric lighting discernible anywhere.

Typically, this formerly backward republic was putting its faith in a tourism boom to generate much-needed revenue. One hotel rejoiced in the name of Ylang-Ylang. Others were springing up aiming to attract young European divers. Late the same night the inbound Air Mauritius 707 from Antanarivo carried us to Nairobi and our conference.

It was sad to see Kenya, once the paragon of independent Africa, in a state of economic decline more pronounced than on my last visit. The beggars knew that a Christian conference was taking place in town, and had learned their spiel well: 'How are you? Do I go to church? Yes. John 3:16. For God so loved the world. I wonder if you could help me? . . .'

But the real cultural lesson (such a better way to put it than 'culture shock', isn't it?) was in how the Africans reacted to the programme, which had 'Made in America' stamped all over it. As I'd seen so often in broadcasting, the technology leaps ahead before we've quite learned to use it in relevant and culturally sensitive ways.

There are a lot of so-called Christian executives in America. They wear suits, get paid comparable salaries to their secular peers, and they administer, direct, or analyse what the 'foot soldiers' do, often overseas. Some of them form an enormous swathe of middle-management, which only an advanced nation with a large percentage of churchgoers could support. Others are figureheads, fundraisers, spokespeople. Many used to have their own cable television shows, or run quasi-political pressure groups, or both. They can all make an excellent presentation (some with slick graphics), but not all get their hands dirty in any direct involvement.

Then there is what I call 'the huge invisible army', the unsung heroes from all walks of life who pray, visit the sick, comfort the bereaved, care for the dying, lend a helping hand, bring hope and healing, proclaim the good news with every fibre of their being . . . and don't seek the limelight. To them, 'Godliness with contentment is great gain.'

Unfortunately even Christian conferences are more often filled with the former than the latter, exchanging business cards, gossip and strategies. The African audience sensed instinctively the nature of some of the speakers and panellists on the big screen, and quietly ignored the proceedings. Mr X, director of this, would introduce Mr Y, director of that. There was only one exception: Billy Graham. At the mention of his name, everyone snapped to attention. Perhaps because his integrity was intact, perhaps because he served as a worldwide symbol of evangelism.

When the singing wasn't loud enough or rhythmic enough on the satellite feed, several of the Africans went downstairs and got the beat going themselves. I liked what I saw. The African Church was underfunded, undereducated, underskilled. Yet it was growing at ten times the rate of the American Church. It must be doing something right.

Outside the conference hall I met a small man with a red bow tie and a beaming smile so broad you'd run into it no matter which side you tried to pass him on. I struck up a conversation with him. His name was Brother David. He was a typist for a local district administrator. With him he had his lunch and all his prized worldly possessions in a yellow box. He showed me: first the pictures, then a notebook.

'This is my wife. These are my six children. Here is my town. This is where I work. This is my testimony, how I became a Christian.' I asked how far he'd come. 'Eight hours.' '*On foot*?' 'Yes.' Had he enjoyed the conference? 'No. I haven't been in. I just found out when I got here that it costs $4 to enter. I can't afford it.' This last was not said the way the beggar said his piece earlier. It was completely matter of fact. I gave him my address, promised to write.

Fourteen months later Shelly and I were in the throes of an overseas move. We'd sold our house in California and life had taken on that edge of apprehension when one certainty is removed before a new one is put in its place. On the last day in our old home a blue air letter landed on the mat. It was from David's pastor.

He said David had told him about meeting me, and how we were friends across the miles. He'd never left Kenya, so he couldn't imagine what life was like in America, but he felt there must be lots of stress. He wanted us to know we were being particularly thought of at this time, that was all. Then he gave some news of their area. It was a wonderful gesture, a letter from someone we'd not met, 8,000 miles away, touching an emotional chord, at just the right time.

I'd hoped to see Bishop Festo Kivengere at the conference. He'd led an underground movement against Idi Amin in Uganda, then had to flee for his life. He was back now with his people. I also had to get to BURUNDI. I managed both at the same time, for Festo came on board my plane out of Bujumbura when it made a stop in Kigali, capital of Rwanda.

Last stop before the South African homelands was ZAMBIA, to see David and Anne Watters, friends from student days in Scotland. We didn't have their correct address. I knew David was a surgeon at the main hospital. Fortunately he'd recently operated on the lady at the information desk, so she got us in touch with him.

Anne's description of robberies, life behind barbed wire enclosures, with guard dogs, and the element of fear ever present, certainly took away some of the perceived glamour of a posting such as theirs; though I dare say I could have had the same conversation with a New Yorker. Anne was trying to juggle the children with doing eye clinics. David was taking lessons for a Private Pilot's Licence, so he could do flying doctor visits in remote areas. I admired them, their guts, the real help they were bringing to people, and the skills they were transferring to nationals.

We were finishing lunch together. Dessert was self-serve fruit from a well-stocked bowl on the table. A pile of paper napkins was by the bowl. David reached over for a mango as we talked, not bothering with a napkin. He leaned forward thoughtfully, placing his elbows directly opposite me on the table, and took a bite from the mango. It was juicy, and juice began to trickle down his left arm.

We kept on talking, then he took another bite. More juice. Down the right arm. Another bite. Juice squirting sideways; trickling slowly to the places on the arms the rest of the juice had missed. A few minutes later he glanced at his watch. 'Got to go,' he said. 'In the theatre at two.' The mango juice had fairly well congealed now on both arms. He hadn't seemed to notice. He got up and left. 'And he's a surgeon,' I thought!

From the Watters' in Lusaka we flew to Livingstone. I sat in the back with the chickens. Shelly was in the middle with eighteen Italians. I asked the pilot in the men's toilet after the flight if he was glad of the new radar at the airport, since it had been a murky approach. 'Oh, that,' he said. 'You can't tell if it's broke or not, so I ignore it.'

Having Shelly with me clearly broke the spell, for unlike my experiences at Niagara and the Taj Mahal, Victoria Falls were turned on. We didn't linger. We were anxious to proceed with our novelty next day of visiting eight countries within one, each of doubtful legitimacy.

# 31

## Eight Countries that weren't

*Bantustans, Chad, West Africa, Atlantic Isles (1985–6)*

We rented a car immediately on arrival in East London, on South Africa's south coast. Well, I say a car. It was a Mini. Shelly quite fancied driving this legendary British automotive product. I was able to fit in because our luggage for this trip was one small knapsack each, so that we could get around more easily, hiking if necessary.

This was real explorational travel. At least ten tribal homelands were created by the South African government, with varying degrees of autonomy, and various agendas on the part of the homeland rulers. But information about them was desperately hard to come by. Maps delineated their boundaries in general terms, but it was rare to see listings of such basic information as the names of their capitals. Not all had boundary signs, or sometimes even road signs, posted.

The outside world didn't recognise them. Tourists didn't visit. Their locations may have been scenic, but they certainly didn't have the best of the land. The average white South African could tell you nothing about them, with the exception of the legalised gambling and (horror of horrors!) entertainment by black stars from overseas in front of mixed audiences, at Sun City, BOPHUTHATSWANA (Bop for short.) If you went further up the National Party hierarchy, however, and allowed an official escort to accompany you, everything you saw and heard came through a government filter.

We decided to go it alone. Was it safe? We were never personally threatened. I don't count the sight of six-foot-tall Zulu warriors walking by the side of the road, spears at the ready, intimidating. Everybody we met, talked to, and asked directions from, was friendly. We did read in the paper two days after we left one village, that a rivalry with a neighbouring group had developed, and an altercation had resulted in several villagers being hacked to death. But, comfortingly, the report added that political factors were not involved.

We started with the ones I'd already been to, Transkei and Ciskei. A quick drive through King William's Town (South Africa), and soon we were eating greasy fish and chips in Umtata (Transkei, or 'across the bridge'). The Transkei immigration officer, as he had done the previous time, reprimanded me for not having a Transkei visa. ('Where do you get one?' was the obvious question, but not being one to upset border officials, I said nothing.) He let us through. These two and Bop were the furthest along, in independence terms. Possibly as advanced was VENDA, right at the other end of South Africa, on the border with Zimbabwe.

On the way back from Bop (easiest to get to; the closest to Pretoria of its seven scattered pieces of territory being barely an hour's drive) and Venda we drove through GAZANKULU, LEBOWA, KWANDEBELE, KANGWANE, KWAZULU, and the one with the most musical name – QWA QWA. I only found it by following a bus with 'Qwa Qwa' written on it to its terminus.

Qwa Qwa had a capital. We were in it, but hadn't noticed anything special about the dirt road leading to it. It was called Phuthaditjhaba. Oh dear! It's hard enough to learn the names of these new states, without having to get your tongue around the capitals, as well. Perhaps that's why their names were withheld from the general public. Much better to have called it Qwa Qwa City, Qwa Qwa. Then everybody would have remembered.

The real beauty of Qwa Qwa was at its southern extremity, where it adjoined Natal. Here the magnificent Drakensberg range (of *King Solomon's Mines* fame) rose to its highest point, almost 11,000 feet. The views were magnificent. Oddly enough, when I struck out for the mountains I realised that I'd been here before, speaking at a summer camp in 1972. Only then it hadn't been a country, or state, or homeland, or self-governing entity, or whatever. Now it was. For how long?

I suspect this is one of those situations where the lethargic win. They don't bother to go to see a new country, then hey, presto! Radical political changes. Apartheid dismantled. Elections. ANC rules OK. The country is reabsorbed into the mother it was born from, and notionally independent of. Now it doesn't exist any more. Back to square one. The intrepid have gone out with pick, shovel and pith helmet (or at least red Mini) to find and identify it. Have they wasted their time? Question: If it was at one time a country, and you visited it then, does that count? Well, all that mattered was that it did count at that time, in the race to go everywhere. The TCC committee that decides such matters hedged its bets, recognising five, and saying the other five would be counted after they attained the same level of independence as the first five.

Pondering that conundrum we dropped off the Mini at Jan Smuts and checked in for the TAP night flight to Portugal. We only intended to go as far as the halfway stop, Brazzaville, Congo. The man at the desk said it was impossible without a waiver and an indemnity. The plane stopped there to refuel, but nobody ever got off there. We did. We were the only two who did. I noticed that the departure for Lisbon was announced on the board, but not the provenance of the flight.

The man in charge of immigration was higher than a kite. Both eyes were bloodshot, and he kept circling around us, making waving motions with his arms. It was quite a challenge to explain to him that we were entering on the Transit Without Visa 3 Day Rule, according to the information set out in the TIM (*Travellers' Information Manual*). He took Shelly's arm, and patted her hand. 'Come this way.'

I rescued her, and we fled into the dark African night. As often with irregular schedules in less-developed nations, there was a three-day wait to catch the once a week UTA French Airlines DC10 up to Ndjamena, CHAD, stopping en route at Bangui, CENTRAL AFRICAN REPUBLIC. We had friends we wanted to visit in Bangui, but couldn't afford another week.

In Chad the Faeroes factor (planned time three days; actual three hours) worked in reverse. The plane carrying us onwards to Dakar, Senegal, an Air Afrique DC8, was already due to be on the ground, so we sweated a little when the UTA jet was tardy in getting away from Brazzaville. (There was no sign of our friend, the night immigration officer, on our departure. I suppose he slept during the day.)

This was the only time in the week when two jets this size crossed paths in Ndjamena. They weren't specifically designed as a connection, since UTA passengers were nearly all bound for Europe from either of the two capitals. The slightest hitch, and I knew we would have to go on to Paris, against our better wishes. Ten other planned stops would fall by the wayside, and with them ten points in the race.

We needn't have worried, even though the UTA landed fifty minutes late. No other plane was in sight. I panicked at first, thinking maybe the schedule had been adjusted by an hour, and we'd just missed it, because we didn't have visas for Chad. It had taken weeks of effort to get the bare minimum number of visas from Washington before leaving, and some of them were only good for ninety days and were now running out. Chad we felt was covered by being in transit for just ninety minutes.

'Relax,' said the lady who finally poked her head through the door of the small arrivals hall, of which we were now the only occupants. She did her best to conceal a broad grin. 'It hasn't left yet. It'll be a while.' I did a mental calculation. It was the return leg of the 'guest workers' special to Saudi Arabia, used by poor landlocked peasants from central Africa lucky enough to find menial jobs in the kingdom.

If it hadn't even taken off from Jeddah for Khartoum, the first stop, it would be another six hours, at least. What I didn't know, but soon discovered, was that it hadn't yet left Dakar on the outbound journey, and would have to make fourteen take-offs and landings before it reached us, a night and a day later.

There was only one other aircraft scheduled during that entire twenty-six hour period: an Air Tchad F27 turbo prop going to Niamey, capital of NIGER, first stop on our route next day, anyway. So far I hadn't even managed to get outside the arrivals hall, so no ticket reissuing could be done. The plane was towed round in front of the window where we were. A rag-tag band of passengers climbed on board, from a departure gate beyond our quarters. Although our door to the rest of the airport was locked, the one leading in from the tarmac, which we arrived through, had never been secured. So we marched out to join the tail end of the passengers boarding.

I wish I'd counted more carefully! We hunted for a free seat. There wasn't one! There were forty-four seats, and forty-six passengers, counting us. So we stood! The engines sprang to life. As we raced down the runway, I adopted the London Tube rush hour stance, letting my imagination supply the missing strap. My half standing, half bending over, would have doubled as the brace position if we'd been flying over water, but of course we were traversing some of the most barren sections of the continent, about as far from the ocean as you could get.

The small stewardess opened the cockpit door and had a hurried conversation with the captain. He performed a long loop over Ndjamena airfield, came in low for touchdown, and dropped us off. We were going to have to wait for the twenty-six hours, and try to make up time once we got to Dakar.

Fortunately we were dropped on the tarmac at the side of the airfield this time, so we didn't have to be locked up in the arrivals hall again. By nightfall a fellow in operations found us a room in a hotel, and kindly drove us into town. The walls of the room were pockmarked with bullet holes from the on-again, off-again civil war. Its progress seemed to depend on how much Colonel Gaddafi got involved.

An overland group, with a just completed crossing of the Sahara Desert under their belts, arrived at the same time as us, and set up camp in the hotel grounds. After South Africa, this was the more rugged part of the trip for us. After the Sahara, it must have been bliss for them!

The hotel chef baked the most delicious French bread, with a slightly burned taste, in an oven in the ground behind our room. French propriety was observed. When we stood outside the dining room door in the evening, waiting for it to open so that we could have our first meal since breakfast, the French-trained manager walked past, and looked very meaningfully at his watch. 'How uncouth,' he was probably thinking. 'Wanting to eat before 8 p.m. Must be British.'

When we boarded the DC8 next day, an amazing scene met our eyes: for two days, it looked as if a tribe of nomadic herders had been making the plane their home, camp, base, everything. They had been carrying with them all but the proverbial kitchen sink. There wasn't any space in the row we'd been assigned to. We clambered over kettles, pots and pans, recumbent bodies, and possessions wrapped in cloth bundles. Then we settled down amongst them as an oddity they could talk about later to their friends.

As well as finally making it to Niger, we stopped at Ouagadougou, and Bobo Dialasso in Burkina Faso. Dakar allowed us to make side trips to Gambia, GUINEA-BISSAU, GUINEA (Conakry), and the CAPE VERDE ISLANDS. Our route home included stops at the beautiful Portuguese islands of MADEIRA and the AZORES.

TAP's flights from Lisbon to New York were all now non-stop, but we chose the Boston one which landed at Terceira. That's when I found out that chivalry can cost you. A lady who was undoubtedly a travel agent reached the door of the 737 that brought us from Funchal to Lisbon at precisely the same moment as I did. 'After you,' I said. She raced down the steps, nipped smartly through the transit hall door and over to the transfer desk where I heard her request seat 1A. I was right behind her at this point. How did she know I was aiming for that seat? She was bound for Boston, too.

I had now definitively been to every single country on the African continent . . . except one, which went by the delightful name of Rio Muni. It was better known by the name of its principal town, Bata, and was really only half of the country of EQUATORIAL GUINEA (capital Malabo on the island of Fernando Poo, a few miles off the Cameroon coast). A visit to either half counted. A former colony of Portugal, the islands of SAO TOME and PRINCIPE, had also become a tiny independent republic, and TAP flew there intermittently. Maybe when I went there, I could find a way of continuing to Malabo, and then my Africa map would really be complete.

# 32

## From Yap to Borneo

*Micronesia, Indonesia (1986)*

The year 1985 had been stupendous, but it was now to do some serious travelling. Even though by most people's standards I'd travelled a lot, there was a long way to go. If I was to claim the prize I wanted – every country – I'd have to cover a lot of territory. I didn't consciously set out to make 1986 a 'year of non-stop travel'. But with my goal now broadened to country collecting I had to be ready. And when a lot of opportunities which I'd been pursuing came up, I snatched them.

I was quite busy. By now I was presenting a weekly radio travel programme called *Going Places*, and I was asked to host two television shows: one interviewing super-successful people: *Money to Burn*; the other a travel show sponsored by the Pacific Asia Travel Association (PATA), called *Destination Pacific*. Fortunately the tour business was looking after itself.

For *Money to Burn* I wore a funny hat, and talked to everybody from Orville Reddenbacher, the 'Popcorn king' to Howard Ruff, gold bug and financial adviser, to the Earl of March, the Queen's cousin, of Goodwood fame. *Destination Pacific*'s budget demanded studio profiles of faraway places, using promotional videos for the most part, with local airline reps being willing interviewees.

It was the radio show, oddly enough, that struck gold, and was of most direct use with contacts to get to places on my list I'd missed out on so far. I did a series on all the dots of islands in

Micronesia with Michael Musto of Guam, and thoroughly fell in love with them from a distance.

I was given a great deal of help by a pan-Latin-American tourism organisation which had no money, but tried awfully hard to promote their members' interests. I was particularly keen on Chile, because it controlled access to Easter Island, and was starting to make noises in the Antarctic, taking tourists in Hercules military planes to Teniente Marsh base on King George Island.

Indonesian tourist officials initiated me over the airwaves to the delights of their hundreds of islands, many of which had autonomous status in the TCC and other lists. Cruise line reps touted their ships, and I screened their upcoming journeys for any destinations I needed to get to.

But of course this wasn't the good old BBC, where the licence payer ultimately sustained the output; this was America. The programme was a commercial undertaking, and had to make ends meet. Enter the New Zealanders! Almost as soon as my show started, I got a call from my friend Stephen Greenfield at Globetrotters in Auckland, saying he would take a series of paid spots on the programme.

He was followed by United Touring, various coach companies, sheep farmers with homestay programmes; in short so many that we had to eventually limit the number of Kiwi advertisers to give others a chance. Apparently the government had wonderful tax incentives for any company promoting the country overseas. My show's invoice to them qualified them for this concession, and, presumably, a free trip to California. How enlightened!

Where the radio programme couldn't help directly, I continued my own researches, spending night after night poring over airline guides to seek out the right connection that would allow me to transit a country for which I might not get a visa, or to maximise the number of stops per itinerary.

I'll be the first to admit that this was the year that travel fever gripped me, and the race to hit each name on the list reached almost obsession status. This wasn't normal choosing of a destination and spending time there; more like an offbeat hobby, where it was countries you collected, not just postcards of them.

But I felt that all my earlier years of deep involvement with countries overseas, when I'd lived abroad, spent student summer vacations working in foreign spots, plied my trade as a journalist and broadcaster, and reached out a helping hand to friends in the second and third worlds, balanced things out. I'd had my years of going back to Russia and China two or three times each, even my years of staying put in America.

Now the scent of the chase was in my nostrils. If there really were this many territories out there, I would go to them. If I hadn't heard of them before, I would get acquainted with them in reality, not just from books, brochures, or the experiences of others. I've no desire to climb mountains, but it must be the same sort of feeling – you have to climb it just because it's there. If it exists . . . visit it!

Three other justifications recommended themselves to me. First, I was still in the travel business, and having actually been to every destination a customer could mention would be a priceless business asset. There was no education in the world for a tour operator that could compare with seeing a place first hand. My visit to any country would ultimately benefit the country, too, because I wouldn't hesitate to recommend it to future travellers, or arrange visits there for clients, if I was impressed.

Second, my writing, television, and radio activities were expanding again, now that I didn't need to be involved full time in the travel business. In my earlier media career I'd grown tired of metaphorically chasing the fire engines – pursuing bad news in other words. Travel and destinations were subjects that fascinated people – surely I would find something to write about in the places I would visit; especially the out of the way ones. In fact, some of these destinations were known to very few people, and would remain so if I didn't go to them, and try to increase the sum of human knowledge about them.

Third, you never really know what's inside the box until you open it. This was true in my personal experience with regard to the Iron, Bamboo, and Sugarcane Curtains. No amount of reading or studying about communism, no amount of news reports could compare with riding the train for six weeks through East Europe, Siberia, and China. I determined to apply that to the pursuit of countries as destinations.

Looking back, there's another pertinent fact that didn't occur to me then. Some of the places I might never have chosen to go to, if they hadn't been on a list to be achieved – in fact might never even have heard of – turned out to be the ones I enjoyed the most. Life's like that sometimes.

So the pattern of the year consisted mostly of research and preparation from February to April, and mostly of the hit-the-ground-running-and-don't-stop type of travel between May and December.

May was Micronesia: JOHNSTON ISLAND, MARSHALL ISLANDS, FEDERATED STATES OF MICRONESIA, CHRISTMAS ISLAND (the other one!), GUAM, REPUBLIC OF BELAU, NORTHERN MARIANAS, NAURU, KIRIBATI, and TUVALU (with my award for best-named capital: Funafuti).

The Continental/Air Micronesia flight I took to Guam is a country collector's dream – six sectors joining five separately counted territories. I got to Honolulu Airport early enough (5 a.m.) to see the specially outfitted 727 having enough seats removed to allow all the cargo to be loaded. At 5.55 a.m. we were taxiing, and by 6.05 up in a cloudless Pacific sky.

Majuro, in the Marshalls, was the only civilian stop out of the first three. All sorts of rumours surround Johnston Island, about the millennium's supply of nerve gas stored there, or the secret experiments; but they remain rumours, for you can't get off to explore. Some Americans get pretty peeved over this, since they'd like to know what their tax dollars are being spent on. A uniformed officer stood at the bottom of the steps to enforce the prohibition.

Kwajalein Missile Base was thoughtfully not testing during our approach and landing. The golf course looked nice, though. I wonder if they have an early warning system for golfers when there's a missile alert – sort of a very loud '*Fore!*'

Ponape offered a speedboat tour of the mysterious thirteenth century ruins of Nan Madol, and in Truk you could cruise round shipwrecks in the world's largest lagoon. These were islands in the FSM (Federated States of Micronesia). When the US trust mandate ran out, and the islanders in this part of the Pacific, having grown accustomed to Uncle Sam's largesse, still wanted the major-league handouts, new names had to be thought of to explain (or disguise) the new arrangements. So 'Trust Territory' began to be replaced with 'Commonwealth', 'Federated States', and so on.

But Yap was the state in the Federated States I wanted to see, and it didn't disappoint. Bare-breasted women parading to the US post office, three steps behind their men. The men wearing loin cloths. A pig squealing his last as he was slaughtered at the street corner for the evening meal. Friendly, happy faces, gums red from incessant chewing of betelnut.

And the doughnut-shaped wheels of limestone which constitute Yap money, some eight feet in diameter, lying around in clearings, and beside trees, safe because of their stupendous weight. Obviously fixed assets, giving new meaning to the idea of rolling over a loan. The letter from the Yap Tourist Bureau was right. 'Tourism,' it said, 'was in its infantry stage of development.' (They meant infancy.) No guns, and what an intriguing 'infant'.

The resort hotel at Belau at which I stayed was everything a piece of paradise in the Pacific should be. Rota, Tinian and Saipan were favoured by Japanese tourists even more than Guam, which is to say a lot. It started with honeymooners. Now all of Micronesia has become popular with single Japanese. For them it's safe and it's clean. And you can see lots of relics from the war. If I were them I wouldn't particularly want to, but there's no accounting for taste!

In Kiribati (pronounced Keerie-bas) there wasn't a great deal of activity going on in the capital, Tarawa. It only seemed to have one paved road, but since it was only a stopover for me on the way to Nauru, I didn't feel disappointed.

Ah, Nauru. Can you name the country where they have to close the road so the two 737s of their national airline can cross? Where there's a great big hole in the middle, because the phosphate deposits have been dug up? Where the locals are starting to suffer from diabetes because they live off tinned food from Hawaii? Where the government of the eight-square-mile atoll owns an office tower that used to be the tallest building in Melbourne? Correct – Nauru.

The final anomaly of this trip was trying to get from one part of Kiribati (the former Gilberts) to the other – the bit in the Line Islands. It's called Kirimati, and when you apply the same pronunciation rules as to Kiribati, you get something which sounds like Christmas (Keerie[s]-mas). The Pacific one, not the Indian Ocean one. (I wonder if anyone's ever gone to the wrong one by mistake?) This is the one with the little red crabs, the one favoured by fishing buffs who know that it has a very low, flat lagoon where they can walk right in and troll for fish.

It was comforting to know that the vice president of the country was trying to do the same thing, but in reverse. I was going from Kiribati to Kirimati; he from Kirimati to Kiribati. If this was his own country, and he couldn't do it any quicker than me, I had to be doing something right! Kiribati (the Gilbertese) did have an airline: it was called Air Tungaru. The problem was it didn't have any planes, at least none with enough range to reach from one part of their country to the other. So every Wednesday they chartered an Aloha Airlines 737 (no time to paint it in Air Tungaru colours of course) and flew the round trip between Christmas and Honolulu to connect with the outside world.

I travelled down one Wednesday with Carol Farrow, who ran the airline, the Captain Cook Hotel, the inbound handling of German fishing groups, and just about everything else of consequence. This meant another 5 a.m. start – ticking off these Pacific islands one by one could be quite exhausting!

Grandpa Farrow was clearly the expert 'big wheel' on Christmas. He poked his stick through the curtain at me, and invited me to sit in the first-class section with him. Air Tungaru only had an economy tariff, but I suppose there wasn't much point chartering a plane that had a first class, if you didn't use it.

A driver was organised to show me all the non-fishing bits of Christmas (the short tour!). This was a type of destination I was going to become more and more familiar with, as I left the more populated air routes. One where your choice of stay was measured either in minutes, or in exact multiples of weeks – Wednesday to Wednesday.

Two hours forty-five minutes in the Aloha (masquerading as Air Tungaru) craft brought me back to Honolulu. This was the end of the Tungaru flight operation for another week. It was also the end of this section of my trip.

But for the vice president of Kiribati, this was only the first hop of a three-hop, three-day journey, just to get to the other part of his own country. He'd take next day's Air Mike to Majuro, and after a two-day layover there, with not a great deal to do – as even some of the guidebooks admit – a final flight on Marshall Island Airways to Tarawa.

Before turning my attention away from Micronesia to Indonesia, I dropped in on the other half of what we used to call the Gilbert and Ellis Islands – the Ellis part of the group, nowadays called Tuvalu.

This was worth doing just to hear people's reactions when you announced: 'I'm off to Funafuti.' Also because it was one of the last scheduled services anywhere in the world utilising the venerable DeHaviland Heron, whose in-service picture I remember gracing the pages of my *World Aircraft Directory* when I was twelve.

I had to make my way from noisy Nadi (jumbos from Australia and America) to sedate Suva, on the other side of Vita Levu, Fiji, where the airfield reminded me of the Nutts Corner of my boyhood – but on a quiet day.

I was totally dependent on Fiji Air, which maintained domestic services linking outer islands, even as far as Rotuma. Funafuti was their only 'international' flight. They ran it just like all their others . . . except for spraying an extra dose of insecticide on landing.

You never quite knew whether the flight to Funafuti was going to operate at all, on schedule, with all, some, or none, of its passengers hanging around for days, then giving up.

So it was something of a relief to find that there were no operational hitches on the day of my flight, and I didn't lose my seat in the sense of being thrown off the plane or left behind – only that from experience I'd intuitively picked the best one, and was told: 'The chief minister usually takes that seat.'

I moved one row, and found myself sitting between two Jehovah's Witnesses. Have you ever been trapped on a slow fourteen-seat plane for three hours with two Jehovah's Witnesses? I suspect they make more converts that way than going door-to-door. If I were them, I'd assign all their task forces to Funafuti flights. Maybe they did! There seemed to be a very high proportion of J.W.s to the population, all things considered.

The landing, after an impressive approach over the lagoon, could only be described as unique. We came to rest on what could best be described as a sort of village green. Definitely grass! The Heron could have been towed to one side, and a cricket match started at any moment. Probably did, after we'd left.

From the aircraft window I saw at once why so many flights were delayed or cancelled. The narrow landing area didn't leave much room for manoeuvre, especially if the winds were up, as they often were. On either side of us lay the wrecks of planes which had miscalculated.

Two highly obsequious expatriate Australians, in the standard colonial lower-level administrator's uniform of pressed shorts and knee-length socks, were waiting at the door of the plane for the chief minister. He heaved his bulk out of what had been my seat, and stood regally listening to their talk of faxes and despatches on this and that subject, putting forth the government's position, responding to messages requesting Tuvalu's opinion, and so on. You'd have thought Funafuti was the new hub of world affairs in the Pacific.

Turning to me, the more obsequious of the two shifted gears immediately. He'd done his grovelling. Now he needed someone to be mean to, to restore his manhood. He barked at me: 'Why have you come here? What do you want? What's your profession?'

There's little worse than a two-bit ex-Aussie colonial servant in shorts on his own patch in the Pacific. The nice ones are good; the bad ones are awful. When you think of how charming a variant of the same breed is in Norfolk, Lord Howe, and closer to their home, it's a pity such surliness is still abroad.

Had he been cordial to me I would have answered his question about why I came by saying I liked the sound of the name 'Funafuti'. Instead, I slapped down my TCC gold card as a dual purpose means of identification and answer to his interrogation. Twenty minutes later I left. The pilot checked to make sure I wanted to return to Fiji, and wasn't back on his Heron by mistake. No Jehovah's Witnesses on the return flight.

Although the next series of territories – KALIMANTAN, SABAH, SARAWAK, SULAWESI, MOLUCCAS, TIMOR, BALI, IRIAN JAYA, and JAVA – were roughly in the same corner of the globe (slightly northwest of Australia, or slightly northeast, respectively) as Tuvalu and the others I'd just been to, logistics dictated a return to base first.

Logistics were everything in the quickened pace of the race for the world. Each territory in the remaining list had a primary access point; some had only one means of access and egress. This meant you had to do a lot of doubling-back. And months of careful, detailed planning.

To reach Funafuti you had to be in Fiji or Kiribati, neither of which were any good for Indonesia and her islands. The two remaining points in Africa (Sao Tome and Equatorial Guinea) required Lisbon and Madrid as starting points. The Madrid flight was weekly; the one from Lisbon once a month only.

Afghanistan, if you could get a visa (which was highly doubtful) could only be reached effectively from Moscow or Delhi, unless you wanted to go trekking with the mujahadeen through the Khyber Pass, and risk being shot at or bombed. Svalbard was accessible only from Tromso, which meant getting to Oslo first.

Since it was pitch black there from October to April, there was obviously only a short window of opportunity in summer to visit. Several phone calls to SAS later, I discovered that there was a four- to five-week-long waiting list for the few flights which existed. They were restricted in the number of passengers they could carry, due to the extra fuel they needed for the long haul up to the Arctic. Coal miners and their families had priority. Maybe I had better get to know the Norwegian Arthur Scargill?

It had seemed such a great achievement to reach, now, 259 countries on the TCC list (more on my own personal list). I qualified for a plaque commemorating the event.

But the remaining forty-nine countries were not going to prove easy. Even though I'd done a great deal of preliminary research that spring on how to reach as many as possible, the results thrown up were more in the nature of what *should* be done, and when, rather than what *could* actually be done.

Visas, permissions, and timing, combined with securing availability on the right flights, seemed to throw up the most hurdles. But there were obstacles aplenty, everywhere you looked.

Anyhow, the die was cast. This year my travel company had organised our own series of agent familiarisations in Australia, and Shelly and I were due to launch them in late May and early June. That provided a framework for my strategy, which, in a nutshell, was to cover all the ground in and near Indonesia as a side trip from my Australia duties, then race back to California to put the finishing touches to preparations for the 'mother of all journeys' in late June and July.

So we welcomed two groups to Cairns, Queensland, sent them on separate days on the Kuranda Railway and the hydrofoil to the Barrier Reef, then left them enjoying Sydney while Shelly and I made the first of eighteen flights on Garuda, the Indonesian airline, and its affiliates, switching to Malaysia Airlines for the northern *Borneo* portions.

We tried to see as much as we could of these exotic regions in a short time: communal long houses on stilts, the Sultan's palace with 2,000 rooms and 250 toilets, his father's Churchill shrine, the lush jungle scenery, Mount Kinabalu.

But I actually most remember the scene in Surabaya, when we arrived after midnight. It seemed the whole town was alive with commerce, even at that hour. Owners and traders did deals in the bar in our overfull and pricey hotel; out in the street thousands of piecework employees and one-man shops produced the cheap textile and other products that were revolutionising world trade. Wherever you looked, not a beat was missed in production. This was the new order of things, as significant as the Industrial Revolution was in its day.

That the focus of world trade and influence was swinging more towards Asia was obvious in the staggering contrasts. The theory was that tourists from rich countries (America, Germany) came to visit stone-age tribes an hour or two inland. But they had to arrive via ultra-modern cities such as Kuching or Kota Kinabalu, and observe in passing that maybe the locals were better dressed than they were, and were enjoying a higher standard of living.

Eight days, nine new territories achieved! But it couldn't have been done without lots of advance planning. The schedules only just meshed. It was worth it, apart from the new territories, for the spicy hot snacks served by Garuda, even on short fifteen-minute hops between islands. They looked like innocuous little balls of rice to roll between your fingers and pop in your mouth. It was only after you swallowed, you felt the fire swirling around your throat from the tiny peppers carefully buried in the glutinous middle of the rice.

The stewardesses looked about nineteen, the pilots about sixteen. But they sure could bang those jets down smack on the centre of a runway! No bothering with any gentle approach, much less warning.

What with the utilisation factor of frequent, short inter-island hops requiring multiple take-offs and landings, and the above described landing techniques of the Indonesian pilots, I speculated that the life of each of their DC9s and F28s must have been short.

As Shelly and I left to return to California, I didn't know whether to be relieved or sorry to say goodbye to these aircraft which had become a second home to us around Banjarmasin, Balikpapan, Jayapura, Bandung, and Ujung Pandang.

I needn't have worried. Not long ago Garuda sold them second-hand to Piedmont Airlines (now US Air) for their intra-Florida services. I wonder if Florida's preponderantly retired senior citizen community which travels these routes now, know of the provenance of the planes in which they're flying?

More to the point, would I be able to overcome all the obstacles in the way of the July trip? I'd soon find out.

# 33

# Freezing Coalminers and a Bomb

*Spitsbergen, Sao Tome, Equatorial Guinea, Sardinia, Melilla (1986)*

I had to subdue the urge to congratulate myself on how far along I was in the 'country' race, because I arrived back to face a raft of problems. Any one of them could have threatened the next immediate journey, which was so crucial. All of them, taken together, looked like they would overwhelm three months of carefully laid plans.

'Your dates will need to be changed,' said the first telex on my desk. 'Sorry we cannot accommodate you,' said the second. 'What you ask is impossible,' said the third.

The word from the Arab Gulf was not encouraging. Normally we had problems booking a shared room in Muslim countries if Shelly used her professional name, and they didn't realise we were married. This time it was beginning to look as if Bahrain and Dubai could make the necessary arrangements for me, but not Shelly (because of her passport, or gender, I wasn't sure).

The silence from embassies about needed visas (Oman, Afghanistan, Iraq) was deafening. Even the normally helpful Russians apologised – they could allow me to go to Tashkent en route to Afghanistan, but had no control over paperwork beyond that point, and couldn't guarantee anything. (So who was running Afghanistan, then?)

Those visas that could conceivably be obtained in the US (Sao Tome, Equatorial Guinea) could only physically be processed if I now stayed around in America for the next two weeks at least, waiting until my passport had made the rounds and come back. That, of course, ruled out the dates already selected. So it was either 'Go, but no permission', or 'Wait and get the permission after it was too late to go'.

I took the decision that could be said to separate a traveller from a tourist. 'I'll go,' I said to myself. 'I'll see what can be worked out for visas en route. If I miss the chance because of waiting for permission which might never come, I'll find it hard to live with myself afterwards.'

That was easy to say. But quicksand is just around the corner when the desert wanderer thinks he's finally found some firm ground. Before I went to Indonesia I'd left the itinerary I needed for July with three different airlines. I'd made all the bookings (except for Svalbard, which stubbornly refused to budge from a long waiting list), but I needed an airline's rate desk to price out each segment, and confirm that they could all be integrated onto one ticket.

You weren't supposed to ask more than one airline at a time. They didn't want you to 'shop' them for a speculative quote, then find something better yourself, leaving them with no revenue despite the work they put in reserving and calculating. I, on the other hand, couldn't simply put myself in the hands of a supplier who said: 'Agree to buy my product. Then I'll work out the price. Whatever it is you must pay.' It was a perpetual dilemma in the travel business, and I'd been on both sides of it.

Then there was the catch-22 if you did surrender and put yourself in the hands of, and at the mercy of, only one carrier. They would ask your date of travel. As soon as you said it was a week or two in the future, you were placed in a queue in which it was hard to get to the front, because there was always somebody leaving today or tomorrow whose quote had priority over yours. It was another way of boxing you into a commitment.

The main upshot was that if I wanted to get to SVALBARD (SPITSBERGEN), I'd have to leave the US a week earlier than the original plan. If I could only get the seat confirmed, I'd jump at it, but even then there was an element of uncertainty. It was just a better chance than waiting until later.

I put aside all other business and spent the rest of the day restructuring the journey, breaking it into bite-sized chunks which each airline could digest.

What I came up with meant I had to leave in two days. SAS would take me to Tromso via Oslo and Copenhagen, and I'd be sort-of-confirmed, sort-of-not, on the Tromso-Spitsbergen flight. Meaning, I suppose, I could still be bumped off the plane at the last minute. It was worth the chance!

Then Iberia and TAP could confirm the flights to Malabo in Equatorial Guinea, and Sao Tome. But, although the two islands were only separated by a little over a hundred miles, there was no connection at all between them, or through any neighbouring country. This meant I'd have to fly up and down to Europe both times, within a few days of each other.

This was good enough for starters. The rest would have to be worked out in London, which was going to be the base for tackling the Gulf, Iraq, Afghanistan, and other possibilities. Maybe at least one of them would work. But all thoughts of this would now have to be suspended, until the first objectives were achieved.

I got to Spitsbergen . . . by the skin of my teeth. The nice trick when they finally said they might be able to confirm me was to suggest I ignore my through ticket (at travel agent's rate) and pay full fare for a separate ticket. It was, I suppose, a comment on the real world, that the closer I got to the end of my list, the more money was required to solve each problem that came up.

I paid up, and flew. Eleven hours from Los Angeles to Copenhagen, non-stop. (I was on my own. Shelly would join me in London on 4th July, after I returned from Equatorial Guinea – if I got there; and we would have a go at the Gulf together.) Two-hour wait, in Copenhagen's excellently designed airport, then another hour and a half to Oslo.

There I called it quits for the day, but jet lag from the nine-hour time difference, and the bright 'midnight sun' effect even at this latitude (what would it be further north?) meant it was hard to sleep.

Next morning was spent snaking up NORWAY's beautiful fjord-indented west coast that I'd first seen from an RAF Shackleton on patrol for Russian submarines out of Kinloss in far north Scotland, in 1969. This time it was in a succession of early-variant DC9s, packed with Scandinavian businessmen.

Ålesund, Trondheim, Bodo, Tromso. Finally, the long-awaited

take off for Longyearbyen, main Norwegian town on Spitsbergen, the most southerly island in Svalbard. I could see why there'd been so much hand-wringing over whether I would be allowed a seat or not. The departure area was packed full, every line was occupied on the manifest, and there was that nervous scrutiny by the handling staff that bespoke their anxiety lest a mistake had been made, and one too many try to squeeze into the available space.

The captain spent an age calculating the figures on his loadsheet. With such a full load the total all-up weight of the aircraft was critical. When we eventually boarded, I was knee-to-knee in the middle seat of three. We took off. I hoped no one was left behind, just because of my desire to see the place. I don't think so. Of course the solution was to put on more flights, as they started to do about four years later. Then it was just the one SAS DC9, and an occasional Aeroflot once every other week in peak season.

After ten minutes in the air, we landed again, right at the North Cape, Norway's northernmost point, 72° North, a long way inside the Arctic Circle. 'What's gone wrong?' I mumbled to myself. 'Don't tell me we're turning back now, after all this effort.'

We weren't. We were so heavily loaded, the captain simply needed to top up with fuel now at his last opportunity, having burned some off even in the brief run thus far.

It would be unduly romanticising to say what greeted me at Longyearbyen was an awe-inspiring sight. Fascinating it was, not awe-inspiring. An element of anti-climax is invariably built into finally arriving somewhere you've tried for so long to get to. Nowhere on earth can quite fulfil the picture our imaginations have painted. Until we get to that big final destination in the sky, which the Author of the Universe assures us is going to be beyond our wildest dreams, nothing is perfect, neither in life nor in travel.

I'm glad though, that I got a glimpse, at least, of this unusual territory, even if the rather sparse buildings and the essentially utilitarian nature of Longyearbyen couldn't begin to match the grandeur of the setting Nature had so bountifully bestowed on it. And what had I expected, from Russian and Norwegian coal miners, working at temperatures down to minus 60° – and in total darkness for half the year?

I think the best way to see Svalbard would be by ship, the

*Nordnorge* supply vessel perhaps, or one of the occasional expedition or cruise ships (especially Russian ones) that venture there nowadays.

That way you would have time to appreciate the grandeur of the mountains close up, and take in Bear Island as well, halfway between Norway and Svalbard. Perhaps also sail all the way around Svalbard's other islands – not just Spitsbergen – and even visit yet another claimant for 'northernmost settlement in the world' – the tiny village of Ny Alesund on the Kong fjordan. (I'm sure there's a challenger in Greenland.)

One reason the plane was so popular, though, was that the harbour at Longyearbyen had a tendency to be ice-bound for a large part of the year. So your cruise could offer spectacular vistas and fail to deliver you to your destination. The SAS DC9, having succeeded in delivering me to one more place on which I could set foot, beckoned me back on board again (one of the factors mitigating against visitors on Svalbard is that there's no hotel!).

This was probably about the longest journey you could make in Europe, from north to south. Longyearbyen to Lisbon, with five en route stops. All by DC9, which I have to say was quite cramped. The other reason I couldn't have stayed in Longyearbyen even if there had been a hotel (assuming an improvement of mammoth proportions in air frequencies), was that the one day in the month that put Sao Tome on the map was about to dawn – 30th June.

This June ABC listed flight TP215 between Lisbon and Sao Tome with the notation: 'Operates June 30 only'. That made it clear. If you wanted to be in Sao Tome, that was the day to aim for, even if you were still in the Arctic Circle the day before.

As I think back, I'm amazed I ran things so close. Yet glad they worked. I pulled myself into seat 1A in TAP's 'Navigator Class'. (Yes, even visiting out of the way spots to add to a country collection can have its perks!).

This was a hammered out agreement, of the sort I loved. Most Europeans know the national carriers of the whole continent, as well as their homeland. Not so in America, where LOT was a 'parking lot', and TAP, well who knows? I noticed both started announcing themselves to the American market as Polish Airlines and Air Portugal. ALIA also transformed itself into Royal Jordanian.

Our method of working with carriers such as this (almost entirely unknown in the American heartland) as well as starting with agent fams as we did with LOT to Russia and ALIA to the Middle East, was to simply say: 'Look, give us the tickets at half price, and we'll promote your airline.'

It didn't always work. But it usually resulted in higher commissions, lower prices or both. Good for the customer, good for the airline, good for us. As US carriers started expanding service overseas in the 1980s, and United and Delta started taking over the places occupied by Pan Am and TWA, something happened. A sea-change in American travel habits occurred, from accepting the concept that Pan Am and a foreign carrier served appropriate gateways, and domestic US carriers made the connections, to expecting to travel all the way from a small American city to an overseas point on the same US airline. This hurt smaller foreign carriers very badly since they had no reach beyond the gateway to compete.

In time, it hurt my company's business, too. We'd steadily built up a wide network of foreign airline contacts, and had cut 'deals' with them for advantageous prices. Alas, the American travelling public is a very patriotic lot, particularly when it comes to membership of frequent flyer schemes and the clamour steadily built up from our passengers for ticketing on their preferred carriers, treating us just like a regular domestic US travel agent.

Lacking the ethnic base of, say, an east coast city, we then weren't able to deliver as many American clients to our partner airlines as we'd have liked. However, one survival of our deals was TAP's two business-class tickets for the price of one (half price in other words) or in my case, half of that again (quarter price).

I didn't get too many opportunities to fly in first or business class, so I enjoyed those I did get. I was thinking of two things as I relaxed in the comfortable seat of the aged, but graceful 707 – the same one that carried all the Portuguese hurriedly home from Angola and Mozambique after independence ten years before.

First was what I'd say to a fellow passenger who asked: 'Why are you going to Sao Tome?' Second was how I'd explain not having a visa. The second reply required much more careful formulation.

My strategy had started out normally enough – apply for one, in the usual way. But, as with Angola, it wasn't necessarily a situation of applying and receiving one. Fairly new small countries, shorn of their colonial status and leaning towards the revolutionary left, had a habit of not actually entertaining seriously a request from a lone Western tourist, who, in their eyes, had no connection with the country or reason for coming that they could readily classify.

Strategy number two evaporated the moment I set foot on the ground. It had been alluring, but not realistic. 'Pretend you're a sort of supernumerary crew member, and go through passport control with the TAP crew from the plane.' I suggested to myself. It failed because I didn't lay any preliminary groundwork in advance in Lisbon. Of course being in the Arctic when I should have been attending to this and speaking broken Portuguese in such a way as to be taken for a Cuban in Angola, were the drawbacks to this approach.

Once on board, the right means of broaching this with crew members somehow never suggested itself to me. Besides, I realised, the list of crew names would already have been telexed to the authorities.

So I stood in the ramshackle terminal in Sao Tome, and watched the crew effortlessly pass through customs, and be whisked away to the comfort of their hotel. The plane stayed on the ground for a full day and night to allow them to rest up. It clearly wasn't practical for TAP to keep a separate crew on hand there for a month. For me, it was ideal: I'd be able to return without delay, but would have ample sightseeing time compared with a normal turnaround.

That's when the third strategy evolved – that of declaring the true nature of my visit. Simply a round trip, Lisbon back to Lisbon. I only wanted to stay as long as the plane was on the ground! I didn't wish to apply for a visa to stay. I'd be returning immediately.

The immigration officer looked me up and down, rolled his eyes, and spread out his wrinkly palms with an expression which said: 'We've got a right Charlie here! Now what shall I do with him?' He motioned to me to wait in a corner, while a colleague was summoned.

Eventually, it all worked out all right. I was allowed 'in', since I was already there. I expected them to perhaps hold my ticket and passport overnight. Instead, they assigned a junior officer to me, who shadowed me throughout my whole stay.

He acted as both guide and jailer, finding me a pension (the one decent hotel up on the hill was full), then magically appearing at the doorway every time I attempted to leave and go for a walk; and accompanying me to a restaurant where I paid for his meals. I did get around a little bit under his supervision. I knew the strategy would likely work – after all, if they chose *not* to let me in, and deport me on the next plane, it was the one I was already booked on! Nevertheless I resolved never to turn up again visa-less . . . if possible!

Would I have bothered going to Sao Tome if it hadn't counted as one more country on the list? Yes, I think I might have. It was one of the best-preserved examples of a former tiny colonial outpost, the sort Maugham or Greene wrote about so well, with the names of big European trading interests sprinkled around the dock, the old-fashioned weighing scales, the verandahs and shutters on the pensions, the crumbling pink facades on the buildings, the slow, lazy pace, the tropical bugs, the ennui.

I never really found out if a visa would have been obtainable, or how long it would have taken. Time had run out, the tantalising prospect of Spitsbergen had loomed, and had to be seized.

My seat (1A) was taken on the way back to Lisbon by a pinstripe suited British businessman, so I slipped into 1B beside him and asked what he'd been doing there, before he got a chance to interrogate me.

'Banknotes,' he said. 'We print for virtually all the former colonies. It's a thriving business, every time there's independence, a revolution, a change of government.'

We stopped in the Cape Verde Islands for an hour to refuel. Sal Island used to be well known to aviation buffs. It was the only point South African Airways could land, between their apartheid stronghold at the bottom of the continent and 'white' Europe, especially once Luanda fell to the MPLA. Praia, one island over, was where you flew to on turbo prop planes from Senegal.

From Lisbon I had to get to Madrid in record time, and set off for Africa again, to a spot that could have been reached from Sao Tome by jet in ten minutes. But, politics being what they were, no connection existed between the tiny dots that had been claimed, one by Spain, the other by Portugal.

All I knew in advance about Equatorial Guinea was that after independence it had had a crazy despot as leader, Macias Nguema, who buried his opponents alive in hot sand. He was said to have slaughtered tens of thousands of innocent citizens. It didn't sound like a place you'd want to stay for long.

This time the Iberia DC10 only planned three hours on the ground. They would stop at Lagos, Nigeria, on the way back up, for a crew change. The three hours would be long enough, I thought, for a quick look around. Unfortunately by the time we meandered around West Africa on the way down, we were that much later in arriving.

On disembarking in Malabo, I surveyed not just the long queue waiting to be processed into Equatorial Guinea by one official with all the time in the world, but also the eager line of outbound passengers who'd already been waiting for three hours to board. They were clutching their stamped clearances, boarding passes and seat assignments, and *already starting to move towards the aircraft*!

Panic set in! If I were to be stuck here for a week, bang would go any hope of the Gulf, Iraq or Afghanistan. Quick action was called for. If I just bolted from one line to another, I'd risk being shot by one of the trigger-happy guards, maybe. But if I just stayed where I was, off would go the once-a-week flight, and I'd be stranded.

The two lines were in parallel formation, but facing in different directions. Neither was exactly straight. I seized my chance, and began a series of crab-like movements that took me from one line to the other – not all at once, just stealthily, a millimetre at a time, like the stills of an animation story board, where you could see each position, yet when transferred to the screen, they acted as one seamless move in the cartoon.

No one seemed to notice. 'Hello again,' said the steward, as I boarded. I saw that somebody was sitting in my seat, so I took another. After I got used to the blinding strobes from the stewardess in the second cabin (Iberia were experimenting with new garishly-striped uniforms) I handed her the coupon from my ticket for the Malabo-Madrid portion, saying simply: 'Give that to the ground staff. They forgot to lift it.' And that's how my map of Africa became completely filled in.

I hadn't counted on a bomb to welcome me back to Europe. An EL AL flight from Tel Aviv landed at Barajas Airport just ahead of ours. Their passengers, including Israel's ambassador to Spain, were going through immigration at the same time as I and 200 Equatorial Guineans.

One of the Israelis and I were jostling for a position nearer the front of the queue, when we heard a loud 'bang', then shrieking and the sounds of running helter and skelter. We passed through customs and ran upstairs. The EL AL check-in desk (and the KLM one next to it) were demolished. Debris was everywhere. Sirens roared.

As we stood contemplating the damage (it looked like no lives were lost, thankfully, though a number of people had serious injuries) the police roared up – three cars, one after the other. The uniformed police jumped out, and appeared to head at random for any dark-skinned or Arab-featured person hanging around. All such were bundled into the police cars and driven off. On the television news that evening, the newscaster announced that quick action by the security forces had pinpointed and arrested those responsible for the bombing. I wonder!

From Spain I hopscotched over to Italy to fill in the last remaining gap in Europe, while I was there: SARDINIA. Then I pulled out the TCC list of Africa to mentally tick off each one, and confirm to myself that, after fourteen journeys to that continent, I could now claim I'd been to every single country there.

That's when I noticed the entry under 'M'. Not just 'Morocco', but 'Morocco, Spanish' (confusingly backwards). I remembered the enclaves of Ceuta and Melilla, on the north coast of Africa, and the story David Watters, my Zambia surgeon friend, told of his near-perilous bus journey between them and the connecting bits of Morocco.

On leaving he'd noticed a lot of people climbing on, then off, the bus. He fought his way through the thick of humanity trying to board, and found a window seat. At each border crossing between SPANISH MOROCCO and (Moroccan) Morocco, and other points besides, soldiers boarded and searched the bus.

When he arrived, another search. As he was getting off, a young local sprinted over to his seat, reached behind it, extricated a bag full of hashish, said 'Hi!' and sprinted off. I decided to give the bus journey a miss, returned to Spain, and went by ferry to Melilla from Algeciras, on the Costa del Sol, returning later the same afternoon.

From Malaga I flew to London to meet Shelly. What news would she have about my onward tickets?

## 34

# Baghdad, Kabul, Al Capone

*Iraq, Afghanistan, Gulf States, St Pierre (1986)*

The only piece of news Shelly brought to London with her was bad – I was cleared for Bahrain and all seven Emirates. She was not.

She'd gone ahead with planning the next series of trips, to the mysterious Bonin Islands, in conjunction with our long-awaited Tibet journey. Our company had received authorisation from Pyongyang to send tourists (in small numbers) to North Korea, so we'd put in a request for the autumn, hoping it might tie in with the Tibet dates already set. Nothing was firm yet on any of these plans.

For now it looked like she'd have to stay put in London, while I took off for the Gulf. First though, a series of futile attempts to provoke the Iraqi, Omani and Afghan Embassies in Kensington into parting with a visa, so that I could add these countries to my Emirates journey.

I got out the *ABC World Airways Guide*, and rifled through the pages for a morning, that stretched into afternoon, then evening. I had now been to 275 countries on the TCC list – halfway between the 250 plaque, and the 300 level, that had once seemed so impossible.

The club recognised the superhuman (and perhaps ultimately unsuccessful) efforts it would take to reach all 308 countries on their 1986 list, so they offered a 'Special award' to anyone who reached the magic 300.

In my case, that meant only twenty-five to go. And, if I could add Bahrain, Oman, Iraq and Afghanistan to the seven emirates of the UAE, that would be eleven – almost halfway to the total.

I put aside thoughts of camel safaris, gliding into harbour in an elegant dhow, visiting old desert fortresses, and other elements of the Gulf visit we'd looked forward to. On my own, I could maybe compress the schedule I'd started with, and see how quickly I could take in each of these places and return to London.

I can't honestly say I 'put aside' fears and worries about the situation I was contemplating launching myself into. I couldn't put them aside, for they'd never seriously entered my head as dangers to contemplate. I knew that Iraq was at war with Iran, and that Baghdad had been subject to aerial bombardment.

I knew that even though the Russians kept a tight hold on Afghanistan, the mujahadeen had managed a few rocket attacks on Kabul Airport. But I reasoned to myself that such were the hazards of a region that seemed to have been embroiled in almost perpetual fighting since biblical times.

My one concession to fear or prudence was to empty my pockets of everything that connected me with America. Just in case!

By midnight my researches had come up trumps. Fifteen separate flights, all eleven new countries included, and only four days in total, if I left on Thursday. It was now the early hours of Wednesday. I drifted off to sleep, knowing that I'd have to be at the airline offices as soon as they opened.

By lunchtime on Wednesday, the tickets were all in my hands. An amazing feat, when you think about the airlines involved. Have you ever tried to get confirmed flights on Iraqi Airways, Ariana-Afghan Airlines, and a brand new airline (Emirates) all in one morning?

Less than twenty-four hours later I was tucking into smoked salmon on the way to Athens, my transfer point for IRAQ. Not satisfied with the security checks in the terminal, the Iraqis performed their own thorough checks airside before the man in olive fatigues at the bottom of the 727's rear steps nudged you with his rifle to indicate you could board.

Being essentially visa-less for the entire journey (including stops that didn't yield a new country, but were necessary for connections, such as Qatar and India meant that I tended always to announce my next-but-one stop as my destination. That usually got me through.

So I told the Iraqis I was bound for Jordan. I was – when I left Baghdad. I told the Omanis I was bound for India, and in India I even managed a domestic flight with no visa, arriving at Bombay and departing from Delhi.

It's hard to think or write about Iraq post-Gulf War and call to mind what you expected from it eight years ago. If, in fact, the legends of Aladdin, Ali Baba, and flying carpets were in your mind, you'd have been better off in Yemen. Only one flying carpet remained, as far as I could see, on a copper sculpture fastened to the wall of the departure lounge of Saddam International Airport. Otherwise, old Baghdad had been flattened to make way for a concrete oil-fed metropolis.

Looking back, I now fondly wish I'd made even more strenuous efforts to obtain a visa, so that I could have seen the Hanging Gardens of Babylon, and the other alluring sights of biblical Mesopotamia, before the country disintegrated. My few hours, plus a partial blackout, didn't give a great deal of scope.

Number 276 safely reached. Thirty-two to go! The mild euphoria was quickly shattered at Queen Alia Airport in Amman in the early hours, when the Emirates flight I was booked on simply didn't operate. No check-in staff, no representative, no mention on the flight indicator.

All was made clear when the Gulf Air ticket agent, to whom I turned for help, spat on my ticket. Apparently the desire of Dubai, the second emirate, to rival Gulf Air (based in Abu Dhabi) on its own territory, did not go down well, and Emirates – which went on to become one of the world's most successful airlines – found itself in its first few months with offices mysteriously shut down, licences withdrawn, permissions withheld, and other obvious hassles.

Not having time to participate in inter-Gulf, inter-emirate internecine fighting, I wiped off the spittle and sought out British Airways, (always a good home port in an overseas storm) who obligingly rerouted my ticket via Doha and Abu Dhabi. So, with ABU DHABI, my first emirate was in the bag, and I wouldn't have to turn south on the round-emirate journey from DUBAI.

I reached the other five emirates by shared taxi in less than a day. SHARJAH was only twenty minutes' drive, then AJMAN, UMM AL

Qaiwain, and (at the northernmost point of my journey), Ras Al Khaimah, overlooking the Strait of Hormuz.

Although united in a loose federation, each emirate had retained its own character to some degree, but all the traditional aspects (dishdasha clothing, fortresses, camels, sand dunes) were eclipsed by the frantic modernisation – skyscrapers, port construction, hundreds of new apartments, soccer stadia, four mammoth airports rivalling each other for international traffic.

My favourite emirate was Fujeirah, where I lunched at the Siji restaruant at the Hilton. Its east-coast beach overlooked the azure Indian Ocean; and the coastal road in both directions led to Oman, north through Khor Fakkan to Dibba, south to Khatmat Malahaw.

In true Murphy's Law style, though, it was either attempt to cross to Oman here and be shot, or return through the flat expanses of desert to the Dubai Hilton, overnight, and fly to Muscat (Oman's capital) next day. I chose the latter, since it also allowed a Bahrain stop.

The Muscat authorities, while being hospitable, allowed my tape recorder and radio to be stolen from my in-transit baggage. The reason I didn't discover this until London was that my luggage began a transit independent of me at Muscat, and I didn't see it again until we both completed our Muscat-Bombay-Delhi-Kabul-Tashkent-Moscow-Frankfurt-London itinerary on the Monday morning.

It was now Saturday afternoon: ten countries since Thursday. Afghanistan would be real seat-of-the-pants. The India part went flawlessly – even the 1 a.m. Bombay-Delhi jumbo, on the first leg of its journey to London and New York. It disgorged me into the transit lounge at Delhi around 4 a.m., and the Ariana flight was scheduled to depart at 8 a.m.

As I approached the 727-100, I observed that whoever painted the new titles on the fuselage ('Bakhtar Afghan Airlines') had not done a very good job. 'Ariana' was still visible underneath. Once on board, the first thing I noticed was the Pan Am logo on the buckle of my seat belt. There was plenty more to come – Spanish signs in the toilets, Indian Airlines cutlery, Czech ('OK Jet') paper napkins.

Breakfast was served while we were still on the ground – somewhat unusual, I thought. But since we'd already been sitting around for an hour before the food was served, eating did help to pass the time during the second hour.

It was when the third hour rolled around that I became really concerned. It was one thing to plan a series of flights to allow an hour or two on the ground in a country that was difficult to reach, but quite another to arrive there after the connection had left, and have to come up with an explanation . . . or worse!

Had I known, I had nothing to worry about. Shortly after our arrival in Kabul, two Ariana flights were indeed scheduled to leave, thirty minutes apart, both for Moscow, one continuing to Prague. No flights for the rest of the week, but two on Sunday morning. It seemed strange, but that was what the timetable said. Sunday was also a popular day for India to Afghanistan flights – as well as ours from Delhi, one was scheduled from Amritsar at about the same time.

What was really happening was as follows: Ariana had two planes – 727s that formed part of Pan Am's original fleet a long time back, and had passed through various hands since then. Since the Soviet invasion, no insurer (not even the archetypical risktaker Lloyds of London) could be found to insure the two planes, and when one was eventually found, at exorbitant cost, its stipulation was that neither plane could remain on the ground in Kabul for more than two hours. Ever!

The insurance reality, the reality that few people apart from me were mad enough to actually pay money to Ariana to fly with them by choice (unless there was an incentive), and the reality of the need for hard-currency income, combined to produce an ingenious solution.

All Western cities had been removed from Ariana's route network, which now only extended to neighbouring India in one direction, and Moscow and Prague in the other. But ferrying Soviets for roubles and Indians for rupees, as well as their own bankrupt citizenry, was not likely to make them rich, so they found a network of unofficial travel agents in the Hindustani community in London and offered them ultra-cheap London-Delhi tickets in return for infusions of much-needed hard currency.

How did they transport people to and from London? I'd chosen their Moscow flight rather than the Prague one because no flight was listed for Prague to London that would connect the same evening with the Ariana arrival into Prague. Apparently they circumvented this by chartering a CSA (Czech) Tupolev for the Prague-London section, thus offering point-to-point travel each way between India and the UK – albeit by the long way round. (Even Aeroflot was quicker if snow didn't divert you to Latvia!)

I learned all this from the Afghan pilot to whom I chatted whilst waiting for take-off. He assured me the other plane would wait at Kabul 'to get the Indians to England'. He said the delay was due to weather concerns about the low-lying mists around Kabul.

More likely, they were waiting to get an all-clear from the missile alert unit in Kabul. The difference between flying into Kwajalein Missile Base, (USA), Marshall Islands, Pacific Ocean, and flying by Ariana into Kabul was that in the latter case, the missiles could come without warning. Plus, it wasn't practice!

The landing at Kabul is best described as hanging aloft in suspended animation for an extended period, followed by a sudden spiralling corkscrew descent. The pilot had obviously practised this manoeuvre on many occasions. The Belgian pilot on loan to Red Sea Airlines used much the same technique, without, in his case, the justification.

I made the most of my two hours in AFGHANISTAN. Not enough time to go into the city, nor to count the number of bombers and Soviet military transports lined up alongside the runway, but enough to play the tourist in a small surreal drama. I sought out a Soviet officier in uniform. We discussed harmless topics such as planes (civil, not military). He led me over to a desk, and pulled open a drawer. Inside were old tourist postcards of Herat and Mazar-i-Sharif, which he offered for sale. I bought a couple and tendered a note to him. 'You'll want your change in sterling,' he said, and counted out the exact number of pence in silver and copper.

Aloft out of Kabul, the panorama below was magnificent: the majestic snow-capped Hindu Kush mountain range, the 11,000-feet-high Salang Pass, the Amu Darya River. At Tashkent we pulled in beside the other Ariana 727 (the one I'd taken from Delhi to Kabul – they switched them in Kabul, the Delhi one going to Prague, the Amritsar one taking me to Moscow) which had landed five minutes earlier. Nobody tried to defect this time.

We both reached Moscow at about the same time which, because of the morning's delay, was too late for my London flight. Its engines were warming up just as we taxied in. The customs man gave me a fearsome look, and an equally fearsome going-over, when I disembarked. He was taken aback, I think, to see a non-Russian, non-Afghan, non-Indian emerge (without a visa, of course) and casually talk of changing planes to complete his Afghanistan to London journey. He couldn't really do anything nasty to me, merely changing planes as I was, but he made me empty out my briefcase *three times* while he meticulously checked it.

Lufthansa found me a flight to Frankfurt that evening, and paid for me to stay at the airport Sheraton before taking the early morning Airbus to Heathrow. Ironically the Indians in the other Ariana plane stayed on board in Moscow (minimising customs interference) then proceeded smoothly via Prague into London, arriving twelve hours before me, and for half the price. Some you win, some you lose.

I was elated now to have achieved 286 countries – twenty-two to go.

On the way back across the Atlantic I made a deviation to take in the one territory I'd missed out on in all of North America. The TCC listed under its 'North America' heading four big ones – Alaska, continental US, Canada, Mexico – and one minnow, St Pierre and Miquelon. I went there with the purpose of ticking off the minnow, and left charmed and captivated by this small maritime redoubt.

St Pierre and Miquelon sit tucked underneath Newfoundland at the entrance to the Gulf of St Lawrence. Originally called 'Islands of the Eleven Thousand Virgins' (the population was now under 6,000), they had been France's consolation prize for losing mainland Canada to the English. Commercial fishing, shipwrecks, and bootlegging under Al Capone, had all disappeared as revenue-earners, to be replaced with tourism, what else?

In Hotel Robert ('St Pierre's largest: 54 rooms') you could see Capone's straw hat, and owner Jean Pierre Andrieux would bend your ear with an illustrated history of the island. I stayed chez Marcel Helene ('panoramic ocean view, English spoken, meals on request'), ambled around the narrow streets, and passed the time of day with the gendarme, who didn't have much crime-stopping to do, at least not out of tourist season.

Then I caught the Air St Pierre HS748 to Halifax, Air Canada to Boston, TWA to San Diego, for my last four weeks at home for some time.

# 35

# Typhoon, DMZ, Mutineers

*Ogasawara, Tibet, North Korea, Pitcairn, R. Crusoe, Tokelau
(1986–7)*

Back home in California, I surveyed the situation. The twenty-one
territories left to be visited were a diverse group. Fifteen were
islands: nine in the vastness of the Pacific Ocean, of varying degrees
of accessibility, four in the Atlantic, one in the Caribbean, one in
the Indian Ocean; four were Antarctic territories; two were my
last countries in Asia, Tibet and North Korea.

Fifteen of them had no regular commercial air service whatsoever; four were restricted military bases declared off-limits to
the public; ten had neither air service nor any form of scheduled
commercial sea passenger service; the six which had no air access
but did have ships calling were served at intervals varying from
every other month to once or twice a year only.

Clearly this was going to be no picnic. Just as the last hundred
countries were much harder to reach than the first 200, so the last
twenty of those hundred were significantly more difficult than the
previous eighty.

The Antarctic territories and the military bases seemed the
hardest nuts to crack. The places with intermittent sea service
always seemed either to be definite that no berths were currently
available, or if not so purposefully negative, very vague about when
space could be confirmed, what the procedure for making definite
bookings was, or both.

Worse, what sea service there was existed primarily for locals, government officials, or people specifically invited to the territory concerned. Tourists and country chasers were a very low priority, viewed merely as a last minute fill-up of any available space. With restricted capacity, and high local demand, space did not always become available – even at the last minute.

Pitcairn seemed to be worst off. There was no airstrip, and no real scheduled shipping. Twice a year, a cargo vessel heading from New Zealand to Southampton through the Panama Canal might anchor a mile off, so that goods could be offloaded. Then it was gone. Every other year the responsible British government official (Pitcairn was Britain's last Pacific colony) chartered a yacht from Mangareva, at the edge of French Polynesia, to look in on this part of the realm.

To get a place on the Tokelau boat from Western Samoa, which operated on an irregular schedule every other month, you first needed to secure a permit from the Department of Tokelau Affairs. This, and waiting for a standby place to open up, could only be done on the spot. So it essentially meant you had to go down to Samoa on spec and hang around.

Although St Helena and Ascension in the Atlantic Ocean had a more regular service – five or even six times per year – only one per year stopped additionally at Tristan da Cunha. The first sailing of the year was the only time the waters in the treacherous South Atlantic were suitable for a landing. That put tremendous pressure on this annual departure, the waiting list for which stretched for two or three years.

The first shipping service to open up for me was that of the Ogasawaramaru, the occasional link (and only means of transportation) between the remote Bonin Islands and Japan. As a variant to our highly successful London-Hong Kong groups by train, my company had been booking a large number of individuals on the westbound Trans Siberian, starting with a sailing from Japan to Nakhodka (the less secretive port than Vladivostok), or a flight from Niigata to Khabarovsk.

Our efficient Japanese agent who arranged these tickets for us, secured September passage for Shelly and me to Ogasawara, and we decided to combine this with the two Asian countries (Tibet and North Korea), both of which had begun to accept our groups.

On the way we stopped in Okinawa, RYUKYU ISLANDS, one of

the last Pacific island groups it would be relatively easy for me to get to by air. This would also positively be the last American military base that could be visited without special permission, which I was to find was not exactly forthcoming.

We had to go the long way round to enter Tibet – through Taipei to Hong Kong, weekly charter flight to Chengdu, then CAAC 707 up to Lhasa, the capital. By the time we'd endured the Chinese pilot's frequent altitude changes, and the four-hour, eighty-mile Land-Rover drive over a pot-holed road from the antiquated airfield, I was quite sick. The height being 13,000 feet didn't help. The road to Shigatse, the second town, was even worse, reaching 17,500 feet.

So what I remember about this mysterious land is mostly being flat on my back, head pounding, and no relief in sight even from the oxygen cylinders supplied in the hotel room. Shelly did the sightseeing for both of us – Drepung Monastery, Potola Palace, Norbulinka Park, former summer retreat for the Dalai Lamas.

It was a privilege to be among the first Western tourists to visit this proud land, with its ancient rituals (only 880 visas had been issued in 1983, slightly more in 1984). The sounds you heard continually had a time-worn feel to them: donkeys and yaks plodding across the earth, the sing-song prayers of lamas, the chants of mantras, the tinkling of bells. And always, the flapping of prayer flags, especially high on the mountain passes, closest to heaven, as if the Tibetans were crying out continually: 'Lord, look down upon us; help us to survive!' It must have seemed to many in that land, that if indeed God was watching them, it was from a distance.


Just before we'd left home we'd had an enigmatic telex from Pyongyang, saying the North Koreans would love to welcome us, but not in October. Could we please come at another time?

Well, we would return in future years, but for now the die was cast. There was only one other point of entry to North Korea that was possible, and that was the Demilitarised Zone (DMZ), thirty-five miles north of Seoul. We hurried to South Korea, very security conscious because of the Asian Games, and boarded a bus for the ninety-minute ride to the border. We were lucky to get on – it was always booked up and passport numbers had to be sent ahead.

After signing a visitors' declaration that we were 'entering a hostile area and risking possible injury or death as a result of enemy action' we were paraded through the Joint Security Area into the Military Armistice Commission building, a drab enough shed which housed the conference table. Two steps around it to the other side, and we'd officially crossed into North Korea. We stared at unsmiling faces all around. Then we got back on the bus to Seoul, and flew to Tokyo.

As we boarded the Ogasawaramaru in Tokyo Bay, we were handed a sheet of paper with our numbers on it. We mistakenly assumed that was to indicate our cabin. It actually indicated the exact position on the dormitory floor on which we could place the cubes of hard plastic surrounded by foam which served as pillows.

We found ourselves the only foreigners, lying prone surrounded by about ninety Japanese, all staring up, not at the sky or stars, but a television screen fastened to the wall at a crazy angle to suit viewing from the floor beneath. If they'd added 'sensurround sound', and if I'd been able to understand the programmes, the overall effect might have been like the Omni-theatre in St Paul, Minnesota, a 360° experience. As it was, I just got a stiff neck.

Shelly got more than a stiff neck. She became very sick. That was before Typhoon Wayne struck with full force, and our brief forays up on deck were first discouraged then prohibited outright. With all hatches effectively battened down, we were reduced to sleeping, watching television which we didn't understand, or walking the few paces to the vending machine on which – though we couldn't read the words – the pictures of seaweed, dried fish etc. gave a reasonable indication of the food on offer.

My wife retreated to the exact mid-point of the ship – the sixth of twelve steps beside the vending machines. Her face turned a shade of green I'd never seen before. Fifty-three hours in a typhoon, living on sushi, seaweed, and rice snack balls, was a dreadful way to clock up another country.

After the ship, sleeping on a tatami mat in a ryokan (traditional inn) on the island and squatting to eat unfamiliar food, was positively heaven. For anyone bound for Ogasawara, or sister islands Volcano or Iwo Jima (known to US Marines), I only have one word of advice: 'You may find that a few words of Japanese will come in handy.'

On the Sunday we dropped into a tiny Christian church, with a congregation of twelve, and a pastor who predated World War II. We couldn't communicate by language, but at least recognised the tunes of some of the hymns they sang. Later the same day we met up with some students who were anxious to be updated on the American top twenty of pop music.

Even with the strangeness of this journey – perhaps because of it – there came an intense ache as we left. For a moment, we'd intersected with a culture that was very different . . . so different that, moving about in it, you felt as if you were alone in the universe, separated from all the familiar things that allowed you not even to stop and think about the basics.

One of the students we'd met came down to the harbour to see us off. As the ship pulled away he got out his trumpet and played, slowly and clearly 'Auld Lang Syne' – each note reverberating in the evening stillness above the water, its intensity gripping you the more as you got further from the hubbub on shore.

It was a song known to the Japanese as 'Hotaru no hikari' ('By the light of the glowworm'). I remember the Ishiharas explaining the story to me when I was twenty-one, and living in Hokkaido for three months in their family.

The little boy's family were poor, too poor to pay for electric light. So he studied: 'by the light of the glowworm'. Since he ultimately succeeded in overcoming his poverty, and passing his exams, the Japanese associated the song with success, achievement, graduation, celebration.

But, as the strains of the tune died away, and an almost perfect sun began to set on the horizon, I couldn't help overlaying on his song the emotions that always came when we'd sing: 'Should auld acquaintance be forgot, And never brought to mind' in Scotland on New Year's Eve.

Each year you never know what the next one will bring, which of your friends you might never see again. And travel magnifies this. You encounter a place, a person, seemingly for a split second, as if you are on a fast-moving carousel at a fair . . . then the music stops and everybody moves on. How important to 'tak' a cup o' kindness' while you have the chance. You will never pass this way again.

We had another reason for remembering Ogasawara. Shelly was not just sea sick. It was morning sickness. Perhaps it was because of the time difference that it seemed to strike all day long! We were going to become parents! Any thoughts of the impact on our travelling patterns were buried in the surge of joy we felt at bringing a new life into the world.

This was our last journey together for quite a time. But we'd acquired far more than new countries to add to our list. We'd received enrichment that would last a lifetime.

Cruising was not my ideal way of travelling, even though the advantages were undeniable. There was still a spark of adventure in landing somewhere off your own yacht, hitchhiking, bussing, even flying by small local plane, and striking out on your own when you got there. But waiting on deck with a hundred others, to be initiated into a packaged experience?

But I had no choice at this stage. I'd reached a critical level: 291 countries, seventeen to go to reach the goal. But even to top 300 I had either to mount a series of separate expeditions myself, or join existing cruise expeditions.

Expedition travel by small ship was one thing cruise lines could do well. I'd been a guest of one line for SOUTH GEORGIA, SOUTH SANDWICH, SOUTH ORKNEYS and SOUTH SHETLANDS, the latter next to King George Island near the tip of the Antarctic Peninsula where Chilean, Argentinian and British contiguous territorial claims, and Chinese, Russian, Polish and American bases in close proximity meant that you could add a number of Antarctic territories to your list in a short time.

But French, Australian, New Zealand, and Norwegian Antarctic were different animals altogether. My enquiries in each area had come to naught. So I grabbed at the chance to be on a unique journey – a half-circumnavigation of the Antarctic continent departing 18th January 1987. It would pass Peter 1 Island, claimed by Norway – a first attempt to do so in at least ten years – and additionally call at McMurdo, next to Scott, the New Zealand base; thus achieving two very difficult destinations out of the four.

In the meantime, the ship would be heading for Pitcairn, Easter Island, and Robinson Crusoe, three Pacific islands I was missing. I flew to Tahiti on 30th October and joined the other passengers for a brief tour before sailing. I was not surprised to see the average age of the passengers was well in excess of seventy.

In fact, quite a few were over eighty, and very active. Gertrude was on her 199th country, and her fourteenth cruise with the same company. Elinor had only managed thirteen cruises because her plane had arrived too late into Tahiti for the previous cruise.

By one of those coincidences in life, these were the two ladies who'd earlier sent the TCC brochure to my office, thinking I'd be interested.

The tour consisted of the usual historical accounts: Captain Cook, missionaries, Polynesian seafarers. At one point the guide took us to a waterfall, leaving several of the older men waiting by the bus. He returned mischievously to say there were graceful 'wahini' (maidens) bathing in the waterfall. Immediately a stampede of male senior citizens descended on the area, all tiredness forgotten.

We sailed through the TUANMOTUS and the AUSTRALES to PITCAIRN. To me one of the incredible experiences of travelling far and wide – even to notch up more countries – was to see with my own eyes places as storied as this.

Anybody who'd watched the movie *Mutiny on the Bounty* knew the basic story, how first mate Fletcher Christian and twenty-four fellow crew seized HMS *Bounty* from Captain William Bligh, and set him and eighteen loyal crew adrift in an open cutter. The mutineers eventually settled on Pitcairn as their new home.

Now here were Christians and Youngs (descendants of the original midshipman) welcoming us, heaving us onto the back of their three-wheeled all-terrain Hondas for the noisy ascent of the steep cliffside track to the hamlet of Adamstown. Here in the square was the quaint church with the Bible from the *Bounty* inside – outside was the anchor.

This was a community of forty-four residents, 3,000 miles from the nearest landmass, with no airstrip, no dock even (the islanders came out to fetch us in aluminium longboats), no doctor; and, many would say, no future and no hope.

Until recently they'd had no telephone, communication with the outside world being by tapped morse code. Emergency operations, if necessary, were performed by the Adventist pastor's wife with a kitchen knife, her only guidance being ham radio instructions from California or England.

The entire population were at least nominally teetotal, vegetarian Adventists, since their first ever reading matter had been a box despatched by Adventist missionaries from America. Judging by the scurrying by the earliest arrivals to purchase several crates of beer from the ship's stocks, things may have relaxed somewhat.

The islanders sold us carvings and stamps – their main revenue earners. We passed the other three islands in the group – Ducie, where they occasionally went shell-hunting, Oeno, and the controversial one, Henderson. This was the one a millionaire coal miner from Virginia attempted to buy from the British government, before he fell prey to the wildlife lobby on behalf of the unique flightless rail, and other birds, flowers and insects known nowhere else.

The islanders, all forty-four of them, came out in their longboat to see us off. 'Send back the empty box, please, when you get back,' shouted the seller of my *Bounty* model, 'we need it!' It was the first time an entire country had seen me off. As we sailed off, their lusty voices chorused: 'In the sweet bye and bye, We shall meet on that beautiful shore,' attesting at one and the same time to their faith, their nautical roots, and what must at times be for them an excruciating loneliness there in the empty regions of the Pacific.

EASTER ISLAND was next – that strange land of giant stone carvings, massive canyons, and legends of 'bird men' diving off sheer cliffs for eggs. Then ROBINSON CRUSOE ISLAND (Juan Fernandez), the exact spot used by Defoe as a model for his hero. I said goodbye to the ship in Chile expecting to see it again in just over a month's time down near Cape Horn for the Antarctic circumnavigation. I flew north on Varig to Recife, in north eastern Brazil. Here at last I found the organiser of charter flights out to FERNANDO DO NORONHA. These flights couldn't be found listed in any timetable, and were only sold locally. Fernando was a Brazilian military base that had been turned into a sort of Butlin's holiday camp. Dolphin-watching and diving were the main attractions.

Two hundred and ninety-five. Only five to go to the magic 300! But those five could be inordinately difficult. Thirteen more and the list would be complete. I'd now completed North, Central and South America, the Caribbean barring one – San Andres and Providenciales – Africa, Asia, Europe, Near East and Mediterranean. Four Antarctic, four Pacific Ocean, three Atlantic, one Indian Ocean and San Andres remained to be tackled. All were remote islands, prohibited military bases, swathes of ice, or a combination. You could hardly call any of them a 'country' without stretching the definition to the limit, but it was too late now to turn back!

A big setback was in store. I developed pneumonia in December, and had to cancel my place on the Antarctic semi-circumnavigation. The fact that guest lecturer James Michener also had to cry off for a hip operation, was cold comfort. There might never be another chance at these thoroughly remote parts of the white continent.

Our son Nathan was born in May 1987. We moved to England. The race for the world was on a back burner for a time largely because of the lack of opportunities to get to the remaining places. I began to lose hope of the overall total. Reaching 300 depended on when a booking would come through on the St Helena ship.

It had been inconveniently timed to coincide with the Antarctic circumnavigation, one being once a year, the other once every ten years. I'd missed both. I determined not to lose out the following year, and motored down to the tiny village in Cornwall, Porthleven, from which Curnow Shipping operated. Mrs Carole Kitchen assured me I was on the waiting list for January 1988 and January 1989. She'd have a better idea closer to departure.

They had to wait and see exactly how many berths would be requisitioned by officials. Also the ship had caught fire and missed one sailing, causing a knock-on effect to the others. The St Helena-Ascension shuttle was always overloaded, she regretted. They carried far, far more passengers than the vessel's licence allowed. But what could they do? It was the islanders' only means of transport.

I did have one small breakthrough. I reached the Tokelau Affairs Office in Samoa by phone, and amazingly they said: 'September looks all right.' Not for a cabin, mind you; they'd long since been booked. But if I didn't mind sleeping on deck?

I didn't, the first night. I happily carved out space amongst islanders, pigs, chickens, and necessary freight. It was on the second night that I knew something was wrong when I cocked one eye open and looked around to find that all my fellow deck-occupiers had scarpered. What did they know or suspect that I didn't? Next minute, *splash*! A gigantic wave, the first of several, burst over my sleeping bag, and thoroughly soaked both it and me.

The food ran out on the fifth day. It was a six-day trip. But the local schools were given a holiday, in honour of the boat's arrival. Or maybe the children just took the time off; I'm not sure! We called at all three islands: FAKAOFO, ATAFU, NUKUNONU. Two of the advantages of the trip were the chance to stay at Aggie Grey's, one of the South Pacific's most famous hostelries, and to visit the grave of 'Tusitala' – storyteller Robert Louis Stevenson.

After Tokelau I flew from Samoa to Fiji to connect with the weekly Air Caledonie flight (in a now rarely-seen French Caravelle jet from the early '60s) to WALLIS and FUTUNA, two French islands I'd not visited before. The Archbishop of the Isles was my seat companion, and a rather drunk local must have been severely conscience-stricken, because he kept coming down to our seat, dropping to his knees, and attempting to kiss the ring on the prelate's finger. After five or six of these sorties, the two stewards grabbed and pinioned him, tying him with rope to an empty seat for the rest of the flight.

My final stop on this unusual Pacific itinerary almost got me into trouble with HM Customs on arriving back into the UK, even though everything was above board! It was San Andres in the Caribbean, which the Colombians used as an entrepot for goods from the US. The check-in lines went on for ever, as each person or family group seemed to have at least twenty cases, boxes, bales or cartons with them.

Sneakily, the UK customs men at Gatwick had a look in my suitcase, where I'd discarded my old flight coupons, before asking me where I'd been, and what was the purpose of my trip. About to say 'Tokelau', I thought better of it (exotica is often disbelieved by officials, strangely!). 'Colombia,' I said, usually a red flag, but the frank upfront admission took them aback, as did my explanation for the suspicious itinerary.

Outside, Shelly was holding up our four-month-old son, in a blue sweater with a big red 'B' on it. Since his name began with 'N', I never did work out what the 'B' was for. He'd been three months old when I left, but seemed like a babe-in-arms. Travelling to the last few countries, and missing any more of his early days, would be hard.

# 36

## First to the Pole

*South Pole (1987–8)*

Just ten to go now! But these last ten would be tough! Three military bases – as yet no word of any way in – three Atlantic islands – fingers crossed for 6th January 1988 (twice: first to get on, second to be able to land at Tristan). Four Antarctic territories: here the prospect was of separate negotiations with each government regarding somehow visiting their slice of the Antarctic pie. Outlook bleak.

With 298 countries to my credit, I was desperate to achieve two more soon and pass the 300 mark. The most likely still looked to be St Helena and her two dependencies, for which I'd have to wait until January. The other seven began to seem unreachable. We made plans to spend Christmas with Shelly's parents, ready to return in early January for the sailing of RMS *St Helena* if I got on.

A flyer for an unusual tour departing 18th November fell into my hands: '16 Days – $35,000 – South Pole'. I laughed. I'd heard about the North Pole trips through upper Canada by Twin Otter, but the South Pole? Wasn't that only for explorers? The whole idea seemed faintly ludicrous.

Besides, I knew something of the background to this expedition. It was being offered to a select roster of up-market cruise clients (and presumably those on the TCC list) by an American company. But they were only packaging under their own label an adventure put together by some very determined Canadian mountain climbers.

These climbers were the daredevils of their profession, if you could call mild-mannered, conservative Canadians daredevils in any meaningful sense. They'd scaled peaks worldwide before deciding the Antarctic was the next frontier to conquer. For the last few years they'd been organising climbing parties to Mount Vinson, deep in the Antarctic interior, concentrating on extending the reach of support of civilian endeavours such as theirs beyond the Antarctic coast.

Perforce, they'd learned a lot about operating under harsh conditions. The two things I remembered hearing were that they'd equipped an old DC3 with a third engine to carry out flights to the Antarctic (it crashed), and that they'd been involved in back-up support last year for the 'Footsteps of Scott' walk to the Pole (their supply ship sank, and the South Pole base chief ordered their immediate evacuation).

Then there was the vexed question of whether going to the South Pole even counted as French, Australian, New Zealand and particularly Norwegian Antarctic. By walking around the actual Pole, you were theoretically walking round the entire world, so you could almost count everything, but especially the wedges of territorial claims, which all narrowed to their apex right at the Pole.

Norway was the difficult one. Its claim was always shown on maps with dotted lines, since its territorial limits had not been defined. But that meant it hadn't been officially determined that its claim didn't reach the Pole either.

All this was very interesting, I mused, but highly theoretical. The tour was due to depart in four days' time, from the southern tip of Chile. The passenger list ('limited to fourteen', said the flyer) would have been long since closed, the $35,000 from each person (half a million dollars all told) no doubt already applied to defray what must have been exceptionally high set-up costs. (My own company's tours had been considered expensive, but you could have gone five times on the train from London to Hong Kong for the price of one South Pole passage.) And the detailed arrangements necessary? The special clothing? Getting a seat in time on a flight all the way down to Punta Arenas?

That night I awakened suddenly from sleep. I sat bolt upright in bed. It was almost 1 a.m.; not quite 5 p.m. the previous day on the West Coast. It was worth a try! My fingers feverishly dialled the US access code, then the number. A pleasant female voice answered.

Yes, somebody was still there in public relations. She'd put me through. A young man with a Scandinavian name but generic American accent came on the line. He listened to my proposal thoughtfully. 'I'll get back to you in a few hours,' he said.

In view of the time difference, I was surprised to find a reply fax already on my machine when I came down to breakfast. It was an acceptance of my proposal to film the attempt on the Pole for network television, made possible, they said, by one of the paying passengers having dropped out at the last moment. But it was in the form of a contract, which had to be signed and returned the same day or the offer was void.

I scanned the conditions and my heart sank. Sixteen pages of waivers and liability releases. A medical exam would be necessary. Even clothing suitable for Antarctic cruises (which I had) would not be suitable. Special boots, special pants, a special parka, and a sleeping bag certified to $-40°$, *must* be obtained. Failure to do so voided the contract. They could not help – their equipment had been especially ordered more than six months ago.

No extra room could be made, or weight allowance increased, for my camera equipment, and it was up to me to protect it against the extreme cold. And I needed to pay for my share of the charter costs, food and fuel. (I later learned that the fuel was costed out at $110 per gallon!) The money clause, with specific wiring instructions, and an injunction against divulging the particulars, was repeated twice.

Ironically, it was the difficulty of meeting all these conditions that galvanised me into saying 'yes'. I wired funds, popped round to my friendly village GP, Jane Woodgate, at the end of her surgery, booked tickets through Brazil to Chile, and started tapping my network in the BBC for technical tips.

These turned out to be more like horror stories – how the tripods snapped during the Reagan-Gorbachev summit, and film froze in the canister in Russia. I phoned contacts at Ted Turner's CNN in Atlanta, partly for their advice, partly to sell them the film of my trip. They'd just had a crew return from the Antarctic, so didn't want any more footage from there. They'd been invited by the National Science Foundation in Washington DC.

Every year selected members of broadly the 'establishment' press and media were given a tour by the NSF. It was by invitation only. By way of contrast, the NSF's attitude to our tour was hostile in the extreme. They went so far as to send a letter to each US participant stating that they had 'serious reservations as to the . . . adequacy of contingency back-up aircraft, alternative recovery and refuge sites, fuel, shelter, provisions and other emergency response capabilities. Our concerns also stem from the absence of aids to navigation, and the paucity of weather, flight level, wind, and other flight support information.' They went on to say they wouldn't allow us to land at the South Pole, and wouldn't rescue us if we got stuck.

The letter was signed by Dr Peter E. Wilkniss, the very same Polar Division Director who'd brought the Scott expedition to an untimely end the previous year. This was sour grapes. The stranglehold of governments (and one government in particular) over the Antarctic was being threatened if private groups could now marshal their own resources. Control could be exercised over who visited and received favours as long as government maintained their monopoly. Science was supposed to be the be-all and end-all of Antarctic endeavour, but there was a lot of politics dressed up as science, scientific support, and national interests.

The night before I left I was contacted by a fellow in Hampshire who'd patented a method of preserving heat during tyre changes in Formula One car racing. He volunteered to construct a customised heating insulation blanket to completely wrap around my camera. He and I stayed up all night until it was finished. The clothing was pure brinkmanship. I phoned the British Antarctic Survey. They gave me the home phone number of their supplier in the north of England. He sized me over the phone, cobbled together items from what he had on hand (including a magnificent pair of Japanese 'Iceman' yellow boots), charged my credit cards, and put the whole package on a night train.

I'd no time to check them over – in fact I saw them for the first time in a box sitting behind a wire grille at Tunbridge Wells Station when I went to pick them up on my way to Heathrow. Since the thick red parka didn't fit into my already bulging suitcase, I wore it on the Tube. I got some funny looks!

After the ulcer-inducing rushing to join the group, it was frustrating to walk into a situation of indefinite delay in Chile. All four engines on the DC4 had to be replaced. Bad weather had delayed the caching of fuel and food. Political sensitivities had to be ironed out. With everyone on a 'high' of expectation on arrival, it was sad to watch the enthusiasm trickle away.

We were due to have returned from the trip by Thanksgiving. December approached, and the final survey flight had not yet taken place. Four years of planning were beginning to unravel. Hope and optimism, so rare at the best of times, evaporated. Giles Kershaw, chief pilot for the expedition, returned to his 'other' job of flying 747s for Cathay Pacific in Hong Kong. Four of our people went on an extended trip around the Chilean and Argentine Lake Districts. Two dropped out of the expedition. I returned to England, a trifle demoralised.

The organisers had promised to summon us back once they had more grounds for optimism about the trip. Our lengthy non-productive sojourn at the tip of Chile had impressed on me the enormity of the task facing the organisers. Remaining in England on almost permanent standby, I began to worry, as Christmas neared, that the South Pole's new dates might come uncomfortably close to the St Helena dates, which were already set in concrete. (They'd effectively moved me up to the top of the waiting list by taking my money.)

Just a day or two before Christmas Eve there was a glimmer of hope about the expedition, but too uncertain in its nature, and coming at much too short notice to make feasible the operation of securing airline seats to South America at such a peak time, never mind dragging participants from all over the world away from their Christmas arrangements.

What actually happened was worse. I gave up on the expedition – at least for the holidays – and booked non-refundable and non-changeable air tickets for myself, my wife and my six-month-old son, to my in-laws'. When word came to be ready to leave from Chile in the days immediately following Christmas, all three of us had to fly back to London on Christmas morning. Have you ever had to walk out on your mother-in-law just as the family is gathering for Christmas dinner, and tell her you're sorry, you've got to go to the South Pole?

There were a few more fits and starts. When I tried to check in at Heathrow on a Pan Am ticket which had been switched to Varig due to the many changes of date, it was a day when Varig had no flight. Swissair said they'd take me and checked my bags, with all my precious clothing, survival gear, and vital camera equipment, on the first leg of the journey to Zurich.

I had to go to the ticket desk to have the coupons exchanged.

That's where they decided they couldn't accept the ticket without an endorsement from Varig, who had no representative at the airport on non-flight days. I rushed back to the check-in counter to retrieve my baggage. Too late! It had gone to Zurich. I immediately paged a supervisor. 'See that my bags are sent direct to Santiago from Zurich,' I told him. 'On the contrary,' he said. 'We have a strict policy with passenger-unaccompanied luggage. It will come back here to its point of origin.' (Too late to join me before I left Punta Arenas for the cold.)

Pondering Swiss intractability, I had to hope that somehow common sense would prevail. I rushed over to British Airways, who had a jumbo leaving for Rio. There I could connect with a Ladeco flight to Santiago. The BA 747 ran an hour late, and was just pulling into its gate as the Santiago plane nosed off. I was stuck for twenty-four hours, my bags were in Switzerland, I'd missed the connecting flight from Santiago down to Punta (by just one day).

Fortunately, there was yet another delay on the Antarctic Airways (as the Canadians had so appositely named their 1945 vintage DC4, leased for them by a Calgary charter operator, since they couldn't muster enough insurance). I made it by the skin of my teeth. So, amazingly, did my bags. If the 'dash' to the Pole (which it now was – after November delays, nobody had the stomach for a long, drawn-out itinerary) was quickly completed, I might even make it – only just! – back to Britain before the RMS *St Helena* left port.

It was not to be. Delays are almost second nature in terrain such as Antarctica, especially with the type of expedition we were trying to mount. As the day came for the *St Helena* to sail south, and we were still on terra firma in South America, I stopped thinking about those potential three territories lost for another year, and mustered all my energy for the present four Antarctic territories.

The air was electric when we eventually got airborne in the hollowed-out shell of the tatty DC4. It had been freed from its northern fire-fighting duties (last in a long line of uses after United retired it in the early '50s) and the inside scooped out to be reconfigured with only twenty seats forward, long-range fuel capability, and masses of space in the hold for cargo and emergency needs. The Chileans jealously guarded whatever military secrets they were hiding and prohibited all departure photography at Punta.

We flew over the Drake Passage, down the peninsula, and deep into the Antarctic continent for an uncomfortable, unpressurised eleven hours, glimpsing ice floes and landmarks below, chatting and snoozing alternately, savouring the experience ahead.

The landing at the edge of the Ellesworth Mountains was on the world's most southerly runway – a sheet of bare ice, 11,000 feet long and 160 feet wide. Kershaw, back from Hong Kong, had already made a dozen proving flights, ferrying in huts, food, fuel and equipment: testing the capabilities of the aircraft and the icefield, the Canadians had reassured us. They didn't tell us how many of the landings were sideways, nor that on the trip made while we were waiting in Punta in November, his Omega navigation equipment had packed up, so he located the field by 'dead reckoning'. Was this adventure or what?

It was the passengers, not the plane, which slipped and skidded on first contact with the ice cap this time. We looked like Laurel and Hardy as we bounced off, rather than disembarked. You don't really get a feel from the air of what the ice cap is like, but once you set foot on it you experience the peculiar mixture of snow your footprints sink into, which isn't like the Christmas card stuff you know, combined with an icy surface which isn't as slick as an ice-skating rink but still demands caution.

Supplies had to be unloaded on the double, onto skidoo-hauled pallets, to avoid excessive cooling of the plane's Pratt and Whitney radial engines. The camp area was in sight of the plane, but the half-mile walk to it was the first test of both gear and human reactions to this inhospitable place, 1,400 miles inside the Antarctic Circle, a good 2,000 miles from what could be called our nearest 'town', Punta, the one we'd just left in Chile, a full 600 miles from the nearest habitation of any kind.

'Welcome to Patriot Hills. 80°20'S,' said the hastily-erected banner. Home was going to be among the oil drums in one of these five orange tents (or 'polar huts', as the organisers preferred to call them) for the next three days, while waiting for optimum weather to fly to the Pole. One of the tents – the combined kitchen, diner, radio room, operations centre, lounge and briefing area – you could stand up in. The toilet's low snow walls gave you privacy on three sides and a fresh breeze on the fourth. Every item, including the plastic bag that served as receptacle here, and all our rubbish to the last sweet wrapper, had to be brought back out of the Antarctic at a cost estimated to be $1,000 for each one of us.

This wasn't the Antarctica of the cruise ships – cute penguins and seals performing for the cameras at the continent's edge, where ice met ocean, and summer temperatures could even rise above zero. Here a walk of a few hundred yards took you into indescribable solitary communion with nature, and the ever-present danger of losing your bearings. You didn't dare wander far. Fierce winds could blow up a storm in seconds, wiping out the horizon.

On the third day, 10th January, just as we were beginning to get used to our surroundings, pilot Henri Peck assembled the first seven of us into one of the two Twin Otters parked at Patriot Hills. The Pole was so close we could smell it. Given favourable weather, we'd make it in five hours. Our watches said it was afternoon, but that didn't mean anything in this land of twenty-four-hour daylight.

We'd been airborne for just over two hours when the weather closed in. 'We're going to make an emergency landing at our other base in the Thiel Mountains,' came back word from the cockpit. As we descended I scanned the horizon for the first signs of something that looked like where we'd just left. Wrong! I saw nothing but one blue Esso drum poking out of the ice, and a range of hills that looked forbiddingly close.

After the propellers came to a stop all was clear. Martyn Williams, expedition leader, and pilot Henri handed out spades. We all started digging in unison, the costliest construction crew ever. The passengers on this journey were paying $7,000 a day to form a protective wall, made from ice blocks! Behind it, we quickly set up our two emergency tents. The other Otter landed behind us.

A forty-knot wind howled and blew around us all that night. Our rations consisted of a chocolate bar, passed through the zippered tent door. No cooking could be contemplated. We felt like the writer of the Old Testament Psalms who first saw God's handiwork in an icy version of the quiet waters and still pastures, then felt the thundering and turbulence of the elements His might had created.

Twenty-six hours later the storm subsided. We breakfasted and strapped in for our take-off run. I will never forget those six attempts at take-off as long as I live. As each of five tries was aborted, just short of the looming hill full in our view, knuckles

turned white, uneasy looks were exchanged, queasy feelings sur-
faced. Airborne on the sixth run, we hovered alarmingly close to
the ground for what seemed an age, before finally gaining height
and leaving the Thiel Mountains behind.

Refuelling was performed in flight. That's why eleven of the
eighteen seats had been removed to make way for rows of the blue
fuel drums that were almost a symbol of our journey by now. It was
an odd experience to drape your arm over the edge of your seat and
find your elbow resting on fifty gallons of aviation gasoline. Odder
still to see a hose pipe emerging from the cockpit, and being asked
to connect it to a floor outlet to start the flow. Most odd of all, to
see a small leak form, sputter onto the floor, and cause the system
to be shut off and start again. Definitely a non-smoking flight!

The tension was palpable as we circled. We were on approach
to the South Pole. It seemed unbelievable. We could see the Stars
and Stripes and the famous silver geodesic dome housing the US
base. An American voice on the radio told us pointedly we weren't
authorised to use their runway. The pilot and expedition leader
being Canadian, they went ahead anyway and nosed down.

Ten men in rust-coloured anoraks surrounded us the moment we
landed. Most of them had walkie-talkies and appeared to be saying
to each other things like: 'Private aircraft has landed. Await instructions.' And: 'Approaching private aircraft. Will report back.'
Followed by: 'Door of private aircraft is being opened and passengers disembarking.'

We must have looked a sight, the first tourists *ever* to the SOUTH
POLE, fumbling with our cumbersome gear, tumbling out of our
cramped, airborne quarters, with expressions on our faces that
hovered between awe, incredulity and defiance. We'd done it!
We'd landed! The first non-government-assisted private expedition
in the history of South Pole travel. The mind-numbing −40°
temperature was momentarily forgotten. Our guide opened the
door and stepped out. Then I backed out, video camera running to
capture people's faces as they emerged. So I suppose, if you don't
count leaders, I was the first tourist at the South Pole.

Our phalanx of guards, with the appearance of those about to
arrest an alien who has strayed onto their planet, quickly transmogrified into a hearty welcoming committee. Yes, the ground rules
had been established in a call a few minutes before to Washington
DC. (A smile of satisfaction crossed the expedition leader's face,

realising that meant Peter Wilkniss would have been roused from bed in the early hours!) We would be invited into the base for a limited time. We could buy a souvenir (limit one per person). We would be entitled to one cup of coffee and one cookie each.

My mind went back to the porter's message at Lincoln College, Oxford – so much for the aircraft charter 'including coffee and biscuits'. This time it was $35,000 *plus* airfare, 'including coffee and biscuit' (singular). The invitation inside the base was appreciated. The restriction on comestibles was churlish, given that it cost the taxpayer just as much to fly a pound of lobster in from Christchurch, New Zealand, as it did a pound of cookies.

No amount of bureaucratic displeasure could dampen the genuine warmth of the welcome accorded to us by base personnel. Manager Mike Constantine was cordial and helpful. We set about doing what tourists everywhere do. Minnesotan Warren Bjorklund exclaimed: 'What a party!'; Pennsylvanian Norman Hahn hunted for a patch; nurse Anna Burton from Key West, Florida unfurled a presentation banner 'from the southernmost city in the US to the southernmost point on earth'; oil company CEO Merle Chambers from Denver chatted to the scientists; eighty-two-year-old Howard Bean from Tuscaloosa, Alabama told onlookers about his North Pole trip; I filmed; Long Islander Carmen Becker stayed with husband Bob and Texan Caroline Ross who were being connected to oxygen bottles and looking slightly piqued.

But, of course, the main business was outside. It required some effort just to walk the few hundred yards to the 'Ceremonial South Pole' (the semi-circle of flags where visiting dignitaries were pictured). The elevation was close to 10,000 feet. It felt like more. The air was thin and ice cold. The survival clothing impeded movement.

Colourful as it was, this pole was not our goal. A short way beyond it a small bronze post protruded from the ice, like a periscope from a submerged submarine. On it was the inscription: 'USGS 90°S'. This was it. From here all directions were north, as far as the eye could see. From here too you could walk around the globe. I did it in a rather slow eleven seconds, then a quicker seven, pausing only long enough to be sure my feet touched the French, New Zealand, Australian and putative Norwegian sectors of Antarctica.

I was elated. Not only had my country count now jumped to 302, I had conquered the odds. Polar travel was still an exclusive preserve. After Robert Falcon Scott's ill-fated 1912 expedition, *no one* went there for forty-four years. I would soon become one of not many more than a hundred people in all of history who'd set feet on *both* poles. And how many of those had been to 300 countries besides?

It was not just the numbers, impressive as it was to look figuratively up at the rest of the globe and realise – three British dots and three American military bases aside – I'd been to every last country and territory out there. It wasn't just for the slices of Antarctic that I'd come to the South Pole. To stand here, at latitude 90° South, was to realise an exploration dream, one that had driven enterprising souls since the continent was first sighted. The quest to reach the southernmost point on earth was the ultimate for the great explorers. Now I'd done it. Granted, not the hard way by huskies, horses or foot. But that didn't take away one whit from the feeling of elation. To this day I don't think I remember any other trip so vividly.

I didn't think then, and I don't think now, that transforming the stuff of legend, heroism, knighthoods, and claims in the name of the sovereign, into something available to anyone who could pay for the ticket was demeaning. Rather it opened up a whole new means of access to a continent that theoretically belonged to no one and was available to all, but in practice had been the preserve of government. But the established organs didn't give up easily. A *New York Times* headline thundered: 'Tourists and Cigarette Butts Make Inroads at South Pole'. (No one in our group smoked during the polar visit!)

An officious American administrator was quoted (anonymously) in another article as saying. 'It's the curse of a leisure class that can afford to go to the uttermost end of the earth to dump its orange peel.' (We didn't consume any fruit at his station, just coffee and *one* cookie. And we left not a single item behind.) The high price tab was sniffed at. Since when has major league travel been cheap? Expeditions, whether in Columbus' time or ours, cost big dollars to put together. So do the salaries and costs of the ninety percent of the US Antarctic programme that supports the ten percent scientific part which is its declared purpose.

Much of the ill-informed comment stemmed from incredulity. That a small mountaineering outfit from British Columbia would be crazy enough to even think of attempting a self-sufficient

South Pole expedition, putting their own 'permanent' camp on the continent, laying in a year's supply of fuel and food, researching and inaugurating the world's southernmost runway, and organising all the necessary logistics. And having thought of it, to actually achieve it – even allowing for a few false starts. There were many doomsayers who averred it couldn't be done; I too was one of the sceptical ones in the early stages. Perhaps it hadn't fully sunk in to outside observers, even when it had been achieved.

The dangers inherent in polar travel, whether government or private, came home to us when we learned that two US Navy fliers crashed on the polar plateau, near our route of flight between the time of our first and second attempts. A short time later Giles Kershaw, our chief pilot and one of the prime architects of our expedition, lost his life too in a crash. No toehold was gained in such a unique and forbidding place without a price being paid.

I came away from the South Pole trip with a great respect for the Antarctic. In my pursuit of countries and a record, in my desire to win a race, I'd discovered a place which, despite enormous logistics, scarce facilities, immense distances, and sometimes appalling weather, took hold of my spirit in a way I'd not seen anywhere else do.

Of course I preferred visiting inhabited regions of the earth, for all the benefits mutual encounters between people could bring. But there was something very special about this last great pristine wilderness, where men had not as yet managed to quite entirely destroy the Creator's handiwork. Who knows what developments the future will see in South Pole tourism? If the critics of our trip are to be believed, there'll be an exponential increase in the number of tourists. But we were the first.

*The going was splendid.*
*So we arrived and were able to plant our flag at the South Pole.*
*God be thanked.*
Roald Amundsen, 14th December 1911

# 37

# Forgotten Colonies

*Ascension, St Helena, Tristan (1988)*

Unfortunately the triumph of the South Pole was about to be lost in a tragedy as far as the country-count was concerned. The RMS *St Helena* had not only left Britain, but would – just at the exact moment I was flying back from the Pole – be steaming out of Tenerife in the Canaries, the last point at which I could have conceivably joined her.

It wasn't as if I could speed up of my own accord, hail Concorde, or anything like that. My penchant for long roundabout routes seemed to stick to me doggedly, even when I needed all haste. Punta Arenas to East Sussex was a complicated journey, since most South America to London flights weren't daily, and the two flights out of Punta were at different times (on different airlines) on different days.

We managed a small anti-climax after the successful Pole visit. Most of us would have kept right on going, as soon as the Otter touched down at Patriot Hills – after all, our mission was accomplished. Only one thing stood in our way: the DC4 was in Punta and had to be summoned to come and pick us up.

Three days we waited, three agonising days, during which I saw all hopes of St Helena slipping away from me. The Canadians made a great point of how radio contact was maintained throughout the expedition. But usually you could only raise Patriot Hills from Chile about midnight. It seemed to work the same way in reverse, only it was every third midnight, it seemed.

Eventually the DC4 pulled in to bring us out. The timing seemed to be more connected with bringing in another fourteen or so tourists to repeat the South Pole trip, now that the inaugural had proved to be a success: this slightly irked those who'd paid a premium to be on the very first flight, when the difference between first and second flights was only a matter of days.

Armies of TCC-types invaded Punta. The price for the second trip was reduced to $25,000 for speedy fill up. Word got around quickly! As I was leaving the Navigantes Hotel for the airport, I could see through the back window of my taxi a bald American lawyer of about seventy running after the cab, slightly breathless. I signalled to the driver to stop. The lawyer leaned in through the window and asked if I could give him my Antarctic gloves, as he didn't have any, and was going to the Pole. I told him I'd lost one on the ice near Patriot Hills, so I could give him one, and maybe he'd be in luck and find the other one. Perhaps the newspapers had a point about certain kinds of tourists after all!

I counted the weary miles (and days!) from Patriot Hills to Punta (hoping no diversion to pick up stranded Chinese scientists at King George Island this time). Arrival too late to get out the same day. Overnight. No early enough flight next day to be in Brazil in time for a direct flight to Europe, so the long haul instead – domestic flight with one stop to Santiago, Buenos Aires (five-hour delay, but excellent steak dinner in the transit lounge); Miami (morning arrival – forced day stop until overnight flight), Cincinnati, Gatwick.

An en route phone call brought me up to date with the St Helena situation. There was one last chance to catch up with it, and that was if I could fly directly (or via the Falklands) on a military plane into Ascension the day the ship was due to arrive in port. I couldn't overnight in Ascension because there was no hotel, and permits weren't given to civilians. (I was going to hear this refrain a lot from military bases in my last territories!) Even to land there required permission from the Ministry of Defence, and since it was a Royal Air Force aircraft which only operated twice a week, getting a seat also required MOD clearance – not lightly given.

At this stage the help of Mrs Gay Denbow, St Helena's UK representative, was invaluable. She was providing facilities for me to film at St Helena. Somehow her intervention broke a logjam, and on arrival at Gatwick I got a message that the RAF would fly me down – provided I paid the civilian rate. Civilian rate was twenty-five times the military dependant rate (maybe I would have a few rows to myself!).

There was still a great deal of paperwork to be done to actually secure a positive booking on the Port Stanley flight, and confusion about exactly when it operated, due to no timetables being published. Actually, it wasn't so much paperwork as endless phone calls to the appropriate 'desk' in Whitehall, and fielding replies which started as evasive and ended as merely vague. It all seemed to be done by a series of oral communications. I was never given any receipt or passenger coupon. You just had to make sure the messages passed through the right channels.

Finally it appeared that a plane was leaving in thirty-six hours, and this was the one I had to be on. I dropped all the survival gear from the North Pole on the floor of my bedroom, repacked for the tropics and took the train to Oxford. I knew, or thought I remembered from student days, that RAF Brize Norton was out in rural Oxfordshire, somewhere west of Witney, and north of Faringdon; but it didn't help that civilian maps tended to overlook it. Maybe the cartographers didn't want to sign the Official Secrets Act!

The sketchy note I had helpfully said military ground transport would operate, but only from Swindon railway station, and a good three hours before flight departure. I missed out on both counts. I took a taxi, and swung in through the gates of the nerve centre of RAF Transport Command.

This was the point from which flights, with defence attachés, ambassadors, and air vice marshals aboard, left for Washington and other world capitals, and where two stately VC10s were on permanent standby to act as conveyors of the royal personage for long distance full-blown tours. It was another RAF convention, like seats facing backwards, to have a complete backup ready to fly, just in case of any trouble with the assigned aircraft: perhaps a wise move in view of the age profile of the Transport Command fleet!

Brize Norton, as well as being famous for sky-diving aerobatics, and air-to-air refuelling, had a very refined system for processing top military brass, government ministers, and important civilians, when they transited through as passengers. Certain categories of passenger were allowed into the VIP lounge after formalities, certain others were driven straight to the lounge, others merited a side entrance to the lounge; the top category was whisked immediately to the steps of the plane.

Even VIPs were divided into VIPs and VVIPs. I never discovered my own status – presumably it wasn't too exalted. The flight was being called even as I arrived, so, still slightly worried about not having a ticket, I assembled with all the troops heading out to Port Stanley, and boarded the L1011 Tri Star waiting amongst six sleek VC10s. Despite the closest scrutiny a dark January night allowed, I failed to determine which were 'the' two.

The Tri Star had a familiar look to it, which I recognised as soon as I saw the Pan Am markings on the seat belts. It was a special purchase for the Falklands run. They'd configured the whole of one side as a flying hospital, complete with stretcher and drip. The stewardesses were stewards, no alcohol was served, and there didn't appear to be any women passengers amongst the 200 on board.

Later on the ship I met a young woman who worked for a Spanish language TV station in Malibu. She'd managed to circumvent the regulations and get a seat on the RAF plane, which goes to show what can be done if you're determined. If US military prohibitions could be overcome with the same vigour, then maybe there was a chance after all of getting to Wake, Midway, and Diego.

In ASCENSION we landed on Wideawake Airfield, a brilliant name for 10,000 feet of asphalt on which you set down after the longest of transoceanic long-hauls from the UK, the Caribbean Basin, or virtually the tip of South America. The aerodrome was devoted to the military (US one side, UK the other). J2s, M2s, and all sorts of other military vehicles picked up their passengers and whisked them away. There was no terminal as such. A civilian felt a mite conspicuous.

I poked my head into the ops room and asked a sergeant how I could get to the ship, or how I could spend the ten hours or so that I had at my disposal here. He said: 'I was just reading about you in the island newspaper. You're the bloke who's going down to make a film in St Helena, aren't you?' Then people started appearing out of the woodwork, offering to show me around. The newspaper editor and the vicar asked why I hadn't told them I was coming, as they could have arranged the necessary sponsorship for a permit and accommodation. Oh well, next time!

As was invariably true with places you were told you weren't allowed to go to, when you got there, people were extremely friendly. I couldn't help noticing that the article the sergeant referred to somewhat overstated my credentials. It *was* true that the TV station for which I was filming was indirectly owned by Time-Warner. The article implied, though, nothing less than a front cover spread for *Time* magazine or a Warner Brothers movie.

Maybe that explained my later encounter with the drunk in the bar of the Consulate Hotel in Jamestown (the hamlet that served as St Helena's only town and capital), when I was filming there. He accosted me out of the blue, but spoke mainly to an audience of fellow drinkers: 'These pictures will be worth *millions . . . millions!*' he screamed, fully confident of the value of at least his share in the take. If he only knew the true price put on an educational programme in a commercial environment!

Actually even a tiny fraction of the British government's annual subsidy to each man, woman and child on St Helena (including the drinker) paid towards my editing budget would have produced a valuable public relations instrument for both the shipping line and the island colonies. I was besieged by officers, crew, passengers, and islanders for a copy of the finished product. Yet I ended up being out of pocket on the project, not helped by the insistence of both beneficiaries that I pay full fare.

The rather specious explanation was that the RMS *St Helena* was a government-controlled and subsidised ship. The taxpayers' money instead was spent on a fleet of junior staffers from Whitehall enjoying an ocean cruise followed by business-class flights home. On the ship I sat through a showing of a home movie with dreadful glitches that was painful to watch. But it was suitably fawning over the colonial administration, I suppose. The experience of coming on this trip was already beginning to tell me something about the fate of these isolated islands at the hands of pen-pushers thousands of miles away, and minor functionaries on the spot.

Someone was rustled up to take me on a round island tour. I'd heard that although nominally a dependency of St Helena, 700 miles to the south, Ascension was actually administered day-to-day by a combination of the USAF, the RAF, and my former employer the BBC. I was keen to see what the BBC especially had done with a volcanic cone a thousand miles from both the African and South American coasts – what surely must be one of the loneliest outposts ever of Britain's once vast empire.

I suppose it wasn't altogether strange that the BBC ended up administering what had for a hundred years or more been referred to by the British Crown as a ship ('HMS Ascension'). The Royal Navy were the first occupiers, in 1815, solely to prevent the French using the island (or ship) as a means of launching a rescue attempt for Napoleon – imprisoned on St Helena. The real story of the early twentieth century on Ascension was its critical geographical position, allowing it to become a hub of sorts in a cable-laying network across the Atlantic, from Cape Town to London, Dakar to Buenos Aires.

But today's Ascension had caught up with the space age. In place of the underwater cables, satellites. In place of the troop ferrying point from America to North Africa in World War II, an extended runway, a missile proving range, a NASA site at Devil's Ashpit, BBC aerials festooning English Bay, power stations, desalination plants, and some said (but in hushed whispers) widespread electronic eavesdropping, both by the British, and on behalf of the US National Security Agency.

The BBC had chosen a bleak, low-lying spot on the northern coast, covered with grey dust, sandstone, black lava and piles of clinker, for their Atlantic Relay Station. It was next to the fuel farm, where oil could be piped straight from supply ships in the bay below to tanks standing on the foundation of a former guano factory.

The workers needed for this new project were housed in a new village at the foot of Green Mountain, Two Boats. This colourful name derived from the ancient stopping place of sailors going to fetch water. Twenty-foot longboats had been upended in the earth, and seats provided on top of them. The *pièce de résistance*, however, was the English farmhouse built high up the mountainside by the early sailors. All the introduced greenery and water supplies prevented a natural inclination to feel that you'd landed on the surface of the moon. All in all, it was a strange mixture of oceanic outpost, Foggy Bottom, Hertfordshire, and out-of-this-world.

Returning from the tour, I joined the new doctor for St Helena in a sort of games room-cum-village hall, and waited for the four-wheel-drive transport down to the embarkation point. The Georgetown jetty was very slippery and slimy. Passengers not allowed off the ship watched our fumbling attempts in and out of the launches through binoculars. It was a recurrent sore point with the few TCC members who made it to the top of the waiting lists, that they were frequently not allowed to land.

The seventy-year-old lawyer who'd chased down my gloves in Punta Arenas had come all the way only to be told conditions were not favourable enough for him to go ashore. In the literature accompanying the passage, the Master made it clear that landings at Ascension and Tristan would not be permitted to those of a certain age (which varied between sixty-five and seventy).

The Royal Mail Ship *St Helena*, a slight, 3,150 ton vessel, built for the coastal waters around Vancouver – and still bearing maps and charts referring to British Columbia – was the successor to the great Union Castle mail ships of the UK-South Africa run in the heyday of ocean travel, before jets and mass tourism. It was a microcosm of the English small-time colonial society it served.

Tea at 4; Divine Service Sunday 10.30 (Anglican of course) followed immediately by the transformation of the lounge from church to pub, complete with darts. The 'Saints' (St Helenans) kept pretty much to themselves. The English socialised by class – the Governor and his circle kept attending parties in each other's cabins to which 'ordinary' paying passengers were not invited. Tourists were at the bottom of the social ladder: Americans below that, even.

The *Daily Information Leaflet* was a work of art. The first item was usually 'Rig of the Day', indicating whether you could expect to see the officers in white uniform or other exotic attire. As well as all the necessary information on 'Today's Events' ('Frog racing in the lounge – a 10p tote will be in operation'), it had a marvellous 'Did you know?' section, explaining to the layman such nautical terms as 'Oil on troubled waters': 'From the seamanship practice, frequently done in salvage work, where a little vegetable oil spread from windward has a remarkable effect in modifying the seas and thus reduces the risk of accidents'; and 'I'm alright Jack': 'The ultimate in self-consideration. In complete form, the expression is "Blow you Jack, I'm inboard". It comes from the standard joke that the first liberty man to climb the ship's side from the boat pulls the rope ladder up behind him.'

But the strangest of the morsels of information relayed by this all-purpose sheet was a request that all Freemasons on board have a meeting. Members were asked to jot down their name and affiliation inside an envelope to be left with Colin, the purser. For greater secrecy, the envelope could be marked 'M'. Nothing was said about handshakes!

Fortunately landing at ST HELENA did not threaten to be too perilous. A helpful note from Curnow in Cornwall drew our attention to the fact that at Jamestown disembarkation would be either via the ship's gangway or rope and a launch to the (slippery) wharf steps. But it gave hope to the old, infirm, or frightened: 'For those passengers who are unable to negotiate comfortably either the gangway or the wharf steps [no mention of the rope!] arrangements can be made for them to be landed in a specially-adapted cargo box which is lowered over the ship's side into a lighter and subsequently lifted from there directly onto the wharf.'

I spent a delightful two days filming on St Helena: interviewing the Governor in his mansion (Plantation House), climbing Jacob's ladder – a series of 700 steps cut into a sheer incline – coaxing Jonathan, the 255-year-old tortoise to perform for the camera, and visiting Napoleon's grave, receiving as a souvenir an authenticated copy of his death certificate from the current parish priest (Napoleon was exiled and died here). If they could solve the access problem, it would be a great draw for tourists from France.

I found a tremendous sadness in the place, a forlornness almost. Even though the RMS (as most of the Saints referred to the refitted *Northland Prince* from Vancouver) had ended their threatened total isolation when the Union Castle ships withdrew in the 1970s, 5,000 miles to the country they looked on as home and a mere five or six fully-booked sailings a year were features virtually guaranteeing their continued remoteness from the affairs of the world. Although living in a British possession, the new British Nationality Act rendered their passports useless for entry to the UK on a long-term basis. Our departure would take away the noise and excitement of one more sailing day, and would leave behind a quiet that was perhaps too quiet.

Before I left I found a monument to a Belfast doctor who'd served on the island in the 1920s, Dr W.J. Arnold. His obelisk was right in the middle of the parade ground, at the bottom of Jamestown's main street. He, of all colonial appointees, was said to have had a true understanding of the islanders' needs, and of their often grinding poverty. He frequently dispensed medicine without charge. He was revered by the Saints: 'The best friend St Helena ever had', read the inscription. A little human kindness went, and still goes, a long way.

The weather was kind enough to us to allow a landing at TRISTAN DA CUNHA. With an average of only one day out of six being favourable, we were fortunate. Landing, however, was quite complicated. Once off the ship and in one of the specially fabricated Tristan boats, you played a waiting game outside the little harbour of Edinburgh of the Seven Seas, until a large enough wave appeared which you could ride up on and crest through the harbour entrance, where hands reached down to haul you up to shore. Ever since I'd heard the story of these islanders, evacuated to Britain after their volcano erupted, and how keen they'd been to return, I'd wanted to meet them and talk to them.

Tristan was an unusual place. Only seven family names existed: Glass, Green, Hagens, Lavarello, Repetto, Rogers, Swain. Each family had their own 'potato patch'. Rock lobster fishing in the surrounding waters was profitable. They really didn't need any longer to be a dependency of St Helena, which in turn was a colony of the UK – one of the last.

But tradition died hard, and four Britons held the positions of administrator, doctor, schoolteacher and agricultural officer, respectively. News of my film hadn't reached the administrator, who'd been on a long home leave in the UK. So my reception in the three islands varied from celebrity status but still permit difficulties (Ascension), to full co-operation in a workmanlike way (St Helena), to official hostility (Tristan). The administrator was still smarting from having been described by a British journalist as more appropriately dressed for a day at the Cheltenham Races, than for the outdoor life on Tristan. Yet the locals greeted me warmly and were cordial throughout my stay.

I did witness a small piece of history. Pat Patterson, from Newcastle, England, had married a local girl, Susan Green, and come to settle, thus starting a new family name for the first time this century. I also climbed up the slopes of the volcano to where the ash was hot to the touch, and was made an honorary member of the (imaginary) Tristan da Cunha golf club, complete with tie.

The voyage ended in Cape Town on 11th February, leaving me three 'countries' ahead – with a total of 305. Only three to go, but to all intents and purposes these three were utterly unreachable.

Or so I thought. By an accident, or bad judgment, as a result of my pneumonia that caused me to cancel the circumnavigation cruise, I was throwing away my best chance to reach one of the three . . . maybe the only chance ever.

# 38

# Prisoners of War

*North Pole, Wake (1988)*

What I'd unwittingly thrown away was a chance to go to Midway – probably the most difficult territory on the TCC list to access.

Since I couldn't obtain a cash refund against the Antarctic circumnavigation, I'd been carrying a credit that had to be used up within the next few months. I decided to cash in my chips. And the only journey on offer was the North Pole!

So, ninety-seven days after standing at 90° South, I found myself helping to raise our own barber's pole (which we'd brought with us from Edmonton) at 90° North.

My scheduled routing from South Pole to North Pole was nothing if not unusual: South Pole-Patriot Hills – (King George) – Punta Arenas – Puerto Montt – Santiago – Buenos Aires – Rio de Janeiro – Miami – Cincinnati – London – Brize-Norton – Falklands – Ascension – St Helena – Tristan da Cunha – Cape Town – Johannesburg – Nairobi – Luxembourg – London – Amsterdam – Toronto – Winnipeg – Vancouver – Calgary – Edmonton – Yellowknife – Cambridge Bay – Resolute – Cornwallis – Magnetic Pole – Eureka – Conger – Eureka – Barbeau – 86° – North Pole.

From our 'Explorer's Inn' base at Resolute, my log entries show the Twin Otter itinerary:

|  | Arrive | Depart |
|---|---|---|
| Resolute |  | 14.00 17th |
| Little Cornwallis Mine | 14.35 17th | 15.00 17th |

| | | |
|---|---|---|
| North Magnetic Pole | 16.45 17th | 17.25 17th |
| Eureka Weather Station | 19.25 17th | 11.00 18th |
| Fort Conger | 13.35 18th | 15.10 18th |
| Eureka Weather Station | 17.25 18th | 19.25 19th |
| Barbeau Peak | 20.50 19th | 21.20 19th |
| Eighty-six North | 23.55 19th | 00.40 20th |
| North Pole | 02.55 20th | 04.05 20th |
| Eureka Weather Station | 08.55 20th | 11.15 20th |
| Grise Fjord | 13.45 20th | 11.00 21st |
| Devon Island | 11.45 21st | 15.00 21st |
| Resolute | 15.40 21st | |

Then two nights and a day to fly home from Resolute via Frobisher Bay-Montreal-Ottawa-Toronto-Amsterdam-London.

There was a lot of *déjà vu*: ski-equipped Twin Otters, Canadian pilots, special clothing, weather-dependent itinerary, no sunsets. The differences were just as intriguing: the landing, instead of being on a huge land-mass covered with thick ice cap, was on the Arctic Ocean, some 14,000 feet deep, with the merest smidgeon of ice (six to twelve feet) on top – enough to hold our aircraft, just! The pilot's first task on landing was to jump out and drill into the ice to establish just how thick it was!

No poles or markers. No scientific bases. Just a few Inuit, hundreds of miles apart. Plenty of animals, unlike the South. Sometimes we would fly low over a herd of musk ox. We had a dog-sled trip, and learned to build an igloo. I got high marks because I'd practised at the South Pole under emergency conditions!

But the overall impression I carried away from the NORTH POLE journey was how easy it all was, after the South Pole expedition. You just seemed to fly further and further north over the ice in Canada and suddenly you were there – the North Pole, last stop before Russia!

The seeming ease I'm sure was due to the practised proficiency of those intrepid Canadian bush pilots, who were now in their seventh year of North Pole service, and to the skill of guide Bezal Jesudason, an Indian who married a Canadian teacher and became the Arctic explorer's friend and outfitter. They too had had their bugs in the early days, the same as we experienced with the South Pole.

The first year (1982) one Twin Otter sank through a layer of soft ice, and plunged two and a half miles to the bottom of the Arctic

Ocean as the passengers watched from a few feet away on the ice, powerless to help. After a couple of hours shivering, a backup plane was despatched, and they were ferried back to shelter. But this time everything went flawlessly, even the part where I was on standby!

That didn't strictly concern the Polar part, but the critical connecting flight from Edmonton up to Resolute via Yellowknife on 16th April. Given the choice of paying $650 for this flight alone on a confirmed basis, or $379 for all my flights within Canada (Toronto, Montreal, Frobisher, Winnipeg, Calgary, Vancouver, Edmonton and Resolute – with Los Angeles thrown in as a bonus) on condition I travelled standby, I plumped for the latter without too much hesitation.

The folly of this registered with me when I learned that Mrs Jesudason's annual shopping list stretched to 12,000 lb of canned goods alone, none of which could be obtained locally. All her fresh vegetables, fruit and salad items had to be flown in on this plane and she was only one of many Far North residents depending on this vital air link. Not surprising, then, that more than half the 737's capacity was allocated to freight, leaving forty seats to be fought over by anybody whose business required them to be in and around the Arctic that next week.

If I'd missed that plane there was no other way whatsoever to join the North Pole flyers. I sweated a little the night before departure and I was definitely the earliest person registering at the desk for Canadian flight 687. I got on. In the light of what I'd missed to get to the North Pole I'd have been a little upset if I'd missed the Pole by trying to save money on the connecting flight. I returned to the UK on 23rd April. Time for a rest.

It was an enforced rest, because just after I'd paid over my circumnavigation credit, and confirmed my North Pole arrangements, I'd learned that a Royal Viking ship was planning a stop at Midway for a few hours on the way to California from the Orient in April. It was unprecedented. (I later heard that they'd sent a bevy of attractive young women out to do the negotiating over a period of months.) The dates clashed. There was no way I could do both Midway and the North Pole, and my money was committed to the Pole.

As the Viking ship was anchoring off the lagoon at Midway for its first and last five hour call on 19th April, I was wrapped up in protective Arctic clothing, hunched over the radio at Eureka Weather Station, waiting for the word which came later that night that conditions were ideal for a Pole attempt. But to be positioned for Midway I'd have had to fly to the Orient a week before, instead of reporting to Resolute Bay via Edmonton. By going to both Poles I had let Midway slip away. I regretted that decision. It looked like it might be a long time before I'd get another chance.

Of the three remaining bases, Wake came through first. That was something of a surprise. There actually was an organisation called 'Survivors of Wake, Guam and Cavite' in Boise, Idaho, run by one Chalas Loveland. It was largely a grouping of the civilian contractors who'd been employed by Morrison Knudsen and other companies to build up US defences in the Pacific just before the outbreak of World War II.

Although I ended up filming a 'special' on Wake, the June trip actually came about because Chalas' group of ex-prisoners of war had been planning a return trip for years and years, and couldn't ever quite muster enough people to charter an entire long-range aircraft to get them there. They had a lock on a Hawaiian Airlines DC8 for four days from 13th June, but needed forty bodies as well as the 132 from their own organisation. Thirteen Marines who'd served there, and twenty-seven TCC members made the numbers come out exactly right.

Schooled in the European side of the war, and hazy about what happened in the Pacific theatre, especially where America was concerned, I didn't know quite what to expect: the trip was an education.

The men who were returning to Wake were mostly in their late sixties and seventies. They'd been teens and early twenties in 1941, caught up in the outbreak of hostilities, forced to endure prison camp longer than almost anyone else during the entire war. Unlike the Marines, these civilians had not been recognised by the US government as participating in the war effort; hence were denied benefits and pensions.

That had been one fight they'd recently won. This trip had a different flavour: it was remembrance, pure and simple. A chance to relive the 'glory days', to expiate the horrors, to revisit an experience indelibly etched on their minds. I'd never been on such a focused journey before, or one of such intensity, where, despite the lightheartedness and continual banter, everyone had a ghost to lay at rest, or a memory to pluck from nearly half a century before, as if it was yesterday.

We started at the Arizona Memorial in Hawaii. The Pearl Harbor attack which launched America into World War II is known more or less worldwide. What I didn't realise was that Wake came under attack later that same day – the first day of hostilities in the Pacific theatre. Because of the International Dateline it's always recorded in history books as one day later: 8th December 1941. It was only four hours after the shelling of Pearl Harbor.

After we'd been to the Punchbowl, one of our number, Robert Curry, stepped up to the wall of names of those entombed when the SS *Arizona* was sunk, and placed a wreath. 'My brother lies there,' he said quietly. It was a very touching moment, so unlike visiting a mere tourist monument. I knew travelling with these men back to Wake was going to be an emotional experience.

The flight next morning almost never made it off the ground. Our engineer was asleep in bed, and Hawaiian Airlines had us listed incorrectly as a 'ferry flight'. The next time I heard those words, the mixup would be of invaluable help in finishing my race to all the countries of the world. For now everyone who'd set their alarms for 4 a.m. just groaned and waited.

When we got off the ground there was much paying for arrangements by those who hadn't and refunding to those who'd overpaid – a surprisingly large number. Our room and board at the air force base on Wake was going to run to the princely sum of $72 per person, sharing four or six to a barracks for the most part. Complimentary cocktails were offered to compensate for the late take-off, and the buzz of chatter became intense long before the dateline was crossed and 13th June became 14th June.

It was the yelling, not the normal announcement by the cabin crew, that alerted me to our imminent landing. A score of voices repeatedly chimed: 'There it is, there it is, there's Wake!' Men bringing their sons to show them the place of their torment, widows travelling in memory of their spouses, hard-bitten Marines, everyone was glued to the DC8's square windows, willing a closer glimpse of the three almost contiguous islets that made up Wake. We bumped down onto the sweltering apron, next to the sign proclaiming: 'Where America's Day Really Begins', and one by one the Wake defenders and friends spilled out, blinking either from the hot sun, or disbelief that their dream of returning was coming true.

On the ground a full dress uniform welcoming ceremony was headed by Major Dave Saunders, USAF. He quickly oversaw the transfer of everybody to the mess hall, where a briefing was laid on. We were not his most distinguished guests, as it turned out. 'In April I had Elizabeth Taylor in the back seat of my car,' was his opening gambit. 'I was in the driver's seat,' he added hastily.

A litany of information about Wake's role followed: the fourteen million gallons of JPY they had available (whatever that was), their participation in the Korean Team Spirit exercise, their recent rescue of sailors from a nuclear submarine that had run into trouble, their constant availability as a contingency measure in case war should break out somewhere in Asia, and how on normal days with nothing spectacular to do, they were implementing 'Operation Beautify' on the less than three square miles that was their charge. One of the journalists travelling with me summed up his speech succinctly: 'He supervises the six Air Force personnel, who supervise the twenty-five civilian American supervisors, who supervise the 152 Thais who do the work.'

Next, information that pertained to us: 'Transport is a big item here . . . mainly because there is so little of it. Basically during your visit it'll be non-existent, except for one formal tour. There are bicycles you can check out, but please don't forget to return them so someone else can use them. The 172 of you double the number of people we normally cater for in the mess hall, so please come an hour after the workers here are fed, and stagger your own arrival: Barracks 11–16 first, Barracks 17–28 last. Dial 211 if you have an emergency, 410 for a fire, and, above all, remember Wake Island Rule Number One: we close at five.' What with the din and all the excitement, nobody paid a blind bit of notice.

This was evident the first morning of our three-day stay on the island. The combination of time change, suppressed excitement, desire to explore old haunts, and the American's need for his awakening shot of caffeine, prompted a queue as far as the eye could see outside the mess hall at dawn – before it even opened. Any of the Thai workers who arrived even seconds later than their normal breakfast time found all their places at the food tables commandeered by hungry and excitable visitors.

My first quest was to see what had become of the Pan Am Hotel.

It had been bombed in what was only the second attack of the war. I crossed the rickety bridge with a couple of fellow aviation enthusiasts to comb through the ruins, and hark back in imagination to the great days of the transoceanic Clippers.

But the men had the bit between their teeth now, and were scurrying as fast as they could in all directions, here searching out a long-repressed memory, there sighting a landmark which prompted a flow of recollections. One man found the wallet he'd buried in the sand forty-seven years previously, and let out a whoop of delight.

Dar Dodds from Florida, who'd been a timekeeper for the contractors in 1941, and Bill Taylor, from Utah, were my informative guides on what was less a drive round Peale, Wilkes, and Wake than a history lesson come alive. 'It's been one-sided up to now,' Dar began, 'not to take anything away from the Marines who were wonderful, but there were 383 of them and 1,156 of us. Sometimes in the fighting that first day and on 11th December it was one sergeant and twelve civilians to a gun. This is acknowledged by Admiral Cunningham, the overall commander, in his book, sadly now out of print.'

Gradually as we shuttled from one part of the island to another, the tale unfolded – the first surprise attack on the 8th. The fierce onslaught on the 11th that was convincingly repulsed, even after Radio Tokyo had announced the capture of Wake, not expecting opposition. The big battle, when they were overrun, on the 23rd.

'They tied our hands with telephone wire, and lined us up in our revetments. Then their planes flew over and strafed the area just in front of us. It was clear they weren't sure quite what to do with us,' Dar and Bill said.

Most were eventually shipped to hellholes of prison camps in China or Japan. The Geneva Convention seemed to have little impact. 'We lost about half our men in the camp,' Al Brueck from Boise told me. 'Some of the younger ones just couldn't take it.' I asked Rich Pagoaga and Joe Goicoechea if they thought they'd ever come out alive. 'Yes,' they said, 'we refused to give in. But it was no picnic.'

A worse fate befell the ninety-eight civilians left on Wake as slave labour, after all their comrades had become POWs in Shanghai or Fukuoka. Whether in retaliation for the American air strikes which were now beginning to hurt, or out of sheer bloodymindedness, all were machine-gunned to death near the only memorial to civilians the island would see for four decades – a coral boulder they'd hand carved themselves in May 1943.

Those ninety-eight were in everyone's mind when the ceremony was held to dedicate the monument that had taken years of effort, and a plea that went all the way through Washington's bureaucracy up to John Leaman, Secretary of the Navy. Congressman Ron Packard, whose father was among the captured, spoke. His father had offered the prayer over the mass grave of the slain on 11th December 1941, on almost the same spot. His prayer was for a just and lasting peace.

'For no one loves peace more than those who have known the ravages of war. No one loves liberty more than the prisoner of war. May we all be a caring and righteous people, for without faith and devotion to God, neither peace nor liberty can be sustained.' Letters were read out from President Reagan and Vice-President Bush. It was a star-spangled occasion, but a very emotional, very moving one.

A faint drizzle fell as Father Joe McDonald, the son of a civilian defender who hadn't lived to see this return, led the religious dedication. 'All creatures need a home to go to at the end of the day, a place of refreshment, company, rest. We also need an eternal home when death brings down the curtain on our daylight. Our faith assures us that we have a home to go to, prepared for us, with many rooms, a home of refreshment, light and peace.' The raindrops ceased.

A slight chill held the air. Jim Lilly of Morrison Knudsen quoted from David Woodbury's book *Builders for Battle*: 'Ordinary men have the ability under stress to do far greater things than they believe they can do. If the summons is clear and urgent, man can become superman. We can rise to great heights if we have to.' It was ordinary men such as these who were being so honoured, men whose memorial, long overdue, was now firmly set in place.

The civilians gave way to a short ceremony for the Marines. Chief Warrant Officer Charlie Holmes presented the flag, saluted, and declaimed:

> They will suffer no more,
> We will remember them.

That was all. But the economy of words belied deep well springs of feeling. There was no mood of bitterness, but there was shared grief, and the easy fellowship that exists between people whose experiences were so intense. Tears flowed freely. I don't know what ghosts were laid to rest by that ceremony for the defenders, but as we left, I felt I'd been privileged to listen in on, and come alongside, for a brief moment, the experience of a whole generation that had been engulfed in a war that changed the world . . . for ever.

Rodney Kephart, one of our group, had awakened at 4.25 a.m. on the morning of the dedication. Like many of the defenders, he must have been turning over and over in his mind the events that made Wake a place of such poignancy. Suddenly a flash of inspiration struck him. He grabbed a pen and notepad, and scribbled down the words as they came to him. He showed me them later on the plane. They were words of reassurance and admonition from an all-knowing Creator God to His children:

> I knew each of you even before you were conceived. You were created for a special task, even those who gave their all these many years ago. Each of you have work to be completed. Some have hours, some days, some weeks, and some months or years. Remember, you are in My Hand and I am the Timekeeper. That which took place here did not escape Me. It all came to pass to fulfil My plan. Unless you forgive you can never forget. If you hold hatred, anger, animosity, and bitterness over what happened here, you are holding it against Me, for I am King of Kings and Lord of Lords. Forgive, My children, that you might forget what is past, so that peace can reign in your hearts.

The balmy shores of Wake had been at peace for forty years now. The gallantry of the men buried there, and the survivors, was at last deservedly commemorated. Wake may have been number 306 on a list of 308, but I think I learned more there about war and peace, about a time to remember, and a time to forget. I wouldn't forget Wake in a hurry.

# 39

## Forbidden Territory

*British Indian Ocean Territory (1991)*

Now that I'd found a way to visit one of the three highly-restricted military bases that had been my biggest challenge, I should have felt more confident about the other two. Yet it was easy to underestimate the difficulty of outwitting the prohibition put on civilian visitors by a powerful military, with the full backing of its government. In the event it was a full three years before I made concrete progress, and then only on one of the two bases.

Royal Viking decided not to repeat the 1988 Midway stop in any subsequent year, and no other shipping line stepped into the breach. That avenue was clearly dead. I petitioned offices of the US Navy in Washington, and at embassies abroad, with singular lack of success. I consulted congressmen, contacted admirals of my acquaintance, and made some headway with the Navy press unit, proposing a film on the upcoming anniversary of the Battle of Midway. They wanted to supply me with archive footage, or video shot by Navy cameramen, though, rather than allow me on to the island.

Major Saunders, the commanding officer on Wake, had been sympathetic, and furnished what information he had. It all came down to a hierarchy within the Navy, where Midway and Diego Garcia, though half a world apart, both held a special enough status to come under the direct command of CINCPAC – Commander in Chief, Pacific. His jurisdiction stretched from Alaska to Kuwait, one of the largest commands imaginable, and his specific permission was needed to access either of my two goals.

I suppose I should have gone and talked to him – if I could have indeed gained an interview. The difficulties inherent in this approach, however, were legion. First, he could turn me down. Second, his remit might force him to give me an official denial, even if he were prepared personally to grant my request. Third, there was the tricky problem of how to couch the request – without a valid reason according to their regulations, you were in effect saying: 'I know civilians are prohibited. I'm a civilian. Can I go?' Fourth, the nasty precedent. Tourists and country collectors were the last people they wanted, and if they let you in on that basis, what would they say to the next similar enquiry? Fifth, the fact that CINCPAC was the ultimate authority meant that exploring other avenues might be more advisable initially, because once he said no, you wouldn't get beyond that.

I couldn't see any immediate hope for Midway. Such few TCC members as had been there were old enough to have seen active service in World War II, or were even older and had made a stopover there on the amphibious planes of the '30s. So I studied books on the island's significant part in the war, learned what I could about the gooney birds for which Midway was famous . . . and waited for inspiration.

No one at all in the roster of members claimed to have been to Diego Garcia. Indeed, with the restrictions placed by both the British and American governments, it would have been surprising if anyone had. I explored every conceivable avenue . . . short of signing on to military life for eight or sixteen years. It seemed the options were limited to being a drummer in a visiting band, a chaplain, a crew member on a contract charter aircraft, or – and I actually met one of these in Indianapolis – a manager of the bank on the base.

I researched where US military aircraft bound for Diego took off from, and what procedures were employed on check-in. True to expectations, the paperwork required in advance to board, and the checking, were both rigorous. One break was when a colleague told me of a friend of his who he thought was serving there. There might be the possibility of an invitation to visit him. When I followed up this lead, he'd already completed his assignment, and returned to the States.

I appeared on a BBC TV programme in 1990, profiling my travels. I mentioned Diego was one place I hadn't been to, and was looking for a way of getting there. After the show I received a phone call from the former commander of the British base there. He said he'd love to take his wife back for a visit, but even he wasn't allowed back, so great was the net of secrecy thrown around the place.

Even the obvious was not neglected in my approaches. I rang up the East Africa Desk at the Foreign and Commonwealth Office in London. They had responsibility for administering the British Indian Ocean Territory – all 21,000 square miles of it. Their sniffy response to my request to visit was to the effect that the 1966 agreement with the United States precluded any civilian visits not on approved government business. It was a complete dead end.

What caused all this super-secretiveness, all these restrictions, which in effect had turned a British colony into an off-limits high-tech military installation? The story was rather sordid, involving a deal done by a bankrupt Labour administration in Britain in the '60s to get a discount of several millions from the Polaris missiles they were buying from the US.

They came up with the nefarious idea of expelling the existing population of copra-plantation workers (some 1,000 or more) from all the islands of the Chagos archipelago, then turning over the southernmost island in the chain – Diego – to the Americans on a long lease to create a monster 'defence' facility, which would be unhindered in its development and expansion by any neighbouring populations.

The plan worked brilliantly – despite opposition from the Organisation for African Unity and Mauritius (to which the Chagos had always been attached, and where the Chagos natives had been unceremoniously dumped). Perceived strategic defence imperatives, with RAF bases further east being abandoned as a result of the new political realities in Singapore, Aden, the Maldives, overruled any squeamishness at the thought of destroying a living community of people.

The defence mandarins now saw a base a thousand miles and more away from interference of any kind, with all arrivals pre-screened and controlled by themselves, no civilian airliners allowed, and the nearest populated islands – Seychelles, Mauritius, the Maldives – all more than four days away by steamer or yacht, with no scheduled link of any kind for freight or passengers. A pity the colony was still listed in respectable publications such as the *Statesman's Yearbook*, and recognised by the TCC!

Little by little the idea grew in my mind that the only way in was by private yacht, and then not to Diego itself, but to one of the dozen or so of the other islands to the north of the base, still within the archipelago. But realising this as theory was one thing; implementing it would take almost more effort than had visiting all my previous countries. For now it would not be a question of merely nosing out opportunities and contacts who could help. I'd already done that, and it wasn't enough. I'd have to take on the full responsibility and liability (financial and otherwise) of organising a chartered yacht, and filling it with enough other people to be a viable proposition.

After too much trial and error I gave up completely on informal arrangements with individual yacht owners. Too often a confident 'I'll be in Singapore in a couple of months, I could take you from there,' became the reality of a dozen changes of mind en route, and a let down. I started phoning appropriate sources in Mauritius (made more difficult by the changing of all telephone numbers on the island from the last issue of the telephone book), Seychelles and the Maldives.

Night after night I spent on the phone from my office in Bellingham, Washington, or at home in Sudden Valley, across the 11,000 miles, eleven time zones, two oceans and three continents, trying to find a vessel that was seaworthy, an owner or agent who was trustworthy, and a price that was not extortionate. Time and again I fell between the small-ship league and the tiny schooner brigade, the former needing many more passengers than I could realistically muster, the latter causing an instinctive foreboding when I tried to imagine its performance in heavy ocean swells.

Suddenly I got a call from Israel, offering a 115-foot luxury motor yacht for a very short window of time in late May, 1991. It was already April, and though I'd had positive responses to the feelers I'd put out, I would need to canvas potential travellers again to be sure they were serious. The Israelis wanted money, a lot of it; and quickly, or no deal. From long experience of travel organising I knew that once signed up, I would have to carry the can. A perfect catch-22 operated, whereby no one wanted to commit if a trip was not absolutely certain, but the trip could only be definite if they committed.

The yacht was bigger than my minimum requirements, and more lavishly appointed. It was also considerably more expensive than I'd budgeted! It was used to celebrities, having lately undertaken voyages with Barbara Walters of ABC, Mort Zuckerman (US News), the President of Estée Lauder, the Vice Chairman of Warner Communications, and Leonard Bernstein, in its home area of the Red Sea. What prompted the call to me was a just completed assignment for *National Geographic* in the Seychelles, leaving the vessel positioned there between trips, and open, as they say, to offers.

My offer was tentatively accepted, based on number of days required to and from Mahe, the Seychellois capital. I quickly rounded up the self-confessed 'lunatic fringe' of the TCC, extracted from them promises of forthcoming payment, and forwarded my own funds to Israel.

Then a protracted series of negotiations started with the yacht owners, that weren't even concluded when we were ready to cast off, two weeks later. They said the quoted price was only good for daytime travel, and as we'd require continuous movement, the price would double. I assumed the deal was a whole charter. They said any new passengers over the six names I gave would be charged extra.

They were so intransigent, sensing a committed party – hence an opportunity to raise the price – that I began to wonder if the whole arrangement would fall through. It did. Months, probably years, of legwork were about to go down the drain. The Israelis said they had another client. They were maybe bluffing, but with only a handful of passengers to divide any extra costs amongst, I couldn't match them as they upped the ante. I said 'Sorry. No thanks.'

For some days I pondered the loss of the yacht and the trip. It had seemed to be in the bag. I'd come so far in my personal race for the world. Was I going to falter now, at the last but one post? And what about the others who were relying on me to fulfil their dreams too?

That's when a strange sensation took hold of me. I'd been reading a book I'd bought from Winnie Crapuchetes, an eighty-year-old former China missionary friend of Gordon and Vera Dunn, neighbours of ours in Bellingham. The book was called *How I Know*

*God Answers Prayer* by Rosalind Goforth, and dealt with the turbulent turn of the century period in China, especially the Boxer Rebellion.

The author was in the midst of savage fighting, where foreigners were sitting ducks. She found herself and her children being mobbed, their lives threatened, every day a new anxiety whether they would survive. Yet when she prayed: 'Dear God, I know that nothing is impossible with You. Save us alive from this maelstrom,' she had the unshakeable conviction that God heard her explicitly, and would completely answer her prayer. The rest of the book was a stirring tale of miraculous escapes and fast-paced true adventures.

I stopped for a moment and thought. There was no comparison, strictly speaking, between my situation and hers. Yet if the main thesis of the book was true, prayer being answered would not be fickle, arbitrary, or a matter of sterile theological debate. It would be real. You would know. Like many Christians, I'd prayed about serious and weighty affairs, spiritual matters, life and death issues. But if the pressing prayer of the moment, for a yacht at the price I could afford, to keep faith with my signed up customers, was answered, then I too would know without a doubt that God answers prayer.

So I prayed. And I got a call from Israel to say they'd agree to a modified price, and the voyage to the Chagos was on. That didn't stop Howard Rosenstein asking me at the last moment to cancel the cheque for final payment I'd sent, and to bring fists full of cash to the boat, or conducting further negotiations with me by phone from Tel Aviv as we sat in dock in Mahe, to squeeze the last drop from the contract. But the young captain, thirty-year-old Eran Donskoy, found a form of words to satisfy both him and me, and we set off to plough an almost straight furrow 1,000 miles east along an imaginary line almost exactly 4° south of the equator towards the British Indian Ocean Territory.

Perhaps it was the continuous movement round the clock. Perhaps it was the constant use of the noisy and rather smelly engines. Perhaps it was the fact that we went straight through the sea, irrespective of what it threw at us, with no deviations to maybe make our course smoother. Perhaps it was the excellent seafood buffet we'd enjoyed on slipping out of Mahe. Perhaps the nervous tension we all felt – would we be allowed to land at our destination?

Or the stress of those financial negotiations with a very determined Israeli. Or a mixture of causes.

Whatever it was, five passengers (we were seven passengers in seven cabins with seven crew) retired below and I didn't see them for the better part of the next two days, as they slept off the effects of seasickness. My own travail was more dramatic. I had just reached the bridge to speak to Eran when the entire contents of my stomach decided to empty themselves over his plush carpet. Smadar, one of the crew, rushed up and issued the two of us still above deck with buckets to carry around for future occurrences.

The swells got worse. On the second and third nights the crew were sprawled out on the floor of the salon, trying to get some relief from the pounding of the sea. When the below-decks passengers began to emerge one by one, most decided not to return to their cabins and took to sleeping on the floor, too.

On the first two days I never counted more than three diners at any meal – and then it was generally for toast and dry biscuits. It was a pity that when we regained our appetites the craft was lurching so violently through the swells. At each meal Elinor, Miri or Netta would set out a beautifully presented serving plate of salads or cold cuts, only to see a sideways roll of the yacht mix the carefully prepared food items into an unintended puree.

Or the soup tureen would arrive, piping hot, and its contents would perform violent sloshes onto both sides of the tablecloth, sending us scurrying for cover. Sometimes the whole tureen, if not held fast by a crew member, would slalom all the way down the table, knocking aside everything in its path before overturning itself into the lap of whoever was sitting furthest away from where its journey commenced.

Night was no relief. I wandered into the kitchen about 2 a.m. at the same time as Delphine was pouring herself a cup of coffee. A sudden wave caught the stern, and Delphine lost her balance. She staggered towards me, emptying her scalding hot coffee onto my bare arm as she did so. She caught hold of me for a moment. The crazy movements of the yacht kept us locked in a dance-like motion for a few seconds. Then the boat rocked violently the other way. Delphine went sliding backwards to the wall. She grabbed a fixture for support. It came away in her hands. Loose cutlery cascaded onto the floor, now made slick by the spilled coffee. We both slid down to our knees and laughed. It was all you could do.

The fifth morning dawned bright and clear. It was a complete contrast to all we'd been through. Danger Island, on the edge of the Great Chagos Bank, was in sight. The zodiacs were launched, the crew put on standby. Once over the reef – too dangerous to approach any closer – it'd be a short way to the island, and we'd all set foot on BRITISH INDIAN OCEAN TERRITORY. Only one snag. Half of the passengers couldn't swim. The crew solved that by half-carrying, half-dragging them through the surf to safety. One passenger arrived on Danger Island minus a shoe, another minus his glasses, and a third minus his trousers. But nobody complained. We stood on the sand, drank a toast, and celebrated – for me – country 307. One to go.

# 40

## A Wing and a Prayer

*Midway (1992)*

The return voyage from Danger Island to Mahe was on such a glacially smooth sea that we wondered if it was the same Indian Ocean on which we'd spent those agonising days during the outbound journey. Everyone was in a good mood because of the goal accomplished. Never mind that the base at Diego Garcia had maintained a discreet silence when we called them up on our radio – maybe it was better that way.

Naturally, talk turned to travel on the way home. Tony entertained us with stories of escaping from pygmies trying to shoot arrows at him for not paying a fee to take their pictures; driving a Volkswagen Combi with no reverse gear through Africa, and other incredible stories. Virtually everyone had an experience of being rescued by an Aeroflot half-price ticket from some out of the way place. Kevin, US Air despatcher, had a fund of airline yarns.

But Midway was uppermost in many minds. Tony had paid a fishing boat owner in Hawaii to take him there, but after more than two weeks on the open sea they were stopped three miles out by a Navy patrol and turned around. He upbraided Sandford for not fighting hard to arrange Midway as an extra stopover on the Wake charter.

Sandford had his own method of reaching Midway. Every two years he joined a specially vetted group of naturalists who counted the laysan albatrosses (gooney birds) – some job, since estimates ran to as many as half a million on the tiny two-mile island. There was general agreement that spending two weeks deep in gooney droppings was a big price to pay to add another country. Besides, this particulary opportunity was now suspended.

Actually Midway consisted of two islands – Sand and Eastern, Sand being the better-known. Its pre-war history had been as a cable relay station, then a stopover for the Pan Am Clippers. War history buffs identified the Battle of Midway as a turning point in the Pacific war. 'Remember Midway' was still a rallying cry to American patriots.

As a practical measure, I'd given up on official military convey-ance as a means of gaining entrance. The military machine, in cases like this, moved – if it moved at all – at only two speeds: slow and terminally slow. Sea approaches as with Diego looked as if they would not work either, so I began to look for planes that could do the journey, and get – or sidestep – the permission.

There was of course the DC8 sitting in Honolulu which had ferried us to Wake. But getting 180 people together, and raising the $90,000 or so that it would take would have been formidable obstacles. And I didn't even have the clout of the veterans. When I investigated smaller capacity planes, I found the root of the problem. None with enough range was based at any Pacific point such as Honolulu. That would easily add another $15,000 of costs, even for the smallest of executive jets, to fly the distance from the West Coast and back; a cost which I guessed my prospective passengers would be reluctant to pay.

Another snag: even if a small plane were found, and it had the range, and the price barrier could be overcome, there was no way the Navy would allow a flight just to land there, drop off its passengers for sightseeing, and return to its point of origin. I tested this several times when phoning operators of private or executive jets. When Midway was mentioned as the destination, they all consulted manuals which clearly stated that no private or chartered civilian flights would be given permission to land. The perennial problem – that of recruiting enough paying passengers to make the operation viable – was of course also there, awaiting solution.

So now I knew what I needed: a six- to fourteen-seat executive jet, that was on the way to somewhere in the Pacific or Asia already (so I wouldn't have to pay to get it out to the general area) that would be prepared to apply for permission to make a transit landing in Midway, departing for a different point than the one it arrived from, be somehow situated to give a massive discount on the normal price (hopefully by having the bulk of positioning costs already paid for), and be able to give me enough notice to round up people by giving them definite dates.

It was this last that became the biggest headache. As I devoted time and energy to this project. I found that I could either have a plane with advance notice, but no permission and too costly, or a plane that was better priced and could sidestep the permissions, but was leaving in a matter of days or hours. Such was the nature of the executive charter business.

At least my researches were now giving me hope. Most months one or maybe two planes of the type I was interested in came to my attention – sometimes after they'd transited Midway, sometimes as they were about to go there on short notice. It could be done! It was just a question of waiting for one with enough notice to put together my passengers to defray the huge cost involved.

Then at last I received just the telephone call I'd been waiting for. It was from ex-President Jimmy Carter's former pilot in Atlanta, who now ran his own Lear Jet service. He had a contract, he said, from the big air force base outside Anchorage, Alaska, the one used as a stopover on state visits to and from Asia, to do some flying training there. It was to last two or three weeks, and would involve two of his Lear 36s. Once the job finished, he'd be happy to send one jet directly back to Atlanta, with all his equipment, while the other could take the longer way round on the way back, via Midway, with myself and party as paying passengers.

The beauty of the suggestion was that we would only have to pay the costs of a one-way journey from Anchorage, and could even get off in San Jose – just what I was looking for. Also, since the jet was finishing a military contract, the necessary permission to land at Midway would be a breeze. The one problem was not knowing the exact date. As soon as their duties were over, the Lear would want to leave. On the other hand, weather or other factors might delay the flying training, so no guarantee of any kind could be given, only that it would be in 'approximately two and a half weeks'.

I looked at the calendar. February 22nd. I plumped for a date, hoping I'd be close enough, and started furiously writing the copy needed to get the word out to the small band of enthusiasts who subscribed to my newsletter *Destination Hotline*, top members of the TCC, and a circle of former clients of the tour company which I'd now sold, plus some media contacts for good measure.

First the headline and sub heads:

PRIVATE EXECUTIVE CHARTER BY LEAR JET
ONLY OPPORTUNITY OPEN TO CIVILIANS TO VISIT
HIGHLY RESTRICTED MIDWAY ISLAND BY AIR
Maximum guests: six more Register without delay
to be part of this historic opportunity.

Then the body of text:

On Wednesday March 11, 1992 at 8.00 a.m. a private Lear Jet Century III-36 will lift off from Anchorage International Airport over the Cook Inlet, fly down the Alaskan peninsula to the edge of the Aleutian Range, and refuel at Cold Bay. From there it will head south 2,000 miles over the Pacific Ocean to its special destination . . . *Midway Island*.

Geographically little more than a dot in the vast expanse of the Pacific, Midway has fascinated 'destination collectors' for decades.

| | |
|---|---|
| REMOTE | 1,250 miles northwest of Hawaii |
| INACCESSIBLE | No air service since the 1950s |
| RESTRICTED | US Navy base; off-limits to civilians |
| SECRETIVE | Top level clearance to visit required |
| HISTORICAL | Battle here was WW II turning point |
| FASCINATING | More gooney birds than anywhere |
| LISTED | A separate Guinness and TCC territory |

After dipping his wings to give the passengers an outstanding view, the pilot will complete two circuits of the approach before landing at the Naval Station Air Terminal. During the hours on the ground there will be time for a short walking tour, basic sightseeing, and photography – subject to permission.

That last one was a big 'subject to'. But I had to be optimistic now that I'd come so far. It wasn't a piece of cake recruiting five fellow adventurers, but within a week the plane was full. Now it was just a case of checking every day with Atlanta, to see if they were keeping up to schedule, and warning the other passengers *not* to make firm bookings on connecting flights up to Alaska. I told them it could be any day that week. Wednesday wasn't certain.

Day after day I checked in with Atlanta. Day after day their ops room told me the same story. They were on schedule as far as they knew, but they couldn't be certain until the last few days of training when the results were evaluated, and they were informed if any extra time was needed. They'd give me a firm forty-eight hours' notice, no matter what.

I suppose I was grateful for that. If departure was the day I'd picked or one day later, we'd be all right. One day earlier or two or more days later I could phone the participants, and give them the new ETD (estimated time of departure). It felt like running a tour on Korean Air into Russia again through shooting down and subsequent boycott.

The cancellation when it came was all the more devastating for being unexpected. It arrived in the form of a curt fax:

DUE TO BIRD STRIKE HAZARD WE MUST DECLINE ANY FURTHER INVOLVEMENT WITH MIDWAY.

Apparently they'd been monitoring any small plane arrivals at Midway since I'd signed up with them. Since these were infrequent, the first one had just taken place. Bad news. The pilot reported that the gooneys were nesting, and several chicks had been born. Both mother and father were busy flying food back to their young.

Since air traffic was intermittent – most days, in fact several weeks, there were no planes at all – the gooneys paid not the slightest heed to the runway, and flew across the take-off path at will. When a heavy military transport (bearing the fortnightly pay cheques) would line up for departure, the control tower would routinely despatch a group of the Thai contract personnel on the base to shoo hundreds of birds off the apron and runway where they'd taken up very comfortable positions.

This had frightened the pilot reporting to Atlanta. Through his cockpit window he could see fifty or sixty of these birds, each weighing over twenty pounds, competing with him for the air space. My Atlanta contact obviously thought this was one additional element he could do without.

With the time difference, he'd given me about fifty-one hours to get something else organised. Twice in the last three months I'd had calls from planes transiting Hawaii offering to do the side trip to

Midway, but *then and there*! Then I'd had the plane ready, but not the people. Now I'd laboriously assembled the people, and had lost my plane. Where would I find another one?

I did some praying, then got out the 500-page-thick *Air Charter Guide*, and went down the listings page by page, phoning every charterer, air taxi operator, executive jet service, even air ambulance that looked even remotely possible. I was on the phone from 6 a.m. until well after 8 p.m. I had no firm leads when I finished, but a fellow called Michael from Northern California had seemed to be the best hope, if a somewhat slim one. On the way to bed I stopped at the fridge for a cold drink. The magnet on the door proclaimed, 'Expect a miracle.' 'All right,' I thought. 'I will!'

In between my first batch of phone calls next morning, I received a message that a Michael had called. I phoned back immediately. 'You said yesterday you weren't sure if your company could get the authorisation to land. Have you had any word back yet?'

I'd been through it all before. Every time they referred the question of a Midway landing higher up (if they hadn't done one before) the answer always came back the same: it was not possible for a public charter to land at Midway, due to the restrictions. Prior approval must have been obtained from the Navy to refuel. It seemed that only a tiny handful of operators were approved and knew the drill – usually because they did contract work for the military.

So I was ready for a negative answer, once more. What I wasn't prepared for was a different Michael with a loud New York Jewish accented voice. 'I didn't call you yesterday. I heard you were looking for a plane to go to Midway. I'll get you one. But I don't touch anything for less than a couple of thousand bucks. So can you wire me the money at once?'

He brushed off all questions of permission, contract, name and provenance of aircraft, exact number of passengers (critical now that it was likely to be a costlier and roomier Lear 35) as mere details that could easily be settled once the essential business of payment was taken care of. To this day I don't remember phoning his company, which was clearly a brokerage lining up other people's planes. But if his sixth sense of business led him to me, or if my angel had brought him into contact with me, I didn't mind. He was in the right place at the right time. Ironic that I'd worked the entire industry 'bible', though, without success. It was the promised miracle!

I quickly wired him the agreed amount, payable to him, from

which he'd withdraw his $2,000. Not bad for a phone call bringing two parties together. He faxed back the outline agreement I sent him, signed. I asked him to guarantee a refund if the plane did not land at Midway. He did. That was confidence for you. The details had to be left up to the pilot, he said.

The downside was that I needed at least two more people to travel to make up the extra cost for the larger plane *and* the fact that we were going out from the West Coast after all. And I needed them by morning. I did some more praying. I got three, and one reserve, Kevin from the Diego trip, who I knew was used to jump seats, and could perhaps be added at the last minute.

It was a bit of a scramble, but we were able to assemble everybody at the Hacienda Hotel, Sepulveda Boulevard, El Segundo on the evening of the 11th, for take-off the following morning. The others should have been pleased, because they now didn't have to pay their way up to Alaska. I was the one doing the running around, because although our first stop next day was Boeing Field, Seattle, ninety-five minutes from my home, I had to fly down to Los Angeles to check everybody on board.

The aircraft was late arriving from Burbank. I shuttled the other eight in a limo over to the private terminal at LAX, next to MGM Grand Air, and went off to find a phone to see what was happening. It's perhaps a good thing that the Lear landed a few seconds after I left, and they commenced the loading process without me. I might have taken my tour leader responsibilities a bit too seriously and fretted. As it was the plane sort of self loaded, as was afterwards explained to me by a bystander.

'The first thing was, I don't know what they were expecting . . . maybe not a 727, but a sort of smaller version of a 727.' He chuckled as he narrated. 'It was a pity that Arab sheik's big jet was parked just in front . . . it did make the Lear look quite small. Anyway because of the curvature of the roof at the back, they found that the only place the man with the lump on his head could sit was right in the back, so everybody just sort of squished in around him. But first there was a lot of backing in and out, and turning sideways. It was like a game of fitting all the objects into the spaces and there was only one possible way they would go.'

I had the drop-down seat by the door, that would have been the toilet if we were only eight, instead of nine. Once I sat down, I could swivel around and put my chin over the pilot's shoulders in one direction, or jostle for leg space with the first passenger on the bench on either side of the plane. I also found the coffee dispenser and food trays were directly over my head, and the bar was under my left elbow. The flight manuals that couldn't fit in the tiny cockpit were under my right elbow. That was after I got in.

Getting in itself was an art form. Here's what you had to do: first collect, while standing on the tarmac, an armful of flight manuals, food trays and anything that normally decorates the toilet seat. Then place those all on the tarmac, clamber in backwards, and swivel around. Then yell for somebody still on the tarmac to pass up to you all the items you had to pass down to get in. To close the door, all the same items have to be moved again, usually by passing them down the plane, until the door swing area is clear, the door shut, and they can be draped in various positions on the floor again. As you'll have gathered, there wasn't much room. This would be our home now for twenty-plus hours of flight.

The rest of the day passed pleasantly: sneaking into line at LAX between Lufthansa, United and Korean jumbos for take-off; spectacular views of Mount St Helens; parking amongst the gleaming new 757s and 767s lined up for export at Boeing Field; an Alaskan King Crab supper in Anchorage; seeing that Esther, the eighty-three-year-old doctor, virtually blind in one eye, found her way to her room in the hotel. I asked her how she made out on the medical tests for tough journeys like the Antarctic. 'No problem,' she said. 'I sign my own doctor's exam.' As to the man sitting where the roof curve began: 'I'd have that lump off him in five minutes at my clinic.'

Next morning I scrutinised everybody closely, for no other reason than that I'd had to guess the weight of each, and total them for our payload, and I wanted to be sure that I wasn't too far off on this critical day when we'd fly far out over the North Pacific, away from any habitation. We performed the same ritual dance to board – it was quicker now. There was just no question of turning back once you'd embarked on the process of heading towards your seat unless you wanted to force the whole cabin to back out also bent double, like a movie scene in reverse.

We put into Cold Bay at the edge of the Aleutians to refuel. Its name was apt. On the sole pay telephone in the waiting room, while I read about fishing charters and the prohibition of weapons at the Reeve Aleutian desk, the pilots got the word that the cheque deposited in their bank account by Michael's outfit had been $2,000 less than they expected. He'd informed me, of course, but it seemed he'd neglected to tell them! They were in jeans and tee shirts today, not the starched white uniforms of yesterday. 'For a reason,' they said, with a knowing look.

During the four and a half hours that it took from Cold Bay to Midway, I thought about all the different methods I'd employed in the race for the world that would soon be over. First there'd been the curiosity of the Irish schoolboy, with perhaps a strong strain of whatever it is that propels so many Irish to emigrate coursing in my blood. Then college days, cheap student charter flights, and long four-month vacations. Friendship with overseas students, and invitations to their countries. Journalism, radio and television work, film-making, the travel and tour business, trips of Christian solidarity, relief missions, journeys involved with human rights.

Then there'd been the race itself, the rather arbitrary TCC list that had become so venerated by some it had taken on the proportions of a golden scroll; and the Guinness Book, unable to decide from one year to the next whether it would accept the TCC reckoning, or compile its own list. I'd regarded it as a bit of fun, a challenge, an extension to a hobby I'd have pursued anyway. Although I wouldn't have chosen to go to some places on the list, on balance I enjoyed most of them. And it was a great excuse to meet and interact with interesting people, both en route and when you got there.

The criticism that to spend only a few hours refuelling or in port was to miss something, was legitimate. But, as an ancient philosopher said: 'It's better to have seen the flowers from horseback than not to have seen them at all.' Naturally I have more fond recollections of places where I was able to get right down and smell the flowers, where I could make some contribution to the people, where I built links that transcended cultures.

Above all, I was proud of the fact that, whereas some of my elderly American rivals in the race constantly denominated the cost of their travels (usually in the $500,000 to $1,000,000 range), I could look back on a penniless dream that kicked it off, and funding that came in creative and work-related ways as I progressed. I wanted to be able to say to young people starting out. 'Follow your dreams as far as you dare. Don't be intimidated by lack of money. For you it may not be travel. Your contribution to your fellow man might be in another area. But seize your chances. You never know where they may lead.'

It may be slightly naive to think that world peace and understanding can be brought about by travel alone. For the record, I don't. I think we'll always have relative rich and relative poor (most poor Westerners have palatial lifestyles compared to the third-world average; many third-world despots have a lifestyle the top five percent in the West can scarcely even imagine). We'll have corrupt politicians as long as we have mankind, and structures of varying degrees of corruption.

But maybe, just maybe, the world will be a better place if a few more people join the Peace Corps, Voluntary Service Overseas, OM, YWAM; if a few more nurses and engineers and agronomists and book-keepers do a stint in a foreign country, and see where it leads them. The Russians didn't look like such ogres when we partnered with them in tourism. Inviting Chinese, Iraqi, Bosnian, Malaysian and Kuwaiti students to tea in your home does wonders for your world view. And now the Koreans and Nepalese are sending out missionaries . . . to the West. Hooray!

My train of thought was broken as the pilot pointed out a speck on the horizon . . . MIDWAY. A surge of adrenalin runs through the cabin. It's real. We're almost there. But will we be allowed to land? We'd better, because there's no source of fuel for a long way. I needn't have worried. In a split second we were on the ground. The door was being opened from the other side by a Navy aircraft handler. Shock was written all over him as he stared into the nine faces at close proximity. 'We weren't expecting any passengers,' he said, forthrightly, 'just an empty ferry flight. But since you're here, come and see round the place.'

We accepted his invitation with alacrity. The museum was opened up for us, and the post office, so that we could frank cards, and mail evidence of landing to the *Guinness Book of Records*. A shop was found with a stock of twenty-nine tee shirts. We bought twenty-seven. We posed with the gooneys and their chicks next to their nests. They were everywhere. Hundreds of thousands on a two-mile strip of sand. The New York Irish policeman who was head of security stood with our group for a picture.

Last business before piling into our sardine can Lear and flying to Honolulu and home was a quiet walk to the side of the apron where we were the only plane in sight. I dropped to my knees on the tarmac and said: 'Thank you God.' My race was over.

# Appendix

# TCC Approved List of Countries

## NORTH AMERICA

Alaska
Canada
Mexico

St Pierre & Miquelon
United States (continental)

## CENTRAL AMERICA

Belize
 (British Honduras)
Costa Rica
El Salvador

Guatemala
Honduras
Nicaragua
Panama

## EUROPE AND MEDITERRANEAN

Aland Islands
 (Mariehamm)
Albania
Andorra
Austria
Balearic Islands
 (Mallorca, Minorca)
Belgium
Berlin
Bosnia & Herzegovina
 (Sarajevo; Yugoslavia)
Bulgaria
Byelorussia
 (Minsk: White Russia)
Corsica
Crete

Croatia
 (Zagreb, Dubrovnik, Yugoslavia)
Cyprus, Republic of
Cyprus, Turkish
Czechoslovakia
Denmark
Dodecanese Islands
 (Rhodes)
England
Esthonia
 (Tallinn)
Faroe Islands
Finland
France
Germany, East
Germany, West
Gibraltar

Greece
Guernsey & Deps.
   (Alderney, Herm, Sark: Channel
   Islands)
Hungary
Ionian Islands
   (Corfu, etc.)
Ireland
   (Eire)
Ireland, Northern
   (Ulster)
Isle of Man
Italy
Jersey
   (Channel Islands)
Latvia.
   (Riga)
Liechtenstein
Lithuania
   (Vilnius)
Luxembourg
Macedonia
   (Skopje)
Malta
Moldavia
   (Kishinev)
Monaco

Montenegro
   (Titograd; Yugoslavia)
Netherlands
Norway
Poland
Portugal
Romania
Russia
San Marino
Sardinia
Scotland
Serbia
   (Belgrade)
Sicily
Slovenia
   (Ljubljana)
Spain
Spitsbergen
   (Svalbard, Bear Island)
Sweden
Switzerland
Turkey in Europe
   (Istanbul)
Ukraine
   (Kiev)
Vatican City
Wales

## AFRICA

Algeria
Angola
   (Portuguese West Africa)
Benin
   (Dahomey)
Bophuthetswana
Botswana
   (Bechuanaland)
Bourkina Fasso
   (Upper Volta)
Burundi
   (Urundi)
Cameroon

Central African Republic
Chad
Ciskei
Congo
   (Brazzaville)
Djibouti
   (French Somaliland, Afars &
   Issas)
Egypt
Equatorial Guinea
   (Rio Muni, Fernando Poo)
Ethiopia
Gabon

Gambia, The
Ghana
   (Gold Coast, British Togoland)
Guinea
   (French Guinea)
Guinea-Bissau
   (Portuguese Guinea)
Ivory Coast
Kenya
Lesotho
   (Basutoland)
Liberia
Libya
Malawi
   (Nyasaland)
Mali
   (French Soudan)
Mauritania
Morocco
Morocco, Spanish
   (Ceuta, Melilla)
Mozambique
   (Portuguese East Africa)
Niger
Nigeria
Rwanda
   (Ruanda)

Sao Tome & Principe
Senegal
Sierra Leone
Somalia
   (Italian Somaliland, British
   Somaliland)
South Africa
Southwest Africa
   (Namibia)
Sudan
Swaziland
Tanzania (Tanganyika)
Togo
Transkei
Tunisia
Uganda
Venda
Western Sahara
   (Spanish Sahara)
Zaire
   (Kinshasa; Belgian Congo)
Zambia
   (Northern Rhodesia)
Zanzibar
Zimbabwe
   (Southern Rhodesia)

## NEAR EAST

Abu Dhabi
Ajman
Bahrain
Dubai
Fujeira
Iran
Iraq
Israel
Jordan
Kuwait
Lebanon

Oman
Qatar
Ras Al Khaima
Saudi Arabia
Sharjah
Syria
Umm Al Qiwain
Yemen Arab Republic
   (Sana'a)
Yemen, People's Democratic
   Republic (Aden)

## ASIA

Afghanistan
Armenia
  (Yerevan)
Azerbaijan
  (Baku)
Bangladesh
Bhutan
Brunei
Burma
China, People's Republic of
  (Peking)
China, Republic of
  (Taiwan, Formosa)
Georgia
  (Tblisi)
Hong Kong
India
Indonesia
  (Java)
Irian Jaya
  (Dutch New Guinea)
Japan
Kalimantan
  (Indonesian Borneo)
Kampuchea
  (Cambodia, Khmer Republic)
Kashmir
Kazakhstan
  (Alma Ata)
Kirghizia
  (Frunze)
Korea, North
Korea, South
Laos

Lesser Sunda Islands
  (Bali, Timor, Indonesia)
Macao
Malaysia
  (Kuala Lumpur)
Moluka
  (Moluccas, Indonesia)
Mongolia, People's Republic of
Nepal
Pakistan
Philippines
Sabah
  (North Borneo)
Sarawak
Siberia
Sikkim
Singapore
Sri Lanka
  (Ceylon)
Sulawesi
  (Celebes; Indonesia)
Sumatra
  (Indonesia)
Tadzhikstan
  (Dushambe)
Thailand
Tibet
Turkey in Asia
  (Anatolia, Ankara, Izmir)
Turkmenistan
  (Ashkhabad)
Uzbekistan
  (Tashkent, Samarkand,
  Bukhara)
Viet Nam

## ANTARCTICA

American
  Palmer, McMurdo Sound, South
  (Pole)
Argentine

Australian Antarctic Territory
  (Mawson, Davis, Macquarie,
  Heard)
Chilean

Falkland Islands Dependencies
  (British Antarctica, Graham
  Land, So. Shetland, So.
  Sandwich, So. Georgia, So.
  Orkney)

French Southern & Antarctic Terr.
  (Kerguelen, Crozet, Amsterdam,
  & St Paul)
Norwegian
  (Bouvet)
New Zealand
  (Ross Dependency)

## INDIAN OCEAN

Andaman-Nicobar Islands
British Indian Ocean Territory
  (Chagos Arch., Diego Garcia)
Christmas Island
Cocos Islands
  (Keeling)
Comoro Islands
  (Anjouan, Moheli, Grand
  Comoro)
Lakshadweep, Union Terr. of
  (Laccadive Is.)

Malagasy Republic
  (Madagascar)
Maldive Islands
Mauritius & Deps.
  (Agalega, St Brandon,
  Rodriguez)
Mayotte
  (Dzaoudzi)
Reunion & Deps.
  (Tromelin, Glorioso)
Seychelles
Zil Elwannyen Sesel
  (Aldabra, Farquhar, Amirante Is.)

## CARIBBEAN

Anguilla
Antigua & Deps.
  (Barbuda, Redonda)
Aruba
Bahamas
Barbados
Cayman Islands
Cuba
Dominica
Dominican Republic
Grenada & Deps.
  (Curriacou, Grenadines)
Guadeloupe & Deps.
  (Marie Galante)
Haiti
Jamaica
Leeward Islands, French
  (St Martin, St Barts)

Leeward Islands, Netherlands
  (Saba, St Eustatius, St Maarten)
Martinique
Montserrat
Netherlands Antilles
  (Curacao, Bonaire)
Puerto Rico
San Andres & Providencias
St Kitts, Nevis
St Lucia
St Vincent & Deps.
  (Bequia, Canouan, Grenadines)
Trinidad & Tobago
Turks & Caicos Is.
Virgin Islands, American
  (St Croix, St John, St Thomas)
Virgin Islands, British (Tortola,
  etc.)

## SOUTH AMERICA

Argentina
Bolivia
Brazil
Chile
Colombia
Ecuador
French Guiana

Guyana
  (British Guiana)
Paraguay
Peru
Surinam
  (Netherlands Guiana)
Uruguay
Venezuela

## ATLANTIC OCEAN

Ascension
Azores Islands
Bermuda
Canary Islands
Cape Verde Islands
Falkland Islands

Fernando do Noronha
Greenland (Kalalik Nunat)
Iceland
Madeira
St Helena
Tristan da Cunha

## PACIFIC OCEAN

Australia
Bismark Archipelago
  (New Ireland, New Britain,
  Bougainville, Admiralty Islands)
Cook Islands
  (Rarotonga, Aitutaki, Penrhyn)
Easter Island
Fiji Islands
French Polynesia
  (Tahiti, Tuamotu, Austral, Gambier)
Galapagos Islands
Guam
Hawaiian Islands
Johnston Island
Juan Fernandez Islands
  (Robinson Crusoe Island)
Kiribati
  (Gilberts, Tarawa, Ocean Island)
Line/Phoenix Islands
  (Palmyra, Fanning, Christmas,
  Canton, Enderbury, Howland)

Lord Howe Island
Marquesas Islands
Marshall Islands, Rep. of
  (Majuro, Kwajalein, Eniwetok)
Micronesia, Federated States of
  (Ponape, Kosrae, Truk, Yap;
  Caroline Islands)
Midway Island
Nauru
New Caledonia & Deps.
  (Noumea; Loyalty Islands)
New Zealand
Niue
Norfolk Island
Northern Marianas
  (Saipan, Tinian)
Ogasawara
  (Bonin, Volcano Island, Iwo
  Jima)
Palau, Republic of
Papua New Guinea

Pitcairn Island
Ryukyu Islands
　(Okinawa)
Samoa, American
　(Pago Pago)
Samoa, Western
　(Apia)
Solomon Islands
　(Guadalcanal, New Georgia,
　Tulagi)
Tasmania

Tokelau Islands
　(Fakaofu, Atafu, Union)
Tonga
　(Nukualofa)
Tuvalu
　(Ellice Islands, Funafuti,
　Vaitapu)
Vanuatu
　(New Hebrides Islands)
Wake Island
Wallis & Futuna Islands

To contact the author, write to:

2 Old Brompton Road, R 257,
LONDON SW7 3DQ U.K.